GLOBAL ENVIRONMENTAL POLITICS: FROM PERSON TO PLANET

GLOBAL ENVIRONMENTAL POLITICS: FROM PERSON TO PLANET

Edited by
Simon Nicholson and Paul Wapner

Paradigm Publishers
Boulder • London

Copyright © 2015 Paradigm Publishers

Published in the United States by Paradigm Publishers, 5589 Arapahoe Avenue, Boulder, CO 80303 USA.

Paradigm Publishers is the trade name of Birkenkamp & Company, LLC,
Dean Birkenkamp, President and Publisher.

Library of Congress Cataloging-in-Publication Data

Global environmental politics : from person to planet / edited by Simon Nicholson and Paul Wapner.
    pages cm
    Includes bibliographical references.
    ISBN 978-1-61205-648-7 (hardcover : alk. paper)—ISBN 978-1-61205-649-4 (pbk. : alk. paper)
    1. Environmental policy—Political aspects.   2. Environmental protection—Political aspects.   3. Environmental protection—International cooperation.   I. Nicholson, Simon (Simon James) editor of compilation.   II. Wapner, Paul Kevin, editor of compilation.
    GE170.G567 2014
    363.7'0561—dc23

                                                                        2014018921

19 18 17 16 15   1 2 3 4 5

For
Liam & Julien
and
Eliza & Zeke

Contents

Part III
From Person to Planet: Into a Livable Future

Acknowledgments

This book is the result of more than two decades of teaching introductory courses in global environmental politics. During this time, we have learned from committed colleagues, benefited from working with remarkable students, and felt the deep joys of loving families. It is a pleasure to express our appreciation.

First, we want to thank the authors whose writings appear on these pages for producing such remarkable work. Their words offer penetrating insight into global environmental challenges and the world is better for their efforts.

Second, we are grateful to our colleagues in the Global Environmental Politics Program at American University and the Environmental Studies Section of the International Studies Association. You have provided steady intellectual friendship in the service of environmental protection, and this has afforded much light in an often-dark world. We would also like to thank our research assistants, Matthew Cannon, Chiara Guzzardo, Anne Kantel, Jonathan Waldrop, and Sijin Xian, for providing exceptional help in bringing this volume to fruition.

We owe a special debt to our students. While both of us enjoy research, our scholarship most takes flight in the classroom. Over the years, we have been challenged by our students to reflect on the most profound dimensions of global environmental politics and to develop accessible, coherent, exciting, and significant ways of presenting material. We are grateful to all who suffered through our presentations, participated in seminar discussions, and answered our most urgent questions with deeper lines of inquiry.

Jennifer Knerr, at Paradigm Publishers, has been a joy to work with. She saw the need for a compelling, fair-minded, and forward-looking text to apprentice students into the world of environmental challenges and skillfully shepherded it through the production process. We are grateful to her and her team at Paradigm for their tireless efforts in support of this volume.

Simon writes: I would like to acknowledge and thank my parents, Alison and Neville, and my sisters, Emma and Sarah, for their unyielding encouragement. I would also like to recognize the intellectual debt I owe to a string of great teachers, most notably Alexander Gillespie, Patrick Thaddeus Jackson,

Anna Strutt, and my partner and collaborator on this book project, Paul Wapner, who I have the honor of calling a mentor and friend. I am blessed every day by the love and support of my wife, Anne-Claire, and my two sons, Liam and Julien. Fatherhood brings with it certain obligations, perhaps the most important of which is to work toward a future filled with possibility for one's children. I would like to dedicate this book to Liam and Julien in small service of such an end.

Paul writes: Since this book is primarily a teaching tool, it seems fitting to acknowledge key teachers in my life. Academically, my deepest gratitude goes to Richard Falk. Among many other things, Richard has taught me that meaningful scholarship must be in the service of creating a more just world. He has certainly demonstrated this in his work, and I strive to follow his example. From a different corner, I'm grateful to Ram Dass, Mitchell Ratner, Jeff Warren, and the land and people of the Lama Foundation for helping navigate the more existential questions. I appreciate their guidance over the years. My greatest teachers are my family. Thank you, Diane, Zeke, and Eliza, for educating me into lifehood. I've learned and continue to learn from your unique ways of being in the world and feel incredibly fortunate that you are the central animators of my life.

Introduction

Living in an Environmental Age

Each person reading this book is a unique individual, with particular likes and dislikes and a novel way of being in the world. At the same time, each is a living part of a much larger, interconnected whole that includes other people, species, and the elements. Reconciling these two identities sits at the heart of global environmental politics and represents the essential challenge of the twenty-first century.

Think for a moment about what it takes to live through a typical day in our lives. We all need to eat, work, share companionship, shelter ourselves, and, if we're lucky, enjoy some entertainment. What is required to support these necessities and efforts? At a minimum, we depend on farmers to grow crops and transportation systems to get the food into our refrigerators. To create and run our computers, cell phones, and other gadgets, we need minerals, petroleum, and often coal or natural gas. To be clothed we need cotton and other fabrics and dyes, and these, like everything else, depend on adequate water, sufficient sunlight, moderate temperatures, ingenuity, and lots of hard work. Any casual look reveals that our lives depend on the functioning of a broad and complex social and biological tapestry.

For millennia, human beings have had the luxury of taking the fabric of life for granted. It has served simply as a backdrop to our endeavors. Even though they are essential to our lives, we have used air, water, soil, and other species in innumerable ways with little thought or concern. The natural world has long appeared as an inexhaustible stock of resources that we could never use up or endanger. Furthermore, we have treated each other with mixed levels of compassion and concern, and all too often have chosen to ignore how our actions detrimentally affect others. Injustice has a long history. In short, the earth has always seemed too vast and productive to imagine that humanity might ever cause widespread environmental harm, and some parts of humanity have always seemed expendable in the effort to advance gains enjoyed over-whelmingly by a few.

No more.

Over the past fifty years or so, our species has grown so large—in numbers and power—and so interconnected through globaliza-tion that our actions are tearing at the threads and, in many cases, shredding the very fabric that supports life. Today dilemmas such as climate change, mass extinction, ozone depletion, soil erosion, and freshwater degradation and scarcity are undermining the lives of many and, in the extreme, threatening the organic infrastructure that supports all life on earth. Furthermore, the processes that drive environmental harm have reached such proportion that ignoring the lot of others condemns almost everyone to a nightmarish future. To put it plainly: the days of not worrying about the earth and our fellow humans are gone. We live inescapably in an environmental age.

What is the character of the ecological predicament? How did we arrive at such a point of planetary and social fragility? What institutions and actors are propelling environmental degradation? How can we turn things around? *Global Environmental Politics: From Person to Planet* explores these questions.

This is a book concerned with planetary politics—policy making and collective action practiced across the globe, focused on global sustainability. It aims to help readers decipher the complexities of how power shapes environmental affairs and how it can be manipulated in the service of global environmental protection. Its point of departure is that environmental dangers are not inevitable consequences of humanity's presence on earth. Plenty of people in the past and many in the present have lived and continue to live ecologically sound lives. Rather, the challenges we face result from certain ways of thinking and acting—ways of organizing and understanding political, economic, and cultural life—that, despite best intentions, are undermining the earth's capacity to sustain us. This book brings these forces into high relief and introduces readers to both the challenges and promises of global environmental politics—a politics that plays out everywhere, from the decisions at international negotiations to the most intimate, personal choices we each make.

HOW CAN I MAKE A DIFFERENCE?

Every semester we hear the same query. Students want to know how they can make the world a better place. Many of our students think, as we do, that deteriorating environmental conditions demand engagement. What does effective environmental action look like?

Each semester we respond by talking about the need for knowledge and the ability to translate knowledge into action. We are convinced that action without knowledge is dangerous, and that knowledge without action is irresponsible. And yet there has always been something unsettling about such a generic answer. How does knowledge best express itself in action? What does action look like when it must engage multiple spheres of influence and project itself across various arenas throughout the world? Moreover, how can individual students find their way into efforts that speak to their unique gifts, proclivities, and passions?

This book represents an attempt to go beyond a generic response to the question of how to make a difference. Anyone who wants to move the world in a more sustainable direction needs to wrestle critically with a few essential things, and those fundamentals give the book its structure. In the following pages we bring together compelling and insightful selections from some of the world's foremost writers and thinkers on the global environmental situation to help readers puzzle through a set of foundational issues and concerns in global environmental politics.

Foremost, we think it is essential for people to know about the environmental state of the world (Sections 1 and 2), the causes of environmental harm (Section 3), and the institutions that drive and can best respond to environmental degradation (Sections 4, 5, and 6). These make up what we consider Global Environmental Politics 101. Much of the book is devoted to such concerns.

Furthermore, we believe that appreciating how the world is wracked by injustices that cut across nations, races, ethnicities, and gender provides insight into the challenges and potential of global environmental protection and is thus essential for assessing one's intentions, perspectives, and abilities to work collectively in the service of sustainability (Section 7).

In addition to such understandings, we also emphasize the ability to analyze different leverage points and make strategic decisions. It is all too easy to pass through life taking steps that one hopes will make a difference, all the while having no real impact or, sometimes, making the situation worse. Discernment creates the difference between wise and simply comfortable action (Section 8).

Finally, we share the view that the greatest deficiency in the world today is not a lack of resources to devote to environmental well-being, genuine commitment to sustainability, or a sense of human solidarity (although the world could certainly use more of each of these). Rather, we lament the poverty of political imagination (Section 9). We live in a world driven significantly by inertia. Conventional ways of harnessing energy, producing food, exchanging and sharing wealth, and disposing of waste are so encrusted in our institutions, norms, and behaviors that it is difficult to envision alternative ways of living together even if current modes are unsustainable. Thus, we end the book by presenting voices committed to stimulating the political imagination as an essential feature to fashioning a livable future.

The conjunction of knowledge and action has a few other important elements, and appreciating these captures the overall orientation of this book. Most crucial is the notion that environmental challenges are not puzzles in need of solutions. That is, just like there is not a single answer to how one can make a difference, there is no solution set to environmental degradation. For as long as any of us or even our children will live, we will still confront the specter of climate change, ozone depletion, species loss, and a whole range of environmental dilemmas. Living mindfully and compassionately on a finite planet is no easy or short-term task. So one might wonder, why bother at all? Here is where turning knowledge into action takes on added significance. We may not be able to right all the world's wrongs or finish the task of environmental protection, but this doesn't relieve us of the responsibility to try. Working to address environmental harm, at this stage of history, is a civilizational vocation. It is where our talents, concerns, and deepest values can meet the world's greatest need. In this sense, environmental dilemmas offer opportunity. They enable us to align our lives with an undertaking that transcends our lifetime and exceeds our individual capabilities. What better chance to see who we are and work for the common but critical good?

DRAWING CONNECTIONS

It is easy to say that environmental engagement is a meaningful endeavor; it is quite another thing to make it real. This is because global environmental politics, almost by definition, is a discipline plagued by abstraction. Think for a moment about climate change. It involves invisible gases moving through invisible air to trap invisible heat, with computer models telling us that this will cause planetary catastrophe. Likewise, current mass extinction is a matter of billions of people trying simply to live their lives, with the consequence that whole swaths of creatures that most of us never see or even know about are wiped off the earth. The same goes for other global environmental problems. The biochemical systems involved are simply too big and the causes and effects too dispersed to grasp them with concreteness.

Abstraction also afflicts political understanding. As they are usually depicted, governing institutions responsible for and best positioned to address environmental dilemmas seem to be made up of anonymous actors operating behind curtains of bureaucratic and official pomp, and standing at such a distance so as to be unreachable. This describes many depictions of the United Nations, negotiating arenas for international environmental diplomacy, boardrooms of major corporate actors, corridors of governmental power, and the financial officers who make the decisions that drive the world economy. Such abstraction can only discourage those wishing to alter environmental affairs and create the illusion that there is no connection between our individual lives and planetary peril.

Global Environmental Politics: From Person to Planet cuts through abstraction by drawing connections. Every section asks readers to understand not only, for example, the architecture of the international state-system and its ability to address global environmental problems, but also how individuals can influence international environmental politics. Likewise, it asks readers to know not only the causes of environmental harm, but also how people can collectively alter the trajectories of causal mechanisms. Moreover, through carefully designed exercises, each section challenges readers to think creatively about how their own lives and engagements can affect global environmental affairs—not merely through lifestyle changes but, more importantly, through collective thinking and action. In short, the book combines the dual tasks of advancing intellectual know-how and exploring the ways each individual reader can see his or her part in addressing the global environmental condition.

A note on the text: To provide a comfortable reading experience, we have deleted footnotes, endnotes, and references but retained in-text citations.

Part I

State of the Planet

Section 1

Species Unbound: Humanity's Environmental Impact

Politics is many things. At its heart, it is about the problems that arise and the virtues that are possible when people live together. We are living together like never before. What was once a smattering of tribes across the vast expanse of the planet is now a teeming population of more than seven billion people knitted together through trade, communication, and globe-spanning concerns. Everywhere we turn—whether physically or virtually—we run into each other. When we do so, wonders and horrors emerge.

The wonders are mind-blowing. Today, cultures are melding to produce pioneering ideas, innovative technologies, and transboundary movements devoted to human betterment. In the palm of our hands we can hold devices that report the weather, provide directions, play music from around the world, and share messages of love independent of geography.

At the same time, the conjunction of billions produces friction. Cultural conflict, economic competition, arguments over scarce resources, and differences of opinion magnify as humanity grows more concentrated and spreads to all corners of the planet. Politics has its work cut out for it in a globalizing world.

Perhaps no virtues and problems are as challenging these days as ecological ones. The earth is our home. Everything we eat, use, or simply come into contact with originates from land, water, soil, air, and other species. For this reason, the earth provides the parameters of human possibility. For millennia, we did not have to pay attention to this because the earth was so vast and our consumptive habits were so circumscribed that we could ignore nature's imperatives with impunity. To be sure, certain parts of the planet suffered as our ancestors depleted fertile soils, polluted particular streams, contaminated air in specific cities, and ruined landscapes in distinct places. But the materiality of the earth itself was never in question. It provided the large backdrop for human activities and thus we neither had to listen carefully to it for enhancing our intellectual, moral, social, or even economic lives nor worry about overshooting its carrying capacity. The earth was the always-giving provider.

This is changing. Humanity has turned into an ecological force in its own right. We have joined the carbon cycle, ocean currents, weather patterns, and even seasons themselves as shapers of the planet's ecosystemic character. This significantly raises the stakes of our actions. At a minimum, we face unprecedented dangers as we inexorably assume more and more of the reins of eco-planetary governance. Concomitantly, greater consciousness about our new status opens the possibility for unparalleled opportunities to direct collective life and build more compassionate, just, and humane societies. Our ability to avoid dangers and create opportunities—to govern—depends upon how skillfully we wield power. The word *governance* means to steer; it involves using power to shape widespread thought and behavior. In a globalized world, we must find ways of steering that both take advantage of and respect the limits of the earth's material gifts.

The measure of our ecological footprint can be gauged along three lines: *sources, sinks,* and *sites.* Sources are those things we use to live our lives. They are the raw materials out of which we build homes, produce paper, fuel vehicles, and cook food. All of them regenerate and thus are not strictly finite, but they do so at tremendously varying rates. For example, trees—which provide wood for paper, construction, and furniture—can regenerate within a few years. In contrast, oil—which is used to create motor fuel, detergents, fertilizers, and plastics—is fossilized life and takes millions of years to produce. Material substances like oil are effectively nonrenewable when viewed from a human timescale. Today, we face diminishing resources. From a global perspective, we are using almost every material resource faster than it can be replaced. Thus, three-quarters of global fisheries face imminent collapse, water tables in all countries are dropping, deforestation claims twenty-five acres per minute, and deposits of easily extractable oil are harder to find. In a globalized world with billions of people increasingly drawing more and more resources from the earth, the planet is reaching its productive and reproductive limits.

If sources have to do with what we draw from the planet, sinks involve what we put back into it. Sinks represent the air, water, soil, and host of organisms that absorb waste. Every act of production and living metabolism generates some type of waste. This is an implication of the second law of thermodynamics. So, while cars burn fuel (and thus use up resources), they also spew out waste in the form of heat, carbon dioxide, nitrous oxide, and other gases. Similarly, while growing food uses fertile soil and seeds, modern methods release fertilizers and often pesticides and herbicides into the air, soil, and waterways. The earth has the ability to absorb some of this; it can dissipate or assimilate waste across various media and organisms. At some point, however, like a kitchen sink when too much stuff flows into it, the earth's absorptive capacity reaches its limit. When this happens landfills grow, air gets polluted, water becomes contaminated, soils lose fertility, and species die off. Today, the earth's key sinks are stopping up. For example, by cutting down trees and burning unprecedented amounts of fossil fuels, humanity has overloaded the planet's carbon system. Forests, oceans, and the atmosphere have assimilated their fill, leading to climate change. Using up sinks in this way leads to significant environmental dangers.

Sites are places of beauty, ecological significance, or simply value. Traditionally, we think of these as mountain ranges, quiet valleys, deep canyons, or open green fields. However, they include any landscape, seascape, or spot on earth that we care about or have come to appreciate. Perhaps all of us have favorite locations that dazzle, calm, or inspire us. For professional ecologists, sites are places of biological significance. They are "ecological hotspots" that house an inordinate number of species, represent a unique ecological expression, or provide a key service to upholding healthy ecosystems. In a globalizing world that spreads its consumptive fingers further across and deeper into the earth for resources, and disseminates its wastes in every nook and cranny of the planet, too many sites are becoming endangered. We are despoiling an increasing number of beautiful, biophysically consequential, and appealing places. The defiling of sites adds an important dimension to environmental harm in that it undermines not just the organic infrastructure of the earth that supports life, but also those amenities of the planet that enhance the quality of life.

In the chapters that make up this section, we have pulled together three voices to help us appreciate today's pressures on sources, sinks, and sites, and more generally provide a sense of the magnitude and character of current environmental affairs. These readings make clear that humanity is having an immense impact on the earth's abilities to sustain life. The effect is so profound that many see us living in a new and distinct geological epoch known as the Anthropocene. The term, as journalist **Elizabeth Kolbert** writes in the first chapter, highlights the fact that human beings have become the central force shaping the planet's condition. Those who look back on the current age from some future time will see indelible signs of our collective activities etched into the planet's geologic features. Our carbon and other forms of pollution will be present in future ice cores and tree rings, our fabrications of steel and copper sandwiched in layers of future rock. The Anthropocene means not only that humanity reigns supreme over the rest of the living world, but that its dominance has achieved geologic significance. This has huge implications for environmental conditions.

Science writer **Charles C. Mann**, in his chapter, traces the roots of the Anthropocene to the "unusual success" of our species. Our big brains and capacity for cooperative social arrangement enabled humanity to develop and practice agriculture, and this was simply the beginning of our ability to take control over and increasingly transform the earth. The problem with this success is that we are collectively pushing up against hard ecological limits. Humanity cannot infinitely colonize the earth's productive and absorptive capacities without severely degrading its biophysical functioning and, in the extreme, threatening large-scale ecosystem collapse. Mann concludes that the earth is in extremely poor health and getting sicker by the day.

What, then, is the nature of the world to come? **Alex Steffen** argues that while the future is certainly not rosy in an ecological sense, there is still a remarkable human capacity for innovation, hope, and even joy. Tapping into such capacity, suggests Steffen, demands that we imagine new ways of being on and with the earth, and this begins with identifying genuine forms of social and political engagement that can make a difference. Steffen outlines the trajectory of such efforts and challenges us to get excited about working on behalf of planetary ecological well-being.

1

Enter the Anthropocene

Elizabeth Kolbert

The path leads up a hill, across a fast-moving stream, back across the stream, and then past the carcass of a sheep. In my view it's raining, but here in the Southern Uplands of Scotland, I'm told, this counts as only a light drizzle, or smirr. Just beyond the final switchback, there's a waterfall, half shrouded in mist, and an outcropping of jagged rock. The rock has bands that run vertically, like a layer cake that's been tipped on its side. My guide, Jan Zalasiewicz, a British stratigrapher, points to a wide stripe of gray. "Bad things happened in here," he says.

The stripe was laid down some 445 million years ago, as sediments slowly piled up on the bottom of an ancient ocean. In those days life was still confined mostly to the water, and it was undergoing a crisis. Between one edge of the three-foot-thick gray band and the other, some 80 percent of marine species died out, many of them the sorts of creatures, like graptolites, that no longer exist. The extinction event, known as the end-Ordovician, was one of the five biggest of the past half billion years. It coincided with extreme changes in climate, in global sea levels, and in ocean chemistry—all caused, perhaps, by a supercontinent drifting over the South Pole.

Stratigraphers like Zalasiewicz are, as a rule, hard to impress. Their job is to piece together Earth's history from clues that can be coaxed out of layers of rock millions of years after the fact. They take the long view—the extremely long view—of events, only the most violent of which are likely to leave behind clear, lasting signals. It's those events that mark the crucial episodes in the planet's 4.5-billion-year story, the turning points that divide it into comprehensible chapters.

So it's disconcerting to learn that many stratigraphers have come to believe that *we* are such an event—that human beings have so altered the planet in just the past century or two that we've ushered in a new epoch: the Anthropocene. Standing in the smirr, I ask Zalasiewicz what he thinks this epoch will look like to the geologists of the distant future, whoever or whatever they may be. Will the transition be a moderate one, like dozens of others that appear in the record, or will it show up as a sharp band in which very bad things happened—like the mass extinction at the end of the Ordovician?

That, Zalasiewicz says, is what we are in the process of determining.

The word "Anthropocene" was coined by Dutch chemist Paul Crutzen about a decade ago. One day Crutzen, who shared a Nobel Prize for discovering the effects of ozone-depleting compounds, was sitting at a scientific conference. The conference chairman kept referring to the Holocene, the epoch that began at the end of the last ice age, 11,500 years ago, and that—officially, at least—continues to this day.

"'Let's stop it,'" Crutzen recalls blurting out. "'We are no longer in the Holocene. We are in the Anthropocene.' Well, it was quiet in the room for a while." When the group took a coffee break, the Anthropocene was the main topic of conversation. Someone suggested that Crutzen copyright the word.

Way back in the 1870s, an Italian geologist named Antonio Stoppani proposed that people had introduced a new era, which he labeled the anthropozoic. Stoppani's proposal was ignored; other scientists found it unscientific. The Anthropocene, by contrast, struck a chord. Human impacts on the world have become a lot more obvious since Stoppani's day, in part because the size of the population has roughly quadrupled, to . . . seven billion. "The pattern of human population growth in the twentieth century was more bacterial than primate," biologist E. O. Wilson has written. Wilson calculates that human biomass is already a hundred times larger than that of any other large animal species that has ever walked the Earth.

In 2002, when Crutzen wrote up the Anthropocene idea in the journal *Nature,* the concept was immediately picked up by researchers working in a wide range of disciplines. Soon it began to appear regularly in the scientific press. "Global Analysis of River Systems: From Earth System Controls to Anthropocene Syndromes" ran the title of one 2003 paper. "Soils and Sediments in the Anthropocene" was the headline of another, published in 2004.

At first most of the scientists using the new geologic term were not geologists. Zalasiewicz, who is one, found the discussions intriguing. "I noticed that Crutzen's term was appearing in the serious literature, without quotation marks and without a sense of irony," he says. In 2007 Zalasiewicz was serving as chairman of the Geological Society of London's Stratigraphy Commission. At a meeting he decided to ask his fellow stratigraphers what they thought of the Anthropocene. Twenty-one of 22 thought the concept had merit.

The group agreed to look at it as a formal problem in geology. Would the Anthropocene satisfy the criteria used for naming a new epoch? In geologic parlance, epochs are relatively short time spans, though they can extend for tens of millions of years. (Periods, such as the Ordovician and the Cretaceous, last much longer, and eras, like the Mesozoic, longer still.) The boundaries between epochs are defined by changes preserved in sedimentary rocks—the emergence of one type of commonly fossilized organism, say, or the disappearance of another.

The rock record of the present doesn't exist yet, of course. So the question was: When it does, will human impacts show up as "stratigraphically significant"? The answer, Zalasiewicz's group decided, is yes—though not necessarily for the reasons you'd expect.

Probably the most obvious way humans are altering the planet is by building cities, which are essentially vast stretches of man-made materials—steel, glass, concrete, and brick. But it turns out most cities are not good candidates for long-term preservation, for the simple reason that they're built on land, and on land the forces of erosion tend to win out over those of sedimentation. From a geologic perspective, the most plainly visible human effects on the landscape today "may in some ways be the most transient," Zalasiewicz has observed.

Humans have also transformed the world through farming; something like 38 percent of the planet's ice-free land is now devoted to agriculture. Here again, some of the effects that seem most significant today will leave behind only subtle traces at best.

Fertilizer factories, for example, now fix more nitrogen from the air, converting it to a biologically usable form, than all the plants and microbes on land; the runoff from fertilized fields is triggering life-throttling blooms of algae at river mouths all over the world. But this global perturbation of the nitrogen cycle will be hard to detect, because synthesized nitrogen is just like its natural equivalent. Future geologists are more likely to grasp the scale of 21st-century industrial agriculture from the pollen record—from the monochrome stretches of corn, wheat, and soy pollen that will have replaced the varied record left behind by rain forests or prairies.

The leveling of the world's forests will send at least two coded signals to future stratigraphers, though deciphering the first may be tricky. Massive amounts of soil eroding off denuded land are increasing sedimentation in some parts of the world—but at the same time the dams we've built on most of the world's major rivers are holding back sediment that would otherwise be washed to sea. The second signal of deforestation should come through clearer. Loss of forest habitat is a major cause of extinctions, which are now happening at a rate hundreds or even thousands of times higher than during most of the past half billion years. If current trends continue, the rate may soon be tens of thousands of times higher.

Probably the most significant change, from a geologic perspective, is one that's invisible to us—the change in the composition of the atmosphere. Carbon dioxide emissions are colorless, odorless, and in an immediate sense, harmless. But their warming effects could easily push global temperatures to levels that have not been seen for millions of years. Some plants and animals are already shifting their ranges toward the Poles, and those shifts will leave traces in the fossil record. Some species will not survive the warming at all. Meanwhile rising temperatures could eventually raise sea levels 20 feet or more.

Long after our cars, cities, and factories have turned to dust, the consequences of burning billions of tons' worth of coal and oil are likely to be clearly discernible. As carbon dioxide warms the planet, it also seeps into the oceans and acidifies them. Sometime this century they may become acidified to the point that corals can no longer construct reefs, which would register in the geologic record as a "reef gap." Reef gaps have marked each of the past five major mass extinctions. The most recent one, which is believed to have been caused by the impact of an asteroid, took place 65 million years ago, at the end of the Cretaceous period; it eliminated not just the dinosaurs, but also the plesiosaurs, pterosaurs, and ammonites. The scale of what's happening now to the oceans is, by many accounts, unmatched since then. To future geologists, Zalasiewicz says, our impact may look as sudden and profound as that of an asteroid.

If we have indeed entered a new epoch, then when exactly did it begin? When did human impacts rise to the level of geologic significance?

William Ruddiman, a paleoclimatologist at the University of Virginia, has proposed that the invention of agriculture some 8,000 years ago, and the deforestation that resulted, led to an increase in atmospheric CO_2 just large enough to stave off what otherwise would have been the start of a new ice age; in his view, humans have been the dominant force on the planet practically since the start of the Holocene. Crutzen has suggested that the Anthropocene began in the late 18th century, when, ice cores show, carbon dioxide levels began what has since proved to be an uninterrupted rise. Other scientists put the beginning of the new epoch in the middle of the 20th century, when the rates of both population growth and consumption accelerated rapidly.

Zalasiewicz now heads a working group of the International Commission on Stratigraphy (ICS) that is tasked with officially determining whether the Anthropocene deserves to be incorporated into the geologic timescale. A final decision will require votes by both the ICS and its parent organization, the International Union of Geological Sciences. The process is likely to take years. As it drags on, the decision may well become easier. Some scientists argue that we've not yet reached the start of the Anthropocene—not because we haven't had a dramatic impact on the planet, but because the next several decades are likely to prove even more stratigraphically significant than the past few centuries. "Do we decide the Anthropocene's here, or do we wait 20 years and things will be even worse?" says Mark Williams, a geologist and colleague of Zalasiewicz's at the University of Leicester in England.

Crutzen, who started the debate, thinks its real value won't lie in revisions to geology textbooks. His purpose is broader: He wants to focus our attention on the consequences of our collective action—and on how we might still avert the worst. "What I hope," he says, "is that the term 'Anthropocene' will be a warning to the world."

2

State of the Species

Charles C. Mann

The problem with environmentalists, Lynn Margulis used to say, is that they think conservation has something to do with biological reality. A researcher who specialized in cells and microorganisms, Margulis was one of the most important biologists in the last half century—she literally helped to reorder the tree of life, convincing her colleagues that it did not consist of two kingdoms (plants and animals), but five or even six (plants, animals, fungi, protists, and two types of bacteria).

Until Margulis's death . . . she lived in my town, and I would bump into her on the street from time to time. She knew I was interested in ecology, and she liked to needle me. Hey, *Charles,* she would call out, are you still all worked up about protecting endangered *species?*

Margulis was no apologist for unthinking destruction. Still, she couldn't help regarding conservationists' preoccupation with the fate of birds, mammals, and plants as evidence of their ignorance about the greatest source of evolutionary creativity: the microworld of bacteria, fungi, and protists. More than 90 percent of the living matter on earth consists of microorganisms and viruses, she liked to point out. Heck, the number of bacterial cells in our body is ten times more than the number of human cells!

Bacteria and protists can do things undreamed of by clumsy mammals like us: form giant supercolonies, reproduce either asexually or by swapping genes with others, routinely incorporate DNA from entirely unrelated species, merge into symbiotic beings—the list is as endless as it is amazing. Microorganisms have changed the face of the earth, crumbling stone and even giving rise to the oxygen we breathe. Compared to this power and diversity, Margulis liked to tell me, pandas and polar bears were biological epiphenomena—interesting and fun, perhaps, but not actually *significant.*

Does that apply to human beings, too? I once asked her, feeling like someone whining to Copernicus about why he couldn't move the earth a little closer to the center of the universe. Aren't we special *at all?*

This was just chitchat on the street, so I didn't write anything down. But as I recall it, she answered that *Homo sapiens* actually might be interesting—for a mammal, anyway. For one thing, she said, we're unusually successful.

Seeing my face brighten, she added: Of course, the fate of every successful species is to wipe itself out. . . .

Why and how did humankind become "unusually successful"? And what, to an evolutionary biologist, does "success" mean, if self-destruction is part of the definition? Does that self-destruction include the rest of the biosphere? What are human beings in the grand scheme of things anyway, and where are we headed? What is human nature, if there is such a thing, and how did we acquire it? What does that nature portend for our interactions with the environment? With 7 billion of us crowding the planet, it's hard to imagine more vital questions. . . .

THE WORLD IS A PETRI DISH

As a student at the University of Moscow in the 1920s, Georgii Gause spent years trying—and failing—to drum up support from the Rockefeller Foundation, then the most prominent funding source for non-American scientists who wished to work in the United States. Hoping to dazzle the foundation, Gause decided to perform some nifty experiments and describe the results in his grant application.

By today's standards, his methodology was simplicity itself. Gause placed half a gram of oatmeal in one hundred cubic centimeters of water, boiled the results for ten minutes to create a broth, strained the liquid portion of the broth into a container, diluted the mixture by adding water, and then decanted the contents into small, flat-bottomed test tubes. Into each he dripped five *Paramecium caudatum* or *Stylonychia mytilus,* both single-celled protozoans, one species per tube. Each of Gause's test tubes was a pocket ecosystem, a food web with a single node. He stored the tubes in warm places for a week and observed the results. He set down his conclusions in a 163-page book, *The Struggle for Existence,* published in 1934. . . .

What Gause saw in his test tubes is often depicted in a graph, time on the horizontal axis, the number of protozoa on the vertical. The line on the graph is a distorted bell curve, with its left side twisted and stretched into a kind of flattened S. At first the number of protozoans grows slowly, and the graph line slowly ascends to the right. But then the line hits an inflection point, and suddenly rockets upward—a frenzy of exponential growth. The mad rise continues until the organism begins to run out of food, at which point there is a second inflection point, and the growth curve levels off again as bacteria begin to die. Eventually the line descends, and the population falls toward zero.

Years ago I watched Lynn Margulis, one of Gause's successors, demonstrate these conclusions to a class at the University of Massachusetts with a time-lapse video of *Proteus vulgaris,* a bacterium that lives in the gastrointestinal tract. To humans, she said, *P. vulgaris* is mainly notable as a cause of urinary-tract infections. Left alone, it divides about every fifteen minutes. Margulis switched on the projector. Onscreen was a small, wobbly bubble—*P. vulgaris*—in a shallow, circular glass container: a petri dish. The class gasped. The cells in the time-lapse video seemed to shiver and boil, doubling in number every few seconds, colonies exploding out until the mass of bacteria filled the screen. In just thirty-six hours, she said, this single bacterium could cover the entire planet in a foot-deep layer of single-celled ooze. Twelve hours after that, it would create a living ball of bacteria the size of the earth.

Such a calamity never happens, because competing organisms and lack of resources prevent the overwhelming majority of *P. vulgaris* from reproducing. This, Margulis said, is natural selection, Darwin's great insight. All living creatures have the same purpose: to make more of themselves, ensuring their biological future by the only means available. Natural selection stands in the way of this goal. It prunes back almost all species, restricting their numbers and confining their range. In the human body, *P. vulgaris* is checked by the size of its habitat (portions of the human gut), the limits to its supply of nourishment (food proteins), and other, competing organisms. Thus constrained, its population remains roughly steady.

In the petri dish, by contrast, competition is absent; nutrients and habitat seem limitless, at least at first. The bacterium hits the first inflection point and rockets up the left side of the curve, swamping the petri dish in a reproductive frenzy. But then its colonies slam into the second inflection point: the edge of the dish. When the dish's nutrient supply is exhausted, *P. vulgaris* experiences a miniapocalypse.

By luck or superior adaptation, a few species manage to escape their limits, at least for a while. Nature's success stories, they are like Gause's protozoans; the world is their petri dish. Their populations grow exponentially; they take over large areas, overwhelming their environment as if no force opposed them. Then they annihilate themselves, drowning in their own wastes or starving from lack of food.

To someone like Margulis, *Homo sapiens* looks like one of these briefly fortunate species.

THE WHIP HAND

No more than a few hundred people initially migrated from Africa, if geneticists are correct. But they emerged into landscapes that by today's standards were as rich as Eden. Cool mountains, tropical wetlands, lush forests—all were teeming with food. Fish in the sea, birds in the air, fruit on the trees: breakfast was everywhere. People moved in.

Despite our territorial expansion, though, humans were still only in the initial stages of Gause's oddly shaped curve. Ten thousand years ago, most demographers believe, we numbered barely 5 million, about one human being for every hundred square kilometers of the earth's land surface. *Homo sapiens* was a scarcely noticeable dusting on the surface of a planet dominated by microbes. Nevertheless, at about this time—10,000 years ago, give or take a millennium—humankind finally began to approach the first inflection point. Our species was inventing agriculture. . . .

Farming converted most of the habitable world into a petri dish. Foragers manipulated their environment with fire, burning areas to kill insects and encourage the growth of useful species—plants we liked to eat, plants that attracted the other creatures we liked to eat. Nonetheless, their diets were largely restricted to what nature happened to provide in any given time and season. Agriculture gave humanity the whip hand. Instead of natural ecosystems with their haphazard mix of species (so many useless organisms guzzling up resources!), farms are taut, disciplined communities conceived and dedicated to the maintenance of a single species: us.

Before agriculture, the Ukraine, American Midwest, and lower Yangzi were barely hospitable food deserts, sparsely inhabited landscapes of insects and grass; they became breadbaskets as people scythed away suites of species that used soil and water we wanted to dominate and replaced them with wheat, rice, and maize (corn). To one of Margulis's beloved bacteria, a petri dish is a uniform expanse of nutrients, all of which it can seize and consume. For *Homo sapiens,* agriculture transformed the planet into something similar.

As in a time-lapse movie, we divided and multiplied across the newly opened land. It had taken *Homo sapiens* 2.0, behaviorally modern humans, not even 50,000 years to reach the farthest corners of the globe. *Homo sapiens* 2.0.A—A for agriculture—took a tenth of that time to conquer the planet. . . .

As any biologist would predict, success led to an increase in human numbers. . . . Rocketing up the growth curve, human beings "now appropriate nearly 40% . . . of potential terrestrial productivity." This figure dates from 1986—a famous estimate by a team of Stanford biologists. Ten years later, a second Stanford team calculated that the "fraction of the land's biological production that is used or dominated" by our species had risen to as much as 50 percent. In 2000, the chemist Paul Crutzen gave a name to our time: the "Anthropocene," the era in which *Homo sapiens* became a force operating on a planetary scale. That year, half of the world's accessible fresh water was consumed by human beings.

Lynn Margulis, it seems safe to say, would have scoffed at these assessments of human domination over the natural world, which, in every case I know of, do not take into account the enormous impact of the microworld.

But she would not have disputed the central idea: *Homo sapiens* has become a successful species, and is growing accordingly.

If we follow Gause's pattern, growth will continue at a delirious speed until we hit the second inflection point. At that time we will have exhausted the resources of the global petri dish, or effectively made the atmosphere toxic with our carbon-dioxide waste, or both. After that, human life will be, briefly, a Hobbesian nightmare, the living overwhelmed by the dead. When the king falls, so do his minions; it is possible that our fall might also take down most mammals and many plants. Possibly sooner, quite likely later, in this scenario, the earth will again be a choir of bacteria, fungi, and insects, as it has been through most of its history.

It would be foolish to expect anything else, Margulis thought. More than that, it would be *unnatural.* . . .

DISCOUNT RATES

By 2050, demographers predict, as many as 10 billion human beings will walk the earth, 3 billion more than today. Not only will more people exist than ever before, they will be richer than ever before. In the last three decades hundreds of millions in China, India, and other formerly poor places have lifted themselves from destitution—arguably the most important, and certainly the most heartening, accomplishment of our time. Yet, like all human enterprises, this great success will pose great difficulties.

In the past, rising incomes have invariably prompted rising demand for goods and services. Billions more jobs, homes, cars, fancy electronics—these are things the newly prosperous will want. (Why shouldn't they?) But the greatest challenge may be the most basic of all: feeding these extra mouths. To agronomists, the prospect is sobering. The newly affluent will not want their ancestors' gruel. Instead they will ask for pork and beef and lamb. Salmon will sizzle on their outdoor grills. In winter, they will want strawberries, like people in New York and London, and clean Bibb lettuce from hydroponic gardens.

All of these, each and every one, require vastly more resources to produce than simple peasant agriculture. Already 35 percent of the world's grain harvest is used to feed livestock. The process is terribly inefficient: between seven and ten kilograms of grain are required to produce one kilogram of beef. Not only will the world's farmers have to produce enough wheat and maize to feed 3 billion more people, they will have to produce enough to give them all hamburgers and steaks. Given present patterns of food consumption, economists believe, we will need to produce about 40 percent more grain in 2050 than we do today.

How can we provide these things for all these new people? That is only part of the question. The full question is: How can we provide them without wrecking the natural systems on which all depend?

Scientists, activists, and politicians have proposed many solutions, each from a different ideological and moral perspective. Some argue that we must drastically throttle industrial civilization. (Stop energy-intensive, chemical-based farming today! Eliminate fossil fuels to halt climate change!) Others claim that only intense exploitation of scientific knowledge can save us. (Plant super-productive, genetically modified crops now! Switch to nuclear power to halt climate change!) No matter which course is chosen, though, it will require radical, large-scale transformations in the human enterprise—a daunting, hideously expensive task.

Worse, the ship is too large to turn quickly. The world's food supply cannot be decoupled rapidly from industrial agriculture, if that is seen as the answer. Aquifers cannot be recharged with a snap of the fingers. If the high-tech route is chosen, genetically modified crops cannot be bred and tested overnight. Similarly, carbon-sequestration techniques and nuclear power plants cannot be deployed instantly. Changes must be planned and executed decades in advance of the usual signals of crisis, but that's like asking healthy, happy sixteen-year-olds to write living wills.

Not only is the task daunting, it's *strange*. In the name of nature, we are asking human beings to do something deeply unnatural, something no other species has ever done or could ever do: constrain its own growth (at least in some ways). Zebra mussels in the Great Lakes, brown tree snakes in Guam, water hyacinth in African rivers, gypsy moths in the northeastern U.S., rabbits in Australia, Burmese pythons in Florida—all these successful species have overrun their environments, heedlessly wiping out other creatures. Like Gause's protozoans, they are racing to find the edges of their petri dish. Not one has voluntarily turned back. Now we are asking *Homo sapiens* to fence itself in.

What a peculiar thing to ask! Economists like to talk about the "discount rate," which is their term for preferring a bird in hand today over two in the bush tomorrow. The term sums up part of our human nature as well. Evolving in small, constantly moving bands, we are as hard-wired to focus on the immediate and local over the long-term and faraway as we are to prefer parklike savannas to deep dark forests. Thus, we care more about the broken stoplight up the street today than conditions next year in Croatia, Cambodia, or the Congo. Rightly so, evolutionists point out: Americans are far more likely to be killed at that stoplight today than in the Congo next year. Yet here we are asking governments to focus on potential planetary boundaries that may not be reached for decades. Given the discount rate, nothing could be more understandable than the U.S. Congress's failure to grapple with, say, climate change. From this perspective, is there any reason to imagine that *Homo sapiens*, unlike mussels, snakes, and moths, can exempt itself from the natural fate of all successful species?

To biologists like Margulis, who spend their careers arguing that humans are simply part of the natural order, the answer should be clear. All life is similar at base. All species seek without pause to make more of themselves—that is their goal. By multiplying till we reach our maximum possible numbers, even as we take out much of the planet, we are fulfilling our destiny.

From this vantage, the answer to the question [of] whether we are doomed to destroy ourselves is yes. It should be obvious.

Should be—but perhaps is not. . . .

3

Humanity's Potential

Alex Steffen

In the last five years, the scope, scale, and speed of the planetary challenges we face seem to have grown and accelerated. The ecological news has gone from bad and distant to terrible and immediate. We now realize that we are in the midst of a crisis that worsens with every passing day, and that things are worse than we thought.

That crisis can be measured. In 2009, a group of scientists led by the Stockholm Resilience Centre determined "planetary boundaries" for nine major natural systems that represent the earth's ability to sustain life, its "biocapacity": greenhouse-gas concentrations in the atmosphere, ozone depletion, ocean acidity, freshwater consumption, deforestation, the global nitrogen cycle, terrestrial biodiversity, chemicals dispersion, and marine ecosystems. They assigned a number for the safe upper limit of human impact on that system, such as the amount of the ozone layer that has been compromised. What they found was that humanity is close to straying beyond every one of these boundaries.

Though the boundaries are the subject of a global debate involving hosts of scientists and advocates, each is a massive issue in its own right, acknowledged to be a serious crisis by the experts involved. Put them together—as we must, since, as part of a single, living planet, they are all interconnected and affect one another—and we begin to see how massive the current ecological crisis is. It's crystal clear that humanity has pushed nature beyond its biocapacity and has overshot the planet's limits.

Signs of overshoot are erupting all around us: melting polar ice caps, freak weather, massive storms, ocean dead zones, wild-fires, food shortages,

24

heat waves, extinctions of species, rising seas, desertification, the spread of invasive plants and animals. The fabric of the biosphere is coming unraveled, and we're tugging on the loose threads.

Our unsustainably intensive uses of the earth have brought the increased risk of passing catastrophic tipping points; indeed, many eminent scientists warn that those tipping points now look less like distant threats than imminent dangers. Ecological damage and the resulting dangers are largely cumulative: add enough together, and the consequences grow far larger than the sum of the individual acts of destruction. We don't know when another day of environmental irresponsibility will set in motion not just a little more ecological destruction but a slide into a profoundly larger and more comprehensive catastrophe. We don't know which snowflake will tip us into an avalanche, but we know that the risk of avalanche is high.

With all of this in mind, it ought to be our goal to have no impact—to bring our ecological footprint below biocapacity, perhaps even to start reweaving the living fabric of the planet before the whole tapestry rips apart. We need to get back within planetary boundaries, and fast.

The concept of planetary boundaries helps us grasp our ecological peril, but it leaves out humanity. People's actions—how we live, how we treat each other, how we build our societies—are the other half of our planetary equation. We can't understand how much is changing without grappling with human aspirations and abilities and the very real generational thresholds looming in front of us.

The global population has mushroomed from 2.5 billion to over 7 billion in just the last sixty years. And we live on a planet where almost half of the population in the least developed countries consists of teenagers and children. There are a lot of young women about to enter their childbearing years (mostly in poor countries), and that means the number of humans is almost certain to grow.

Huge strides are being made toward slowing the population explosion—by educating young women, providing them with economic opportunities, and making sure they have access to family-planning information: the three best means of slowing population growth. But the odds are good that most young women will still want to have families, as we nearly all do. Even in the best-case scenarios we are headed toward a peak population of at least 9 billion people shortly after mid-century, before population growth levels off and population slowly begins to decline.

Almost all of those 9 billion people will aspire to greater prosperity, reaching for what they see as the good life. The Global North and the Global South—the "developed" and "developing" worlds—now live around the corner from each other and are mutually dependent. Everywhere in the world, the poor see how the rich live, if not out their windows, then on TV. People who live in shanties can compare the material quality of their own lives with that of people who fly over them in jets.

Kids from Cape Town to Caracas to Novosibirsk—and everywhere in between—want globally middle-class lives. They want refrigerators, scooters, smart phones, and the latest fashions. They want education, health care, good jobs, and governments that help them solve their problems. We can be sure that every one of the billions of kids now growing up wants a better life and has his or her own dreams.

Unfortunately, the model that people in the Global North used to get rich is no longer replicable. As a famous 2002 report, the *Jo'burg Memo,* put it, "There is no escape from the conclusion that the world's growing population cannot attain a Western standard of living by following conventional paths to development. The resources required are too vast, too expansive, and too damaging to local and global ecosystems."

There's no way the whole world could get rich the way Americans and Europeans did, even if we didn't care about the consequences. We're already beyond the planetary boundaries, and business as usual now has prohibitive environmental effects. We're running out of places to dump and spew waste without dire human cost. We've also used up a tremendous share of the planet's easy bounty—from old trees to cheap oil to big fish to virgin metals—meaning that conventional resource and energy use will largely depend on supplies that are increasingly difficult to obtain (and often more and more ecologically costly).

The combination of declining stocks (less good stuff to use) and shrinking sinks (fewer places to safely put the bad stuff) will make development as usual far more difficult for the world's poor. The "Western model" of development is bankrupt.

We need to replace that model of development with a new one. For a new model to work in the real world, it must be rugged and shockproof—because the world's a rough place these days:

More than 2 billion people have no access to electricity. About the same number have no safe means of disposing of their sewage. More than 1 billion drink fetid water. Over 1.2 billion don't always have enough to eat, and at least 840 million are suffering from chronic hunger and are only one bad harvest away from mass starvation. Hungry people don't have the energy to work as hard—economists estimate that somewhere between $64 billion and $12.8 billion is lost annually from developing-world economies because of malnutrition. Hungry people are sick people, and sick people, in turn, slide further into poverty.

Common, preventable diseases like childhood diarrhea kill millions of people every year, and other diseases are growing epidemic in a world where hundreds of millions have no medical care at all. AIDS alone is expected to kill 68 million people by the year 2020, leaving at least 20 million children orphaned. Some countries, like Botswana and Zimbabwe, will have lost half their adult population to the disease by the end of the decade.

Amid these sorts of societal holocausts, all other services decline, especially education: more thon 800 million people worldwide are illiterate, 60 percent of them women. And uneducated people are, in turn, less likely to understand good hygiene, to be able to master new farming techniques, or to participate in democracy in any meaningful way (where it exists at all). For the poorest 1 billion people, life has become a series of vicious deteriorations and inescapable traps. For 2 billion of their neighbors, who are doing slightly better, this poverty creates instability and a nasty backdraft, making it harder to effect any progress at all. This is part of the context in which the environment is unraveling. . . .

Already, we see a huge gap between the laws and practices the nations of the world profess to embrace and the reality on the ground, where laws go unenforced and people are powerless to challenge the business interests that are destroying the systems upon which they must depend to live. Often those destructive projects are funded and advised by banks and development agencies in the Global North, in the name of fighting poverty. But poor people living in toxic landscapes of industrial waste or amid the burnt stumps of what were once forests can see in concrete terms the meaning of Paul Hawken's condemnation that we have an economy where we "steal the future, sell it in the present, and call it G.D.P."

Exploitation and corruption make the challenge more difficult—so much so that any new model of sustainable prosperity needs not only to take them into account, but to work to mitigate them. If the answer to our ecological crisis doesn't also lead to greater security for everyone and help spread democracy, rule of law, and open government and business practices, it is, in fact, no answer at all.

The other side of the corruption and exploitation coin is the ongoing waste of human potential and the growing cost of lost opportunities to engage the world's poor and young in transforming their own situations. A planet full of young people means a world of fresh starts, but a child today must be helped today: twenty years from now may be too late.

Another two decades of the status quo will make many of our goals nearly impossible. Needless deaths, injuries, sicknesses, and malnutrition today will impose astronomical costs on us over the coming decades. Missed opportunities to educate children (especially girls) leave lifetimes of limited options. The traumas of conflict and collapse, of natural disasters and family tragedies, combine with the strains of living in extreme poverty to leave hundreds of millions with lifelong difficulties with coping.

The disillusionment of a generation of young people, who find themselves trapped in corrupt or failing states, or simply shut out of opportunities for dignity and work in the global economy, can turn them away from productive engagement with the problems around them and lead some of them toward extremism and terror. As much as we want to believe in an endless potential for human transformation, the reality is that people's energy, spirit, and capacity for growth are themselves limited resources.

Right now, we're squandering their hopes in mind-boggling proportions. Every passing year makes it more difficult to raise billions of people out of poverty to become parts of stable, democratic states with functioning economic, legal, and health systems. Meanwhile, climate vulnerabilities, food shortages, and rising energy costs begin to undermine even the progress much of the developing world has managed so far. There are generational thresholds for change, and we may not be acting boldly enough to move through them.

The brutal reality is that failure is possible in human societies as well as in ecological systems. There are points beyond which societal problems start to become impossible to solve. And when you combine the two—an ongoing societal meltdown with massive ecological degradation—the result can be real, catastrophic failure that lasts for generations, perhaps effectively forever.

But failure is not the only option.

If we can tap into the best that people have to offer, we have the capacity to transform both our social and our ecological problems at once. If we spend the next two decades in action, we may be surprised at how much different life will be in forty years.

We may be on the verge of creating a bright green model of development that not only reduces the ecological impact of prosperity, but is available to billions more people in ways that increase their resilience to disaster and help make their social and political systems more rugged. Just how dramatically different that model is, though, is indicated by how strange its essential characteristics may seem to us today. And its first characteristic is that people living in a bright green world cause essentially no ecological harm.

It is simple common sense that practices that are unsustainable cannot continue, and we know that propping up unsustainable practices with nonrenewable resources has even more dramatic consequences. And yet we are currently growing rapidly less sustainable, and using more and more nonrenewable resources to keep the ecological consequences at bay. This must stop. All of this is just plain speaking, and ought to be obvious to any informed observer.

To say, however, that the standard of zero impact is not widely understood and endorsed would be a whopping understatement. Most people rarely see the things they do, buy, and use as being directly part of the living systems of the planet. Few of those people who do think of their connection to nature have ever thought through what their lives would feel and look like if they were designed to have no impact at all. For most people, a 10- or 20-percent improvement sounds like a big deal—in large part because the improvements they're most familiar with involve giving things up. When they do encounter it, the idea of "zero" looms like a giant wall of deprivation.

But zero-impact living, done right, is the good life. It doesn't have to be a sacrifice; it may, in fact, make us wealthier, healthier, and more satisfied. (It will certainly make our children and grandchildren happier than they'd be on a ruined planet.)

Some of the changes a zero-impact future will demand are solutions we've only just recently come to accept but that are mainstreaming fast, like converting from fossil fuels to wind and solar energy. Some of them are innovations that are only now unfolding around us, like radical energy efficiency and completely recyclable products. Some of them are healthy lifestyle choices, like eating less meat and becoming more strategic about how and why we shop, buying less stuff at a better quality.

Already, many of these types of clean technologies and sustainable designs pay for themselves in cost savings and in better health. But this first generation of green solutions is just the beginning of the story. The main plot of that story is how we build the places where we live.

Because cities are the funnels through which raw materials and energy flow to create prosperity (and generate waste), environmental problems increasingly boil down to the structure of cities and the way urban dwellers' needs are met. Cities define the global economy as well, and for most of humanity, living in an innovative, dynamic, well-governed city means the difference between the most marginal existence and poverty alleviation, greater access to education and health services, and a better life for their children. From population growth to climate emissions, human security to public health, the driving forces of the twenty-first century will be defined on the streets of the world's cities and made manifest in their communities, infrastructures, and buildings.

How we build these communities and engineer the infrastructure systems that support them is going through extreme changes. The idea that contemporary suburban American lifestyles—with their McMansions, SUVs, and big-box stores—somehow represent the best form of prosperity we could possibly invent has become obviously ludicrous. But many of us are completely unprepared for the transformation that lies ahead in the next four decades.

To understand that transformation, we need to remember that more than half of humanity already lives in cities, with 200,000 new urban dwellers being added every day. This equates to roughly an urban area the population of Seattle every three days. By 2050, 70 percent of all humans, or 6 billion people, will live in cities. That means building roughly four thousand Seattles in the next forty years.

Even that shocking figure understates the reality that nearly all of humanity will live less than a day's travel from a midsize city. "Rural" life—as the opposite of urban life, disconnected from the global flow of information and trade—will simply cease to exist in all but the most remote corners of the earth. Whether this is a good or a bad thing is open to debate; whether it will happen is not.

Humanity will be an overwhelmingly urban species, and the making of the cities we call home will propel the global economy for the next forty years, transforming existing cities and driving the creation of new ones. By 2030, for example, China is expected to have more than 220 cities with populations larger than 1 million people. Asia as a whole may have more than four hundred. By comparison, all of Europe today has only thirty-five.

City-building at that scale will, of necessity, trigger a massive outburst of urban innovation. There will be no alternative to bright green designs and technologies to meet the consumption demands of 6 billion urbanites for everything from food to housing to transportation. And since most of the systems serving these new cities will themselves be new creations, we have the opportunity to deploy the smartest, most sustainable available technologies and designs. The emerging cities of the Global South could be far more sustainable than the cities of the Global North today, precisely because they are new and poor, and can't afford to use anything but the best possible solutions.

Cities offer us the chance to reinvent prosperity. We know that cities are the best leverage point we have for transforming the impacts of prosperity. At the city level, systems are big enough to make a difference on big problems like climate change and materials depletion, yet small enough to grasp. We can build zero-impact cities, and we need to. If carbon-neutrality and zero-waste systems are going to develop, they'll be led by cities.

We've never had more tools at hand for changing how cities are built. From Copenhagen to Curitiba, Melbourne to Vancouver, urban leaders are showing that both new developments and city centers can be rebuilt to promote compact urbanism, vibrant main streets, welcoming public places, a high quality of life, even car-free communities. Whether the task is retrofitting a historic building, building bike lanes, designing a solar-powered apartment block, or creating infill on a residential street with a cozy home on a small lot, a wealth of innovations have already been proven in the world's leading cities, and thousands more are on the way.

With radical new architectural designs, we're capable of making structures that use 90 percent less energy than the ones the last generation built. With approaches like green infrastructure and district energy, we can use water and power in far more sustainable ways. With new communications technologies suffusing our streets, we're able to forge entirely new relationships with our neighborhoods and redefine how and why we move around them.

And with new cultures of urban living, we're seeing the growth of innovative arrangements for providing for our needs, from car sharing to co-owning household products to providing community support for area farmers in exchange for fresh veggies on a weekly basis. We're even beginning to understand how to remake fraying suburbs into walkable towns, proving that even the most unsustainable places offer opportunities to create thriving metropolitan regions.

For those of us in the Global North, these new tools also highlight the fact that we have a job to do. We bear responsibility for most of the planetary harm humanity has so far caused (Americans alone, for instance, have contributed almost one third of all the greenhouse gases now heating up our planet). We're also much wealthier, with an inheritance of universities and intellectual institutions that gives us a much greater capacity for innovation than the rest of the world.

These realities—our responsibility and our capability—combine to make urban reinvention our duty. We need to lead the way in redefining what urban life can mean. We need to expand the tool set, invent new models, increase our technological abilities, provide case studies and proofs-of-concept, and, ultimately, show positive evidence that bright green urbanism works so that these emerging cities can adopt it as they grow. The urban future demands trailblazers.

The kicker is that all of these changes offer unexpected upsides. Bright green cities are not just more responsible to our obligations to the future: piles of research show that they also are more economically competitive, generate more innovation, are healthier and safer for their citizens, are better braced to withstand climate chaos, and are easier to make resilient in a turbulent world. We won't just live more virtuously in a bright green city, we'll live better.

That presents us with an amazing opportunity. If we think big, we have a chance, now, to improve our own lives, do the right thing, and help ensure that the future our kids inherit is one we'll want them to live in.

If we squander that opportunity, no amount of virtuous living, not even a tidal wave of small steps, will make up for it. Without action that responds to the scope, scale, and speed of the challenges we face, nothing else much matters. In that light, our personal behavior is essentially meaningless, especially if it isn't part of a larger effort to identify ways of changing our cities, transportation, agriculture, and energy systems to function much more sustainably. If we want to change our impacts, we need to change our systems, and on a scope we almost never talk about—stretching through essentially every aspect of our society.

We're not alone in that work. We may be facing an unprecedented planetary crisis, but we're also in a moment of innovation unlike any that has come before. We find ourselves in a time when all over the world, millions of people are working to invent, use, and share worldchanging tools, models, and ideas. We live in an era when the number of people working to make the world better is exploding. Humanity's fate rests on the outcome of the race between problem solvers and the problems themselves. The world is getting better—we just have to make sure it gets better faster than it gets worse.

We don't need a miracle to win this race; we need a movement. We need millions more people who are committed to doing their part to embrace good ideas, find new solutions in their own work, and live and share what they learn.

Each of us has a role to play, and each of us can be part of that movement to change the world. What's needed is not unflinching loyalty to some supreme leader or mystical adherence to some cult's belief system, but millions of us doing our best to think for ourselves and share what we know. . . .

If you're ready to change the world, the planet needs you and there's no time to lose. The crucial first step is to begin to imagine the future you'd like to see, because you can't build what you can't imagine. . . . Find ideas that speak to you. Wonder about the possibilities ahead of us. Think about what life could be like in a bright green future—what your life could be like, in the city where you live, in a world improved by better ideas and new solutions.

Why is thinking about solutions important? Because we're starving for better thinking. The media bombards us with pessimism about the world's problems, portrays the world as a hostile place, urges us to define ourselves as consumers, and lauds political cynicism and mistrust of academia, science, and government. The average newscast is a lesson in isolated despair.

Pessimism and cynicism sap our willingness to confront the wrongs in the world. They make us fearful. They make us small. Optimism, on the other hand, makes us bigger. It helps us envision a better future, connects us to new friends and allies, turns our hopes into strengths: optimism makes us worldchanging. . . .

Section 1 Exercise

The Time Machine

For centuries, people in the West have looked to the future with a sense of promise. The future held the prospect of a better life—one of more comfort, higher levels of material well-being, less sickness, and more happiness. For some people now, however, the Anthropocene casts this orientation into question. The future is laden not with hope, but with extraordinary uncertainty.

Imagine that you are sitting in a time machine. You are required to make a choice. You can go back 300 years or forward 300 years. You can't stay in the present, and once you have made your decision, you're not coming back. If you choose to go back 300 years, it is to the place and condition in which your ancestors lived. You will live with and among them. If you choose to go forward 300 years, it is to your present town or city, as you imagine the ecological and social conditions will be. In both cases, you will be giving up all that you know now and will adopt what is known at your place of arrival.

Which would you choose? Would you go forward or back? Why? On a piece of paper, make two columns. In column A, list the reasons for your choice. In column B, list any regrets you might have in your choice.

If you are completing this exercise in a classroom setting, share your thoughts with a partner, then with the class as a whole.

What's the impulse driving your decision to go backward or forward in time? How much does fear play a role? What about excitement? Over which aspects of the choice do you experience most conflict? Note the implication of your decision: you're choosing to leave the Anthropocene or to go deeper into it. What do your decision and the factors that drove it tell you about our present moment on earth?

Section 2

Four Planetary Challenges:
Climate, Extinction, Water, and Food

One of the most iconic, and perhaps overused, images in environmental studies shows the earth as seen from the moon. Taken in 1968, the photograph below, titled "Earthrise," shows the planet awash in a swirl of white clouds, blue oceans, and gray landmasses.

Earthrise. (Photograph courtesy of NASA)

Many credit the photograph with helping to jump-start the environmental movement since it shows the finitude and therefore the fragility of the planet, and the oneness of life on earth. The photograph shows a little ball surrounded by the vastness of space but with no political boundaries, ethnic differences, species differentiation, or any of the other divisions that suggest one part of life is more important than another.

The photograph's title may be more pregnant than its originators understood. The photo takes us out of our everyday lives. It literally "rises" us out of personal, communal, national, and even international concerns, and calls on us to understand existence from one of the widest angles possible. "Earthrise" represents the virtues of abstraction.

The previous section of this book was an exercise in abstraction. By focusing on the Anthropocene, we stepped away from individual challenges and sought to understand the historical predicament of humanity at this unique time characterized by rapidly worsening environmental stress. This section deepens that exercise by, ironically, going in the other direction. The astronauts who snapped the earth's image could not stay in space. They carried only so much oxygen and food with them on *Apollo 8*. This should remind us that it is difficult to stay at high levels of abstraction. If we want to make a difference in global environmental affairs, we cannot simply stay in the intellectual exosphere, but must return to the concrete world of real-life challenges. This is a crucial part of an environmental education. As the saying goes, one must both marvel at the whole and know one's zip code. Likewise, appreciating the magnitude of planetary ecological dangers is essential for understanding what is, in fact, going on these days; but such knowledge is empty and therefore less useful if it isn't also tied to actual concrete expressions of environmental change. In the service of making such connections, this section parses out a series of key threats to global environmental well-being.

Yes, we live in the Anthropocene, but how do we get a handle on this? In the following pages, selections from a set of eminent authors examine four dimensions of planetary life, paying specific attention to how human actions are undermining them. We focus first on the atmosphere and concentrate on how emissions of carbon dioxide and other greenhouse gases are altering the climate. Second, we look at the world of living creatures and note how humanity is endangering biological diversity. Third, we focus on water—essential to all life—and on how overextraction, pollution, and misuse are endangering freshwater resources. Finally, we look at the soil itself and the way humans are undermining the global food system.

These four systems do not exhaust the list of environmental harms. One could easily choose other ecosystemic foci. However, the atmosphere, biosphere, hydrosphere, and pedosphere capture the main domains that constitute earthly existence, and an understanding of what is happening in each of them can provide an analytical handle on other specific environmental problems.

Author and activist **Bill McKibben** is an important voice on climate change. His writings have made the intricacies of climate science accessible to a popular audience, and the organization he founded, 350.org, has been a leader in the movement to respond to climate change in a meaningful way. In his chapter, McKibben makes clear that climate change is not a future problem; it is already with us. It will take all of the political coordination and muscle that can be mustered to make sure that the problem does not worsen. He points out that oil companies already own the rights to enough fossil-fuel reserves to cause runaway, catastrophic climate change. Therefore, he pleads with the world's citizens to do everything that can be done to ensure that these fuels stay in the ground.

Stephen M. Meyer, a former professor of political science at MIT, draws stark attention to the ways humanity is wiping out other species at inordinate rates. Meyer explains how overharvesting, exploiting, and despoiling essential habitat, and the spread of non-native, invasive species across the planet, are fueling an extinction crisis that rivals even the most dramatic in the fossil record. He argues that human efforts to stem the crisis are too feeble to reverse the trend and that we are thus stuck with living in a biologically impoverished world. While the picture he paints is obviously dark, Meyer doesn't just leave us with handwringing. He calls on us to marshal a moral, rigorous effort to protect what is left of the more-than-human world.

Maude Barlow, one of the world's most well-known writers and activists focusing on freshwater, sounds another alarm. Water supplies across the planet are under significant strain. Barlow argues that the water crisis is not about a lack of knowledge, but rather is indicative of a lack of political will. This provides some cause for optimism. Barlow sees us sitting at a moment of opportunity in which enlightened and effective water governance can protect billions from the ravages of water poverty.

Finally in this section, we hear from **Lester Brown**. Brown is the founder of the influential Worldwatch Institute, and now serves as president of the Earth Policy Institute in Washington, DC. For Brown, most of the world's environmental problems register themselves as pressures on humanity's ability to grow enough healthy food to support a growing population. In this essay he underlines how contemporary pressures are forcing countries into desperate actions and fostering public unrest over rising food prices and diminishing food availability. According to Brown, this is the future. Such pressures seem set to grow, casting a grave shadow over humanity's food future.

The authors in this section provide illuminating angles into climate change, species extinction, water dangers, and food vulnerability. In doing so, they provide details of environmental degradation and help us understand and appreciate the concrete challenges of building a sustainable world. Our work as students of global environmental politics, however, would be incomplete if we simply stopped and focused solely on this level of environmental knowledge. The issues described in this section are not isolated dangers, but instead should be seen as domains of socio-ecological reality that meld into and influence each other. Just as the photo of the earth from the moon makes clear, there are no discrete biophysical features on earth. Likewise, no single environmental challenge is separate from another. Climate change, for instance, affects all water systems; water availability has tremendous ramifications for supporting a world of diverse creatures; and biodiversity is essential for protecting human food resources.

In fact, when it comes right down to it, the planet is an ecological whole. It functions as a single organism in which all its parts are knitted together through biophysical, chemical, and, in the Anthropocene, social connections. As environmentalist John Muir once wrote, "When we try to pick out anything by itself, we find it hitched to everything else in the Universe." This is not simply a poetic locution, but an empirical fact. Thus, this section of the book should be read in combination with the preceding as an analytical exercise that encourages us to move continually back and forth from the abstract to the concrete. We need to see the whole and the parts. Doing so not only provides a fuller picture of environmental conditions, but as subsequent sections of this volume make clear, also enables us to engage meaningfully and effectively with environmental dangers. The ability to connect the person and the planet is premised on understanding both discrete challenges and how they fit into a larger and wilder whole.

4

Global Warming's Terrifying New Math

Bill McKibben

If the pictures of those towering wildfires in Colorado haven't convinced you, or the size of your AC bill this summer, here are some hard numbers about climate change: June [2012] broke or tied 3,215 high-temperature records across the United States. That followed the warmest May on record for the Northern Hemisphere—the 327th consecutive month in which the temperature of the entire globe exceeded the 20th-century average, the odds of which occurring by simple chance were 3.7×10-99, a number considerably larger than the number of stars in the universe.

Meteorologists reported that this spring was the warmest ever recorded for our nation [the United States]—in fact, it crushed the old record by so much that it represented the "largest temperature departure from average of any season on record." The same week, Saudi authorities reported that it had rained in Mecca despite a temperature of 109 degrees, the hottest downpour in the planet's history. . . .

When we think about global warming . . . the arguments tend to be ideological, theological and economic. But to grasp the seriousness of our predicament, you just need to do a little math. For the past year, an easy and powerful bit of arithmetical analysis first published by financial analysts in the U.K. has been making the rounds of environmental conferences and journals, but it hasn't yet broken through to the larger public. This analysis upends most of the conventional political thinking about climate change. And it allows us to understand our precarious—our almost-but-not-quite-finally hopeless—position with three simple numbers.

THE FIRST NUMBER: 2° CELSIUS

If the movie had ended in Hollywood fashion, the Copenhagen climate conference in 2009 would have marked the culmination of the global fight to slow a
changing climate. The world's nations had gathered in the December gloom
of the Danish capital for what a leading climate economist, Sir Nicholas Stern
of Britain, called the "most important gathering since the Second World War,
given what is at stake." As Danish energy minister Connie Hedegaard, who
presided over the conference, declared at the time: "This is our chance. If we
miss it, it could take years before we get a new and better one. If ever."

In the event, of course, we missed it. Copenhagen failed spectacularly.
Neither China nor the United States, which between them are responsible
for 40 percent of global carbon emissions, was prepared to offer dramatic
concessions, and so the conference drifted aimlessly for two weeks until world
leaders jetted in for the final day. Amid considerable chaos, President Obama
took the lead in drafting a face-saving "Copenhagen Accord" that fooled very
few. Its purely voluntary agreements committed no one to anything, and even
if countries signaled their intentions to cut carbon emissions, there was no
enforcement mechanism. "Copenhagen is a crime scene tonight," an angry
Greenpeace official declared, "with the guilty men and women fleeing to
the airport." Headline writers were equally brutal: COPENHAGEN: THE
MUNICH OF OUR TIMES? asked one.

The accord did contain one important number, however. In Paragraph 1,
it formally recognized "the scientific view that the increase in global temperature should be below two degrees Celsius." And in the very next paragraph, it
declared that "we agree that deep cuts in global emissions are required . . . so
as to hold the increase in global temperature below two degrees Celsius." By
insisting on two degrees—about 3.6 degrees Fahrenheit—the accord ratified
positions taken earlier in 2009 by the G8, and the so-called Major Economies
Forum. It was as conventional as conventional wisdom gets. The number first
gained prominence, in fact, at a 1995 climate conference chaired by Angela
Merkel, then the German minister of the environment and now the center-
right chancellor of the nation.

Some context: So far, we've raised the average temperature of the planet
just under 0.8 degrees Celsius, and that has caused far more damage than
most scientists expected. (A third of summer sea ice in the Arctic is gone, the
oceans are 30 percent more acidic, and since warm air holds more water vapor
than cold, the atmosphere over the oceans is a shocking five percent wetter,
loading the dice for devastating floods.) Given those impacts, in fact, many
scientists have come to think that two degrees is far too lenient a target. "Any
number much above one degree involves a gamble," writes Kerry Emanuel
of MIT, a leading authority on hurricanes, "and the odds become less and
less favorable as the temperature goes up." Thomas Lovejoy, once the World
Bank's chief biodiversity adviser, puts it like this: "If we're seeing what we're

seeing today at 0.8 degrees Celsius, two degrees is simply too much." NASA scientist James Hansen, the planet's most prominent climatologist, is even blunter: "The target that has been talked about in international negotiations for two degrees of warming is actually a prescription for long-term disaster." At the Copenhagen summit, a spokesman for small island nations warned that many would not survive a two-degree rise: "Some countries will flat-out disappear." When delegates from developing nations were warned that two degrees would represent a "suicide pact" for drought-stricken Africa, many of them started chanting, "One degree, one Africa."

Despite such well-founded misgivings, political realism bested scientific data, and the world settled on the two-degree target—indeed, it's fair to say that it's the only thing about climate change the world has settled on. All told, 167 countries responsible for more than 87 percent of the world's carbon emissions have signed on to the Copenhagen Accord, endorsing the two-degree target. Only a few dozen countries have rejected it, including Kuwait, Nicaragua and Venezuela. Even the United Arab Emirates, which makes most of its money exporting oil and gas, signed on. The official position of planet Earth at the moment is that we can't raise the temperature more than two degrees Celsius— it's become the bottomest of bottom lines. Two degrees.

THE SECOND NUMBER: 565 GIGATONS

Scientists estimate that humans can pour roughly 565 more gigatons of carbon dioxide into the atmosphere by midcentury and still have some reasonable hope of staying below two degrees. ("Reasonable," in this case, means four chances in five, or somewhat worse odds than playing Russian roulette with a six-shooter.)

This idea of a global "carbon budget" emerged about a decade ago, as scientists began to calculate how much oil, coal and gas could still safely be burned. Since we've increased the Earth's temperature by 0.8 degrees so far, we're currently less than halfway to the target. But, in fact, computer models calculate that even if we stopped increasing CO_2 now, the temperature would likely still rise another 0.8 degrees, as previously released carbon continues to overheat the atmosphere. That means we're already three-quarters of the way to the two-degree target. . . .

We're not getting any free lunch from the world's economies, either. With only a single year's lull in 2009 at the height of the financial crisis, we've continued to pour record amounts of carbon into the atmosphere, year after year. In late May, the International Energy Agency published its latest figures—CO_2 emissions last year rose to 31.6 gigatons, up 3.2 percent from the year before. America had a warm winter and converted more coal-fired power plants to natural gas, so its emissions fell slightly; China kept booming, so its carbon output (which recently surpassed the U.S.) rose 9.3 percent; the Japanese shut down their fleet of nukes post-Fukushima, so their emissions edged up 2.4 percent. "There have been efforts to use more renewable energy and improve energy efficiency," said Corinne

Le Quéré, who runs England's Tyndall Centre for Climate Change Research. "But what this shows is that so far the effects have been marginal." In fact, study after study predicts that carbon emissions will keep growing by roughly three percent a year—and at that rate, we'll blow through our 565-gigaton allowance in 16 years, around the time today's preschoolers will be graduating from high school. "The new data provide further evidence that the door to a two-degree trajectory is about to close," said Fatih Birol, the IEA's chief economist. In fact, he continued, "When I look at this data, the trend is perfectly in line with a temperature increase of about six degrees." That's almost 11 degrees Fahrenheit, which would create a planet straight out of science fiction.

So, new data in hand, everyone at the Rio conference renewed their ritual calls for serious international action to move us back to a two-degree trajectory. . . . Even scientists, who are notoriously reluctant to speak out, are slowly overcoming their natural preference to simply provide data. "The message has been consistent for close to 30 years now," [William] Collins [a senior climate scientist at the Lawrence Berkeley National Laboratory] says with a wry laugh, "and we have the instrumentation and the computer power required to present the evidence in detail. If we choose to continue on our present course of action, it should be done with a full evaluation of the evidence the scientific community has presented." He pauses, suddenly conscious of being on the record. "I should say, a *fuller evaluation* of the evidence."

So far, though, such calls have had little effect. We're in the same position we've been in for a quarter-century: scientific warning followed by political inaction. Among scientists speaking off the record, disgusted candor is the rule. One senior scientist told me, "You know those new cigarette packs, where governments make them put a picture of someone with a hole in their throats? Gas pumps should have something like that."

THE THIRD NUMBER: 2,795 GIGATONS

This number is the scariest of all—one that, for the first time, meshes the political and scientific dimensions of our dilemma. . . . The number describes the amount of carbon already contained in the proven coal and oil and gas reserves of the fossil-fuel companies, and the countries (think Venezuela or Kuwait) that act like fossil-fuel companies. In short, it's the fossil fuel we're currently planning to burn. And the key point is that this new number—2,795—is higher than 565. Five times higher. . . .

Think of two degrees Celsius as the legal drinking limit—equivalent to the 0.08 blood-alcohol level below which you might get away with driving home. The 565 gigatons is how many drinks you could have and still stay below that limit—the six beers, say, you might consume in an evening. And the 2,795 gigatons? That's the three 12-packs the fossil-fuel industry has on the table, already opened and ready to pour.

We have five times as much oil and coal and gas on the books as climate scientists think is safe to burn. We'd have to keep 80 percent of those reserves locked away underground to avoid that fate. Before we knew those numbers, our fate had been likely. Now, barring some massive intervention, it seems certain.

Yes, this coal and gas and oil is still technically in the soil. But it's already economically aboveground—it's figured into share prices, companies are borrowing money against it, nations are basing their budgets on the presumed returns from their patrimony. It explains why the big fossil-fuel companies have fought so hard to prevent the regulation of carbon dioxide—those reserves are their primary asset, the holding that gives their companies their value. It's why they've worked so hard these past years to figure out how to unlock the oil in Canada's tar sands, or how to drill miles beneath the sea, or how to frack the Appalachians.

If you told Exxon or Lukoil that, in order to avoid wrecking the climate, they couldn't pump out their reserves, the value of their companies would plummet. John Fullerton, a former managing director at JP Morgan who now runs the Capital Institute, calculates that at today's market value, those 2,795 gigatons of carbon emissions are worth about $27 trillion. Which is to say, if you paid attention to the scientists and kept 80 percent of it underground, you'd be writing off $20 trillion in assets. The numbers aren't exact, of course, but that carbon bubble makes the housing bubble look small by comparison. It won't necessarily burst—we might well burn all that carbon, in which case investors will do fine. But if we do, the planet will crater. You can have a healthy fossil-fuel balance sheet, or a relatively healthy planet—but now that we know the numbers, it looks like you can't have both. Do the math: 2,795 is five times 565. That's how the story ends.

So far, as I said at the start, environmental efforts to tackle global warming have failed. The planet's emissions of carbon dioxide continue to soar, especially as developing countries emulate (and supplant) the industries of the West. Even in rich countries, small reductions in emissions offer no sign of the real break with the status quo we'd need to upend the iron logic of these three numbers. Germany is one of the only big countries that has actually tried hard to change its energy mix; on one sunny Saturday in late May, that northern-latitude nation generated nearly half its power from solar panels within its borders. That's a small miracle—and it demonstrates that we have the technology to solve our problems. But we lack the will. So far, Germany's the exception; the rule is ever more carbon.

This record of failure means we know a lot about what strategies *don't* work. Green groups, for instance, have spent a lot of time trying to change individual lifestyles: the iconic twisty light bulb has been installed by the millions, but so have a new generation of energy-sucking flatscreen TVs. Most of us are fundamentally ambivalent about going green: We like cheap flights to warm places, and we're certainly not going to give them up if everyone else is still taking them. Since all of us are in some way the beneficiaries of cheap fossil fuel, tackling climate change has been like trying to build a movement against yourself—it's as if the gay-rights movement had to be constructed entirely from evangelical preachers, or the abolition movement from slaveholders.

People perceive—correctly—that their individual actions will not make a decisive difference in the atmospheric concentration of CO_2; by 2010, a poll found that "while recycling is widespread in America and 73 percent of those polled are paying bills online in order to save paper," only four percent had reduced their utility use and only three percent had purchased hybrid cars. Given a hundred years, you could conceivably change lifestyles enough to matter—but time is precisely what we lack.

A more efficient method, of course, would be to work through the political system, and environmentalists have tried that, too, with the same limited success. They've patiently lobbied leaders, trying to convince them of our peril and assuming that politicians would heed the warnings. Sometimes it has seemed to work. Barack Obama, for instance, campaigned more aggressively about climate change than any president before him—the night he won the nomination, he told supporters that his election would mark the moment "the rise of the oceans began to slow and the planet began to heal." And he has achieved one significant change: a steady increase in the fuel efficiency mandated for automobiles. It's the kind of measure, adopted a quarter-century ago, that would have helped enormously. But in light of the numbers I've just described, it's obviously a very small start indeed.

At this point, effective action would require actually keeping most of the carbon the fossil-fuel industry wants to burn safely in the soil, not just changing slightly the speed at which it's burned. And there the president, apparently haunted by the still-echoing cry of "Drill, baby, drill," has gone out of his way to frack and mine. His secretary of interior, for instance, opened up a huge swath of the Powder River Basin in Wyoming for coal extraction: The total basin contains some 67.5 gigatons worth of carbon (or more than 10 percent of the available atmospheric space). He's doing the same thing with Arctic and offshore drilling; in fact, as he explained on the stump in March [2012], "You have my word that we will keep drilling everywhere we can. . . . That's a commitment that I make." The next day, in a yard full of oil pipe in Cushing, Oklahoma, the president promised to work on wind and solar energy but, at the same time, to speed up fossil-fuel development: "Producing more oil and gas here at home has been, and will continue to be, a critical part of an all-of-the-above energy strategy." That is, he's committed to finding even more stock to add to the 2,795-gigaton inventory of unburned carbon. . . .

So: the paths we have tried to tackle global warming have so far produced only gradual, halting shifts. A rapid, transformative change would require building a movement, and movements require enemies. As John F. Kennedy put it, "The civil rights movement should thank God for Bull Connor. He's helped it as much as Abraham Lincoln." And enemies are what climate change has lacked.

But what all these climate numbers make painfully, usefully clear is that the planet does indeed have an enemy—one far more committed to action than governments or individuals. Given this hard math, we need to view the fossil-fuel industry in a new light. It has become a rogue industry, reckless like no other force on Earth. It is Public Enemy Number One to the survival of our planetary civilization. "Lots of companies do rotten things in the course of their business—pay terrible wages, make people work in sweatshops—and we pressure them to change those practices," says veteran anti-corporate leader Naomi Klein. . . . "But these numbers make clear that with the fossil-fuel industry, wrecking the planet is their business model. It's what they do." . . .

They're clearly cognizant of global warming—they employ some of the world's best scientists, after all, and they're bidding on all those oil leases made possible by the staggering melt of Arctic ice. And yet they relentlessly search for more hydrocarbons—in early March, Exxon CEO Rex Tillerson told Wall Street analysts that the company plans to spend $37 billion a year through 2016 (about $100 million a day) searching for yet more oil and gas. . . .

You could argue that this is simply in the nature of these companies—that having found a profitable vein, they're compelled to keep mining it, more like efficient automatons than people with free will. But as the Supreme Court has made clear, they are people of a sort. In fact, thanks to the size of its bankroll, the fossil-fuel industry has far more free will than the rest of us. These companies don't simply exist in a world whose hungers they fulfill—they help create the boundaries of that world. . . .

Environmentalists, understandably, have been loath to make the fossil-fuel industry their enemy, respecting its political power and hoping instead to convince these giants that they should turn away from coal, oil and gas and transform themselves more broadly into "energy companies." Sometimes that strategy appeared to be working—emphasis on appeared. Around the turn of the century, for instance, BP made a brief attempt to restyle itself as "Beyond Petroleum," adopting a logo that looked like the sun and sticking solar panels on some of its gas stations. But its investments in alternative energy were never more than a tiny fraction of its budget for hydrocarbon exploration, and after a few years, many of those were wound down as new CEOs insisted on returning to the company's "core business." In December [2012], BP finally closed its solar division. Shell shut down its solar and wind efforts in 2009. The five biggest oil companies have made more than $1 trillion in profits since the millennium—there's simply too much money to be made on oil and gas and coal to go chasing after zephyrs and sunbeams.

Much of that profit stems from a single historical accident: Alone among businesses, the fossil-fuel industry is allowed to dump its main waste, carbon dioxide, for free. Nobody else gets that break—if you own a restaurant, you have to pay someone to cart away your trash, since piling it in the street would breed rats. But the fossil-fuel industry is different, and for sound historical reasons:

Until a quarter-century ago, almost no one knew that CO_2 was dangerous. But now that we understand that carbon is heating the planet and acidifying the oceans, its price becomes the central issue. . . .

There's only one problem: Putting a price on carbon would reduce the profitability of the fossil-fuel industry. After all, the answer to the question "How high should the price of carbon be?" is "High enough to keep those carbon reserves that would take us past two degrees safely in the ground." The higher the price on carbon, the more of those reserves would be worthless. The fight, in the end, is about whether the industry will succeed in its fight to keep its special pollution break alive past the point of climate catastrophe, or whether, in the economists' parlance, we'll make them internalize those externalities. . . .

So pure self-interest probably won't spark a transformative challenge to fossil fuel. But moral outrage just might—and that's the real meaning of this new math. It could, plausibly, give rise to a real movement.

Once, in recent corporate history, anger forced an industry to make basic changes. That was the campaign in the 1980s demanding divestment from companies doing business in South Africa. It rose first on college campuses and then spread to municipal and state governments; 155 campuses eventually divested, and by the end of the decade, more than 80 cities, 25 states and 19 counties had taken some form of binding economic action against companies connected to the apartheid regime. "The end of apartheid stands as one of the crowning accomplishments of the past century," as Archbishop Desmond Tutu put it, "but we would not have succeeded without the help of international pressure," especially from "the divestment movement of the 1980s."

The fossil-fuel industry is obviously a tougher opponent, and even if you could force the hand of particular companies, you'd still have to figure out a strategy for dealing with all the sovereign nations that, in effect, act as fossil-fuel companies. But the link for college students is even more obvious in this case. If their college's endowment portfolio has fossil-fuel stock, then their educations are being subsidized by investments that guarantee they won't have much of a planet on which to make use of their degree. (The same logic applies to the world's largest investors, pension funds, which are also theoretically interested in the future—that's when their members will "enjoy their retirement.") "Given the severity of the climate crisis, a comparable demand that our institutions dump stock from companies that are destroying the planet would not only be appropriate but effective," says Bob Massie, a former anti-apartheid activist who helped found the Investor Network on Climate Risk. "The message is simple: We have had enough. We must sever the ties with those who profit from climate change—now." . . .

Meanwhile the tide of numbers continues. The week after the Rio conference limped to its conclusion, Arctic sea ice hit the lowest level ever recorded. . . . [O]n a single weekend, Tropical Storm Debby dumped more than 20 inches of rain on Florida—the earliest the season's fourth-named cyclone has ever arrived. At the same time, the largest fire in New Mexico history burned on, and the most destructive fire in Colorado's annals claimed 346 homes in Colorado Springs—breaking a record set the week before in Fort Collins. This month [July 2012], scientists issued a new study concluding that global warming has dramatically increased the likelihood of severe heat and drought—days after a heat wave across the Plains and Midwest broke records that had stood since the Dust Bowl, threatening this year's harvest. You want a big number? In the course of this month [July 2012], a quadrillion kernels of corn need to pollinate across the grain belt, something they can't do if temperatures remain off the charts. Just like us, our crops are adapted to the Holocene, the 11,000-year period of climatic stability we're now leaving . . . in the dust.

5

End of the Wild

Stephen M. Meyer

For the past several billion years evolution on Earth has been driven by small-scale incremental forces such as sexual selection, punctuated by cosmic-scale disruptions—plate tectonics, planetary geochemistry, global climate shifts, and even extraterrestrial asteroids. Sometime in the last century that changed. Today the guiding hand of evolution is unmistakably human, with earth-shattering consequences.

The fossil record and statistical studies suggest that the average rate of extinction over the past hundred million years has hovered at several species per year. Today the extinction rate surpasses 3,000 species per year and is accelerating rapidly—it may soon reach the tens of thousands annually. In contrast, new species are evolving at a rate of less than one per year.

Over the next 100 years or so as many as half of the Earth's species, representing a quarter of the planet's genetic stock, will either completely or functionally disappear. The land and the oceans will continue to teem with life, but it will be a peculiarly homogenized assemblage of organisms naturally and unnaturally selected for their compatibility with one fundamental force: us. Nothing—not national or international laws, global bioreserves, local sustainability schemes, nor even "wildlands" fantasies—can change the current course. The path for biological evolution is now set for the next million years. And in this sense "the extinction crisis"—the race to save the composition, structure, and organization of biodiversity as it exists today—is over, and we have lost.

This is not the wide-eyed prophecy of radical Earth First! activists or the doom-and-gloom tale of corporate environmentalists trying to boost fundraising. It is the story that is emerging from the growing mountain of scientific papers that have been published in prestigious scientific journals such as *Nature, Science,* and the *Proceedings of the National Academy of Sciences* over the past decade.

THE REAL IMPACT

Through our extraordinary capacity to modify the world around us, we human beings are creating a three-tiered hierarchy of life built around human selection. The great irony here is that this anthropogenic transformation of the biosphere springs as much from our deliberate efforts to protect and manage the life around us as it does from our wanton disregard for the natural environment.

At one extreme we are making the planet especially hospitable for the *weedy species*: plants, animals and other organisms that thrive in continually disturbed, human-dominated environments. . . . Many of these organisms are adaptive generalists—species that flourish in a variety of ecological settings, easily switch among food types, and breed prolifically. And some have their needs met more completely and efficiently by humans than by Mother Nature. In the United States, for example, there are five times as many raccoons (*Procyon lotor*) per square mile in suburban settings than in corresponding natural populations in "the wild."

From dandelions to coyotes, weedy species will enjoy expanding populations, spatial distribution, ecological dominance, and opportunities for further speciation into the far future. Many of these species have become so comfortable living with us that they have been labeled pests, requiring stringent control measures: the common (Norway) rat (*Rattus norvegicus*) and white-tailed deer (*Odocoileus virginianus*) come immediately to mind.

Living on the margins in ever-decreasing numbers and limited spatial distribution are *relic species*. Relic species cannot thrive in human-dominated environments—which now nearly cover the planet. Facing the continual threat of extinction, relic species will linger in either ecologically marginalized populations (e.g., prairie dogs and elephants) or carefully managed boutique populations (e.g., pandas). Most, including the Sumatran rhinoceros (*Dicerorhinus sumatrensis*), the California condor (*Gymnogyps californianus*), and virtually all of Hawaii's endemic plants, will require for survival our permanent, direct, and heavy-handed management, including captive breeding and continuous restocking.

Other relics, such as rare alpine plants, may survive in isolated patches through benign neglect. Over time they will experience progressive genetic erosion and declining numbers, and will rapidly lose their *ecological* value. In essence, they will be environmental ornaments.

But a large fraction of the non-weedy species will not be fortunate enough to have special programs to extend their survival or will be incapable of responding to such efforts. These are the *ghost species*—organisms that cannot or will not be allowed to survive on a planet with billions of people. Although they may continue to exist for decades, their extinction is certain, apart from a few specimens in zoos or a laboratory-archived DNA sample.

Some, such as the East Asian giant soft-shell turtle (extirpated except for one left in the wild) and the dusky seaside sparrow (extinct), are incapable of adapting their highly specialized needs rapidly enough to keep up with human-induced pressures. Others we intentionally try to eradicate. Although they are now protected, wolves and black-tailed prairie dogs in North America were once hunted for extermination as part of federal and state animal-control programs (and unofficially, they still are). In Africa, the lion population has plunged from over 200,000 in 1980 to under 20,000 today due to preemptive eradication by livestock herders.

Still other prospective ghosts we simply consume beyond their capacity to successfully reproduce—for food, for commercial products, or as pets. Recent reports suggest that we have consumed 90 percent of the stocks of large predatory fish, such as tuna and swordfish, in the world's oceans. And while 10,000 tigers live as private pets in the United States, fewer than 7,000 live in the wild throughout the world!

A great many of the plants and animals we perceive as healthy and plentiful today are in fact relics and ghosts. This seeming contradiction is explained by the fact that species loss is not a simple linear process. Many decades can pass between the start of a decline and the collapse of a population structure, especially where moderate-to-long-lived life forms are involved.

Conservation biologists use the term "extinction debt" to describe this gap between appearance and reality. In the past century we have accumulated a vast extinction debt that will be paid, with interest, in the century ahead. The number of plants and animals we "discover" to be threatened will expand out of control as the extinction debt comes due.

Thus, over the next hundred years, upwards of half of the earth's species are destined to become relics or ghosts, while weedy species will constitute an ever-growing proportion of the plants and animals around us. By virtue of their compatibility with us, weedy species can follow us around the planet, *homo*genizing (in both plausible interpretations of the word) the biosphere by filling in the spaces vacated by relics and ghosts. More and more we will encounter on every continent remarkably similar, if not the very same, species of plants, insects, mammals, birds, and other organisms.

HOW DID WE GET HERE?

Although we have been aware of species losses for decades, only recently has it become apparent that the biotic world as we have known it is collapsing.

The causes, varied and complex, fall into three broad disturbance categories: landscape transformation, geochemical modification (pollution), and biotic consumption and manipulation. Each reflects some aspect of human-induced manipulation of the environment. . . .

Consider the plight of a simple, undemanding, and modestly adaptable creature: the California tiger salamander (*Ambystoma californiense*). These amphibians live most of the year underground in upland fields and woodlands. Each winter they migrate thousands of feet to their natal breeding pools to find mates and lay eggs. After several weeks of carousing they return to their underground burrows in the surrounding uplands.

The key to the breeding success of these salamanders is the ephemeral nature of the pools. The pools exist as dry depressions for six months of the year. Then, as heavy spring rains flood the region, these shallow basins fill with water, creating vernal pools. Tiger salamanders have come to rely on these temporary pools because, since they are dry part of the year, they cannot support naturally occurring fish populations. Thus, the salamanders' eggs are relatively safe from predation. As the eggs hatch, the larvae find themselves immersed in a bath of food: the water is bursting with millions of planktonic organisms. The salamander larvae grow rapidly—and they need to, because with the rains gone the pools dry up quickly, and unless the juvenile salamanders mature and move out into the surrounding terrain they will die. And so it has been for millions of years.

But not anymore. Today the California tiger salamander is disappearing. First, the upland habitat where it lives is prime real estate for residential, commercial, and agricultural development. Between 50 and 75 percent of its native habitat has already been lost, and more than 100 development projects are pending in the remaining areas. Woodlands are cut down and fields plowed up to make room for houses, lawns, schools, shopping centers, and roadways. Many vernal pools themselves are simply filled.

Where pools are spared bulldozing they are pressed into service as roadside storm basins to collect runoff from lawns, roads, and driveways—water saturated with fertilizers, herbicides, pesticides, and heavy metals. The nitrogen and phosphorus in the runoff stimulates massive algal blooms that drive oxygen levels in the pools down to deadly levels, suffocating a large proportion of the animals. High concentrations of herbicides and pesticides in the runoff kill many juveniles and, in lower doses, alter metabolic chemistry in ways that bizarrely change sexual development, immune function, and even limb development.

Even setting aside local sources of contamination, the water in the pools is increasingly laden with a cocktail of toxic compounds (e.g., the herbicide atrazine) that are not used locally. Blowing in from industrial and agricultural sites many hundreds of miles away, these endocrine-disrupting compounds significantly reduce breeding success and foster grotesque developmental abnormalities.

Then there is the army of alien species—bullfrogs, crayfish, and other predators— that have been introduced intentionally into the landscape. These voracious hunters consume huge numbers of salamander larvae and juveniles, further decimating the tiger salamanders. In some instances, non-native salamanders (former pets) have been released into local pools, reducing breeding success and posing the risk of hybridization. And fish are frequently added to the temporary pools to devour mosquitoes during the wet season. While this makes life more comfortable for nearby human inhabitants, it exhausts the young salamanders' food supply.

But the assault does not end there. The regularity of spring rains is being replaced by recurrent three- and four-year droughts. Several generations of tiger salamanders therefore never emerge to replace the animals lost to natural and unnatural causes. In the past, tiger salamanders persisted despite climate variations by virtue of wandering individuals who trundled aimlessly through networks of wetlands until they chanced upon new vernal pools and restarted the population. But that is no longer possible because the matrix of connecting wetlands has been eliminated, and habitat fragmentation makes the chance encounter with a car tire many orders of magnitude greater than an encounter with either a suitable mate or a suitable habitat.

Finally, where residual populations of tiger salamanders have survived despite the odds in still isolated locations, they have become a target of the pet trade. Children are paid 25 cents per salamander to collect these highly prized animals, which are then sold for $15 a piece in U.S. pet shops and for more than $200 overseas. In fact the global trade in "exotics" such as tiger salamanders is growing explosively, especially for reptiles and amphibians. Probably one in a thousand salamanders survives the commerce and perhaps one in a thousand of these survives a few years in captivity.

This story is neither fictional nor unique. It is, in fact, the rule. One could tell similar stories of the red-crowned crane (*Grus japonensis*), the leatherback sea turtle (*Dermochelys coriacea*), the Lesothan succulent *Aloe polyphylla,* and most other species in decline. Relic species generally face an overwhelming web of threats that are impossible to disentangle.

Further complicating the picture are two meta-disturbances: global climate change and economic globalization. Climate change will make many areas inhospitable to their present inhabitants. Entire biotic communities will be evicted: coastal wetlands will be permanently submerged, many cloud forests will dry out, some dry savannas will become lush while others become deserts. Studies suggest that the types of climate shifts we can expect over the next century are well within the experiential history of most species that have survived the last two million years. In the past, most could have moved to new regions. But today only weedy species have the capacity to migrate and reestablish thriving populations in new habitats, which invariably are human-disturbed areas. For the rest, there is . . . no place to go because acceptable habitat has been reduced to a few isolated patches surrounded by a sea of human development. There is no way for non-weedy species to get to potentially more suitable locations (if they exist) hundreds of miles away because of interposed cities, roadways, subdivisions, shopping centers, and airports.

Economic globalization exacerbates the species-loss problem in several ways. Globalization increases the demand for natural resources in remote and undeveloped regions. In locations previously occupied by subsistence villages, labor towns spring up to support foreign timber and mining operations. As foreign capital flows into undeveloped regions it inflates the price paid for local goods, thereby increasing incentives for over-exploitation to feed the lucrative export market. Timber from the Malaysian and Indonesian rainforests bought and paid for by Japanese firms brings a much higher return than the same lumber sold in local markets. Over 80 percent of these rainforests have now been logged, with the consequence that the orangutan population is now less than ten percent of what it was decades ago.

Perhaps most importantly, the booming trade of the globalized economy accelerates the pace of alien species being transported around the globe. Breaking down economic barriers effectively breaks down geographic, ecological, and biotic barriers as vast numbers of plants and animals are shipped worldwide to support the pet and horticultural trades. Although presently only about five percent of these aliens take hold and flourish in their new environs, five percent of an exploding number is itself a large number. (As a reference point, 25 percent of the vascular plants in the United States today are alien species.) . . .

Thus, climate change and economic globalization are powerful agents of human selection that amplify and make irreversible the traditional and localized human disturbances that undermine biodiversity.

WHY THERE IS NOTHING WE CAN DO

As our awareness of the extinction crisis has grown, we have taken some ameliorative actions. In the United States we have imposed rules upon ourselves to try to halt the loss. The U.S. Endangered Species Act prohibits the taking, harm, or harassment of some 1,300 plants and animals designated by the U.S. Fish and Wildlife Service. . . .

Since the early 1990s the European Union has had its Habitat Directive, which makes it illegal to kill or harm about 700 protected species or to disrupt 168 specially designated habitats. Approaching the problem from a different angle is the Convention on the International Trade of Endangered Species (CITES), which, as the name implies, is an attempt by the international community—presently over 150 countries—to limit the global trade in threatened species. About 30,000 plants and animals are on the CITES list. Thousands of species are added annually.

Meanwhile, nations, acting individually and through international conventions, have attempted to set aside biologically valuable landscapes and ocean areas as wildlife refuges and bioreserves. More than ten percent of the earth now has some form of protected status. . . . The Northwestern Hawaiian Islands Coral Reef Ecosystem Reserve, encompassing over 400,000 square kilometers of ocean, protects about 70 percent of the coral reef ecosystems in the United States. Over 7,000 marine species are associated with this area, of which 25 percent are found nowhere else on the planet.

Recognizing that governments have limited political and fiscal resources, nongovernmental organizations have moved to impede the flow of species loss through land protection, public education, litigation, and policy advocacy. The Nature Conservancy claims to have helped to preserve over 117 million acres of wildlife habitat over the past 50-plus years. . . .

Unfortunately, such efforts are far too little and far, far too late. In fact these and similar apparent success stories reflect a much more insidious process that is reshaping the living earth. Our most common tools for preserving biodiversity—prohibitory laws and regulations, bioreserves, and sustainable-development programs—are themselves powerful engines of human selection, tweaking (for our pleasure) but not fundamentally altering the outcome: massive species loss.

Prohibitory regulation. Virtually by definition all regulatory efforts at species protection and recovery are focused on relics and (unknowingly) ghosts, which have no chance of true recovery. . . .

The very notion that we could regulate ourselves out of the extinction crisis—that government could force the wild to remain wild—is based on a fundamentally false premise: that the causes of species extinction are finite and reducible and that the number of true threatened species is reasonably limited. When the U.S. Endangered Species Act was recrafted in the early 1970s, wildlife experts naively believed that at most a few hundred species would require protection. Although the current U.S. list of domestic "endangered species" tops 1,300, the list would contain almost 5,000 entries if politics did not prevent it. . . .

More to the point, the great irony is that the U.S. Endangered Species Act is the very institutionalization of human-driven evolution. We decide which species get on the list for protection and which are kept off. We decide which habitats of listed species will be labeled critical. We decide the recovery goals: how many of a given plant or animal should be allowed to persist, in how many "populations," and where they should (and should not) be distributed across the landscape. The official recovery goal for wild bison is for a total population in the low thousands, not their original numbers in the tens of millions. The wolf recovery plan envisions several dozen packs confined to carefully delineated refuges in a few key states, not free-roaming wolf packs in every state that would reflect their true former range. And the government still shoots both species if they wander off designated lands. Recovery goals for plants (for which the U.S. Fish and Wildlife Service spends less than five percent of what it spends on animals) are limited to restoring populations in the locations where they are presently growing as relics and ghosts, not to restoring their former range.

Similarly, International Whaling Commission rules, CITES, and other international conventions convert human values into biotic structure; they are not regimes designed for ecological restoration. How many minke whales are sufficient to allow hunting? How many zoo requests for gorillas should be honored? Fundamentally, the determination of which species make it onto these protection lists and the timing of those listings is more about what appeals to us in an aesthetic and charismatic way and economics than about pivotal ecological roles and biology. Pandas get lots of attention and support; the many thousands of disappearing aquatic invertebrates do not.

Although legal prohibitions and strict enforcement can preserve some relic species at the margins and temporarily forestall the extinction of ghost species, they cannot prevent or even slow the end of the wild. Regulation, then, does little more than transform nature into a product of the human imagination.

Refuges and preserves. Biologists and ecologists have long recognized the limitations of species-specific preservation and have lobbied instead for the creation of protected areas that would shield ecosystems and all the plants and animals within. The idea behind refuges, bioreserves, and the like is to somehow wall off the wild from the harmful disturbances of humanity. Set aside 20,000 acres, limit human activity, and allow nature to proceed unhindered in its special space. And for a while this appears to work. But this too is largely an illusion. The refuges and bioreserves we set aside are no more than our paltry conception of an ecosystem, and the species within their boundaries are in most instances part of the extinction debt and all the while in decline. . . .

Direct and indirect human encroachment into bioreserves is relentless and, with ever expanding populations in the developing world, unavoidable. Mexico's Montes Azules Biosphere Reserve, North America's last remaining rain forest, extends across 820,000 acres and is home to half of Mexico's bird species. Having already lost a quarter of its tree cover in the last 30 years to illegal logging by local residents (which Mexican authorities have ignored) the park has become a magnet for those looking for land to clear and till. In Africa and Asia, bioreserves have become the preferred hunting grounds for poachers and bush-meat traders: that is, after all, where the animals are!

Bioreserves will always be too small and too isolated from each other to accomplish their stated goal of preserving the wild as it is today. Embedded in a matrix of human habitation—cities, towns, farms, mining and logging operations—they cannot be insulated from broader human disturbances in the region, even if their own boundaries remain inviolate.

Consider one of the world's favorite eco-tourist destinations: the Monteverde Cloud Forest Preserve. This ecologically significant area covers more than 30,000 acres and hosts more than 2,500 plant species, 100 mammalian species, 400 bird species, 120 reptilian and amphibian species, and thousands of insects. The problem is that the cloud forest appears to be drying out. Deforestation is the apparent cause, but not from logging in the preserve. Rather, the clearing of lowland areas outside the preserve for agriculture is causing changes in the local patterns of fog and mist formation, thereby altering cloud formation up in the preserve. Thus, despite strong protections within its boundaries, the cloud forest may soon lack its defining feature: clouds. And the multitude of species that depend on that moisture will go the way of the extinct golden toad.

This weakness in the call for specific ecosystem preservation becomes all the more apparent in the context of climate change. The creation of a network of isolated, independent bioreserves assumes that the global environment—in particular the global climate—is relatively static. For the past 11,000 years this would have been a fair assumption. But this has changed. . . .

Ultimately the transformation of wilderness into a patchwork of static bioreserves is just another tool of human selection—the antithesis of the wild.

Sustainable communities. Much has been said and written about sustainable communities as a social approach to easing the extinction crisis. Sustainability has been something of a crusade for the UN, various international agencies, and many nongovernmental environmental organizations. The argument goes that if local communities could learn to live within the carrying capacity of their environs, the pressures on terrestrial and marine ecosystems would be eased. And of course this is true.

But in the context of the extinction crisis, sustainable development is an anthropocentric resource-use policy, not an ecological model. Consumptive demand measured against resource supply, not ecosystem function, determines the limit of sustainability. What is the maximum amount of mahogany, or tuna, or leopard pelts that can be harvested and still allow projected human demand for the product to be met for the foreseeable future? The demands of the ecosystem are not truly part of the equation. . . .

Moreover, if there was ever a hope for this strategy, even at a limited level, economic globalization destroyed it. Consider what might be regarded as an exemplar of sustainable development: Brazil-nut harvesting in the Amazon. Originally the idea was to protect the rain forest by creating a local economy based on the collection and sale of Brazil nuts. Initially this was quite successful. But today, local residents in the Brazilian Amazon harvest over 45,000 tons of nuts from the forest floor each year, yielding some $43 million in global trade. Unfortunately, nut gatherers harvest so many nuts that few if any seedlings are taking root. As aging Brazil-nut trees die off, they will not be replaced. Global demand for this environmentally friendly and sustainable crop drives the harvest and has made it unsustainable in the long term. . . .

The notion of sustainable communities, then, is not about the wild. It is about long-term economic efficiency and the wise use of natural resources. . . .

A REASON TO DO NOTHING?

We cannot prevent the end of the wild. Absent an immediate 95-percent reduction in the human population (a truly horrendous thought), we cannot change our current course. This leads us to the question, If we are unalterably moving to a world in which half the currently existing species will be relics or ghosts, why should we continue to do anything to preserve biodiversity? Why not rescind national and international laws protecting endangered species, eliminate bioreserves, and let the unfettered market determine how and where we consume natural resources? By bowing to the serendipitous elements of human selection in setting the course of biotic development and evolution we could happily bulldoze, pave, or grass over every square inch of the planet in the pursuit of human progress. But it is not that simple.

This why-bother strategy would greatly magnify the scale, scope, and destructive consequences of the end of the wild. First, it would effectively bifurcate the earth's biota into two groups: weedy species and ghost species, the latter subsuming virtually all relics. . . .

Second, this human-selected biosphere will not necessarily be a human-friendly one. Without direct management many species that we view as key natural resources, such as timber trees and marine fish stocks, would be consumed out of existence. The invisible hand of the market is all too invisible when it comes to the exploitation of natural commodities. . . .

Third, this approach would almost certainly increase the predominance of pests, parasites, and disease-causing organisms among the weedy species. . . .

Fourth, the global spread of invasive species would explode if left unchecked. Ecological concerns such as biotic homogenization aside, the economic toll would be disastrous. The economic harm caused by the 50,000 non-native invasive plants, animals, and other organisms already in the United States is approaching $140 billion per year. Florida's government alone spends $45 million annually battling invasive species, which cause some $180 million in agricultural damage. . . .

In the end, the notion that we could let nature take its course in a world so dominated by humanity is as dangerous as it is self-contradictory. Like it or not, nature now works for us. If humanity is to survive and prosper on such a planet then we have no choice but to at least try to manage the fine details of the end of the wild.

Since we cannot possibly restore relic and ghost species to their former status, nor do we have the knowledge to pick evolutionary winners and losers, we should focus on two core concerns: (1) safeguarding future evolutionary processes and pathways and (2) preserving ecosystem processes and functions. . . .

The end of the wild does not mean a barren world. There will be plenty of life. It will just be different: much less diverse, much less exotic, far more predictable, and—given the dominance of weedy species—probably far more annoying. We have lost the wild. Perhaps in 5 to 10 million years it will return.

6

Where Has All the Water Gone?

Maude Barlow

Three scenarios collude toward disaster.

Scenario one: The world is running out of freshwater. It is not just a question of finding the money to hook up the two billion people living in water-stressed regions of our world. Humanity is polluting, diverting and depleting the Earth's finite water resources at a dangerous and steadily increasing rate. The abuse and displacement of water is the ground-level equivalent of greenhouse gas emissions, and likely as great a cause of climate change.

Scenario two: Every day more and more people are living without access to clean water. As the ecological crisis deepens, so too does the human crisis. More children are killed by dirty water than by war, malaria, HIV/AIDS and traffic accidents combined. The global water crisis has become a most powerful symbol of the growing inequality in our world. While the wealthy enjoy boutique water at any time, millions of poor people have access only to contaminated water from local rivers and wells.

Scenario three: A powerful corporate water cartel has emerged to seize control of every aspect of water for its own profit. Corporations deliver drinking water and take away wastewater; corporations put massive amounts of water in plastic bottles and sell it to us at exorbitant prices; corporations are building sophisticated new technologies to recycle our dirty water and sell it back to us; corporations extract and move water by huge pipelines from watersheds and aquifers to sell to big cities and industries; corporations buy, store and trade water on the open market, like running shoes. Most importantly, corporations want governments to deregulate the water sector and allow the market to set water policy. Every day, they get closer to that goal. Scenario three deepens the crises now unfolding in scenarios one and two.

Imagine a world in twenty years in which no substantive progress has been made to provide basic water services in the Third World; or to create laws to protect source water and force industry and industrial agriculture to stop polluting water systems; or to curb the mass movement of water by pipeline, tanker and other diversions, which will have created huge new swaths of desert.

Desalination plants will ring the world's oceans, many of them run by nuclear power; corporate-controlled nanotechnology will clean up sewage water and sell it to private utilities, which will in turn sell it back to us at a huge profit; the rich will drink only bottled water found in the few remaining uncontaminated parts of the world, or sucked from the clouds by corporate-controlled machines, while the poor will die in increasing numbers from a lack of water.

This is not science fiction. This is where the world is headed unless we change course—a moral and ecological imperative.

But first we must come to terms with the dimension of the crisis.

WE ARE RUNNING OUT OF FRESHWATER

. . . [T]he world is facing a water crisis due to pollution, climate change and a surging population growth of such magnitude that close to two billion people now live in water stressed regions of the planet. Further, unless we change our ways, by the year 2025, two-thirds of the world's population will face water scarcity. The global population tripled in the twentieth century, but water consumption went up sevenfold. By 2050, after we add another three billion to the population, humans will need an 80 percent increase in water supplies just to feed ourselves. No one knows where this water is going to come from.

Scientists call them "hot stains"—the parts of the Earth now running out of potable water. They include Northern China, large areas of Asia and Africa, the Middle East, Australia, the Midwestern United States and sections of South America and Mexico.

The worst examples in terms of the effect on people are, of course, those areas of the world with large populations and insufficient resources to provide sanitation. Two-fifths of the world's people lack access to proper sanitation, which has led to massive outbreaks of waterborne diseases. Half of the world's hospital beds are occupied by people with an easily preventable waterborne disease, and the World Health Organization reports that contaminated water is implicated in 80 percent of all sickness and disease worldwide. In the last decade, the number of children killed by diarrhea exceeded the number of people killed in all armed conflicts since the Second World War. Every eight seconds, a child dies from drinking dirty water.

Some wealthier countries are just beginning to understand the depth of their own crisis, having adopted a model of unlimited consumer growth based on industrial, trade and farming practices that are wasting precious and irreplaceable water resources. Australia, the driest continent on Earth, is facing a severe shortage of water in all of its major cities, as well as widespread drought in its rural countryside. Annual rainfall is declining; salinity and desertification are spreading rapidly; rivers are being drained at an unsustainable rate; and more than one-quarter of all surface water management areas now exceed sustainable limits. Climate change is accelerating drought and causing freak storms and weather patterns just as the population is set to expand dramatically in the next twenty years. (Ironically, this is, in part, to take in the climate change refugees such as the inhabitants of the Solomon Islands, who will lose their lands to the rising seas.)

Many parts of the United States are also experiencing severe water shortages. Pressure is mounting on the Great Lakes governors to open up access to the lakes to the burgeoning megacities around the basin. In 2007, Lake Superior, the world's largest freshwater lake, dropped to its lowest level in eighty years and the water has receded more than fifteen meters from the shoreline. Florida is in trouble. The state's burgeoning population, with a net influx of 1,060 people every day, relies almost entirely upon its dwindling groundwater sources for its water supplies. To keep its fast-spreading lawns and golf courses green, the Sunshine State is sucking up groundwater at such a rate that it has created thousands of sinkholes that devour anything—houses, cars and shopping malls—unfortunate enough to be built on them. . . .

Because of the wealth of these countries, most of their populations are still not suffering from water shortages. That is not so for those in the global South—hence the term *water apartheid.* The world's poor who are living without water are either in areas that do not have enough water to begin with (Africa), where surface water has become severely polluted (South America, India) or both (Northern China). Most of the world's megacities—those with ten million or more inhabitants—lie within regions experiencing water stress. These include Mexico City, Calcutta, Cairo, Jakarta, Karachi, Beijing, Lagos and Manila. . . .

Not surprisingly, there is a huge gulf between the First World and the Third World in water use. The average human needs fifty liters of water per day for drinking, cooking and sanitation. The average North American uses almost six hundred liters a day. The average inhabitant of Africa uses six liters per day. A newborn baby in the global North consumes between forty and seventy times more water than a baby in the global South.

These appalling disparities have rightly created a demand for more water equity and a commitment to providing water for the 1.4 billion people currently living without it. The UN Millennium Development Goals include reducing by half the proportion of people living without safe drinking water by the year 2015. While laudable, this initiative is failing not only because the UN has worked with the World Bank to promote a flawed model for water development, but also because it assumes that there is enough water for everyone without seriously addressing the massive pollution of surface waters and the consequent massive overmining of groundwater supplies.

OUR SURFACE WATERS ARE POLLUTED

We were all taught certain fundamentals about the Earth's hydrologic cycle in grade school. There is a finite amount of available freshwater on the planet, we learned, and it makes its way through a cycle that ensures its safe return to us for our perpetual use. . . . About four hundred billion liters of water are cycled through this process every year. In this scenario, the planet could never "run out" of water.

But this cycle, true for so many millennia, did not take into account modern humans' collective capacity for destruction. In the last half-century, the species has polluted surface waters at an alarming and accelerating rate. The world may not exactly be running out of water, but it is running out of clean water. Ninety percent of wastewater produced in the Third World is discharged, untreated, into local rivers, streams and coastal waters. As well, humans are now using more than half of accessible runoff water, leaving little for the ecosystem or other species.

In China, 80 percent of the major rivers are so degraded they no longer support aquatic life, and an astonishing 90 percent of all groundwater systems under the major cities are contaminated. China is now home to seven of the ten most polluted cities in the world. The World Health Organization reports that 700 million of the 1.3 billion people of China drink water that doesn't even meet the most basic minimum safety standards set by that world body. . . .

This scenario is repeated in many parts of Asia. A 2005 nationwide survey in Pakistan revealed that less than 25 percent of the population has access to clean drinking water due to massive pollution of the country's surface waters. The Indonesian Environment Monitor reports that Indonesia has one of the lowest sanitation rates in the world. Less than 3 percent of Jakarta's residents are connected to a sewer, leading to severe pollution of nearby rivers and lakes and the contamination of 90 percent of the city's shallow wells. Almost 65 percent of Bangladesh's groundwater is contaminated, with at least 1.2 million Bangladeshis exposed to arsenic poisoning. . . .

According to the European Commission, 20 percent of all surface water in Europe is "seriously threatened," and the UN adds that only five of the fifty-five major rivers in Europe can be considered "pristine" anymore. Belgium's water is singled out as particularly bad, due to heavy pollution by industry. The Rhine, the Sarno and the Danube rivers are all in peril. Recent and regular droughts have European leaders very worried about water availability. Southern Spain, southeastern England and western and southern France are all viewed as chronically vulnerable, while fears are growing in Portugal, Italy and Greece. . . .

Forty percent of U.S. rivers and streams are too dangerous for fishing, swimming or drinking, as are 46 percent of lakes due to massive toxic runoff from industrial farms, intensive livestock operations and the more than one billion pounds of industrial weed killer used throughout the country every year. Two-thirds of U.S. estuaries and bays are moderately or severely degraded. The Mississippi River carries an estimated 1.5 million metric tons of nitrogen pollution into the Gulf of Mexico every year. Every year, one-quarter of the U.S. beaches are under advisories or closed due to water pollution. The U.S. government refuses to ban the herbicide Atrazine, an endocrine disrupter banned in many countries around the world and widely linked to cancer. In Canada, more than one trillion liters of untreated sewage is dumped into waterways each year, a volume that would cover the entire 7,800-kilometer length of the Trans-Canada Highway, six stories high. . . .

Thousands of Angolans died in a 2006 cholera outbreak caused by filthy water. Only one in six Luandan households have basic sanitation services, and the city's 4.5 million residents live in the midst of mountains of garbage and open sewers in the streets. Eighty percent of South Africa's rivers are imperiled by pollution, and every year, residents (usually women) have to walk farther and farther to find clean water. The women of South Africa now collectively walk the equivalent of the distance to the moon and back sixteen times a day for water.

One inevitable result of the massive pollution of surface waters in poor countries is that sewage water is increasingly being used to fertilize crops. In 2004, the Sri Lankan bureau of the International Water Management Institute undertook the first global survey on the hidden practice of wastewater irrigation. It found that fully one-tenth of the world's irrigated crops—from lettuce and tomatoes to mangoes and coconuts—is watered by sewage, most of it completely untreated, "gushing direct from sewer pipes into fields at the fringes of the developing world's great megacities." The sewage is added to fields complete with disease-causing pathogens and toxic waste from industry. In some Third World metropolises, all food sold is grown in sewage.

OUR GROUNDWATER SOURCES ARE DEPLETING

To deal with this vast pollution and the resulting effect of reduced clean water supplies, farms, cities and industries all over the world are turning to groundwater sources, using sophisticated technology to drill deep into the Earth and pull up ancient aquifer water for daily use. This is a second piece of the "running out" puzzle. We are taking water from where it is accessible—in aquifers and other groundwater sources—and putting it where it gets used and lost, such as in mass irrigation of deserts, to make cars and computers, or to produce oil from tar sands and coal methane beds where it becomes polluted or actually lost to the hydrologic cycle.

The current practice of "water mining" is different from the sustainable use of well water that has served farmers for generations. Today, groundwater is seen as a finite resource such as a mineral—a deposit to be mined until it is gone, allowing the searcher to move on to new sites—rather than a renewable resource that must be managed and replenished. The exponential mining of groundwater is largely unregulated, and no one knows when the limit will be hit and the supply depleted within a certain community or region.

We do know that the use of groundwater for daily living is growing very fast. About two billion people—one-third of the world's population—depend on groundwater supplies, withdrawing approximately 20 percent of global water annually. Groundwater aquifers are being overpumped almost everywhere in the world and are also being polluted with chemical runoff from industrial farming and mine tailings, as well as being invaded by saltwater from careless drilling practices. . . .

In the First World, much of the groundwater extraction is due to big industrial agribusiness taking massive amounts of water using huge industrial bores. In the Third World, the problem is caused by millions and millions of small farmers using personal pumps.

Groundwater mining can be traced in great part to the famous Green Revolution and the use of flood irrigation to mass-produce food. Since 1950, the global acreage of land under irrigation—the driving factor behind the Green Revolution—has tripled. Using vast amounts of water, scientists developed high-yield crop varieties to meet the needs of developing nations. While the "revolution" produced more food, it used way too much water and also depended on copious amounts of dangerous pesticides and fertilizers. Some countries abandoned past sustainable farming practices and started "double cropping," whereby crops are grown during the dry season and the wet season, adding to the demands on water.

As British environmentalist Fred Pearce points out, irrigated farming gave us twice as much food but used three times as much water, and did more harm than good. He lists the world's major rivers that no longer reach the sea: the Colorado and the Rio Grande in the United States; the Nile in Egypt; the Yellow River in China; the Indus in Pakistan; the Murray in Australia; the Jordan in the Middle East and the Oxus in Central Asia. They have been depleted from damming, overuse and the mining of the groundwaters that feed them. . . .

[I]t is in Asia that the coming crisis can be seen most clearly. The London-based *New Scientist* reported scientists' findings on what it called a "little-heralded crisis" all over Asia with the unregulated and exponential drilling of groundwater. Farmers are drilling millions of pump-operated wells in an ever-deeper search for water and are threatening to suck the continent's underground reserves dry, setting the stage for "untold anarchy." Vietnam has quadrupled its number of tube-wells in the past decade to one million, and water tables are plunging in the Pakistani state of Punjab, which produces 90 percent of the country's food. . . .

China has less water than Canada and forty times more people. In Northern China, groundwater depletion has reached catastrophic levels. Across the northern half of the country—China's breadbasket—groundwater pumping amounts to some thirty billion cubic meters a year. This is due to massive overpumping for agriculture but also because government planners divert large amounts of water from farming to industry every year, to fuel China's economic "miracle." The water table beneath Beijing has fallen nearly two hundred feet in the past twenty years, which has led some planners to warn that China may have to choose another city for its capital.

Drought-related sandstorms are already plaguing China. In the first half of 2006, thirteen major sandstorms had hit Northern China. In April 2006, one storm swept across an eighth of the country and even reached Korea and Japan. On its way, it dumped a mind-boggling 336,000 tons (about 305 million kilograms) of dust on Beijing, forcing people to walk around with facemasks for protection. Every year, a new desert the size of Rhode Island is created in China.

THE PLANET IS DRYING UP

Melting Glaciers

China's crisis is exacerbated by the rapid melting of the Tibetan glaciers, which are vanishing so fast (due to climate change) that they will be reduced by 50 percent every decade, according to the Chinese Academy of Sciences. Each year, enough water melts from the 46,298 glaciers of the plateau to fill the entire Yellow River. But rather than adding freshwater resources to a thirsty country, the furious pace of this melting is actually creating desertification. Instead of steadily feeding the great rivers of Asia—the Yangtze, the Indus, the Ganges, the Brahmaputra, the Mekong and the Yellow—as the Himalayan glaciers have done for millennia, the fast-melting water running off the plateau increases soil erosion, allowing the deserts to spread, and then evaporates before it reaches the thirsty rivers. . . .

The state of the world's mountains—the source of half of humanity's drinking water, now referred to by scientists and environmentalists as "water towers"—should be a major concern to us all as global warming strips away their ancient glaciers. Receding glaciers at sea are another loss of freshwater, as they melt into saltwater and add to the rising of the oceans. Glacier melt is yet another piece of the "running out" puzzle—another example, such as groundwater mining, where water is removed from where it has been stored for millennia to provide life for humans and nature, and ends up lost to both.

Virtual Water Trade

Water is also massively displaced through the trade in what is called *virtual water,* a term that describes the water used in the production of crops or manufactured goods that are then exported. Israeli economists first used the term *virtual* or *embedded* water in the early 1990s when they realized that it didn't make sense from an economic point of view to export scarce Israeli water. This is what was happening, they said, every time water-intensive oranges or avocados were exported from their semi-arid country. Because of poor water management systems used around the world (more than half of all water used in flood irrigation is lost to seepage or evaporation), even a small bag of salad takes three hundred liters of water to produce. It takes about a thousand liters to produce a kilogram of wheat and five to ten times as much to produce a kilogram of meat. Up to thirty thousand liters of water are used to produce one kilogram of cotton.

Water that is used in the production of food is "virtual" because it is not contained anymore in the product, even though a great deal of it was used in the production process. If a country exports a water-intensive product to another country, it amounts to exporting water in a virtual form, although no water is technically being traded or sold. . . . For some water-rich countries such as Canada, this practice may appear to be benign. But many poor countries are exporting huge amounts of water through virtual water trade because of a desperate need for income and because they have been strongly pushed by the World Bank and the International Monetary Fund to pay off their debts through monoculture crop exports, even if it means using their best, most arable land and their remaining water supplies to do so.

India, with its water crisis on the doorstep, is a major virtual water ex-porter, as is Thailand. Vietnam is destroying its water table to grow coffee for export. Africa supplies much of Europe with out-of-season fruits and vegetables, just as Latin America provides for North America. Kenya is destroying the wa-ters of Lake Naivasha to grow roses for export to Europe. Scientists predict the lake, the source of water for Africa's largest population of hippopotamuses, will be a "putrid muddy puddle" within five to ten years if its draining for flower irrigation is not halted. (Knowing this, the big European flower companies are already planning to relocate to Ethiopia and Uganda.) . . .

Many poor countries are exporting their way to drought. Between 15 and 20 percent of the water used in the world for human purposes is not for domestic consumption but for export, according to the UN, in what is consid-ered by many to be a conservative estimate. But with the continued emphasis of the World Bank and other global financial institutions on export growth, this practice is bound to increase and, with it, the transfer of water from the poor to the rich. Oddly, two wealthy but water-stressed countries are also major virtual water exporters: the United States and Australia. Net exports of water from the United States amount to one-third of the total water withdrawal in that country and are a major factor in the drying out of the American Mid-west and Southwest. Not coincidentally, both Australia and the United States have governments in denial about their water crises and completely wedded to economic globalization and its false promise of unlimited growth.

Urbanization and Deforestation

Yet another answer to the question of where the world's water has gone is that it is displaced from the hydrologic cycle by massive urbanization and paving over of natural environments. In a groundbreaking study, Slovakian scientist and Goldman Prize–winner Michal Kravčik showed that when water cannot return to fields, meadows, wetlands and streams because of urban sprawl and the removal of green spaces, there is less water in the soil and local water systems and, therefore, less water to evaporate from land. It is as if the rain is falling on a large cement umbrella, which carries it out to sea. The destruction of water-retentive landscapes means that less precipitation remains in river basins and continental watersheds; this in turn equates to less water in the hydrologic cycle. . . .

The problem is exacerbated by deforestation. In a March 2005 study by the Australian Nuclear Science and Technology Organization, scientists analyzed variations in the molecular structure of rain along the Amazon River. This allowed them to "tag" the water as it flowed into the Atlantic, evaporated, blew back inland to fall again as rain and finally returned to the river. The study showed that since the 1970s, when intensive deforestation began, the ratio of the heavy molecules found in the rain over the Amazon had declined significantly. The only possible explanation was that the molecules were no longer being returned to the atmosphere to fall again as rain because the vegetation was disappearing. The team found a clear connection between the degraded forest and reduced rainfall—an association with a long anecdotal history but lacking in scientific proof until the Australian study.

Desertification and Climate Change

. . . The U.S. National Center for Atmospheric Research (NCAR) reports that the percentage of the Earth's land area stricken by serious drought more than doubled between the 1970s and 2005. Widespread drying occurred over much of Europe, Asia, Canada, western and southern Africa and eastern Australia. In Nigeria, two thousand square kilometers is becoming desert every year. . . .

There are several ways in which climate change affects freshwater sources. As seas rise, they will take out more wetlands, which are already under siege. Wetlands have been called the kidneys of freshwater systems, as they filter and purify dirt and toxins before they reach rivers, lakes and aquifers. (Forests are the lungs of the water system, absorbing pollution and preventing flooding.) Further, as global warming raises the temperature of the Earth, the soil water needed to sustain the freshwater cycle will evaporate more readily. Water in lakes and rivers will evaporate more quickly as well, and the snow packs and ice cover that replenish these systems will become more rare.

So here, then, is the answer to the question, Can we run out of freshwater? Yes, there is a fixed amount of water on Earth. Yes, it is still here somewhere.

But we humans have depleted, polluted and diverted it to such an extent that we can now actually say the planet is running out of accessible, clean water. Fast. The freshwater crisis is easily as great a threat to the Earth and humans as climate change (to which it is deeply linked) but has had very little attention paid to it in comparison. . . .

Every day, the failure of our political leaders to address the global water crisis becomes more evident, Every day, the need for a comprehensive water crisis plan becomes more urgent. If ever there was a moment for all governments and international institutions to come together to find a collective solution to this emergency, now is that moment. If ever there was a time for a plan of conservation and water justice to deal with the twin water crises of scarcity and inequity, now is that time. The world does not lack the knowledge about how to build a water-secure future; it lacks the political will.

But not only are our political leaders following the false promises of a quick technological fix, they are abdicating the real decision-making about the future of the world's depleting water supplies to a group of private interests and transnational corporations that view the crisis as an opportunity to make money and gain power. . . . [T]hese big players know where the water is. They simply follow the money.

7

The Global Food Crisis

Lester Brown

The price of wheat is setting an all-time high in the United Kingdom. Food riots are spreading across Algeria. Russia is importing grain to sustain its cattle herds until spring grazing begins. India is wrestling with an 18-percent annual food inflation rate, sparking protests. China is looking abroad for potentially massive quantities of wheat and corn. The Mexican government is buying corn futures to avoid unmanageable tortilla price rises. And on January 5, the U.N. Food and Agricultural organization announced that its food price index for December hit an all-time high.

But whereas in years past, it's been weather that has caused a spike in commodities prices, now it's trends on both sides of the food supply/demand equation that are driving up prices. On the demand side, the culprits are population growth, rising affluence, and the use of grain to fuel cars. On the supply side: soil erosion, aquifer depletion, the loss of cropland to nonfarm uses, the diversion of irrigation water to cities, the plateauing of crop yields in agriculturally advanced countries, and—due to climate change—crop-withering heat waves and melting mountain glaciers and ice sheets. These climate-related trends seem destined to take a far greater toll in the future.

There's at least a glimmer of good news on the demand side: World population growth, which peaked at 2 percent per year around 1970, dropped below 1.2 percent per year in 2010. But because the world population has nearly doubled since 1970, we are still adding 80 million people each year. Tonight, there will be 219,000 additional mouths to feed at the dinner table, and many of them will be greeted with empty plates. Another 219,000 will join us tomorrow night. At some point, this relentless growth begins to tax both the skills of farmers and the limits of the earth's land and water resources.

Beyond population growth, there are now some 3 billion people moving up the food chain, eating greater quantities of grain-intensive livestock and poultry products. The rise in meat, milk, and egg consumption in fast-growing developing countries has no precedent. Total meat consumption in China today is already nearly double that in the United States.

The third major source of demand growth is the use of crops to produce fuel for cars. In the United States, which harvested 416 million tons of grain in 2009, 119 million tons went to ethanol distilleries to produce fuel for cars. That's enough to feed 350 million people for a year. The massive U.S. investment in ethanol distilleries sets the stage for direct competition between cars and people for the world grain harvest. In Europe, where much of the auto fleet runs on diesel fuel, there is growing demand for plant-based diesel oil, principally from rapeseed and palm oil. This demand for oil-bearing crops is not only reducing the land available to produce food crops in Europe, it is also driving the clearing of rainforests in Indonesia and Malaysia for palm oil plantations.

The combined effect of these three growing demands is stunning: a doubling in the annual growth in world grain consumption from an average of 21 million tons per year in 1990–2005 to 41 million tons per year in 2005–2010. Most of this huge jump is attributable to the *orgy of investment* in ethanol distilleries in the United States in 2006–2008.

While the annual demand growth for grain was doubling, new constraints were emerging on the supply side, even as longstanding ones such as soil erosion intensified. An estimated one third of the world's cropland is losing topsoil faster than new soil is forming through natural processes—and thus is losing its inherent productivity. Two huge dust bowls are forming, one across northwest China, western Mongolia, and central Asia; the other in central Africa. Each of these dwarfs the U.S. dust bowl of the 1930s.

Satellite images show a steady flow of dust storms leaving these regions, each one typically carrying millions of tons of precious topsoil. In North China, some 24,000 rural villages have been abandoned or partly depopulated as grasslands have been destroyed by overgrazing and as croplands have been inundated by migrating sand dunes.

In countries with severe soil erosion, such as Mongolia and Lesotho, grain harvests are shrinking as erosion lowers yields and eventually leads to cropland abandonment. The result is spreading hunger and growing dependence on imports. Haiti and North Korea, two countries with severely eroded soils, are chronically dependent on food aid from abroad.

Meanwhile aquifer depletion is fast shrinking the amount of irrigated area in many parts of the world; this relatively recent phenomenon is driven by the large-scale use of mechanical pumps to exploit underground water. Today, half the world's people live in countries where water tables are falling as overpumping depletes aquifers. Once an aquifer is depleted, pumping is necessarily reduced to the rate of recharge unless it is a fossil (nonreplenishable) aquifer, in which case pumping ends altogether. But sooner or later, falling water tables translate into rising food prices. . . .

The Arab Middle East is the first geographic region where spreading water shortages are shrinking the grain harvest. But the really big water deficits are in India, where the World Bank numbers indicate that 175 million people are being fed with grain that is produced by overpumping. In China, overpumping provides food for some 130 million people. In the United States, the world's other leading grain producer, irrigated area is shrinking in key agricultural states such as California and Texas.

The last decade has witnessed the emergence of yet another constraint on growth in global agricultural productivity: the shrinking backlog of untapped technologies. In some agriculturally advanced countries, farmers are using all available technologies to raise yields. In Japan, the first country to see a sustained rise in grain yield per acre, rice yields have been flat now for 14 years. Rice yields in South Korea and China are now approaching those in Japan. Assuming that farmers in these two countries will face the same constraints as those in Japan, more than a third of the world rice harvest will soon be produced in countries with little potential for further raising rice yields.

A similar situation is emerging with wheat yields in Europe. In France, Germany, and the United Kingdom, wheat yields are no longer rising at all. These three countries together account for roughly one-eighth of the world wheat harvest. Another trend slowing the growth in the world grain harvest is the conversion of cropland to nonfarm uses. Suburban sprawl, industrial construction, and the paving of land for roads, highways, and parking lots are claiming cropland in the Central Valley of California, the Nile River basin in Egypt, and in densely populated countries that are rapidly industrializing, such as China and India. . . .

Fast-growing cities are also competing with farmers for irrigation water. In areas where all water is being spoken for, such as most countries in the Middle East, northern China, the southwestern United States, and most of India, diverting water to cities means less irrigation water available for food production. California has lost perhaps a million acres of irrigated land in recent years as farmers have sold huge amounts of water to the thirsty millions in Los Angeles and San Diego.

The rising temperature is also making it more difficult to expand the world grain harvest fast enough to keep up with the record pace of demand. Crop ecologists have their own rule of thumb: For each 1 degree Celsius rise in temperature above the optimum during the growing season, we can expect a 10 percent decline in grain yields. This temperature effect on yields was all too visible in western Russia during the summer of 2010 as the harvest was decimated when temperatures soared far above the norm.

Another emerging trend that threatens food security is the melting of mountain glaciers. This is of particular concern in the Himalayas and on the Tibetan plateau, where the ice melt from glaciers helps sustain not only the major rivers of Asia during the dry season, such as the Indus, Ganges, Mekong, Yangtze, and Yellow rivers, but also the irrigation systems dependent on these rivers. Without this ice melt, the grain harvest would drop precipitously and prices would rise accordingly.

And finally, over the longer term, melting ice sheets in Greenland and West Antarctica, combined with thermal expansion of the oceans, threaten to raise the sea level by up to six feet during this century. Even a three-foot rise would inundate half of the riceland in Bangladesh. It would also put under water much of the Mekong Delta that produces half the rice in Vietnam, the world's number two rice exporter. Altogether there are some 19 other rice-growing river deltas in Asia where harvests would be substantially reduced by a rising sea level.

The current surge in world grain and soybean prices, and in food prices more broadly, is not a temporary phenomenon. We can no longer expect that things will soon return to normal, because in a world with a rapidly changing climate system there is no norm to return to. . . .

Section 2 Exercise

Fries with That? Tracing Personal Consumption

"Do you want fries with that?" This is the kind of innocuous question that is often appended to our daily consumption decisions. As we live, and especially as we shop, we are inundated with choices: what to wear, what to watch, what to drink. Such conundrums are at the heart of our modern-day consumer lifestyles.

It's hard to imagine that something as routine and everyday as deciding what to eat can be connected to the global environmental challenges that you have been reading about. Yet as this exercise will demonstrate, there are connections, both basic and profound.

The average box of French fries purchased in the United States is the product of a long chain of actions. To grow a potato requires earth, water, and sunshine. It has also come to require carefully bred seeds, various petrochemicals, and masses of fossil-fuel-powered farm and transportation equipment. Potatoes, on their way to becoming French fries, are planted, grown, harvested, processed, frozen, shipped, cooked, packaged, and consumed in ways that have tangible, identifiable implications for the functioning of the earth's living systems.

As it goes for French fries, so it goes for most everything else in our lives. The objects with which we come into contact each day have environmental histories and destinies. They have stories to tell, if we care to listen. It is through objects that we most directly touch global environmental processes and thus, by reflecting on objects, we can begin to unpack and untangle global environmental challenges that otherwise appear distant and abstract.

Your task with the following exercise is to compose the story of an everyday object. (The exercise is constructed for a classroom setting, but can easily be modified for an individual.)

Step 1: Break into groups of four or so. Each of you should then select an object that you have with you in the classroom (e.g., pen, cell phone, bottle of juice, piece of clothing, book, etc.). Pass the object among your group members and explain its significance. Why do you have the object? What is it used for? How often do you use it?

Step 2: Have your group choose one of the objects. On a large sheet of paper or a whiteboard, use images, diagrams, and/or words to trace the story of your object—from its earliest beginnings to its predicted future. What are your object's constituent parts? Where do they originate? How do they come together to make the object that you are holding? What are the object's uses? What will happen to the object when you are done with it?

Step 3: On a separate sheet of paper, draw, describe, or otherwise explain one of the four global environmental problems discussed in this section of the book. Now make the connection. How do the various stages of an object's origination, construction, transport, and disposal impact the environmental problem you have chosen?

Section 3

Causes of Environmental Harm

In the last two sections, we implicitly rendered a diagnosis of the planet's ecological health and found it troubling. No matter where we look, we see signs of severe ecological degradation. What now? What do we do with such information? We are often told that with knowledge comes responsibility. How do we respond to global environmental problems?

For some people, the information is so worrisome that they bury their heads and pretend the facts are simply untrue. For them, ignorance is bliss: what I don't know can't hurt me. This accounts for some of the environmental skepticism we hear downplaying the risks posed by climate change, loss of biological diversity, water contamination, and food insecurity. Others react with a sense of desperation. Animated by rightful outrage but also unfocused anger, they flail around unable to find an entry point for engagement. Untrained to decipher the political landscape, they become cynical of all possible routes to change and wallow in the darkness of ecological pain. Even those who feel less desperate and able to navigate political challenges can fall into a trap of ineffectiveness as they adopt a can-do attitude that simply wants to "get on with it." Uninterested in mindful reflection, they engage in idiosyncratic projects aimed at "saving the planet," with little more than hope that their efforts will add up to productive engagement.

As professors of environmental politics, we understand indignation. As the bumper sticker says, "If you're not outraged, you're not paying attention." But, given the various routes outrage can take, we also feel it is important to steer responses in meaningful directions. Thought without action won't help things. And action without thought, however well intentioned, may make things worse. How do we move forward? This is where analysis comes in. Analysis allows us to get our heads around environmental issues in pursuit of appropriate responses. It enables us to become responsible.

Responsibility is about developing an *ability* to respond. We begin to develop this ability by asking about the causes of environmental harm. Why is the world in dire ecological straits? How did things get so bad? Why is practically every ecological indicator pointing downward? What dynamics are involved?

We can get a handle on these questions by dividing the sources of environmental harm into two categories: *material* and *ideational.* Material causes are the physical drivers—such as economic wealth, technological capacity, or population numbers that can push the overuse of resources, saturation of sinks, or despoiling of sites. Ideational ones involve cultural mindsets—for instance, consumerism, a belief that humans can exploit nature with impunity, or societal tolerance of environmental injustice. We start in this introduction by focusing on material drivers and finish by examining ideational ones. Both are relevant for explaining the causes of ecological degradation.

More than two centuries ago, Reverend Thomas Malthus worried that unchecked population increases would overwhelm the planet's ability to provide enough food. He famously wrote, "The power of population is indefinitely greater than the power in the earth to produce subsistence for man." World population stood at roughly one billion at the time Malthus was writing. Today it stands at more than seven billion and, although the rate of population growth is declining, absolute numbers continue to rise. We are, in population terms, adding another New York City every six weeks, an Egypt every year, and close to three additional United States every decade. More people involves more mouths to feed, bodies to be housed, waste to be absorbed, and so forth. Rising population is a key source of environmental degradation.

Human numbers alone, though, don't tell the whole story. Our individual ability to consume resources, generate waste, and damage beautiful places turns on our economic capabilities. When Malthus was writing, world annual economic output stood at around $200 billion (measured in 1990 dollars). By 1950, it was close to $5 trillion. These days it grows more than $5 trillion every three years. This is, in one sense, good news for the world, especially for the impoverished, who deserve better living standards and enhanced life chances. But greater affluence has its downside. Think about what we do when we have more money: we eat more lavish food, buy more things, travel to more places, and otherwise extend our ecological footprint. Economic growth, by this reckoning, is a central driver of environmental decay.

A third material cause of environmental harm is technological capability. Technology extends our reach into the earth's ecosystems. It allows us to fly through the sky, dig into the ground, power across water, and produce synthetic materials alien to the earth's natural systems. As our technological capabilities grow, so do the power, intensity, and scope of our enterprises. Malthus didn't own a cell phone, car, or computer. Had he, he would have used many more resources, produced more waste, and negatively impacted the landscape through associated production processes. Although it is hard to measure, technological innovation is growing faster than economies and populations. The speed of such innovation is one of the factors leading not simply to "fast food," but "fast clothes," "fast electronics," and fast consumer goods in general, in which production and consumption follow increasingly shorter life spans animated by fashion trends rather than longevity, durability, and sustainability. The consequences of this are marked on the face of the earth itself as greater demands are placed on the earth's overstretched sources, sinks, and sites.

Some analysts point to the conjunction of population, economic capability, and technological change as the main causes of environmental problems. Famously known as the *IPAT formula,* scholars explain how P (population) × A (affluence) × T (technology) = environmental I (impact). Given that each of these factors has been growing over the past decades at incredible speeds, the IPAT formula helps us chart and explain, at least in a rudimentary sense, the chief material causes of environmental harm.

The chapters in this section each make use of the IPAT formulation. The first chapter comes from journalist **Thomas Friedman.** Friedman takes us to far-flung corners of the world to show us the growing pervasiveness of the American way of life. The "Americans" Friedman finds wherever he travels—meaning those who consume at the levels of people in the United States—are rapidly growing in number, with troubling implications for the world's already stressed natural systems.

Writer and activist **Bill McKibben** demonstrates the explanatory power of IPAT by asking three critical questions: How many of us are there? How big are we (in an ecological sense)? How big is the earth? By walking us through these three questions, McKibben demonstrates that the IPAT formula can help us see how expanding human numbers and appetites can push up against hard ecological limits in increasingly profound and troubling ways.

Friedman and McKibben demonstrate that an understanding of the IPAT formula helps to capture the materialistic dimensions of environmental degradation. These forces do not, however, operate in a vacuum, but are embedded in and animated by the second of our analytic categories: ideational factors that steer material arrangements in certain directions. Put differently, demographic, economic, and technological trends are partly governed by ruling ideas that determine the pace, direction, and quality of collective change.

Worldwatch staff researcher and writer **Erik Assadourian** illustrates the power of ruling ideas by identifying how most societies now subscribe to a consumerist mentality that sees the good life tied to high patterns of consumption. For Assadourian, environmental harm comes not simply from increases in population, affluence, or technology, but also from the cultural context in which they operate.

From a different angle, journalist **John Tierney** emphasizes how the cultural context influences the material causes of environmental harm. For Tierney, affluence is not necessarily a bad thing; it depends on how one understands wealth and the purposes to which it is directed. If used to fund green technologies such as solar energy, efficient water systems, and electric cars, for instance, affluence can work in the service of environmental protection. Faith in directing wealth in these directions leads Tierney to write, "The richer everyone gets, the greener the planet will be in the long run."

One can make the same argument about technology and even population. Technological change is not bad in itself; it depends on the type of innovation and its employment. If the global energy system were reconfigured to be powered by wind farms rather than coal-burning plants, or if high-speed rail lines and bicycle lanes largely replaced automobiles, we might see the green side of technology. Likewise, if we decided to educate, medically care for, and communally support each newborn—such that each person could contribute his or her emerging knowledge and expertise to addressing environmental dilemmas—we would, conceivably, see the greener side of population increases.

The good news about understanding both material and ideational causes of environmental harm is that it provides a map for responding to environmental problems. Increases in population, affluence, and technology spell doom for the planet unless we find ways of steering them in green, just directions. This is where cultural politics comes into focus. Shifting societal priorities—through governmental action, market mechanisms, and norms—is essential for governing the material drivers of environmental degradation. The IPAT formula and an appreciation for its current cultural context are a crucial first step for identifying leverage points.

8

Too Many Americans?

Thomas Friedman

Affluenza is a term used by critics of consumerism, a portmanteau of affluence and influenza. Sources define this term as follows:

affluenza, n. a painful, contagious, socially transmitted condition of overload, debt, anxiety and waste resulting from the dogged pursuit of more. (de Graaf) affluenza, n. 1. The bloated, sluggish and unfulfilled feeling that results from efforts to keep up with the Joneses. 2. An epidemic of stress, overwork, waste and indebtedness caused by the pursuit of the American Dream. 3. An unsustainable addiction to economic growth. (PBS)

—Wikipedia

In the fall of 2007, I visited two cities you may have never heard of—Doha and Dalian. They are two cities you should know about if you want to understand how and why the meeting of flat and crowded has helped tip us over into the Energy-Climate Era. Doha is the capital of Qatar, a tiny peninsular state off the east coast of Saudi Arabia. Population: around 450,000. Dalian is in northeast China and is known as China's Silicon Valley, because of its software parks, verdant hillsides, and tech-savvy mayor, Xia Deren. Population: around six million. I have gone to both cities several times, so I knew them pretty well, but I had not been to either one for over three years when I happened to visit them two weeks apart.

I barely recognized them.

In Doha, since I had been there last, a skyline that looked like a mini-Manhattan had sprouted from the sands like a big desert wildflower after a flash rainstorm. Whatever construction cranes were not working in Shanghai and Dubai must have been working in Doha. In fact, there were so many cranes poking up through the city skyline, it looked like Doha needed a haircut. This once-sleepy Persian Gulf port had given birth to a whole extended family of glass-and-steel skyscrapers, in various states of construction, thanks to a sudden massive injection of oil and gas revenues.

The Dalian I knew already had a mini-Manhattan. But when I returned, I saw that it had given birth to another; this one included a gleaming new convention complex built on a man-made peninsula: the Dalian Xinghai Convention & Exhibition Center, said to be the biggest in Asia. It was, indeed, bigger, more luxurious, and more whiz-bang modern than any convention center I've ever visited, and it is located in just one of the forty-nine cities in China with over one million people—forty-seven of which you've probably never heard of.

But this, alas, is not a tale of tourism. It's a tale of energy consumption in a flat world, when so many more people are starting to prosper, consume energy, and emit carbon dioxide at the same levels as Americans. Seeing Doha and Dalian made me worry that we'll never get our collective arms around climate change. Can you imagine how much energy all these new skyscrapers in just two cities you've never heard of are going to consume and how much CO_2 they, and the vehicles going to and from them, are going to emit? I hardly can.

I'm glad that many people in the United States and Europe have switched from incandescent light bulbs to long-lasting compact fluorescent light bulbs in their homes. That has saved a lot of kilowatts of energy. But the recent growth in Doha and Dalian just ate all those energy savings for breakfast. I'm glad that many people are buying hybrid cars. But Doha and Dalian devoured all those gasoline savings before noon. I'm glad that the U.S. Congress decided to boost U.S. mileage-per-gallon requirements up to European levels by 2020. But Doha and Dalian will have those energy savings for lunch—maybe just as the first course. I'm glad that solar and wind power are "soaring" toward 2 percent of U.S. energy generation, but Doha and Dalian will guzzle all those clean electrons for dinner. I am thrilled that people are now doing the "twenty green things" to save energy suggested by their favorite American magazine. But Doha and Dalian will snack on all those good intentions like popcorn before bedtime.

Doha and Dalian show what happens when flat meets crowded. Not only will the world's population grow from around three billion in 1955 to a projected nine billion by 2050, but—much, much more important—we will go from a world population in which maybe one billion people were living an "American" lifestyle to a world in which two or three billion people are living an American lifestyle or aspiring to do so. . . . [T]he metric to watch is not the total number of people on the planet—it's the total number of "Americans" on the planet. That is the key number and it has been steadily rising.

I certainly don't blame the citizens of Doha or Dalian for aspiring to an American lifestyle or for opting to build it on the same cheap-fossil-fuel foundation that we did. We invented that system. We exported it. Others are entitled to it every bit as much as we are, if not more, since we've been enjoying this kind of growth and consumption for decades and others are just getting their first taste of it. Growth is not negotiable, especially in a flat world where everyone can see how everyone else is living. To tell people they can't grow is to tell them they have to remain poor forever.

As an Egyptian cabinet minister remarked to me: It is like the developed world ate all the hors d'oeuvres, all the entrees, and all the desserts and then invited the developing world for a little coffee "and asked us to split the whole bill." That's not going to happen. The developing world will not be denied.

We Americans are in no position to lecture anyone. But we are in a position to know better. We are in a position to set a different example of growth. We are in a position to use our resources and know-how to invent the renewable, clean power sources and energy efficiency systems that can make growth greener. Both Europe and Japan have demonstrated that it is possible to live a middle-class lifestyle with much less consumption. In a world that is both flat and crowded, if we, as Americans, do not redefine what an American middle-class lifestyle is—and invent the tools and spread the know-how that enable another two or three billion people to enjoy it in a more sustainable fashion—we will need to colonize three more planets. Because we are going to make planet earth so hot, and strip it so bare of resources, that nobody, including us, will be able to live like Americans one day.

"It took all of human history to build the seven-trillion-dollar world economy of 1950; today economic activity grows by that amount every decade," notes Yale's James Gustave Speth in *The Bridge at the Edge of the World*. "At current rates of growth, the world economy will double in size in a mere fourteen years."

"Americans" are popping up all over now—from Doha to Dalian and from Calcutta to Casablanca to Cairo, moving into American-style living spaces, buying American-style cars, eating American-style fast food, and creating American levels of garbage. The planet has never seen so many Americans.

Cities all over the world have caught America's affluenza—surely one of the most infectious diseases ever known to man. Tom Burke, a founding director of E3G—Third Generation Environmentalism, a nonprofit green consultancy—has invented a whole new unit of measure to illuminate the problem. He calls it the "Americum." Yes, think of America as a unit of energy. So one "Americum," as Burke puts it, "is any group of 350 million people with a per capita income above $15,000 and a growing penchant for consumerism." For many years, there were only two Americums in the world, says Burke—one in North America and another in Europe, with small pockets of Americum-style living in Asia, Latin America, and the Middle East.

"Today," he notes, "there are Americums taking shape all over the planet." China has given birth to one Americum and is pregnant with a second, which is due in 2030. India has one Americum now and also has another on the way, also due by 2030. Singapore, Malaysia, Vietnam, Thailand, Indonesia, Taiwan,

Australia, New Zealand, Hong Kong, Korea, and Japan constitute another Americum. Russia and Central Europe are nurturing another Americum, and parts of South America and the Middle East still another. "So, by 2030," says Burke, "we will have gone from a world of two Americums to a world of eight or nine."

These are America's carbon copies.

While in Dalian, I met up with my friend Jack Hidary, a young New York–based Internet and energy entrepreneur. He told me about a tour he had just taken, with his official Chinese hosts, to the nearby port of Dayao, Dalian's gateway to the Pacific. He toured the new port complex built by the Chinese government with help from Norway and Japan. It included China's largest crude oil terminal—a stainless-steel forest of oil and gas pipelines, storage tanks, and oil tankers flying Middle East flags.

"I just looked at that and turned to my Chinese hosts and said, 'Oh my God, you've copied us—why have you copied us?'" Hidary recalled. "'You didn't do it with telephony. You leapfrogged us with cell phones. There's only 5 percent landline penetration in China. So why did you copy us here?' I was so depressed. They saw what we did and they could have taken a detour around our pothole and they didn't."

There is still time for China and others to adopt a different approach, but, again, it is unlikely to happen unless we show them the way, This is more urgent than you might imagine, because if the currently developing world locks in American-style consumption, building, and transportation patterns, we will be living with, and limited by, the energy and climate implications for decades.

We have been limited before in history by the logic of disease or hunger or war, but never by "the ecological logic of capitalism," argues Jeff Wacker, the futurist for Electronic Data Systems Corporation. You know that you are in the Energy-Climate Era when the eco-logic of capitalism becomes an important, if not the most important, restraint on our growth.

"Our prosperity is now threatened by the very foundation of that prosperity"—the nature of American capitalism, said Wacker. "We have to fix the foundation before we can live in the house again. China's foundation cannot be the same foundation we built America on. And America's foundation can no longer be the same. We have reached the physical limits of building on this foundation. It has to be a different foundation."

The problem is that we have not invented that new foundation yet. . . .

Even a country like India is now groaning under a powerful new growth trend. After independence, from about 1950 to 1980, India's leaders instituted a socialist-style planned economy, with a dose of free-market capitalism on the side, persuaded that what came to be called the "Hindu rate of growth"—3.5 percent a year—was sufficient. They did so even though that rate of growth barely kept ahead of India's 2.5 percent annual population growth rate, and didn't leave much in the way of rising living standards for most of its people.

Although India, as a democracy, has been slower to take advantage of the collapse of socialist ideology and the flattening of the world than China has, it is catching up fast. India has almost tripled the old Hindu rate of growth and is now motoring along at around 9 percent a year. The impact this is having on both the buying power and building power of the Indian economy is staggering, as illustrated through some revealing comparisons by the Indian economics writer Salil Tripathi on the *Guardian Unlimited* Web site (June 13, 2006):

> To put Indian growth in perspective: when it grew at 7.5% last year, India's income rose by an amount higher than the total income of Portugal ($194 billion), Norway ($183 billion), or Denmark ($178 billion) that year. It was the equivalent of adding a rich country's economy to a very poor one. . . . What it also means is that even though India added 156 million more people to its population during that decade—a figure combining the total populations of Britain, France and Spain put together—during that period, the number of poor people in India actually fell by 37 million, or the size of Poland. Had the poverty level remained the same, there would have been 361 million poor in India. Instead, the Indian economy had lifted 94 million people out of absolute poverty during that period—that's 12 million more people than the entire population of Germany, the most populous state in the European Union.

Ho-hum: add a Germany here, a Poland there—all in fifteen years. . . .

When you visit India today, you can literally see and touch the rise in living standards happening around you, which is beautiful—as long as you're not in a car caught in traffic. In Hyderabad in October 2007, I was going by car through the city's busy downtown when we passed a group of about fifty men sitting cross-legged at the foot of what looked to be a new bridge. A Hindu priest in a colorful outfit was walking among them, swinging a lantern with burning coconut shells and reciting some chants (an Indian friend in the car with me explained) to bring good tidings to the people who would travel on that bridge. Local politicians had also gathered around the ceremony for a photo op. They were dedicating a just-completed overpass that would lift traffic off the streets of Hyderabad and ease the gridlock. The overpass was two years in the making. I was happy to see the progress. Over breakfast at my hotel the next morning, I was flipping through the *Sunday Times of India* (Hyderabad edition, October 28, 2007) when my eye caught a color photograph of totally gridlocked traffic—motor scooters, buses, cars, and yellow, three-wheeled motorized rickshaws, all knotted together.

The headline over the picture read: "No flying over, only snarls." The caption read: "Traffic ends in bottleneck on the Greenlands flyover which was opened in Hyderabad on Saturday. On day one, the flyover was chock-a-block with traffic, raising questions over the efficacy of the flyover in reducing vehicular congestion."

That was my overpass! In one day, an overpass that had taken two years to build was devoured by India's growth without a burp. Now that India's Tata Group has started mass-producing a $2,500 four-passenger car I shudder to think what that bridge looks like today.

Sheila Dikshit, chief minister of the Indian capital territory of Delhi, once told a conference of the World Economic Forum and the Confederation of Indian Industry about what it was like to try to run a city of sixteen million inhabitants that attracts 500,000 new migrants every year: "Each one of them, when they live in Delhi, they want more water, more power, they want more wages, more oil." The article went on to say that no Indian politician dared to deny their people cheap fuel, noting that in the fiscal year 2007, "the Indian government will spend an estimated $17.5 billion, or 2 percent of national output, on fuel subsidies—because it refuses to "pass on the greatly increased world price of energy to its citizens" out of fear of a political backlash (*The Financial Times*, December 6, 2007).

Don't think this phenomenon is confined to just the hot economies of China, Russia, and India. In June 2008, I visited the thousand-acre olive farm owned by Khalil Nasrallah and Sarah Gauch, located on the Cairo-Alexandria highway, about thirty miles from the Pyramids. Khalil, a Lebanese entrepreneur, had bought this property in 1991. He later met Sarah, an American freelance writer and journalist, and they married and had children, setting up homes both in Cairo and out on the farm.

"This is what it looked like when we first came here," said Khalil, opening a photo album to a page with a view from their roof. What I saw was the green swatch of his olive farm surrounded by empty desert on both sides. There wasn't even a water well here when they arrived. Khalil bought the land on spec and discovered the water later—abundant water. "We were really out here alone," he says wistfully.

When you go up to the roof of their desert home today, "alone" is not the word that comes to mind.

Khalil and Sarah are now basically surrounded by gated communities filled with McMansions on quarter-acre lots—gated communities with names like Moon Valley, Hyde Park, Richmont, Riviera Heights, and Beverly Hills. The one immediately to his right has a ninety-nine-hole golf complex. There is a French-based Carrefour big-box store and modern supermarket around the corner. Over the horizon to the left is another gated community and beyond that another golf course. They are all populated by Egyptians who have worked hard and made money in the Gulf or who are part of the globalized business class in Cairo. They are entitled to their golf courses and McMansions as much as Americans living in Palm Desert, California, are. But the energy and water implications of all these new gated communities is one reason the Middle East is increasingly consuming, rather than exporting, so much of its own oil. . . .

I don't know when we will hit the wall. But the steady rise in energy, food, and other commodity prices since 2000 is surely a sign that the world, at present levels of science and technology, is straining to supply all the raw materials for the growth of so many Americums. Without a dramatic improvement in sustainable energy and resource productivity, China, India, and the Arab world's strategy of just aping the resource-wasting development model of America is unviable. The old way is not replicable on the China-India scale in a flat world, without irreparable harm to planet earth.

"Every previous economic spurt and takeoff in history by one country or a region was nurtured by an unexploited biological commons," argues Carl Pope, referring to a region of vast untapped natural resources. "Northern Europe was taken into capitalism by the cod fishermen of the North Atlantic in the seventeenth century. Europe at the time did not have many sources of protein, until it discovered the Grand Banks fishing grounds. It was how they provided protein for all the people who left farms and moved to cities to engage in industry, textiles, and trade. Britain's fleet, by the way, was made possible by the virgin pine forests of North America and hardwood forests of India."

The Industrial Revolution in the eighteenth and nineteenth centuries, added Pope, was fed, in part, "by the American Midwest, an unexploited commons for producing grain, and by Britain exploiting India to grow tea that was shipped to China to obtain Chinese silver and silks. Parts of Africa were exploited for slaves to grow sugar in the Caribbean. [The Japanese] in the early twentieth century stoked [their] growth with tungsten from Indonesia, rubber from Malaysia, rice from China. When that failed after [Japan lost World War II], they fueled their postwar industrial revolution by harvesting all the fisheries in the world to feed the Japanese salarymen making Toyotas."

The bad news for today's rising economic powers and new capitalists is that there are few virgin commons left to fuel their takeoff into capitalism. "That is why China is now reduced to stealing manhole covers," said Pope. "Yes, it is unfair, but it's the reality."

Either they will devour themselves, or they will use globalization like a straw to suck every drop of resources out of the last corners of Africa, Latin America, and Indonesia, or, ideally, we will find a more sustainable growth model for a world that is hot, flat, and crowded.

"The good news is that there is another way to grow," argues Carl Pope. "Today we can substitute knowledge for raw materials in so many more ways." No, you can't build a building with computer bits and bytes like cement bricks and mortar, but with smarter materials and smarter designs you can build a building with a lot fewer bricks and a lot less mortar. You can build a building with tighter windows and a lot better insulation. You can make steel with so much less iron ore and so much less heat. You can make buildings that retain heat or cooling so much more efficiently. You can grow more food per acre. *All it takes is knowledge.* Innovation around sustainable energy and resource productivity is our only way out of this problem. China and India have to become much more knowledge-intensive in everything they produce much faster than the West did in its day, so they can grow with fewer resources. They are trying. But they cannot afford a 150-year learning curve, and neither can we—not when so many of them are going to be living like Americans. If they take even fifty years to get around to the best practices, said Pope, "it's all over."

So how can we encourage economic growth in a world in which natural resources are limited, not growing? One of the most innovative ways to think about this challenge is the "cradle to cradle" concept the architect William McDonough and the chemist Michael Braungart describe in their book *Cradle to Cradle: Remaking the Way We Make Things.* They argue that our current approach to recycling is that we take bigger and higher quality computers, electronics, boxes, and cars and turn them into lower quality, less sophisticated products—and then we throw them away. It is not really recycling, they say, but "downcycling"—just slow-motion waste and resource depletion. In *Cradle to Cradle,* they argue that we can and must make every TV set, chair, carpet, piece of furniture, and computer screen out of materials that can be either completely reusable in other products or completely biodegradable, so that they can be used as fertilizer. All product components, they insist, can be designed for continuous recovery and reutilization as biological or technical nutrients—"eliminating the concept of waste."

I visited McDonough in his office near the University of Virginia and he elaborated on the concept, pointing to the chair in which I was sitting: "Cradle to cradle means, in counterdistinction to cradle to grave, that we close all the cycles, so we don't just send things to landfills and incinerators, we put them into closed cycles so that we can use them over and over again. . . . Like this chair you're sitting on is aluminum and fabric. The fabric goes back to soil. The aluminum goes back to industry, so nothing is ever wasted. We eliminate the concept of waste—everything is in a closed cycle. . . . We look at all these materials, [and] instead of worrying about where they're going to end up in a landfill or incinerator, we design them to be completely safe, so they go back to nature or back to industry forever. And importantly, this creates a massive new opportunity for job creation—in our own country, because in the future, as labor costs begin to level out, logistics will be the most expensive thing and the local will become not only the most cost-beneficial but the necessary. So imagine, today there are 4.5 billion pounds of carpet that get thrown away every year in America. Instead of throwing it away to a landfill, shipping it to China, or incinerating it, what if it all could become carpet again because you designed a cradle-to-cradle product. Not only would you be able to change your carpet as often as you wanted without guilt, but you would be producing massive amounts of jobs in America."

One day, McDonough suggested, all appliances could be leased—refrigerators, microwaves, television sets, even all cars—and returned to their manufacturers to be completely recycled, over and over and over: not cradle to grave, but cradle to cradle. Some variation of this approach is the only viable solution for economic growth in a flat world.

Unfortunately, instead of rethinking and redesigning what it means to be an American, in many areas we Americans are still intensifying, expanding, and plain old doubling down on our old energy-guzzling model. . . .

9

A Finite Earth?

Bill McKibben

Not far from the office where I used to work in Midtown Manhattan, a store-front window offered passersby a look at a "population clock," a kind of human odometer relentlessly tallying our growing numbers. The ever-increasing total looked ominous—about 3 new people each second, 10,000 an hour, a quarter million a day. Since the mid-1960s, we've lived with the idea that there is a "population bomb" or a "population explosion" or, at the very least, a "population crisis." If children of a slightly earlier generation expected to end up buried beneath radioactive debris, children of my generation expected in somewhat the same unspoken way that eventually people would stand shoulder to shoulder on their own few feet of land in a desperately overcrowded world.

To figure out if we're nearing certain limits, the first question you need to ask is, how many of us are there? So here is the first piece of news that may alter the way you see the planet. . . . Oddly enough, it is, at least at first blush, a hopeful indicator: *new demographic evidence shows that it is at least possible that a child born today will live long enough to see the peak of human population.*

Around the world people are choosing to have fewer and fewer children—not just in China where the government forces it on them, but in almost every nation outside the poorest parts of Africa. Population growth rates are lower than at any time since World War II. . . . If this keeps up, the population of the world will not quite double again—the United Nations guesses it will top out at between 10 and 11 billion . . . and the peak could be even lower. The world is still growing, growing at nearly a record pace: we add a New York City every month, nearly a Mexico every year, almost an India each decade. But we may be over the top of the rollercoaster—that growth is no longer "exponential," "unstoppable," "inexorable," "unchecked," "cancerous." If current trends hold, population growth will all but end before the twenty-first century is out.

And that will be none too soon; there is no way we could keep going as we have been. The increase in human population in the 1990s exceeded total population in 1600. There has been more population growth since 1950 than during the previous 4 million years. . . .

The reasons for our recent rapid growth are pretty clear. For most of human history it took more than a millennium for population to double; the Industrial Revolution speeded that considerably, but it was really the public health revolution, and its spread to the Third World at the end of World War II, that set us galloping. "Before then India was elephants in our mind, and so was Africa—we just had vague notions of these places," said Cari Haub, chief demographer for the Population Reference Bureau. "But then the United Nations started very effective campaigns to raise health standards." Vaccines and antibiotics came all at once, and right behind came population. In Sri Lanka life expectancy was rising two years every twelve months. How much difference did this make? Consider the United States: if people still died at the same age and rate as they did at the turn of the [20th] century, America's population would be 140 million, not 270 million [now 310 million]. . . .

Right now women in the developing world are averaging four children apiece, down from six; the U.N. projections assume that number will quickly drop to two, the rate at which population growth eventually stabilizes. If fertility levels stall, at current levels, population would reach the absurd figure of 296 billion by 2150. Even if it drops to 2.5 kids per woman and then stops falling, the population would still reach an only slightly less absurd 28 billion.

But let's trust that this time the nose-counters have got it right. Let's trust that we're in the home stretch, that we've come around the corner. Let's trust that the planet's population really will double only one more time. Even so, this is a good news–bad news joke. The good news is, we won't grow forever; we won't each of us have to stand on our own small patch of soil, surrounded by a sea of brethren. This has led some to say that we don't need to worry about population. Ben Wattenberg, writing in *The New York Times Magazine* last November, declared, "The population explosion is over."

But the bad news is that there are 6 billion [now 7 billion] of us already, a number the world strains to support. One more near-doubling—4 or 5 billion more people—will nearly double that strain. Will these be the 5 billion straws that snap the camel's back?

We've answered the question "How many of us will there be?" But to figure out how near we are to any limits, we need to ask something else: How big are we? Which is not so simple. Not only do we vary vastly one from another in how much food and energy and water and minerals we each consume, but we vary over time. Someone once tried to calculate the amount of energy we used each day. In hunter-gatherer times, it was about 2,500 calories, all of it food we—yes—hunted or gathered. That is the energy equivalent of the daily intake of a common dolphin. Modern human beings use 31,000 calories apiece, most of it in the form of fossil fuel. That's the equivalent of a pilot whale. And the average American uses six times as much as that—as much as a sperm whale. We have become, in other words, different people than we used to be. Not kinder or unkinder, not deeper or more stupid—our natures seem to have changed little since Homer. We've just gotten bigger. We appear to be the same species with the same-sized stomachs, but we aren't; it's as if we're each trailing a big Macy's parade balloon around behind us, feeding it constantly. We are sperm whales cleverly disguised as *Homo sapiens.*

So it doesn't do much good to stare idly out the window of your 737 as you fly from New York to Los Angeles and note that there's plenty of empty space down there. Sure enough, you could crowd lots more people into the nation or the planet. The entire world population could fit into Texas and each person could have an area equal to the floor space of a typical U.S. home. Hell, if people were willing to stand, everyone on earth could fit comfortably into half of Rhode Island. Holland is crowded and it's doing just fine.

But this ignores the balloons above our heads, our hungry shadow selves, our sperm whale appetites. As soon as we started farming, we started setting aside extra land to support ourselves. Now each of us needs not only our own little plot of cropland and our own little pasture for the meat we eat, but our own little forest for our timber and paper, our own little mine, our own little oil well. Giants have big feet. Some Vancouver scientists tried to calculate this "footprint," and found that while 1.7 million people lived in the 400,000 hectares surrounding their city, they required 8.7 million hectares of land to support them: wheat fields in Alberta, cornfields in Juarez, oilfields in Arabia, cattle fields in Ecuador, tomato fields in California. People exist in Manhattan the same way people exist on the *Mir* space station.

That balloon above our heads can shrink or grow, depending on how we choose to live. Last fall I visited a friend of mine, David Kline, an Amish farmer and writer in rural Ohio. The corn harvest was underway, and we spent the morning cutting stalks and loading them on a horse-drawn wagon for the trip to the silo; we spent the noon hour eating a communal lunch with the other men, a lunch slaughtered and harvested and milked within a few hundred yards of the room we sat in. I spent the heat of the afternoon lying on my back under a big old tree, listening to the cattle lowing in the barn and the clop of hooves on the road. My friend David Kline was not big, in the sense I've been using big; he could have a dozen children and as long as they stayed near the farm, their impact on the world would be fairly small. (And of course, the Amish do have many children—at the small school I visited, they were sitting two to a desk.)

At the moment, though, the prevailing wind blows from the other direction, and at gale force. Around the earth, people who once were tiny are, understandably, suddenly growing like Alice when she ate cake. In China in the last decade, per capita income has doubled. Though to us still Lilliputian, people there are twice their old size. They eat much higher on the food chain than they used to—China slaughters more pigs than any nation on earth—and of course a pig takes four pounds of corn to produce one pound of pork. . . .

In 1986 . . . Stanford biologist [Peter Vitousek] decided to calculate how much of the earth's "primary productivity" went to support humans. He added together the grain we ate ourselves, the corn we fed our cows, and the forests we cut for timber and paper; he added in the losses in food as we overgrazed grassland and turned it into desert. And when he was done adding, the number he came up with was 40 percent. We used 40 percent of everything the world's plants don't need to keep themselves alive; directly or indirectly we eat 40 percent of what's possible to eat. "That's a relatively large number," says Vitousek. "It should give pause to people who think we are far from any limits." . . .

When we think about overpopulation, we usually think first of the developing world, because that's where 90 percent of new humans will be added during this final doubling. In *The Population Bomb,* the 1968 book that revived the Malthusian debate, Paul Ehrlich wrote that he hadn't understood the issue emotionally until he traveled to New Delhi, until he climbed into an ancient taxi hopping with fleas for the trip to his hotel. "As we crawled through the city, we entered a crowded slum area . . . the streets seemed alive with people. People eating, people washing, people sleeping. People visiting, arguing, and screaming. . . . People, people, people, people."

But as Harvard's Amartya Sen points out, we fool ourselves when we think of population as a brown problem. The white world simply went through its population boom a century earlier (when Dickens was writing the same kind of descriptions of London). If the U.N. calculations are correct, and Asians and Africans make up just under 80 percent of humanity by 2050, then they would simply have returned "to being proportionately almost exactly as numerous as they were before the Industrial Revolution."

And of course, Asians and Africans and Latin Americans are much smaller human beings, in the sense that we've been using the term—the balloon that floats above their heads is tiny in comparison with ours. Everyone has heard the statistics time and again, usually used in an attempt to make us feel guilty. But hear them one more time, with an open mind, trying to think strategically about how we will stave off the dangers to this planet. Pretend it's not a moral problem, just a mathematical one:

- An American uses seventy times the energy of a Bangladeshi, fifty times that of a Malagasy, twenty times that of a Costa Rican.
- Since we live longer, the effect of each of us is further multiplied. In a year, an American uses three hundred times the energy of a Malian; over a lifetime, we'll actually use five hundred times as much.

- Even if you factor in all other effects—such as the burning of forests—and attribute them to poor peasants, those who live in the poor world are typically responsible for the release of half a ton of carbon annually, compared with an average 3.5 tons for each resident of the "consumer nations" of western Europe and North America. The richest tenth of Americans—the people most likely to be reading this book—each emit eleven tons of carbon annually.
- During the next decade India and China will each add to the planet about ten times as many people as will the United States—but the stress on the natural world caused by those new Americans may exceed that from the new Indians and Chinese combined. The 57.5 million northerners expected to be added during this decade will add more greenhouse gases to the atmosphere than the roughly 900 million southerners.

These statistics are not eternal. Though inequality between north and south has steadily increased, the economies of the poor nations are now growing faster than those of the West. . . .

For the moment, though (and it is the moment that counts), the United States is in a real sense the most populous nation on earth, and the one with the highest rate of growth. Though we only add about 3 million souls a year through both births and immigration, those new Americans are on average forty or fifty times the size of people born in the Third World. My daughter, four at this writing, has already used more stuff, added more waste to the environment, than most of the world's residents in a lifetime. In my thirty-six years, I've probably outdone small Indian villages.

Population growth in Rwanda, in Sudan, in El Salvador, in the slums of Lagos, in the highland hamlets of Chile can devastate those places. Growing too fast may mean that they run short of cropland to feed themselves and start planting erodible hillsides, of firewood to cook their food, of school desks and hospital beds. But population growth in those places doesn't devastate *the planet.* By contrast, we seem easily to absorb the modest annual increases in our population; in terms of our daily lives America seems only a little more crowded with each passing decade. You can still find a parking spot. But the earth simply can't absorb what we are adding to its saturated sinks.

So if it's "us," at least as much as "them," that need to bring this alteration of the earth under control, the question becomes, how? Many people who are sure that "controlling population" is the answer overseas are equally sure that there's a different answer here. If they are politicians and engineers, they're in favor of us living more *efficiently*—of building new cars that go much farther on a gallon of gas, or that don't use gas at all. If they're vegetarians, they support living more *simply*—riding bikes or buses instead of driving cars.

Both groups are utterly correct. I've spent much of my career writing about the need for cleverer technologies and more humble aspirations. That's because environmental damage can be expressed as the sum of Population $\times$ Affluence $\times$ Technology. Surely the easiest solution would be to live more simply and more efficiently, and not worry too much about the number of people.

But I've come to believe that those changes in technology and in lifestyle are not going to happen easily and speedily; they'll be begun but not finished in the few decades that really matter. . . . We're stuck with making real changes in how we live. We're stuck with reducing dramatically the amount of fossil fuel we use. And since modern westerners are a kind of machine for burning fossil fuel, since virtually everything we do involves burning coal and gas and oil, since we're wedded to petroleum, it's going to be a messy breakup.

So we need to show, before returning again to population, why simplicity and efficiency won't save the day by themselves. . . .

If you could gather all world leaders into a single room, the one thing that every last socialist, Republican, Tory, monarchist, and trade unionist could agree on was [former U.S. president] Clinton's original campaign theme: "It's the economy, stupid." We've come to idolize economic growth. Turn on the evening news tonight. Anchormen who would never dream of backing one party or the other will gaze doe-eyed at the camera and say: "Good news today from the Commerce Department: the gross national product has grown at an annual rate of 4.5 percent." And of course, in some ways it is good news. Not only does it mean jobs for people, it means more money to do useful things, even some environmental things: the air over L.A. is cleaner than the air over Bangkok because we have the cash for catalytic converters. We've made great strides against air and water pollution in the last few decades even as our population and our economy have grown.

But the anchorman could just as easily say: "Sobering news tonight from the Commerce Department: we bought 4.5 percent more stuff this quarter than we did a year ago." Because for this other type of pollution represented by carbon dioxide, growth has so far been a cause, not a solution. Build more stuff, sell more stuff—use more energy. . . .

The most fearsome environmental damage comes from things going as they're supposed to go, just at much too high a level. Reducing that damage will mean, literally, an end to business as usual.

It's not just the abstract idea of growth that we adore, however; it's also all its individual components. Take cars, for instance. If America is going to do anything about really reducing the cloud of CO_2 it puffs each year, it will have to burn far less gasoline. Technology has helped us in the past; on average, an American car gets twice as many miles to the gallon now as it did at the time of the first oil shock. Unfortunately, due to population increases, longer commuting distances, a decline in carpooling, and so forth, we have twice as many cars, and we drive them twice as far, completely canceling out the gain from all that new technology. . . .

People drive farther (miles traveled grew by 2 percent in 1995) and they drive faster (the average ticketed speed along the New York State Thruway near my home went from 73 to 76 miles per hour between 1995 and 1996). Engineers even design cars to rumble more loudly because people like the sound of excess power. We don't like the sound of conversation, though—18 million jobs were created between 1980 and 1990, but 22 million people started commuting by car in the same period. Only 5 percent of people get to work by bus or rail, down 35 percent since 1970. In fact, buses roll so empty through the streets that one UC-Berkeley study found cars are more fuel-efficient in some places than buses.

I'm not saying we should give up trying to change people's driving habits; I'm not saying it's hopeless. We will doubtless come up with new technologies that will help; if we would spend the money to make bus systems convenient, many more people would ride them. All I'm saying is that the momentum in the wrong direction is deep and powerful, and to think that by themselves such lifestyle and technological changes will stop the flow of carbon dioxide in time is romantic.

It's romantic because consumerism—consumption—is by now an ideology, nearly a faith. It's barely a choice; it's deep in our bones, the way that religion was deep in the bones of your average fourteenth-century peasant. . . .

And even as we're consuming at levels that would have stunned a medieval monarch, consuming more than any people in any place at any time, most of us don't feel particularly rich, which makes it still less likely we'll make huge changes. Partly, the anthropologists tell us, this is because "a person's sense of well-being depends less on the objective reality of material affluence than on how his or her position compared to the reference group." And in a television-dominated nation, there's no chance that we might be unaware, even for a day, that someone has more somewhere else. Advertising never ceases, not in the airport or the supermarket or the school or on the Web. Soon, promises *Wired* magazine, "push media," Internet-type messages that come across our wrist-watches or eyeglass lenses or pagers, will "penetrate environments that have, in the past, been media-free—work, church, the solitude of a country walk." Where I live in the Adirondack Mountains we're surrounded by wild places, lakes, rivers; life can be very sweet. But increasingly my neighbors, especially the kids, live in the generic suburbia of the tube and feel its pull, like salmon tugged upstream by some primal urge. The same signals go out around the world. . . .

Changing the ways we live has to be a key part of dealing with these new environmental dilemmas, if only because it is impossible to imagine a world where all 10 billion people consume at our levels. All I'm saying is, as we calculate what must happen over the next few decades to stanch the flow of CO_2, don't count on a conversion to simpler ways of life doing the trick by itself. Don't try to calculate carrying capacity for saints; an awful lot of angels could dance on the earth without doing much damage, but we're not angels. You'd think offhand that compared to changing fertility—the number of kids we bear—changing consumption patterns would be a breeze. Fertility, after all, seems biological—hard-wired into us in deep Darwinian ways. But in fact,

I would guess that it's easier to change fertility than lifestyle. For better or for worse, we live in a culture that can say "that's enough" in regard to children at least as easily as it can regarding cars.

But perhaps our salvation lies in the other part of the equation, in the new technologies, new efficiencies, that could make even our wasteful lives benign and make moot the issue of our population. We are, for instance, converting our economy from its old industrial base to a new model based on service and information, and surely that should save some energy, should reduce the clouds of carbon. Writing software, after all, seems no more likely to damage the atmosphere than writing poetry.

Forget for a moment the hardware requirements of that new economy . . . ; just keep in mind that even a hospital or an insurance company or a basketball team requires a substantial physical base. Even the highest-tech office is built with steel and cement; it's filled with pipes and wires. And the money that's earned by people working in services will be spent on all sorts of things—more software, sure, but also more sport utility vehicles. As Department of Energy economist Arthur Rypinski says, "the information age has arrived, but even so people still get hot in the summer and cold in the winter. And even in the information age it tends to get dark." . . .

The United Nations issued its omnibus report on sustainable development in 1987. Chaired by Norwegian prime minister Gro Harlem Brundtland, an international panel concluded that the world's economy would need to grow five to ten times larger to meet the needs of the poor world. And that growth won't mainly be in software. As the Department of Energy's Arthur Rypinski points out, "where the economy is growing really rapidly, energy use is too." In Thailand, in Tijuana, in Tanzania, every 10 percent increase in economic output requires 10 percent more fuel. "In the Far East the transition is from walking and bullocks to cars. People start out with electric lights and move on to lots of other stuff. Refrigerators are one of those things that are really popular everywhere. Practically no one, with the possible exception of people in the high Arctic, doesn't want a refrigerator. As people get wealthier they tend to like space heating and cooling, depending on the climate."

In other words, if you're doing the math about how we're going to get out of this fix, you better figure in some unstoppable momentum in the rest of the planet from people who want the very basics of what we call a decent life. Even if we airlift solar collectors into China and India—which we should— those nations will still be burning more coal and oil. "What you can do with energy conservation in those situations is sort of at the margin," says Rypinski. "They're not interested in $15,000 clean cars versus $5,000 dirty cars. It was hard enough to get Americans to invest in efficiency; there's no feasible amount of largesse we can provide to the rest of the world to bring it about." . . .

Carbon emissions from powering Chinese refrigerators alone increased from 25.6 million tons in 1985 to an estimated 558 million tons in the year 2000. "You can't tell the people of Beijing that they can't buy a car or an air-conditioner because of the global climate-change issue," said Li Junfeng, a senior energy researcher for the State Planning Commission in Beijing. "It's just as hot in Beijing as it is in Washington, D.C." The most the experts dare hope is that China will only double, not treble, its output of CO_2 in the next thirty years. Even that, they stress, "would require a huge mobilization of capital, technology, and political commitment." Instead, the chairman of Exxon recently went to Beijing to urge developing nations to avoid environmental controls that would hinder their development. "The earth's temperature often changes," he said, citing the Ice Ages as an example.

The numbers are so daunting they're hard to imagine. Say, just for argument's sake, that we decided to cut world fossil-fuel use 60 percent, the amount that scientists say would stabilize world climate. And then say we shared that fossil fuel equally. Each human would get to produce 1.69 metric tons of carbon dioxide annually. Which would allow us to drive the average American car nine miles a day. By the time the population increases to 8.5 billion, in about 2025, we'd be down to six miles a day. Of course, if you carpooled, you'd have about three pounds of CO_2 left in your daily ration, enough to run a highly efficient refrigerator. Forget your computer, your TV, your stereo, your stove, your dishwasher, your water heater, your microwave, your water pump, your clock. Forget your light bulbs, compact fluorescent or not.

I'm not trying to say that conservation, efficiency, and new technology won't help. They will help—but it will be slow and expensive. The tremendous momentum of growth will work against it. Say someone invented a new furnace tomorrow that used half the oil of old furnaces. How many years would it be before a substantial percentage of American homes were retrofitted with the new device? And if it cost more? And if oil stays dirt cheap? Changing basic fuels—to hydrogen, say—would be even more expensive. It's not like running out of white wine and switching to red. . . . One day [in November 1997] *The New York Times* ran a special section on energy, featuring many up-and-coming improvements: solar shingles, basement fuel cells. But the same day, on the front page, William K. Stevens reported that international negotiators had all but given up on preventing a doubling of the atmospheric concentration of CO_2. The momentum of growth was so large that diplomats said the changes required to really slow global warming would be like "trying to turn a supertanker in a sea of syrup." . . .

There are no silver bullets against a problem this systemic. Electric cars won't save us by themselves, though they would help. We simply won't live efficiently enough soon enough to solve the problem. Vegetarianism won't cure our ills, though it would help. We simply won't live simply enough soon enough to solve the problem.

Reducing the birthrate won't end all our troubles either. It, too, is no silver bullet. It's just that it, too, would help.

. . . So it's the task of those of us alive right now to deal with this special phase, to squeeze us through these next fifty years. That's not fair, no more than it was fair that earlier generations had to deal with World War II or the Civil War or the Revolution, with the Depression or with slavery. It's just reality. We need, in these fifty years, to be working simultaneously on all parts of the equation—on our ways of life, on our technologies, and on our populations. We need to be electing the right politicians, boycotting the wrong companies, recycling, riding bikes, buying tiny little cars. If we can open up a bit more margin by having fewer kids, that will help. It's like trying to make sure your car has 60,000 miles instead of 90,000 a decade after you got it. It's still not a new car. The difference between 60,000 and 90,000 is subtle. But it's real, too. . . .

As Gregg Easterbrook points out in his book *A Moment on the Earth,* if the planet does manage to reduce its fertility, "the period in which human numbers threaten the biosphere on a general scale will turn out to have been much, much more brief" than periods of natural threats like ice ages. True enough. It's just that the period in question happens to be our time. It's what makes this moment special, and what makes this moment hard.

10

Consequences of Consumerism

Erik Assadourian

Human beings are embedded in cultural systems, are shaped and constrained by their cultures, and for the most part act only within the cultural realities of their lives. The cultural norms, symbols, values, and traditions a person grows up with become "natural." Thus, asking people who live in consumer cultures to curb consumption is akin to asking them to stop breathing—they can do it for a moment, but then, gasping, they will inhale again. Driving cars, flying in planes, having large homes, using air conditioning . . . these are not decadent choices but simply natural parts of life— at least according to the cultural norms present in a growing number of consumer cultures in the world. Yet while they seem natural to people who are part of those cultural realities, these patterns are neither sustainable nor innate manifestations of human nature. They have developed over several centuries and today are actively being reinforced and spread to millions of people in developing countries.

Preventing the collapse of human civilization requires nothing less than a wholesale transformation of dominant cultural patterns. This transformation would reject consumerism—the cultural orientation that leads people to find meaning, contentment, and acceptance through what they consume—as taboo and establish in its place a new cultural framework centered on sustainability. In the process, a revamped understanding of "natural" would emerge: it would mean individual and societal choices that cause minimal ecological damage or, better yet, that restore Earth's ecological systems to health. Such a shift—something more fundamental than the adoption of new technologies or government policies, which are often regarded as the key drivers of a shift to sustainable societies—would radically reshape the way people understand and act in the world.

Transforming cultures is of course no small task. It will require decades of effort in which cultural pioneers—those who can step out of their cultural realities enough to critically examine them—work tirelessly to redirect key culture-shaping institutions: education, business, government, and the media, as well as social movements and long-standing human traditions. Harnessing these drivers of cultural change will be critical if humanity is to survive and thrive for centuries and millennia to come and prove that we are, indeed, "worth saving." . . .

To understand what consumerism is, first it is necessary to understand what culture is. Culture is not simply the arts, or values, or belief systems. It is not a distinct institution functioning alongside economic or political systems. Rather, it is all of these elements—values, beliefs, customs, traditions, symbols, norms, and institutions—combining to create the overarching frames that shape how humans perceive reality. Because of individual cultural systems, one person can interpret an action as insulting that another would find friendly—such as making a "thumbs up" sign, which is an exceptionally vulgar gesture in some cultures. Culture leads some people to believe that social roles are designated by birth, determines where people's eyes focus when they talk to others, and even dictates what forms of sexual relationships (such as monogamy, polyandry, or polygamy) are acceptable. Cultures, as broader systems, arise out of the complex interactions of many different elements of social behaviors and guide humans at an almost invisible level. They are, in the words of anthropologists Robert Welsch and Luis Vivanco, the sum of all "social processes that make the artificial (or human constructed) seem natural." It is these social processes—from direct interaction with other people and with cultural artifacts or "stuff" to exposure to the media, laws, religions, and economic systems—that shape people's realities.

Most of what seems "natural" to people is actually cultural. Take eating, for example. All humans eat, but what, how, and even when they eat is determined by cultural systems. Few Europeans would eat insects because these creatures are intrinsically repulsive to them due to cultural conditioning, though many of them would eat shrimp or snails. Yet in other cultures, bugs are an important part of cuisine, and in some cases—like the Sago grub for the Korowai people of New Guinea—bugs are delicacies.

Ultimately, while human behavior is rooted in evolution and physiology, it is guided primarily by the cultural systems people are born into. As with all systems, there are dominant paradigms that guide cultures—shared ideas and assumptions that, over generations, are shaped and reinforced by leading cultural actors and institutions and by the participants in the cultures themselves. Today the cultural paradigm that is dominant in many parts of the world and across many cultural systems is consumerism.

British economist Paul Ekins describes consumerism as a cultural orientation in which "the possession and use of an increasing number and variety of goods and services is the principal cultural aspiration and the surest perceived route to personal happiness, social status, and national success." Put more simply: consumerism is a cultural pattern that leads people to find meaning, contentment, and acceptance primarily through the consumption of goods and services. While this takes different forms in different cultures, consumerism leads people everywhere to associate high consumption levels with well-being and success. Ironically though, research shows that consuming more does not necessarily mean a better individual quality of life.

Consumerism has now so fully worked its way into human cultures that it is sometimes hard to even recognize it as a cultural construction. It simply seems to be natural. But in fact the elements of cultures—language and symbols, norms and traditions, values and institutions—have been profoundly transformed by consumerism in societies around the world. Indeed, "consumer" is now often used interchangeably with person in the 10 most commonly used languages of the world, and most likely in many more.

Consider symbols—what anthropologist Leslie White once described as "the origin and basis of human behavior." In most countries today people are exposed to hundreds if not thousands of consumerist symbols every day. Logos, jingles, slogans, spokespersons, mascots—all these symbols of different brands routinely bombard people, influencing behavior even at unconscious levels. Many people today recognize these consumerist symbols more easily than they do common wildlife species, birdsong, animal calls, or other elements of nature. One study . . . found that British children could identify more Pokémon characters (a brand of toy) than common wildlife species. And logos are recognized by children as young as two years old. One investigation of American two-year-olds found that although they could not identify the letter M, many could identify McDonald's M-shaped golden arches.

Cultural norms—how people spend their leisure time, how regularly they upgrade their wardrobes, even how they raise their children—are now increasingly oriented around purchasing goods or services. One norm of particular interest is diet. It now seems natural to eat highly sweetened, highly processed foods. Children from a very early age are exposed to candy, sweetened cereals, and other unhealthy but highly profitable and highly advertised foods—a shift that has had a dramatic impact on global obesity rates. Today, fast-food vendors and soda machines are found even in schools, shaping children's dietary norms from a young age and in turn reinforcing and perpetuating these norms throughout societies. According to a study by the U.S. Centers for Disease Control and Prevention, nearly two thirds of U.S. school districts earn a percentage of their revenue from vending machine sales, and a third receive financial awards from soda companies when a certain amount of their product is sold.

Traditions—the most ritualized and deeply rooted aspects of cultures—are also now shaped by consumerism. From weddings that cost an average $22,000 in the United States to funeral norms that pressure grieving loved ones to purchase elaborate coffins, headstones, and other expensive symbolic goods, consumerism is deeply embedded in how people observe rituals. Choosing to celebrate rituals in a simple manner can be a difficult choice to make, whether because of norms, family pressure, or advertising influence.

Christmas demonstrates this point well. While for Christians this day marks the birth of Jesus, for many people the holiday is more oriented around Santa Claus, gift giving, and feasting. A . . . survey on Christmas spending in 18 countries found that individuals spent hundreds of dollars on gifts and hundreds more on socializing and food. In Ireland, the United Kingdom, and the United States—the three with the largest expenditures—individuals on average spent $942, $721, and $581 on gifts, respectively. Increasingly, even many non-Christians celebrate Christmas as a time to exchange gifts. In Japan, Christmas is a big holiday, even though only 2 percent of the population is Christian. As Reverend Billy of the tongue-in-cheek consumer education effort The Church of Stop Shopping notes: "We think we are consumers at Christmas time. No! We are being consumed at Christmastime." Consumerism is also affecting peoples' values. The belief that more wealth and more material possessions are essential to achieving the good life has grown noticeably across many countries in the past several decades. One annual survey of first-year college students in the United States has investigated students' life priorities for more than 35 years. Over this time the importance of being well off financially has grown while the importance of developing a meaningful life philosophy has fallen. And this is not just an American phenomenon. A study by psychologists Güliz Ger and Russell Belk found high levels of materialism in two thirds of the 12 countries they surveyed, including several transitional economies.

While consumerism is now found in nearly all cultures, it is not without consequences. On this finite planet, defining success and happiness through how much a person consumes is not sustainable. Moreover, it is abundantly clear that this cultural orientation did not just happen to appear as a byproduct of growing incomes. It was engineered over several centuries. Today, since consumerism has been internalized by many societies, it is self-perpetuating to some extent, yet institutions within society—including businesses, the media, governments, and educational facilities—continue to prop up this cultural orientation. These institutions are also actively working to expand markets around the world for new consumer goods and services. Understanding the role of these institutional drivers will be essential in order to cultivate new cultures of sustainability.

INSTITUTIONAL ROOTS OF CONSUMERISM

As long ago as the late 1600s, societal shifts in Europe began to lay the groundwork for the emergence of consumerism. Expanding populations and a fixed base of land, combined with a weakening of traditional sources of authority such as the church and community social structures, meant that a young person's customary path of social advancement—inheriting the family plot or apprenticing in a father's trade—could no longer be taken for granted. People sought new avenues for identity and self-fulfillment, and the acquisition and use of goods became popular substitutes.

Meanwhile, entrepreneurs were quick to capitalize on these shifts to stimulate purchase of their new wares, using new types of advertising, endorsements by prominent people, creation of shop displays, "loss-leaders" (selling a popular item at a loss as a way to pull customers into a store), creative financing options, even consumer research and the stoking of new fads. For example, one eighteenth-century British pottery manufacturer, Josiah Wedgwood, had salespeople drum up excitement for new pottery designs, creating demand for newer lines of products even from customers who already had a perfectly good, but now seemingly outdated, set of pottery.

Still, traditional social mores blocked the rapid advance of a consumerist mindset. Peasants with extra income traditionally would increase landholdings or support community works rather than buy new fashions or home furnishings—two of the earliest consumer goods. Workers whose increased productivity resulted in greater pay tended to favor more leisure time rather than the wealth that a full day at increased pay might have brought them.

But over time the emerging consumerist orientation was internalized by a growing share of the populace—with the continued help of merchants and traders—redefining what was understood as natural. The universe of "basic necessities" grew, so that by the French Revolution, Parisian workers were demanding candles, coffee, soap, and sugar as "goods of prime necessity" even though all but the candles had been luxury items less than 100 years earlier.

By the early 1900s, a consumerist orientation had become increasingly embedded in many of the dominant societal institutions of many cultures— from businesses and governments to the media and education. And in the latter half of the century, new innovations like television, sophisticated advertising techniques, transnational corporations, franchises, and the Internet helped institutions to spread consumerism across the planet.

Arguably, the strongest driver of this cultural shift has been business interests. On a diverse set of fronts, businesses found ways to coax more consumption out of people. Credit was liberalized, for instance, with installment payments, and the credit card was promoted heavily in the United States, which led to an almost 11-fold increase in consumer credit between 1945 and 1960. Products were designed to have short lives or to go out of style quickly (strategies called, respectively, physical and psychological obsolescence). And workers were encouraged to take pay raises rather than more time off, increasing their disposable incomes.

Perhaps the biggest business tool for stoking consumption is marketing. Global advertising expenditures hit $643 billion in 2008, and in countries like China and India they are growing at 10 percent or more per year. In the United States, the average "consumer" sees or hears hundreds of advertisements every day and from an early age learns to associate products with positive imagery and messages. Clearly, if advertising were not effective, businesses would not spend 1 percent of the gross world product to sell their wares, as they do. And they are right: studies have demonstrated that advertising indeed encourages certain behaviors and that children, who have difficulty distinguishing between advertising and content, are particularly susceptible. . . .

[M]arketing strategies, taken alone, stimulate interest in a single good or service. Together these diverse initiatives stimulate an overall culture of consumerism. As economist and marketing analyst Victor Lebow explained in the *Journal of Retailing* over 50 years ago, "A specific advertising and promotional campaign, for a particular product at a particular time, has no automatic guarantee of success, yet it may contribute to the general pressure by which wants are stimulated and maintained. Thus its very failure may serve to fertilize this soil, as does so much else that seems to go down the drain." Industries, even as they pursue limited agendas of expanding sales for their products, play a significant role in stimulating consumerism. And whether intentionally or not, they transform cultural norms in the process.

The media are a second major societal institution that plays a driving role in stimulating consumerism, and not just as a vehicle for marketing. The media are a powerful tool for transmitting cultural symbols, norms, customs, myths, and stories. As Duane Elgin, author and media activist, explains: "To control a society, you don't need to control its courts, you don't need to control its armies, all you need to do is control its stories. And it's television and Madison Avenue that is telling us most of the stories most of the time to most of the people."

Between television, movies, and increasingly the Internet, the media are a dominant form of leisure time activity. . . . In countries that belong to the Organisation for Economic Cooperation and Development, 95 percent of households have at least one television, and people watch about three to four hours a day on average. Add to this the two to three hours spent online each day, plus radio broadcasts, newspapers, magazines, and . . . movie tickets . . . , and it becomes clear that media exposure consumes anywhere from a third to half of people's waking day in large parts of the world.

During those hours, much of media output reinforces consumer norms and promotes materialistic aspirations, whether directly by extolling the high-consumption lives of celebrities and the wealthy or more subtly through stories that reinforce the belief that happiness comes from being better off financially, from buying the newest consumer gadget or fashion accessory, and so on. There is clear evidence that media exposure has an impact on norms, values, and preferences. Social modeling studies have found connections between such exposure and violence, smoking, reproductive norms, and various unhealthy behaviors. One study found that for every additional hour of television people watched each week, they spent an additional $208 a year on stuff (even though they had less time in a day to spend it).

Government is another institution that often reinforces the consumerist orientation. Promoting consumer behavior happens in myriad ways—perhaps most famously in 2001 when U.S. President George W. Bush, U.K. Prime Minister Tony Blair, and several other western leaders encouraged their citizens to go out and shop after the terrorist attacks of September 11th. But it also happens more systemically. Subsidies for particular industries—especially in the transportation and energy sectors, where cheap oil or electricity has ripple effects throughout the economy—also work to stoke consumption. And to the extent that manufacturers are not required to internalize the environmental and social costs of production—when pollution of air or water is unregulated, for example—the cost of goods is artificially low, stimulating their use. Between these subsidies and externalities, total support of polluting business interests was pegged at $1.9 trillion in 2001.

Some of these government actions are driven by "regulatory capture," when special interests wield undue influence over regulators. In 2008, that influence could be observed in the United States through the $3.9 billion spent on campaign donations by business interests (71 percent of total contributions) and the $2.8 billion spent by business interests to lobby policymakers (86 percent of total lobbying dollars).

A clear example of official stimulation of consumption came in the 1940s when governments started to actively promote consumption as a vehicle for development. For example, the United States, which came out of World War II relatively unscathed, had mobilized a massive war-time economy—one that was poised to recede now that the war was over. Intentionally stimulating high levels of consumption was seen as a good solution to address this (especially with the memory of the Great Depression still raw). As Victor Lebow explained in 1955, "our enormously productive economy demands that we make consumption our way of life, that we convert the buying and use of goods into rituals, that we seek our spiritual satisfactions, our ego satisfactions, in consumption."

Today, this same attitude toward consumption has spread far beyond the United States and is the leading policy of many of the world's governments. As the global economic recession accelerated in 2009, wealthy countries did not see this as an opportunity to shift to a sustainable "no-growth" economy—essential if they are to rein in carbon emissions, which is also on the global agenda—but instead primed national economies with $2.8 trillion of new government stimulus packages, only a small percentage of which focused on green initiatives.

Finally, education plays a powerful role in cultivating consumerism. As with governments, in part this is because education seems to be increasingly susceptible to business influence. Today schools accept classroom materials sponsored by business interests, like the "bias-balanced" energy education materials by groups representing oil companies in Canada. And Channel One News, a 12-minute daily "news" program with 2 minutes of commercials and some segments sponsored by products or companies, is now shown in

8,000 middle and high schools across the United States, exposing 6 million students—nearly a quarter of all American teens—to marketing and product placements with the tacit support of educators.

Perhaps the greatest critique of schools is that they represent a huge missed opportunity to combat consumerism and to educate students about its effects on people and the environment. Few schools teach media literacy to help students critically interpret marketing; few teach or model proper nutrition, even while providing access to unhealthy or unsustainable consumer products; and few teach a basic understanding of the ecological sciences—specifically that the human species is not unique but in fact just as dependent on a functioning Earth system for its survival as every other species. The lack of integration of this basic knowledge into the school curriculum, coupled with repeated exposure to consumer goods and advertising and with leisure time focused in large part on television, helps reinforce the unrealistic idea that humans are separate from Earth and the illusion that perpetual increases in consumption are ecologically possible and even valuable.

CULTIVATING CULTURES OF SUSTAINABILITY

Considering the social and ecological costs that come with consumerism, it makes sense to intentionally shift to a cultural paradigm where the norms, symbols, values, and traditions encourage just enough consumption to satisfy human well-being while directing more human energy toward practices that help to restore planetary well-being.

In a 2006 interview, Catholic priest and ecological philosopher Thomas Berry noted that "we might summarize our present human situation by the simple statement: In the 20th century, the glory of the human has become the desolation of the Earth. And now, the desolation of the Earth is becoming the destiny of the human. From here on, the primary judgment of all human institutions, professions, and programs and activities will be determined by the extent to which they inhibit, ignore, or foster a mutually enhancing human-Earth relationship." Berry made it clear that a tremendous shift is necessary in society's institutions, in its very cultures, if humans are to thrive as a species long into the future. Institutions will have to be fundamentally oriented on sustainability.

How can this be done? In an analysis on places to intervene in a system, environmental scientist and systems analyst Donella Meadows explained that the most effective leverage point for changing a system is to change the paradigm of the system—that is to say, the shared ideas or basic assumptions around which the system functions. In the case of the consumerism paradigm, the assumptions that need to change include that more stuff makes people happier, that perpetual growth is good, that humans are separate from nature, and that nature is a stock of resources to be exploited for human purposes.

Although paradigms are difficult to change and societies will resist efforts to do so, the result of such a change can be a dramatic transformation of the system. Yes, altering a system's rules (with legislation, for instance) or its flow rates (with taxes or subsidies) can change a system too, but not as fundamentally. These will typically produce only incremental changes. Today more systemic change is needed. . . .

Having a vision of what values, norms, and behaviors should be seen as natural will be essential in guiding the reorientation of cultures toward sustainability. Of course, this cultural transformation will not be easy. Shifting cultural systems is a long process measured in decades, not years. Even consumerism, with sophisticated technological advances and many devoted resources, took centuries to become dominant. The shift to a culture of sustainability will depend on powerful networks of cultural pioneers who initiate, champion, and drive forward this new, urgently needed paradigm.

Perhaps in a century or two, extensive efforts to pioneer a new cultural orientation will no longer be needed as people will have internalized many of these new ideas, seeing sustainability—rather than consumerism—as "natural." Until then, networks of cultural pioneers will be needed to push institutions to proactively and intentionally accelerate this shift. Anthropologist Margaret Mead is often quoted as saying: "Never doubt that a small group of thoughtful, committed citizens can change the world. Indeed, it's the only thing that ever has." With many interconnected citizens energized, organized, and committed to spreading a sustainable way of life, a new cultural paradigm can take hold—one that will allow humanity to live better lives today and long into the future.

11

Use Energy, Get Rich, and Save the Planet

John Tierney

When the first Earth Day took place in 1970, American environmentalists had good reason to feel guilty. The nation's affluence and advanced technology seemed so obviously bad for the planet that they were featured in a famous equation developed by the ecologist Paul Ehrlich and the physicist John P. Holdren, who is now President Obama's science adviser.

Their equation was I=PAT, which means that environmental impact is equal to population multiplied by affluence multiplied by technology. Protecting the planet seemed to require fewer people, less wealth and simpler technology—the same sort of social transformation and energy revolution that will be advocated at many Earth Day rallies. . . .

But among researchers who analyze environmental data, a lot has changed since the 1970s. With the benefit of their hindsight and improved equations, I'll make a couple of predictions:

1. There will be no green revolution in energy or anything else. No leader or law or treaty will radically change the energy sources for people and industries in the United States or other countries. No recession or depression will make a lasting change in consumers' passions to use energy, make money and buy new technology—and that, believe it or not, is good news, because . . .
2. The richer everyone gets, the greener the planet will be in the long run.

I realize this second prediction seems hard to believe when you consider the carbon being dumped into the atmosphere today by Americans, and the projections for increasing emissions from India and China as they get richer.

Those projections make it easy to assume that affluence and technology inflict more harm on the environment. But while pollution can increase when a country starts industrializing, as people get wealthier they can afford cleaner water and air. They start using sources of energy that are less carbon-intensive—and not just because they're worried about global warming. The process of "decarbonization" started long before Al Gore was born.

The old wealth-is-bad IPAT theory may have made intuitive sense, but it didn't jibe with the data that has been analyzed since that first Earth Day. By the 1990s, researchers realized that graphs of environmental impact didn't produce a simple upward-sloping line as countries got richer. The line more often rose, flattened out and then reversed so that it sloped downward, forming the shape of a dome or an inverted U—what's called a Kuznets curve.

In dozens of studies, researchers identified Kuznets curves for a variety of environmental problems. There are exceptions to the trend, especially in countries with inept governments and poor systems of property rights, but in general, richer is eventually greener. As incomes go up, people often focus first on cleaning up their drinking water, and then later on air pollutants like sulfur dioxide.

As their wealth grows, people consume more energy, but they move to more efficient and cleaner sources—from wood to coal and oil, and then to natural gas and nuclear power, progressively emitting less carbon per unit of energy. This global decarbonization trend has been proceeding at a remarkably steady rate since 1850, according to Jesse Ausubel of Rockefeller University and Paul Waggoner of the Connecticut Agricultural Experiment Station.

"Once you have lots of high-rises filled with computers operating all the time, the energy delivered has to be very clean and compact," said Mr. Ausubel, the director of the Program for the Human Environment at Rockefeller. "The long-term trend is toward natural gas and nuclear power, or conceivably solar power. If the energy system is left to its own devices, most of the carbon will be out of it by 2060 or 2070."

But what about all the carbon dioxide being spewed out today by Americans commuting to McMansions? Well, it's true that American suburbanites do emit more greenhouse gases than most other people in the world (although New Yorkers aren't much different from other affluent urbanites).

But the United States and other Western countries seem to be near the top of a Kuznets curve for carbon emissions and ready to start the happy downward slope. The amount of carbon emitted by the average American has remained fairly flat for the past couple of decades, and per capita carbon emissions have started declining in some countries, like France. Some researchers estimate that the turning point might come when a country's per capita income reaches $30,000, but it can vary widely, depending on what fuels are available. Meanwhile, more carbon is being taken out of the atmosphere by the expanding forests in America and other affluent countries. Deforestation follows a Kuznets curve, too. In poor countries, forests are cleared to provide fuel and farmland, but as people gain wealth and better agricultural technology, the farm fields start reverting to forestland.

Of course, even if rich countries' greenhouse impact declines, there will still be an increase in carbon emissions from China, India and other countries ascending the Kuznets curve. While that prospect has environmentalists lobbying for global restrictions on greenhouse gases, some economists fear that a global treaty could ultimately hurt the atmosphere by slowing economic growth, thereby lengthening the time it takes for poor countries to reach the turning point on the curve.

But then, is there much reason to think that countries at different stages of the Kuznets curve could even agree to enforce tough restrictions? The Kyoto treaty didn't transform Europe's industries or consumers. While some American environmentalists hope that the combination of the economic crisis and a new president can start an era of energy austerity and green power, Mr. Ausubel says they're hoping against history.

Over the past century, he says, nothing has drastically altered the long-term trends in the way Americans produce or use energy—not the Great Depression, not the world wars, not the energy crisis of the 1970s or the grand programs to produce alternative energy.

"Energy systems evolve with a particular logic, gradually, and they don't suddenly morph into something different," Mr. Ausubel says. That doesn't make for a rousing speech on Earth Day. But in the long run, a Kuznets curve is more reliable than a revolution.

Section 3 Exercise

Where Do Babies Come From?
The Causes of Population Growth

Whether to have children and, if so, how many, are among the most intimate decisions a person can make. In the best cases, it is usually done in the privacy of one's romantic relationships and has to do with one's personal view of a meaningful life. And yet, the accumulative effect of such decisions has profound implications for public, collective well-being. Whether the world has nine or twelve billion people in the following decades is of critical ecological importance. When it comes to reproduction, the personal is definitely political.

Family size is political in yet another sense. While we think that we can choose our reproductive options in the privacy of our bedrooms, it is clear that broad material and ideational factors inform our decisions. Traditions about the optimal number and spacing of children, the economic need and costs of having children, access to birth control, conventions about the age of mothers, and so forth quietly yet powerfully influence our choices.

In this exercise, we'd like you to reflect on the factors that influence your thoughts about having children, and draw connections between these factors and the population challenges the world currently faces. (This exercise is configured for a classroom setting, but can easily be adjusted to serve as an individual thought experiment.)

Step 1: Organize into groups of three and take turns answering the following questions:

1. Do you have children or do you want to have children?
2. If you want to have children, at what age would you prefer to do so (or at what age did you have them)?
3. How many would you like to have?

Step 2: Discuss which factors influenced your answers. Is the decision entirely a personal one? What does that even mean?

Step 3: Ninety-five percent of population increases are currently taking place in the global South (the world's developing countries). Imagine you are a poor farmer or shopkeeper living in a part of the world in which people earn less than US$2/day (a condition that describes close to 33 percent of the world's population). How would you answer the preceding questions? Would your answers differ from your original responses? If so, how?

Step 4 (to be read only after Step 3): How much did ecological factors, or your concern for the present and future environmental condition, play into your decision making? Given what you know about the nature of the environmental situation and about the factors that drive environmental deterioration, is it selfish to have kids or is it selfish not to?

Part II

**States, Markets, and Society:
Geopolitical Responses
to Unsustainability**

Section 4

International State System

The last section suggested that although the waters ahead are undoubtedly rough in environmental terms, humans can still find more or less effective ways to proceed in ecologically sound directions. We now turn to the question of how to do that. This is where the politics of global environmental affairs comes into high relief. Politics is about power. How does one identify the reins of power that animate large-scale trends of unsustainability, and then maneuver them in new directions? That is, how does one govern in the service of global sustainability?

The term *governance* comes from the Greek root *kybernan,* which means to steer or pilot. It originally had to do with navigating a ship, but has since become associated with all forms of directing, ruling, or guiding. To be concerned with governance is to strive to understand how different people and groups shape widespread thought and behavior or, put differently, wield power in the context of public affairs.

When thinking about governing on a global scale, our minds often spin as we recognize the many levels, complexities, and sheer volume of activity involved. Political thinkers bring clarity to the challenge by partitioning the political world into three overlapping and interconnected realms of governance: *state, economy,* and *civil society.* These categories disaggregate different but related spheres of collective life. In the following three sections, we focus on each of these in turn. The aim is to appreciate how power operates in each, and the promises and perils involved. As you will see in the sections to follow, the world has made some significant strides toward sustainability but, as the biophysical evidence explained in earlier parts of this book suggests, it has a long way to go before we can feel that we are sailing in ecologically safe waters. Understanding this dual reality is essential for making sense of contemporary global environmental politics and for responding in effective ways.

We start, in this section, with the state. The state (or government) is an institution that rules over a given territory. States are effective governors because they usually enjoy legitimacy among their citizens and therefore can get people to follow their directives voluntarily. In the absence of legitimacy, states can still rule but do so through coercive power wherein militaries and police compel compliance. The combination—often referred to as "law backed by force"—represents the key form of state power. Whether it is stopping at a traffic light, not stealing from one's neighbor, or abiding by environmental rules, citizens generally comply with state laws because they either believe in the common-sense logic or inherent validity of such laws, or fear the punishment that lies behind disobedience. The idea that states get to set and enforce laws within their territorial boundaries is a basic component of sovereignty. In our world, sovereign political communities form the international state system.

This section examines the promises and perils of state governance. It notes that states have the ability to set environmental rules within their territories—and this is extraordinarily important for establishing environmental governance over particular parcels of the earth. However, it also explains how states face tremendous challenges beyond their borders. At the international level, there is no world government or other body to coordinate global affairs and this makes it extremely difficult to establish consistent environmental protection throughout the world.

States may enjoy sovereignty over their territories, but the building blocks of ecological systems—air, water, soil, and species—pay little attention to political boundaries. Birds do not put on the brakes as they approach a border; neither do running waters, swirling air currents, or shifting soils. This creates difficulties since so many environmental problems these days are transboundary and, in the extreme, global in character. Indeed, each of the issues we studied in earlier sections—climate change, loss of biological diversity, and the like—threatens not simply a portion of the planet, but world-spanning systems that maintain planetary health. Sovereignty does little to address this. In fact, it frustrates cooperative attempts insofar as it fragments political authority when we increasingly need unity. To put the matter differently, the international state system sets up a mismatch between the *quality of the problem* and the *character of the response mechanism.* Global environmental issues are unitary while the state system is fragmentary. This mismatch accounts for many of the challenges associated with addressing global environmental problems.

States try to overcome this mismatch by negotiating agreements designed to tackle particular environmental issues. This consists of setting up bureaucratic bodies like the different agencies of the United Nations that have some rulemaking and agenda-setting capacities, and establishing and abiding by treaties or norms of international behavior. Such actions have led to marked successes. The world community has made strides on a host of issues, such as ozone depletion, long-range air pollution, and ocean protection. However, one would be naïve not to notice that much work remains to be done. Too many transboundary problems escape the coordinating capabilities of sovereign states and these pose huge dangers. For some, this elusiveness is so severe that they would say the state system, as it currently stands, is a central impediment to effective environmental action.

Our first reading, the **Rio Declaration**, a document agreed upon by states at the 1992 United Nations Conference on Environment and Development, reveals the promise of the state system. It lists a set of twenty-seven principles to guide global environmental governance. These include calls for states to develop national laws and cooperate internationally to address environmental harm, and to adopt focused measures to ensure that development is part and parcel with environmental efforts. It represents the international community at its best.

The second reading, by scholars **Jennifer Clapp** and **Peter Dauvergne**, charts the evolution of international environmental protective efforts. It explains the emergence of the more than 1,100 multilateral environmental agreements and modifications that currently establish acceptable behavior for treating the environment—spanning issues as diverse as climate change, trade in endangered species, ocean pollution, and toxic waste. Like the Rio Declaration, this reading provides evidence that states can cooperate and put into place meaningful rules for governing global environmental affairs. Taken together, the Rio Declaration and the excerpt from Clapp and Dauvergne's book *Paths to a Green World* suggest that the international system is able to address environmental dangers. To be sure, the documents do not claim that the state system is perfect; both indicate that much more work needs to be done. (Indeed, the Rio Declaration simply outlines principles; it makes no promises about states actually heeding its imperatives.) But they implicitly support the political status quo or at least do not call for altering the structure or character of the sovereign state system.

Political scientist **Paul Harris** is less sanguine. Focusing on diplomacy around climate change, Harris points out the limitations of the state system. While he acknowledges the importance of the United Nations Framework Convention on Climate Change for setting the political context for addressing global warming, he notes how individual states concerned with their narrowly defined national interests have stymied progress on climate protection by refusing to assume more aggressive measures to reduce greenhouse-gas emissions. He blames the inclination of states to focus on the short term when defining their interests, and implies the need for reforms to state-level diplomatic efforts that could help states better recognize their common but differentiated responsibilities.

Our final reading in this section is by international-law scholar **Richard Falk**. In this classic piece from his highly influential book, *This Endangered Planet,* Falk condemns the structure of the state system as the fundamental obstacle to global environmental well-being. He shows how the structure prevents the kinds of reforms that Harris and others recommend, and thus advances a radical critique of international environmental efforts. To Falk, our condition is too dire to accept the status quo and too urgent to embrace incremental reform. Falk's analysis suggests that the only way toward genuine global environmental protection is system transformation. We need a completely different world-order system to shepherd us into a livable future.

This section, then, presents a range of viewpoints on the international system, starting with ideas for minor tweaks to the status quo and ending with ideas for large-scale reform. You will see a similar range of views expressed by authors in the two sections that follow. Promises and perils exist not only with the state system, but with the world economy and civil society as well.

12

Rio Declaration on Environment and Development

The United Nations Conference on Environment and Development,

Having met at Rio de Janeiro from 3 to 14 June 1992,

Reaffirming the Declaration of the United Nations Conference on the Human Environment, adopted at Stockholm on 16 June 1972, and seeking to build upon it,

With the goal of establishing a new and equitable global partnership through the creation of new levels of cooperation among States, key sectors of societies and people,

Working towards international agreements which respect the interests of all and protect the integrity of the global environmental and developmental system,

Recognizing the integral and interdependent nature of the Earth, our home,

Proclaims that:

Principle 1
Human beings are at the centre of concerns for sustainable development. They are entitled to a healthy and productive life in harmony with nature.

Principle 2
States have, in accordance with the Charter of the United Nations and the principles of international law, the sovereign right to exploit their own resources pursuant to their own environmental and developmental policies, and the responsibility to ensure that activities within their jurisdiction or control do not cause damage to the environment of other States or of areas beyond the limits of national jurisdiction.

Principle 3
The right to development must be fulfilled so as to equitably meet developmental and environmental needs of present and future generations.

Principle 4
In order to achieve sustainable development, environmental protection shall constitute an integral part of the development process and cannot be considered in isolation from it.

Principle 5

All States and all people shall cooperate in the essential task of eradicating poverty as an indispensable requirement for sustainable development, in order to decrease the disparities in standards of living and better meet the needs of the majority of the people of the world.

Principle 6

The special situation and needs of developing countries, particularly the least developed and those most environmentally vulnerable, shall be given special priority. International actions in the field of environment and development should also address the interests and needs of all countries.

Principle 7

States shall cooperate in a spirit of global partnership to conserve, protect and restore the health and integrity of the Earth's ecosystem. In view of the different contributions to global environmental degradation, States have common but differentiated responsibilities. The developed countries acknowledge the responsibility that they bear in the international pursuit of sustainable development in view of the pressures their societies place on the global environment and of the technologies and financial resources they command.

Principle 8

To achieve sustainable development and a higher quality of life for all people, States should reduce and eliminate unsustainable patterns of production and consumption and promote appropriate demographic policies.

Principle 9

States should cooperate to strengthen endogenous capacity-building for sustainable development by improving scientific understanding through exchanges of scientific and technological knowledge, and by enhancing the development, adaptation, diffusion and transfer of technologies, including new and innovative technologies.

Principle 10

Environmental issues are best handled with the participation of all concerned citizens, at the relevant level. At the national level, each individual shall have appropriate access to information concerning the environment that is held by public authorities, including information on hazardous materials and activities in their communities, and the opportunity to participate in decision-making processes. States shall facilitate and encourage public awareness and participation by making information widely available. Effective access to judicial and administrative proceedings, including redress and remedy, shall be provided.

Principle 11

States shall enact effective environmental legislation. Environmental standards, management objectives and priorities should reflect the environmental and developmental context to which they apply. Standards applied by some countries may be inappropriate and of unwarranted economic and social cost to other countries, in particular developing countries.

Principle 12

States should cooperate to promote a supportive and open international economic system that would lead to economic growth and sustainable development in all countries, to better address the problems of environmental degradation. Trade policy measures for environmental purposes should not constitute a means of arbitrary or unjustifiable discrimination or a disguised restriction on international trade. Unilateral actions to deal with environmental challenges outside the jurisdiction of the importing country should be avoided. Environmental measures addressing transboundary or global environmental problems should, as far as possible, be based on an international consensus.

Principle 13

States shall develop national law regarding liability and compensation for the victims of pollution and other environmental damage. States shall also cooperate in an expeditious and more determined manner to develop further international law regarding liability and compensation for adverse effects of environmental damage caused by activities within their jurisdiction or control to areas beyond their jurisdiction.

Principle 14

States should effectively cooperate to discourage or prevent the relocation and transfer to other States of any activities and substances that cause severe environmental degradation or are found to be harmful to human health.

Principle 15

In order to protect the environment, the precautionary approach shall be widely applied by States according to their capabilities. Where there are threats of serious or irreversible damage, lack of full scientific certainty shall not be used as a reason for postponing cost-effective measures to prevent environmental degradation.

Principle 16

National authorities should endeavour to promote the internalization of environmental costs and the use of economic instruments, taking into account the approach that the polluter should, in principle, bear the cost of pollution, with due regard to the public interest and without distorting international trade and investment.

Principle 17

Environmental impact assessment, as a national instrument, shall be undertaken for proposed activities that are likely to have a significant adverse impact on the environment and are subject to a decision of a competent national authority.

Principle 18

States shall immediately notify other States of any natural disasters or other emergencies that are likely to produce sudden harmful effects on the environment of those States. Every effort shall be made by the international community to help States so afflicted.

Principle 19
States shall provide prior and timely notification and relevant information to potentially affected States on activities that may have a significant adverse transboundary environmental effect and shall consult with those States at an early stage and in good faith.

Principle 20
Women have a vital role in environmental management and development. Their full participation is therefore essential to achieve sustainable development.

Principle 21
The creativity, ideals and courage of the youth of the world should be mobilized to forge a global partnership in order to achieve sustainable development and ensure a better future for all.

Principle 22
Indigenous people and their communities and other local communities have a vital role in environmental management and development because of their knowledge and traditional practices. States should recognize and duly support their identity, culture and interests and enable their effective participation in the achievement of sustainable development.

Principle 23
The environment and natural resources of people under oppression, domination and occupation shall be protected.

Principle 24
Warfare is inherently destructive of sustainable development. States shall therefore respect international law providing protection for the environment in times of armed conflict and cooperate in its further development, as necessary.

Principle 25
Peace, development and environmental protection are interdependent and indivisible.

Principle 26
States shall resolve all their environmental disputes peacefully and by appropriate means in accordance with the Charter of the United Nations.

Principle 27
States and people shall cooperate in good faith and in a spirit of partnership in the fulfilment of the principles embodied in this Declaration and in the further development of international law in the field of sustainable development.

13

Brief History of International Environmental Cooperation

Jennifer Clapp
and Peter Dauvergne

What has the global community done to tackle . . . environmental problems . . . ? Although there is a rich history of formal actions on the part of states
to address these problems in the international arena, we must also remember
that the history of global environmental politics is inextricably tied to contests
of ideas: battles of worldviews and discourses. We have seen new environmental
ideas and language enter into mainstream discourse as global awareness rises
and as environmental conditions deteriorate. These views are also affected by
wider developments in the global political economy. . . .

The first part of this chapter provides a brief history of the globalization of
environmentalism with a focus on the past sixty years, highlighting connections
of this diplomatic, interstate history to events in the global economy and to
the emergence of different perspectives on the global environment. The second
part of the chapter outlines the various mechanisms of global environmental
governance put into place over this period, and highlights the significance of
each in today's global environmental discourse.

THE EVOLUTION OF GLOBAL DISCOURSE ON
ENVIRONMENT AND DEVELOPMENT

. . . The global economy boomed for nearly twenty years after World War
II, ultimately fueling the environmental movement. Concern with the

environmental abuses of rapid industrialization gained momentum in the First World in the 1960s. There were protests against nuclear weapons and chemical pollution. The WWF [World Wildlife Fund] was founded in 1961 to work to preserve global biodiversity. Rachel Carson's bestseller *Silent Spring* (1962) was particularly influential with the public. Her message was a powerful one: the increasing use of chemicals, particularly pesticides, was killing nature and wildlife. It told of a future spring without the songs of birds. The scientific community lost no time in attacking Carson in the media, accusing her and her supporters of overstating the case against DDT (dichlorodiphenyltrichloroethane) and other chemicals. But the strength and simplicity of her message endured with the general public, and indeed research has since shown that her concern over DDT and other synthetic chemicals, many of which are now banned from production and use, was warranted.

The need to protect nature (so that, e.g., people could enjoy the "outdoors") remained a significant concern for the environmental movement in the First World. But increasing public concern with the effects of industrial production began to give the movement a new focus. Also emerging were worries among environmentalists about the cumulative impact of local problems on the health of the planet. More and more people began to see the planet as fragile and interconnected, an image reinforced as pictures of earth from space became more common. For many, the most memorable picture was the one that became available as astronauts Neil Armstrong, Michael Collins, and Edwin Aldrin journeyed to the moon in July 1969. Even today, the image of the earth from space—Spaceship Earth with no visible borders and a common atmosphere and oceans—remains a powerful symbol for global environmental consciousness [see the photo at the start of Section 2].

Other developments shaped the discourse in equally profound ways. The early 1960s saw rapid economic growth and greater global integration of trade and investment. Global growth rates were as high as 5–6 percent in the early to mid-1960s (though this growth was not evenly distributed among countries or regions). The global economic infrastructure codified by the International Monetary Fund (IMF), the World Bank, and the General Agreement on Tariffs and Trade (GATT)—all set up at the end of World War II—was widely seen as critical to fostering this growth and integration. Advances in communication and transportation technologies also contributed to the economic growth in this period. The wave of decolonization in Asia and Africa from the late 1940s to the late 1960s put many newly independent colonies on the global stage. Most joined the global economic institutions in an effort to promote economic growth. It was a time of optimism, and many countries believed that development (often understood as rapid industrialization and economic growth) would follow automatically from participation in the global economy.

But by the late 1960s and early 1970s, many of these "developing" countries realized that replicating the industrialization in the First World was far from automatic. Global growth rates had been strong, but the Third World still lagged far behind the First World in terms of industrialization and industrial exports. Critics from developing countries began to argue that the postwar global economic infrastructure still reflected colonial and imperial interests. . . .

Environmentalism in rich countries at this time began to reflect the economic theme of mutual (North–South) vulnerability. Books like Paul Ehrlich's, *The Population Bomb* (1968), became popular bestsellers. Ehrlich argued that population growth in the developing world, spurred in part by its economic predicament, would one day threaten the globe's resource base. Inequalities would continue to grow in such a world, although both the rich and the poor would eventually suffer from mass starvation, violence, and ecological destruction. He warned, "It is obvious that we cannot exist unaffected by the fate of our fellows on the other end of the good ship Earth. If their end of the ship sinks, we shall at the very least have to put up with the spectacle of their drowning and listen to their screams." The book sold three million copies and went through twenty-two printings in the three years following its release. Coming from a scientific framework and focusing on unsustainable population levels, Ehrlich was one of the key thinkers in the emerging bioenvironmentalist perspective, which began to gain popularity in industrialized countries.

Environmental concern continued to rise in the North in the late 1960s and early 1970s. On November 30, 1969, Gladwin Hill of the *New York Times* reported on the situation in the United States: "Rising concern about the environmental crisis is sweeping the nation's campuses with an intensity that may be on its way to eclipsing student discontent over the war in Vietnam." Twenty million rallied in the United States at the first Earth Day on April 22, 1970, one of the biggest organized demonstrations in the history of the United States. In that year the U.S. government established the Environmental Protection Agency (EPA). Canada followed a year later with a Department of the Environment. The Canadian group Greenpeace made headlines in the same year when it sailed toward Amchitka Island, Alaska, to protest against underground nuclear tests.

Feeding into this rising interest in environmentalism in the North was another bestselling and controversial book, *The Limits to Growth*. This book reported in more popular language the findings of a technical study by a research team at the Massachusetts Institute of Technology. It was part of a wider project of the Club of Rome, an international research and policy group. Its conclusions were similar to Ehrlich's. Using formal modeling and computers, it simulated future prospects for five major, interconnected trends: industrialization, human population growth, natural resource depletion, malnutrition, and pollution. It predicted that if these trends continued, the earth would reach its limits within one hundred years. If allowed, the book argued, "The most probable result will be a sudden and uncontrollable decline in both population and industrial capacity." But the authors did not forecast inevitable doom. They felt it was possible to alter the growth trends to foster sustainability, both ecologically and economically. . . .

These views on population, consumption, and limits to growth in the 1960s and 1970s . . . have been a strong continuing influence in the environmental movement in the North. Though the ecological collapse predicted by many early bioenvironmentalists did not occur, thinkers in this tradition—such as Paul and Anne Ehrlich, Lester Brown (founder and president of the Earth Policy Institute), and William Rees—continue to argue that population pressures and limits to growth do exist, and that human activity is imperiling the future of the planet. . . .

The Stockholm Conference and the 1970s

Debates over the links between the global economy, population growth, and environmental change on the one hand, and the sense of mutual interdependence and vulnerability on the other, were at the core of the United Nations Conference on the Human Environment, held in Stockholm, Sweden, in June 1972. This was the first global-level UN conference on the environment as well as the first world conference on a single issue. Delegates from 113 governments attended. Canada's Maurice Strong was chair. Three parallel NGO conferences—the Environment Forum (with official UN support), the Peoples Forum, and Dai Dong—took place alongside the official proceedings. . . .

The initial purpose of the conference, announced in 1968 by the UN General Assembly, was to discuss "problems of the human environment" and "identify those aspects of it that can only, or best be solved through international cooperation and agreement." The focus was on environmental problems arising from industrialization, of particular concern to Northern governments. This was expanded, however, to include broader development concerns to gain the support of developing countries. . . .

The focus of many of the debates at Stockholm, then, was on how to reconcile the economic development demanded by the South with the perceived need of the North to protect the global environment. The phrase "the pollution of poverty" was coined at Stockholm as developing countries . . . argued that the greatest environmental threat was poverty. At the same time developing countries were skeptical of the North's environmental agenda, worrying it would deny poorer countries the benefits of economic growth and industrialization. Brazil, for example, declared that it had little interest in discussing industrial pollution, which it saw as a "rich man's" problem. The representative from the Ivory Coast went as far as to state that the country would welcome more pollution if this would allow it to industrialize. Developing countries further argued that exploitation by global capitalists was a core reason for their high levels of poverty in the first place. Global economic institutions were singled out for pushing them to export raw materials on declining terms of trade. Many developing countries called for global economic reforms as part of efforts to solve global environmental problems.

Official conference documents at Stockholm, however, did not reflect these calls. At most, these documents acknowledged the unique problems of developing countries, but no real remedies were offered. The conference produced a Declaration on the Human Environment, which contained 26 principles, an Action Plan for the Human Environment, which included 109 recommendations, and a Resolution on Institutional and Financial Arrangements. These measures were "soft" international law—that is, they did not legally bind the signatory states—yet they did signal a growing concern among national governments over the global environment. The Stockholm Conference is also credited with the creation of the United Nations Environment Programme (UNEP). Officially launched in 1973, UNEP was headquartered in Nairobi, Kenya; Maurice Strong was named its first executive director. . . .

The economic turbulence of the 1970s relegated environmental issues to the back burner in many countries, especially poorer ones. Yet states still negotiated important global environmental treaties in this period, partly as a result of processes set in motion by the Stockholm Conference. These include the Convention on the Prevention of Marine Pollution by Dumping of Wastes and Other Matter (the London Convention, 1972), the Convention on International Trade in Endangered Species of Wild Fauna and Flora (CITES, 1973), and the Convention for the Prevention of Pollution by Ships (MARPOL, 1973). . . .

The Brundtland Report and the 1980s

The 1980s brought more turmoil for Third World economies. A foreign debt crisis, in which the South is still mired, was first openly acknowledged in August 1982 when Mexico announced it could not repay its international debts. While other developing countries followed Mexico into a debt crisis in the early 1980s, First World economies began to recover. This relatively strong performance in the North bolstered the global spread of the values and neoliberal economic ideologies of Prime Minister Margaret Thatcher in Britain and President Ronald Reagan in the United States. Neoliberal economic prescriptions at this time called for deregulation, stressing the need for free and open markets as the best way to organize an economy. Neoliberalism advocated liberalization of trade, investment, and financial policies as a way of integrating the global economy, and—it was presumed—of stimulating economic growth. The spread of neoliberal economic thinking in the early 1980s strengthened support for the market liberal view of the environment, which saw these policies as compatible with environmental protection. . . .

Over the course of the 1980s and 1990s, policies shifted worldwide to reflect the ascendancy of neoliberal economic thought. Though the global economy was widely seen in the 1970s as at least partly responsible for the South's weak economic growth, by the 1980s there was a shift toward the view that global economic integration into free markets was the best path to enhance economic growth. In other words, elites increasingly perceived the domestic failure to open economies as the reason for the economic troubles in developing countries, rather than pointing to a failure of the global economy to provide equal benefits. Institutions like the World Bank and IMF were seen as critical sources of support for the transition to globally integrated free-market economies. The Third World debt crisis was viewed as a crucial test for the neoliberal economic policies of these institutions. In return for emergency loans, the IMF and the World Bank required developing countries to implement economic reforms, commonly known as "structural adjustment." These reforms included liberalization of trade, investment, and exchange-rate policies, devaluation of currencies, government spending cutbacks, and privatization of public enterprises.

The rise of neoliberalism and the realization of the severity of the Third World debt crisis shaped the work of the World Commission on Environment and Development (WCED). The UN General Assembly established this commission in 1984 to examine the relationship between the environment and global economic development. It is commonly known as the Brundtland Commission after its chair, Norway's prime minister Gro Harlem Brundtland. Its report, *Our Common Future,* published in 1987, went further than any official international document to provide a new definition of development with the environment at its core. The report, too, was careful to set its analysis in the context of the global political economy.

The Brundtland Report changed the discourse of global environmentalism. The commission tried to chart a middle ground between the North and the South. . . . It proposed a global development and environment strategy designed to be palatable to all. It did not see further economic growth and industrialization as necessarily harmful to the environment, and thus did not foresee any necessary "limits" to growth. At the same time, it argued, very much in line with Third World sentiments at Stockholm, that poverty harmed the environment as much as industrialization. This poverty was in large part due to the place of developing economies within the global structure. The best way to move forward, the report contended, was to promote economic growth—not the kind of growth seen in the 1960s and 1970s, however, but environmentally sustainable growth. With this recommendation, the report popularized the term *sustainable development,* which it defined as development that "meets the needs of the present without compromising the ability of future generations to meet their own needs." This definition of development did not pose a fundamental challenge to the neoliberal economic ideology of the time, because it did not suggest a need to slow the pursuit of economic growth or to slow the process of global economic integration. . . .

Alongside the work of the Brundtland Commission, the world continued to negotiate global environmental treaties. These were generally in direct response to urgent environmental problems (often generating considerable media attention). These include the 1985 Vienna Convention for the Protection of the Ozone Layer and the 1987 Montreal Protocol on Substances That Deplete the Ozone Layer, as well as the 1989 Basel Convention on the Transboundary Movement of Hazardous Wastes and Their Disposal. The Basel Convention arose in response to the revelations in the mid-1980s of hazardous waste being shipped from rich to poor countries for disposal, raising both ecological and ethical concerns. . . .

The Earth Summit and the 1990s

In 1989 the UN General Assembly, following the recommendations of the Brundtland Report, passed a resolution to hold another world conference on the environment, the UN Conference on the Environment and Development (UNCED), to be held in 1992 in Rio de Janeiro, Brazil. Significant backdrops to UNCED, popularly known as the Earth Summit, included the ongoing debt crisis in the Third World, the collapse of the Eastern Bloc, and the accelerating pace of economic globalization. Politicians at this time saw green politics as a popular issue, and the axis at the global level for politics of this nature had shifted from East–West to North–South.

The Earth Summit was held on the twentieth anniversary of the Stockholm Conference. The secretary general of the meeting was Maurice Strong, who, as mentioned earlier, organized the conference in Stockholm. The Rio Earth Summit was the largest UN conference to date, with 179 countries participating and more than 110 heads of state attending. There were 2,400 nongovernmental representatives as well as another 17,000 in a parallel NGO forum. The recommendations in the Brundtland Report dominated discussions at Rio, especially the notion of sustainable development. Governments at the conference found it politically easy to adhere to the Rio goals of promoting more growth with more environmental protection. Who would deny these goals when presented as mutually compatible? . . .

Many developing countries, however, worried about taking on additional environmental commitments without concrete assurances of economic assistance to fund environmentally sustainable growth. Debates over financial transfers for sustainable development split along North–South lines. Developing countries felt strongly that industrialized countries should foot most of the extra costs of "green growth," and that this should be over and above current levels of assistance. Donors, on the other hand, were reluctant to take on further financial commitments. Related to this theme, developing countries also wanted to ensure receipt of environmental technologies without extra cost, as well as ensure that industrialized countries would not be able to use environmental regulations to restrict developing-country exports.

What, then, were the main outcomes of the Rio conference? Perhaps most important, it put environment and development on the agendas of global leaders. It also reaffirmed the Brundtland view that more growth will bring a better environment. . . . Participating governments adopted and signed the Rio

Declaration on Environment and Development, a set of twenty-seven principles outlining the rights and responsibilities of states regarding the promotion of environment and development. These principles included far more of the South's concerns about the right to development than did the Declaration on the Human Environment adopted at Stockholm twenty years earlier. Agenda 21, a three-hundred-page action program to promote sustainable development, was also adopted. The majority of the text of Agenda 21 was negotiated at four separate preparatory committee meetings (PrepComs) in the two and a half years prior to the Earth Summit, and only the last 15 percent was finalized in Rio. The conference also adopted a nonbinding Statement of Forest Principles to promote the sustainable management of tropical, temperate, and boreal forests. It was a compromise document, because it proved impossible to reach agreement on a legally binding forest treaty. The conference also opened two legally binding conventions for signature: the UN Framework Convention on Climate Change and the Convention on Biological Diversity. Further, the conference established the UN Commission on Sustainable Development to monitor and evaluate the progress on meeting the Rio objectives. Negotiations also began at Rio on a treaty on desertification. Finally, Rio was a "trigger" for the restructuring of the Global Environment Facility (GEF), set up to finance efforts in developing countries to protect the global environment. These global cooperative agreements were very much products of institutionalist influence at the conference.

There were some conspicuous failures at Rio, too. The estimated annual cost to implement Agenda 21 globally was US$625 billion, yet relatively little funding was pledged at Rio. Moreover, the developed countries were asked to cover just US$125 billion. This amount is roughly equal to 0.7 percent of their total gross national product (GNP), a theoretical target the UN set for development assistance back in the 1970s, and one that most donors have never been close to reaching. In total, GEF had allocated only US$8.26 billion in grants by 2009 (although it has leveraged US$33.7 billion in cofinancing).

Many NGO participants at Rio were skeptical of the official agenda. The focus on Brundtland-style solutions—in particular, the promotion of economic growth and industrialization as compatible with sustainability—was widely criticized. Social green critics, many of whom were at Rio with more radical NGOs such as Greenpeace and the Third World Network, argued that the world community was ignoring the environmental consequences of economic globalization—inequality, industrialization, economic growth, and overconsumption—at its peril. Despite a record number of NGOs in atten-dance at the global conference, many felt that industry had far more influence on the official agenda, partly because of the close ties to Maurice Strong and industry's funding of the event. A number of critics saw Rio as entrenching a "managerial" approach to solving environmental problems from above, while paying inadequate attention to local solutions from below. These social green critics saw the nod to the role of the poor, women, and indigenous peoples in the official Rio documents as woefully inadequate. . . .

Despite the critiques and the failure to attract significant extra financing to support the goal of implementing sustainable development, most analysts agree that UNCED did achieve some notable successes, especially in terms of raising environmental awareness among the general public in both the North and South. Five years later a special session of the UN General Assembly, known as the Earth Summit +5, reviewed global progress with the implementation of Agenda 21. The conclusions were largely disappointing: the world had not met most of the Agenda 21 goals. Earth Summit +5 failed to inject new enthusiasm into reaching them.

Johannesburg . . . and Beyond

Economic globalization accelerated in the years following the Rio Earth Summit. Trade and investment as a proportion of the economies of both rich and poor countries grew markedly. The GATT concluded the Uruguay Round of trade negotiations in 1994, and the World Trade Organization (WTO) was established in 1995. The WTO has more power to enforce decisions in dispute settlement than the previous procedure under the GATT did, and many viewed this as a prioritization of trade goals above others in the global arena. Despite rapid economic growth in some parts of the world, such as India and China, global economic inequalities remain. Some contend that these inequalities have worsened as a direct result of globalization. A global coalition of nongovernmental forces emerged in the late 1990s to oppose globalization. These groups began to protest at global economic meetings, such as the annual meetings of the IMF, the World Bank, and the WTO. . . .

The antiglobalization sentiment of activists, as well as the steadfast support for globalization among governments and international economic institutions, were continually in the background during the preparations for the 2002 World Summit on Sustainable Development (WSSD), held in Johannesburg, South Africa, ten years after the Rio Earth Summit. The goal was to evaluate the progress toward the Rio goals and set concrete targets to improve implementation. It also aimed to build on the International Conference on Financing and Development, held in March 2002 in Monterrey, Mexico, as well as to develop a strategy to implement the UN's Millennium Development Goals. The WSSD was the biggest ever UN meeting to that date. Over 180 nations and 100 heads of state attended. There were over 10,000 delegates, 8,000 civil society representatives (i.e., representing nongovernmental interests), 4,000 members of the press, and countless ordinary citizens. The secretary general was Nitin Desai, an Indian diplomat with the UN who served as deputy secretary general of UNCED under Maurice Strong, and who continued to work at the UN at the undersecretary general level on policy coordination and sustainable development.

Much like Rio and Stockholm, the conference adopted official documents about the need for global sustainability as well as a plan for implementation.

These are the Johannesburg Declaration on Sustainable Development, which outlines both the challenges and general commitments for the global community, and the Johannesburg Plan of Implementation, an action plan for implementing these goals. Negotiations for these documents began long before the meeting, yet one-quarter of the text was still in dispute at the start of the conference. One of the most contentions issues, as was the case in Rio, was financing. But new and equally difficult items were added at Johannesburg: globalization's role in sustainable development, as well as timetables and specific targets for meeting goals. In the end, the Johannesburg Declaration on Sustainable Development was somewhat different from previous global declarations on environment and development. Economic inequality was recognized as a major problem not only in terms of justice and human well-being, but also in terms of global security. And globalization was mentioned as a new challenge for achieving sustainable development.

The Plan of Action, a sixty-five-page document, was much less ambitious than Rio's Agenda 21 and largely restated the areas where more action was needed to meet the Rio goals, as well as other previously agreed-upon goals such as the Millennium Development Goals and development financing goals. The Plan of Action did include a few more specific goals and targets, focusing on several main priorities, such as water, agriculture, energy, health, and biodiversity. The Commission on Sustainable Development, created after Rio, was reaffirmed as the agency that would monitor progress on this implementation.

The conference also highlighted and promoted a new instrument for implementing sustainable development. These are public–private partnerships (dubbed PPPs, or "Type II" arrangements—"Type I" being government-to-government) between governments, NGOs, and business. These are voluntary agreements that involve stakeholders directly. The aim is to encourage the transfer of funds and technology to areas of critical need. Several hundred such partnerships were identified prior to and during the Summit, and many more have been initiated since. . . . This focus on PPPs gave the Johannesburg Summit a greater focus on the role of business in promoting sustainable development than either Stockholm or Rio had. The Plan of Action mentions the need to promote corporate accountability and responsibility, and the Johannesburg Declaration stresses the duty of business to promote sustainable development. This focus on business as a partner in sustainable development has remained prominent in the years since the WSSD. On the business side, this has contributed to a significant increase in policies and partnerships to promote corporate social responsibility (CSR), with advocates seeing this as a way toward a green economy.

Was Johannesburg a success? Many business participants saw the outcome as constructive and realistic. Many nongovernmental participants were disappointed with the "weak" targets and timetables, noting that the conference added little to global efforts to enhance sustainability. New targets were set on access to clean water and sanitation, as well as on halting depletion of fish stocks, but beyond these, not much new was added in terms of global commitments. The debate over the role of corporate globalization was divided, with industry and most governments on the one hand seeing it as positive, and many environmental and development NGOs on the other seeing it as negative. In the end, the official documents make bland and noncommittal statements about the importance of this issue without offering guidance on how to proceed.

Some argue that the Johannesburg Summit highlights the waning impact of environmentalism in global discourse. Part of the reason that many of the debates at the WSSD did not make much progress was the clash of diverse views on the causes and consequences of global environmental change. . . .

Global Environmental Governance

The global discourse on environment and development shapes, and is shaped by, institutions and policies—from global to local, and public to private. The history of global environmental discourse and diplomacy, as presented in the first part of this chapter, highlights the fact that over time, there have been significant changes to the key actors. In today's world, not just states, but also international institutions, firms, markets, NGOs, foundations, communities and regions, and individuals shape global environmental governance. These actors also employ an increasingly diverse range of policy tools. Thus, it is hardly surprising that we see a wide range of views on how to best pursue global environmental protection. Some even characterize this plethora of actors and arrangements as a "fragmentation" of global environmental governance, away from states as the primary holders of authority and legitimacy. Here, to provide a more comprehensive view of the globalization of environmentalism, we provide a very brief discussion of states, regimes, NGOs, corporations, and subnational and multiscale actors in the context of emerging patterns of global environmental governance.

States

States are core actors in global environmental governance. This is natural, given that state sovereignty, consisting of both rights and duties, has long been considered the guiding principle of international politics. The Treaty of Westphalia, signed in 1648, gave a state supreme authority to act within its territory. Foreign powers could not dictate what states can and cannot do within their borders. At the same time, to preserve these sovereign rights, states are obliged to respect the sovereignty of other states as well as protect their own citizens. States, as a glance at the wars of the last 350 years shows, do not always respect the sovereignty of other states. Nor do states always protect their citizens. Nevertheless, all states have guarded their sovereign rights with vigor and resolve, a fundamental feature of global environmental politics.

There are obvious tensions between the sovereign-state system and the natural environment. Perhaps the most visible is that environmental problems commonly spill across the political boundaries of states. The actions needed to manage the global environment—to act in the interests of the planet—may well clash with state interests. This partly explains the global community's struggle to deal with problems like climate change. But if the sovereign-state system grants states the right to control activities within their borders, what are their duties toward other states if their activities damage the environments of other states or the global commons? Principle 21 of the Stockholm Declaration addresses this question, declaring that states do have a right to exploit their own resources or pollute their own environments, but only as long as this does not affect other states directly. It is, however, difficult to prove that the actions of one state harm the environment of another state (or states) or the global commons. Can it be proven, for example, that deforestation in Costa Rica harms the United States because it decreases the global capacity to sink carbon dioxide? And who is to blame: the Costa Rican government, Costa Rican cattle ranchers, or the consumers of steaks and hamburgers? Because of this difficulty of proof, in practice little beyond moral pressure tends to be applied to hold states to this principle.

A second tension between the sovereign-state system and the natural environment is the tendency for environmental problems to develop over a long period of time. The existence of some problems, such as depletion of the ozone layer by CFCs, took years not just to discover, but also to prove with enough certainty to convince states to act. Environmental problems also tend to be circular and dynamic in nature. They rarely have a single cause, and efforts to deal with one part of an environmental problem can easily create new problems in the future. This long-term and circular nature of environmental problems contrasts sharply with the short-term and results-oriented political lives of those in power in democratic nations. It is naturally difficult for politicians to gain the funding and support for long-term action with political cycles typically lasting five years or less.

Many recognize the contradictions and tensions of the state system for effective global environmental management. Most assume that it is unrealistic, perhaps even counterproductive, to try to replace it (with, e.g., a federal world government). Instead, virtually every state has now created an environment department with national and global responsibilities. States have embraced economic globalization, which strengthens the power of the global market to transfer environmental funds and technology across state borders (although, as we have seen, many argue that this also transfers more environmental harms across borders). States have passed the authority for some environmental issues to global institutions. And finally, states have relinquished some sovereign rights by signing onto hundreds of global environmental agreements. States still dominate global environmental governance. But, as the next section shows, international institutions and regimes have grown in importance.

International Institutions/Regimes

Since Stockholm, global institutions have become increasingly active in promoting global environmental protection. UNEP is a catalyst for global action among states as well as other actors to mitigate specific environmental problems. It does this in part by supporting research on and negotiation of new international environmental agreements. Other arms of the UN also promote sustainable development. The Commission on Sustainable Development (CSD) monitors the implementation of Agenda 21 as well as other internationally declared environmental goals and targets. The United Nations Development Programme (UNDP), the World Health Organization (WHO), the World Bank, and the Food and Agriculture Organization of the United Nations (FAO), just to mention a few, have also—if in a less direct fashion—shaped global environmental management. . . .

International environmental regimes encompass established rules of international cooperation, either through a formal international treaty or agreement, or through a less formal set of rules and norms (established practices that states generally adhere to). States have signed and ratified a remarkable number of global environmental agreements over the past forty years, with an especially large number signed between the Stockholm and Rio conferences. In 1972, there were only a couple of dozen multilateral environmental treaties; today there are more than four hundred.

Are these agreements and regimes working? . . . [S]ome, such as the ones to solve depletion of the ozone layer, have been reasonably successful. At a minimum, the secretariats to the conventions are able to disseminate critical information as well as influence a state's level of concern about an environmental issue. Through aid and training, the secretariats also help raise the national capacity of developing countries struggling to comply with global agreements. Many observers, however, remain skeptical of the value of international agreements, arguing that many do not in fact alter state and corporate behavior. States that do not sign or ratify are not bound by a treaty, creating obvious problems of free riders (a general drawback of international law). It is exceedingly difficult to design effective agreements and enforce compliance. It is also becoming increasingly tricky to coordinate the plethora of sometimes overlapping institutional arrangements for global environmental management. It is, moreover, often unclear that full compliance with a treaty will genuinely improve environmental conditions (a point commonly made about the Kyoto Protocol).

Nongovernmental Organizations and Activist Groups

We define NGOs as organizations that are autonomous from governments, and are generally nonprofit (thus excluding corporations), though the lines are not always clear. International NGOs can include a wide variety of types of groups, such as large transnational organizations (like Greenpeace or Friends of the Earth International), regional groups (like the Third World Network or PANNA, the Pesticide Action Network North America), and local and grassroots groups and international networking groups that facilitate coordination of such groups (like the International Rivers Network and the many local NGOs around the world networked with it), as well as research institutes (like the International Institute for Sustainable Development, or the Worldwatch Institute) and private foundations (such as the Bill and Melinda Gates Foundation). Some of these groups have significant budgets. In 2010, the endowment assets for charitable activities of the Bill and Melinda Gates Foundation was more than US$35 billion. The budget of Greenpeace (including national offices) was close to US$150 million in 2001. The budget of the WWF (including national organizations) in 2000–2001 was around US$350 million. This compared favorably to UNEP's budget in 2001 of about US$120 million. . . .

Corporations and Private Governance Mechanisms

Firms have also increased their role and influence in the global environmental arena, in part as a response to the enhanced role of environmental NGOs. Both business advocacy groups, such as the International Chamber of Commerce (ICC) and the World Business Council for Sustainable Development, and individual transnational corporations (TNCs), like DuPont and Monsanto, have been actively engaged in global discussions on the environment and development.

Like environmental NGOs, corporate actors also play a diplomatic role in an effort to enhance interstate cooperation on environmental issues. Lobbying before state delegations head to international environmental negotiations has enabled firms to influence governmental positions from behind the scenes. Business actors have . . . increasingly begun to lobby at the international level as well, through industry associations and industry representatives with observer status at global environmental meetings. The presence of these actors at global negotiations is now routine—for example, during negotiations on the waste trade, climate change, ozone depletion, biosafety, and persistent organic pollutants. Business actors make fewer public interventions than environmental NGOs do (e.g., in plenary sessions and smaller meetings), but they are active in the corridors, lobbying and shaping the positions of states. Business representatives also end up on national delegations. This trend can be seen in both positive and negative lights. . . .

Corporate actors . . . influence global environmental governance through other international forums as well. Firms have helped shape private forms of global environmental governance, such as industry-set voluntary codes of environmental conduct as well as market-based governance mechanisms such as carbon trading at both the national and international levels. TNCs also exert influence in more diffuse ways, such as through their role in the global discourse over defining key terms, such as sustainable development, and through their economic weight, which influences state decisions in an indirect way.

Multilevel and Multiscale Actors

Until recently, most of the scholarship on global environmental governance focused on NGOs, business actors, states, and institutions working internationally. There is now growing recognition of the important role played by subnational actors, particularly cities and regional governments, as well as individuals, who are increasingly networking across borders at multiple scales to implement more local-level legislation and initiatives that work toward meeting global environmental goals. Actors at the subnational level are not merely responding passively to international environmental norms and agreements. Increasingly, they are the leaders and innovators in environmental governance. Such activity at the subnational level has been especially apparent on issues such as climate change, where networks of cities, partly in response to weak efforts among national governments, have emerged as leaders in promoting reductions of carbon emissions. Similarly, efforts to address problems with a global reach but without an international agreement, such as growing volumes of plastic waste in the world's oceans, have seen local governments around the world banning and legislating to reduce the use of plastic shopping bags.

In addition to cities and regions, informal networks of individuals are also becoming increasingly influential on the global stage. In some cases, these networks form as like-minded individuals lobby for change (such as fewer automobiles), different or new consumer products (such as organic food), or new lifestyles (such as voluntary simplicity). The rapid spread of the Internet over the last decade, which provides a cheap, quick, easy, and decentralized tool for people from different backgrounds and places to communicate for collective action, has allowed a vast array of direct-action and social networks to deepen and spread globally. The Internet is also enabling larger numbers of individuals to communicate about—and recognize—the global environmental consequences of daily choices and activities.

Sometimes these informal networks can combine with more formal processes—such as people wanting to consume more responsibly with ecolabeling or Fair Trade programs—to increase global reach and influence. Other times these networks of individuals remain spontaneous and organic. One example, among many, is the Critical Mass global cycling movement. Emerging in San Francisco in the early 1990s, this movement is leaderless, decentralized, and memberless. Its only formal structure is to arrange for a time (often the last Friday of every month) and a place for cyclists to gather for a noncompetitive and festive protest ride through a city. Generally, these rides occur worldwide without any coordination, although sometimes they correspond with another environmental event, such as Earth Day on April 22; often, although not always, the group follows a spontaneous route. The idea is to bring together enough riders for a "critical mass" able to disrupt traffic and highlight the dangers of cycling in cities designed for cars and trucks. Direct-action movements like Critical Mass also weave into a tapestry of other movements. One example is Reclaim the Streets, a nonviolent grassroots protest movement to oppose corporate capitalism (especially automobiles) that started in London in 1991 and has now spread worldwide, from the United States to Australia, Canada, Finland, and Mexico. Another example is the "guerrilla gardening" movement, in which individuals, sometimes as part of Reclaim the Streets, illegally plant seeds or seedlings in urban spaces, such as on traffic medians, back alleys, vacant lots, and commercial land. Although difficult to track and not a "global actor" in a traditional sense, these multilevel and multiscale networks are becoming increasingly important to the fabric of environmental governance, influencing policy choices, NGO strategies, consumption patterns, and corporate decision making. . . .

To fully understand the rise of sustainable development and the current structures and norms (i.e., established practices and understandings) of environmental governance, we have argued that it is equally critical to examine the broader trends in the global political economy. Global economic shifts—in the generation and distribution of wealth—have been key in influencing the evolution of perspectives not just on the economy, but also on the relationship between the global economy and the environment. . . .

14

What's Wrong with Climate Politics

Paul Harris

THE INTERNATIONAL SYSTEM

The nature and impact of the Westphalian system of sovereign nations fundamentally influences the course of climate politics at all levels. Nation-states have been the default actors in the world's responses to climate change, and it has been cooperation among nations—or lack of it—that has largely determined what has been done to address the problem, and to what degree. This is a normal response to a global problem requiring collective action because the world remains dominated by sovereign nation-states, particularly in official thinking and discourse. Governments have for centuries responded to collective action problems by trying to cooperate at the international level. Given the international (that is, transboundary) nature of climate change, governments have turned to diplomacy and specifically to the United Nations to find solutions, especially in the form of agreements among nations. This is a logical outgrowth of the Westphalian state system. Indeed, it would have been highly unusual, even radical, if the world had responded to climate change much differently, for example by looking for bottom-up solutions among people and organizations before turning to states for leadership, or by letting people rather than governments decide how to respond. The response to climate change has been consistent with official responses to other problems over the centuries, despite climate change being much less about nation-states than most traditional issues addressed by them (such as border and trade disputes).

The Westphalian international system that dominates world order is not natural. It was crafted by statesmen over centuries and as such is a manmade outgrowth of the historical evolution of relations among groups of people. The Westphalian system may be defined narrowly as the various relationships among the fundamental actors in the system, namely nation-states (such as Britain, China, India, Mexico). Nation-states by definition are political entities, each with a government having sole political authority over a territory and the people living there. A sovereign nation is normally recognized by (most) other nations and nowadays by the United Nations.

While nations had declared their sovereignty at earlier points in history, the modern international system is routinely dated to the Peace of Westphalia of 1648, which ended the Thirty Years War of religion in Europe (1618–1648). The Peace of Westphalia was (and remains) significant because it was premised on those principles that make up the modern global order: parties to the Peace were recognized as being their own masters, rather than being the subjects of foreign religious or imperial powers. Each nation was recognized as being equally legitimate in the eyes of international law, and each agreed to accept, at least in principle, that what happened inside other nations was not their concern. Wars in Europe and elsewhere continued, but diplomacy and international law among mutually recognized nation-states became norms that continue to dominate the world today.

Central to the system of nation-states—the international system—are the principles of sovereignty and noninterference. The government of each nation is recognized as having sovereignty—sole and supreme legal and political authority—in its territory; there is no higher authority than that of the sovereign nation unless a government or governments agree to relinquish sovereignty in specific issue areas, usually by treaty. Fundamental to the system is the principle of noninterference: while nations may take an interest in what happens in other countries (although even doing this can provoke criticism today, especially from China), in principle they have no right to intervene in the internal affairs of another nation without justification. What happens within a particular nation is legally the business of that nation and no other, and each nation has the sole right to conduct its own affairs internally and to conduct its relations with other nations (its foreign affairs).

In reality, of course, these fundamental tenets of the international system are often practiced in the breach; nations are routinely concerned about what happens in other countries and frequently intervene in a variety of ways, ranging from diplomatic protest all the way to military intervention. However, the fundamental principles are self-sustaining simply because nations have a key interest in maintaining them. Very significantly, the Westphalian system creates and reinforces an obsession with the interests of the nation-state above all else.

One cannot understate the power of these principles in the context of climate change. The dominant discourse around the problem, among diplomats, scholars, and even ordinary people, is routinely defined in terms of "state-centric territorialization." Climate change, from this dominant perspective and according to the prevailing discourse, is a problem for nation-states, greenhouse gas emissions are measured in terms of nations, climate negotiations are of course among nations, obligations and interests are of nations, the problem is perceived to create security challenges for nations, the scientists in the IPCC [Intergovernmental Panel on Climate Change] are nominated by governments of nations, and so forth. This "territorial trap" greatly narrows the options for thinking about climate change and finding political and policy solutions to it. For example, the question about how to allocate the distribution of greenhouse limitations has become "unambiguously a statist project, which starts from, and reinforces, the conception that it is states that have both rights and responsibilities in relation to the rest of the world," of course with diplomats negotiating responses to climate change while assuming the sovereign equality of nations.

Some nations take the Westphalian principles to extremes. For example, at the 2009 Copenhagen conference of the parties to the climate convention, China refused to accept outside monitoring of even its voluntary pledges to improve energy efficiency, justifying this refusal on the grounds of sovereignty and noninterference in its internal affairs. Others were suspicious of China's pledges: could it be trusted to keeps its word if, when giving that word, it simultaneously refused everyone the right to verify it? Whether that lack of trust was justified is not the point. The point is that the norms of the Westphalian system were powerful at the level of diplomatic negotiations and therefore affected their outcome, in this case contributing to a very weak agreement at the conclusion of the Copenhagen conference.

Crucially for our understanding of nations' responses to climate change, in the Westphalian system each nation seeks to promote its "national interests," usually interpreted as the most important objectives of those ruling and living within that political community. Foremost for each nation is its continued existence and the protection of its territorial integrity, without which there would be no sovereign nation-state in the traditional sense. This helps to explain why nations are so protective of controlling their borders: clear territorial boundaries reaffirm the sense of statehood that was codified at Westphalia. Key national interests include economic vitality and all that it entails, including a strong national economy, jobs, financial prosperity, and connections with the world through trade, as well as what we might call the nation's "way of life"—the collection of language, culture, political system, often religion, and other characteristics that define a particular nation and its population's sense of collective identity and purpose. Governments are seen to be legitimate insofar as they are able, at the very least, to defend these vital national interests, and more often than not it is necessary for them to be seen to be doing so by their populations, especially but not exclusively in democratic states in which governments must periodically face the national electorate.

It would be a slight exaggeration to say, especially in this day and age, that national governments and their citizens do not care at all about what happens in other nations. Often they do, as evidenced by, for example, foreign aid regimes, support for international development programs, and the willingness of governments to go to war to aid other countries and even people for humanitarian reasons. But it is also the case that all governments are very heavily inclined to promote the perceived interests of their own nations, whether that is the perceived interests of their citizens in democracies or the interests of the ruling Party or elites in authoritarian states. In times of crisis, such as economic recession and when threatened with aggression, the interests of other nations are naturally pushed aside. As some political "realists" might describe it, it is every nation for itself much of the time, and nearly all of the time when the going gets tough. This has real implications for the world's responses to climate change. Climate-related policies have the potential to adversely affect economies and certainly will affect powerful interest groups, leading to political resistance, whereas the effects of climate change will bring great suffering to many nations, harming economic development and human health, and even posing an existential threat to some island countries, of course leading them to push for more urgent action.

Throughout history, communities have sought to protect their survival and promote their other interests through a variety of means. In international relations, a balance of power often arises whereby weaker countries ally together to defend themselves against more powerful potential (and real) adversaries. This is most obvious in wartime—US interventions in Europe during the two world wars of the twentieth century are potent examples—but it also obtains in other issue areas, for example when developing countries teamed up in the 1970s to form the Group of 77 ("G-77") to fight for their economic interests vis-à-vis the western industrial powers. A balance of power of sorts has also been manifested in international negotiations on climate change, with most developing nations allying together to push for action by developed countries, although the traditional "North–South" (rich-nation/poor-nation) dichotomy is breaking down as developing nations divide along lines of responsibility for climate change, capability to respond to it, and vulnerability to its effects.

In addition to balances of power to protect their vital interests, nations have always sought to address problems requiring collective action through international cooperation, often brokered by the United Nations and its agencies, and through the creation of international regimes, defined by scholars as "principles, norms, rules and decision-making procedures around which actors' expectations converge in a given area of international relations." Perhaps the most visible example of this can be found in the World Trade Organization (and its predecessor, the General Agreement on Tariffs and Trade) and the many norms and rules for trade associated with it. Naturally, governments have responded to climate change in the same manner: by negotiating agreements and developing norms of behavior intended to address climate change in ways that are consistent with the more fundamental underlying Westphalian norms of the international system and the protection of national interests. Alas, the latter norms are often more powerful than the desire to protect the environment.

A key premise of the international system—sovereignty—has always been challenged by war and other forms of intervention, but since about the 1970s it has been put under stress on a continuing and increasing basis by globalization. Globalization, which can be defined in one sense as the erosion of governments' sovereign control over what happens within and across their borders, has engendered the conditions that undermine the ability of nations to shape events, whether individually or even through cooperation. Manifestations of globalization include the increasing integration of national economies through transnational trade, production, and finance, and a speeding up and deepening of connections among economies and people. Globalization is pushed by a western conception of capitalism that unquestionably promotes economic integration of the entire world. It has enabled people to easily and remotely share information and interact almost instantly. It has been accelerated by the microelectronic revolution, manifested in technologies such as desktop and mobile computers, blogs on the World Wide Web, mobile "smart phones," voice-over-internet telephony and the like.

While economic globalization has received most of the world's attention over the last several decades as global trade and finance have accelerated and affected almost every corner of the world, it is the effects of much of that trade—pollution and adverse changes to the global environment, including climate change—that are the most profound manifestations of globalization. This is because globalization is as much about the increasingly massive extraction, transport, and consumption of natural resources as it is about mobile phones and the internet. Put another way, environmental globalization, particularly climate change, has challenged national sovereignty like almost nothing else. Indeed, for some small-island nations, climate change—and specifically resulting sea-level rise—will likely wipe them off the map one day, making them nations without territories. For them, climate change is the ultimate erosion of sovereignty; it is an existential threat. One argument is that only by cooperating can nations address such a challenge. But with such an enormous collective action problem, it is possible that nations cannot achieve their objectives without expanding the scope of "national" interests to include the natural environment at home and abroad.

CLIMATE CHANGE DIPLOMACY

What has the international response to climate change looked like? Governments have come to recognize that there is indeed a tragedy of the atmospheric commons, and they have responded to it as they have responded to so many other widespread challenges affecting more than one country: by trying to work together collectively to formulate and implement solutions. In practice, this has resulted in agreement to study the problem, followed by a framework convention (treaty) that was then refined by protocols and recurring diplomatic conferences and meetings. . . . That international negotiating process resulted in the signing of the climate convention at the 1992 UN Conference on Environment and Development (the "Earth Summit") held in Rio de Janeiro.

The primary objective of the climate convention was (and is) the "stabilization of greenhouse gas concentrations in the atmosphere at a level that [will] prevent dangerous anthropogenic interference with the climate system. Such a level should be achieved within a time-frame sufficient to allow ecosystems to adapt naturally to climate change, to ensure that food production is not threatened and to enable economic development to proceed in a sustainable manner." The climate convention came into force in 1994 after ratification by 50 nations. As part of the convention, developed countries agreed to reduce their emissions of greenhouse gases to 1990 levels by 2000. This emissions-reduction pledge was voluntary. Not surprisingly, therefore, it was not honored by governments, and greenhouse gas emissions continued to increase for most countries, and, where they declined, it was for reasons quite unrelated to the convention, for example due to falls in emissions from within the former communist nations of Eastern Europe as their economies collapsed during the 1990s. . . .

[T]he general trend of climate diplomacy prevails: national interests trump climate-related ones. It seems that the world remains quite far from the turning point toward, let alone being willing to move swiftly down, a path of concerted action by enough nations. Generally speaking, throughout the climate change negotiations, beginning in the late 1980s when the climate convention was being devised, the relatively narrow and short-term perceived interests of major nations have prevented the international community from agreeing to the robust policy responses that are required to avert the most serious consequences of climate change, least of all implementing such policies. . . .

Sovereignty and the protection of the exclusive interests of people within national borders worked to address many transborder problems in the past, and often they still do, explaining why Westphalian norms took hold and persist. But in the modern world, plagued as it is by worsening climate change, "the national interest" can no longer be separated from "the interests of all nations" and those who live in them. By definition, global environmental problems, chief among them climate change, do not respect borders. It is impossible for any one nation, or even a small group of them, even the most powerful ones, to stop climate change. Greenhouse gas emissions that permeate the earth's atmosphere mean that pollution from within any given nation's territory affects other nations. If those nations most affected are unable to adapt, the consequences can be quite severe, even profound. The interests of people within borders mean that a responsible nation-state must consider ways to address greenhouse gas pollution originating in other nations. Practical sovereignty, at least in this context, is a thing of the past. . . .

Put succinctly, the diplomatic response to climate change has revealed a fundamental clash between the global interest of addressing climate change, largely by averting its worst effects through a massive cutback in global greenhouse gas emissions, and the selfish interests of nations that prefer business as usual. One of its key features has been to largely ignore the rights and obligations of human beings—an incredible shortfall considering that protecting human rights and ensuring the common good (at least within borders) is supposedly the *raison d'être* of any state.

The failure of international negotiations to achieve agreements that will do more to avert catastrophic climate change—their stated objective from the outset—can be largely attributed to the cancer of Westphalia. The norms that serve as the oasis of international relations have proved to be more powerful than the nascent and evolving norm of environmental stewardship. This cancer affects the entire body of the climate change regime. The cancer has not prevented international cooperation. Indeed, it largely explains why the response to climate change is so much about nations and their interests. But the cancer has made that response feeble relative to the seriousness of the problem. . . .

15

State Sovereignty Endangers the Planet

Richard Falk

The planetary crisis is an outgrowth of certain basic patterns of human behavior and political organization. These patterns need to be clearly understood before we can even begin to work out a better future for the human race. At this stage, groping for understanding is the necessary prelude to constructive action. Our point of departure is not a happy one. Despite the marvels of the modern world, there is an increasing realization that mankind has strayed from the pursuit of its own welfare, perhaps decisively, with little prospect of recovery and a growing appreciation of urgency. The French poet, Paul Valéry, put the situation very clearly some years ago: ". . . we are blind and impotent, yet armed with knowledge and power, in a world we have organized and equipped, and whose inextricable complexity we now dread." We seem entrapped in this central paradox of unprecedented knowledge and power on the one side and of unprecedented helplessness and danger on the other side.

The State System: A world of sovereign states is unable to cope with endangered-planet problems. Each government is mainly concerned with the pursuit of national goals. These goals are defined in relation to economic growth, political stability, and international prestige. The political logic of nationalism generates a system of international relations that is dominated by conflict and competition. Such a system exhibits only a modest capacity for international cooperation and coordination. The distribution of power and authority, as well as the organization of human effort, is overwhelmingly guided by the selfish drives of nations. . . .

Sovereign states can sometimes cooperate in situations where *perceived* common interests exist. The idea of an alliance against a common enemy is by far the most successful form of international cooperation. We need only to compare the great effort and resources invested by the United States in the North Atlantic Treaty Organization . . . with the trivial level of attention given to the work of the United Nations to grasp the extent to which international cooperation is itself dominated by ideas of competition and conflict. The vitality of international cooperation against a common enemy has long prompted science-fiction writers to invent stories about world government arising in response to a credible threat of aggression from a distant planet. Writing in 1928, André Maurois even went so far as to conjure up a conspiracy among world leaders consisting of a world-government movement. The essence of the conspiracy was to use the mass media to convince people everywhere that the earth was threatened by an invasion from the moon. . . . One can imagine the countries of the earth banding together in a single political unit to stave off extraterrestrial aggression, but under almost no other circumstances. Maurois ended his story on an ironic note, with the discovery that there really was an extraterrestrial enemy ready and willing to attack the earth from the moon. For the first time the people of the earth are confronted by a common danger, but it remains doubtful as to whether a situation as diffuse and abstract as the ecological crisis can arouse the political imagination sufficiently to serve as the equivalent of a personified enemy aggressor. Somehow the history of man is so bloody and internecine that only a personified enemy seems able to produce fear and a sense of emergency. In this respect, the earlier mentality of man in which the forces of nature were identified with (and personified by) gods was much better suited to waging a war of planetary survival. The rational consciousness of modern man has emptied nature of personality, and has deprived man of any sense of personal kinship with nature. The rejection of pantheism, animism, and polytheism makes it more difficult to engage the survival instincts of man in this struggle to rehabilitate life on earth.

Except for cooperation against an enemy, states have been able to cooperate effectively only on matters of non-vital concern, such as postal service, safety at sea, telecommunications, the extension of commercial credit, and the like. In many areas of international life international law has played a positive and important role by creating an orderly framework for routine competition and rivalry, but such a role is to be distinguished from achieving common policies on common problems. In the area of endangered-planet concerns there has been some effort to formulate a world interest in relation to the prevention of war, the resistance to population growth, and the curtailment of environmental pollution. But the world interest to date has been formulated only in highly general terms designed neither to prohibit dangerous behavior nor to implement positive goals. The formation of a world moral consensus and awareness is part of a move toward understanding, but by itself it is a feeble development considering the seriousness of the situation and the urgency of the need to begin curative action now.

And here is where sovereignty as the organizational basis of world society burdens the struggle for human survival. States have priorities distinct from one another that lead them to perceive the issues of the endangered planet in very diverse ways. As a consequence, it is virtually impossible to obtain agreement even on an agenda of concerns. National governments formulate *planetary priorities* to reflect the ranking and character of *national priorities.* Diversities of power, wealth, ideology, and history create the basic diversity of outlook on the part of national governments. For most governments, especially those with mass poverty, the primary concern is to raise GNP [gross national product] at a satisfactory rate and to secure internal security in relation to rebellion and external security in relation to potential aggressors. Any other concern seems remote and may be viewed with the suspicion that it is nothing but a malicious distraction from the business of the day. . . .

The paradox of aggregation arises out of the conflict between individual benefit and collective benefit. This conflict is present in many critical areas of human choice and has a peculiar relevance to the circumstances of the endangered planet. The paradox of aggregation is relevant whenever an actor has a schedule of priorities that is inconsistent with the priority schedule of the community. In circumstances of abundance—of space, time, resources—the operation of the paradox of aggregation is of far less social and political consequence.

A corporate manager or shareholder is primarily interested in securing a maximum profit from his industrial operations. To achieve maximum profitability often depends on having a cheap way to get rid of waste by discharging it either into the atmosphere or into water. For a long period of time no sense of conflict emerges. The environment seems able to absorb the waste products without suffering general deterioration. Local pollution hazards may result, and may lead to a struggle between the community and the industrial firm. Already at the end of the nineteenth century Henrik Ibsen, the Norwegian playwright, explored the ferocious dynamics of this kind of conflict in *An Enemy of the People,* showing the extent to which the politics and perceived "welfare" of a community become identified with the selfish interests of its richest members, but also with those of poorer people whose livelihood was dependent on the profitable operation of the polluting tannery. It is very difficult to persuade those who destroy the environment to take serious protective action if profits are diminished, especially if antipollution methods of production put a particular firm at a disadvantage vis-à-vis its competitors. . . . A material culture generally gives priority to considerations of profitability and attendant disasters tend to be viewed as the unavoidable costs of industrial progress. . . . Progress is measured, as has been noted, in terms of GNP and GNP per capita. A typical defense of this outlook has been made by an economist, C. E. Ayers:

> Industrial society is the most successful way of life mankind has ever known. Not only do our people eat better, sleep better, live in more comfortable dwell-

ings, get around more and in far greater comfort, and—notwithstanding all the manifold dangers in the industrial way of life—live longer than ever done before. Our people are better informed than ever before. At the height of the technological revolution we are now living in a golden age of scientific enlightenment and artistic achievement.

Such an outlook is resistant to information about the mounting dangers to the planet that arise out of the very processes described as beneficial, and tends to be confident about the capacity of technology to overcome the hazards and harms of technology. . . .

The paradox of aggregation is a subtle and fundamental social process. An imaginative and provocative biologist, Garrett Hardin, . . . has evolved an effective metaphor of this process from a historical experience, the destruction of the common pastures of English country towns in the 1700's and 1800's through overgrazing herds. "The tragedy of the commons" occurs because each farmer calculates his own advantage by reference to the enlargement of his own herd. The gain that results from each additional animal added to the herd is a definite increment to the farmer's wealth and profits, whereas the decision to forgo expansions of the herd in view of the limited grazing capacities of the commons is ineffectual to prevent other less conscientious farmers from adding to their herds. When the sum of the separate herds pushes up against the carrying capacity of the land, then the logic of the paradox of aggregation takes over. It does not help much even to crystallize the community interest and appeal to the conscience of farmers or to demonstrate that only by population control can their collective longer-term interests be protected. Unless the appeal is uniformly successful, a very unlikely outcome as it requires farmers of unequal wealth to forgo immediate private gain, then its results are merely to reward the less socially responsible members of the community at the expense of the more socially responsible. In this kind of setting, the temptation to maintain or enlarge one's own share of the pie is difficult to resist. Inequality is important, as it tends to vindicate a position of less restraint by poorer farmers and a consequent lessening of restraint by all relevant landholders. The typical outcome in such a situation then is, as with the commons, the exhaustion of the common resource by overuse to the detriment of *all* users. Only a common plan of conservation that allocates quotas and effectively punishes violations can hope to protect the collective interests under conditions of scarcity.

As Hardin argues, the deepest problems of the endangered planet arise out of similar conflicts between the pursuit of private gain and the protection of the public good. Decisions as to family size, or as to the use of insecticides or detergents, or as to resource extraction, all involve the exercise of unguided discretion in a context where the public good requires restraint and community control. Even where the public good has been carefully and clearly defined there exists a great deal of pressure to neglect its relevance in the definition of private good. My decision to have two, three, or six children is so insignificant in relation to the total world population as to have no bearing, nor does my use or nonuse of DDT have any discernible effect on the prospects for the survival of hawks and pelicans. Under such circumstances why shouldn't I have as many children as I want to have or protect my garden from the annoying presence of insect pests? To add or subtract a gram of sand from the beach is a decision without social importance. The paradox of aggregation, especially in societies whose mythology exalts a cult of individual initiative, gives an ethical reinforcement to patterns of action that involve the satisfaction of private wants.

To protect public concerns is the task of government. . . . The notion of "the invisible hand" guiding private action toward the automatic fulfillment of the public good and the belief in a laissez-faire role for government inhibit collective action that regulates individual choice. . . . [T]he individual actor is concerned with private gain and is not often inclined to sacrifice private gain for the sake of public good, or to defer benefits so as to uphold the patrimony of future generations.

There are many kinds of rationalizations for widespread indifference to these issues, even aside from callousness and greed. In discussions with socially sensitive friends I have noticed a general disposition to assume that the problems are not so serious, that the dangers are being exaggerated, and that the issues are too vast to think about. If pressed, many people seem to assume that "something will turn up," that technology can solve the problems that technology creates, that earlier warnings about resource shortages have always been exaggerated. . . .

A political variant of this confidence in the capacity of science to turn up solutions at the brink of disaster—that is, when the problems grow really serious—is the feeling that the government will step in effectively to uphold the public welfare before things get completely out of hand and a breakdown occurs. We feel so helpless in the face of the awesomeness of these issues that we base our sense of well-being on the capacity and willingness of our governors to rescue us before the situation deteriorates beyond recall. But why? The history of government is one long record of a failure by political leaders to take curative action in time to safeguard an endangered society or civilization. Political leaders are often beholden to the wrongdoers and are certainly hemmed in by an assortment of pressures, interests, and traditions; resistance to change is fierce, especially on the part of those who expect to bear its main burdens. Today, the scale of danger is greater and the failure by principal industrial societies to make adjustments imperils not only themselves but all forms of life everywhere on the globe. . . .

In conclusion, then, there are powerful motivations underlying exploitative activity. The aggregate effect of this activity is to generate a multi-faceted ecological crisis of planetary proportions. A response to this crisis requires more than a formulation of world interests and an appeal for voluntary compliance. An adequate response requires a public policy that takes into account the varied interests of different sectors of the community and provides effective mechanisms for prompt and uniform enforcement. The paradox of aggregation generates a call for governmental planning and enforcement on a planetary scale. But even should such a call be answered, there is no reason for confidence. All our experience with government . . . suggests that it is no panacea. More specifically, experience with government regulation of business interests should make us wary of placing too much faith in the capacity of government to carry out its mandate to uphold the public good. In case after case, the regulatory agency becomes subverted by the industry or activity that it is supposed to regulate and ends up as the exponent of the industry rather than as its overseer. . . .

Section 4 Exercise

Talking with the United Nations

Scenario: A new UN secretary-general has just been installed. You wish to send a congratulatory text wishing the secretary-general a productive tenure in bringing more peace, economic vitality, social justice, and environmental well-being to the world.

How would you do so? That is, how would ensure that your text ended up in the hands of the secretary-general?

The first thing you want to do is establish contact with the secretary-general in a way that will matter. You can do this by finding a personal connection—so you could tell the secretary-general, "so and so encouraged me to get in touch." Who would "so and so" be? Starting from your hometown, who would you first call or email to make a connection with the secretary-general (perhaps a city council member, county executive, congressional, or district representative)? Go on the Internet and find the person's contact information. Then, who do you think that person would suggest you contact next? Follow the chain of command up through the ranks, as it were, to see who you can eventually call upon to lend his or her name to your efforts. (Note: don't jump straight to the United Nations website to find the email address for the secretary-general's office. The point here is to think about the lines of authority and influence that connect you to the secretary-general.)

Now draft your text to the secretary-general. In addition to congratulations, offer some advice. Assuming that you would wish the secretary-general to advance the cause of environmental sustainability, what would you say about the prospects for global environmental protection? If the secretary-general had a magic wand, which institutional or structural feature(s) of the international system would you suggest changing?

Section 5

Economy

International state action, as the preceding section made clear, provides an important but limited avenue for responding to transnational and global environmental challenges. However, the state is not the only actor on the world stage. There are other important players, and other domains from which governance emanates. In this section, we consider the economy—the system by which goods and services are produced, distributed, and consumed. Although lacking the authoritative and coercive power of government, the way products are made, traded, used, and discarded significantly affects ecological conditions. The economy is like the lifeblood of our material lives: it circulates and determines the magnitude of humanity's impact on the earth.

At the global level, the world is now more economically connected than ever before. The raw materials for products are often mined in one area, designed and manufactured in other places, and then transported and consumed in yet other geographical regions. Furthermore, capital, which financially fuels and determines production and consumption, moves around the globe at astonishing speeds, as investors ignore boundaries in search of the highest possible returns. In such a world, multinational corporations wield enormous influence and often, through their practices, contribute to significant environmental harms. It is frequently said that of the world's 100 largest economies, around half are countries and around half are companies. While comparing countries and companies in these terms is an imperfect analytical conceit, it is revealing of a world in which corporate actors wield significant influence.

Corporate actors are not the only players in the economy. All of us are. Think about how many times and why you choose to eat one kind of food rather than another, or purchase one type of item over another. Similarly, think about why so many people choose certain jobs, entertainment options, or even acquaintances. So often we make decisions based to some extent on financial costs or other economic considerations. In fact, economically motivated analysis appears, for many, to be the most constant form of authority shaping thoughts and behaviors. Here, the source of power is not an official institution steering our lives in one direction rather than another, but rather personal economic preferences that inform everyday decisions. Economic incentive may not be as brazenly coercive as state power, but it nevertheless exerts tremendous influence over people's lives and contributes in profoundly important ways to environmental harm or well-being. In this sense, the economy, including the various incentives that give form to economic decisions, is an essential form of environmental governance.

How can we steer the economy toward environmental sustainability? Where are its levers of power and how easily are they able to be manipulated? Different thinkers provide varying perspectives. Some see little need to alter economic affairs because consumers and corporations are already going green. At best, we only need to convince people and companies to see that choosing environmental goods and services improves the bottom line: we can protect the planet and make money. Others see the issue as being less about consumers and corporate leaders than about the market itself. The market often fails to link environmental and economic benefits and thus we need to adjust market incentives for greater environmental protection. Finally, other thinkers believe the entire market economy is fundamentally anathema to environmental well-being. Capitalism, the dominant way of organizing economic life throughout the entire world, will never align with environmental protection since the incentive to profit calls for constant exploitation that robs the earth of resources, fills up sinks, and otherwise drives ecological harm. In short, just as in the book's prior section analysts of the international state-system offered conservative, reformist, and transformist prescriptions for advancing international environmental diplomacy, observers in this section suggest various perspectives on the relationship between economy and ecology.

This section begins with a selection from global environmental-politics researchers **Peter Dauvergne** and **Jane Lister**. The excerpt is from a book that argues that big business is mainly the enemy of environmental sustainability because, even if it's green, it is still committed to the endless production and consumption of products. However, the book also opens a window into the possibility of businesses contributing to a greener world. In the following edited selection, we read about the pro-business case. This orientation assumes that the global economy is functioning in productive ways that can be modified in the service of sustainability. In this sense, the excerpt can be read as supporting the status quo, or at most calling for relatively minor reforms.

Next, Nobel Prize–winning economist and *New York Times* columnist **Paul Krugman** offers a more reformist argument. Krugman suggests that environmental degradation comes about when the free operation of the market is distorted, either because the full social and environmental costs of particular activities are not properly captured by prices or because the market in other ways fails to function effectively. In such situations, environmental economists propose that the state should step in to impose particular kinds of taxes or regulations aimed at correcting market failures. Krugman argues that reforms of this kind ultimately allow and encourage economic actors to find efficient, market-based solutions to environmental harm. Such government interventions are seen by Krugman as preferable to top-down "command and control" approaches that mandate or prohibit certain kinds of activities.

Finally, this section presents a transformist perspective from journalist and activist **Naomi Klein**. She argues that, far from counting on capitalism to come to the rescue of the environment, capitalist efforts themselves are at the root of environmental challenges like climate change. Klein asserts that the only way to tackle climate change, and by extension other environmental challenges, is to move the world onto a radically different economic trajectory. In this way Klein offers a vision of the future and a plan for action that are markedly different from the visions in the two preceding selections and places her sharply at odds with those who see a better world resting on ever higher levels of economic growth.

16

The Promise of Corporate Environmentalism

Peter Dauvergne
and Jane Lister

Zero waste. 100 percent renewable energy. Zero toxics. 100 percent sustainable sourcing. Zero deforestation. These are just some of the grand promises that multinational companies such as Walmart, Nestlé, Nike, McDonald's, and Coca-Cola are now making as they claim to lead a corporate charge toward "sustainability." "We're integrating sustainability principles and practices into everything we do," Nike tells us boldly.

What is going on? Why are these companies making such promises? Why do they seem to be accelerating their efforts? Is this merely crafty marketing? Are they using feel-good rhetoric to placate governments, activists, and consumers? Some of what we are seeing is definitely "greenwash" and business as usual. But . . . these iterations of "corporate sustainability" have more powerful drivers and motives, and more varied consequences, than previous iterations, which tended toward peripheral, one-off, reputation-saving responses. . . .

Eco-business is likely to keep rising in importance as a global force of change—a trend that global governance analysts and practitioners will have to watch closely. Some are applauding this trend, seeing it as valuable for the mainstreaming and scaling up of sustainability that global solutions will require. Executives of big-brand companies also are making this case, arguing they are "sustainability leaders" and that states now are the "laggards." They are quick to provide example after example of savings, efficiencies, social responsibility, and more transparency and accountability within supply chains. On the surface, the benefits of eco-business do seem to be advancing environmental improvements—and . . . many governments and environmental groups are now rushing to partner with big brands. For those wanting to hear some good news for a change, it is easy to find the apparent gains reassuring. . . .

THE RISE OF ECO-BUSINESS

. . . Corporate efforts to find and gain environmental efficiencies date back decades. The year 2005, however, saw a shift in the strategies of multinational retailers and manufacturers. General Electric launched its Ecomagination program, linking its growth strategy to clean water, energy, and technology, doubling its research-and-development budget to $1.5 billion, and setting a revenue target of $25 billion over the next five years from growing its green-design products—twice the rate of growth of total company revenue. Later that year, Walmart set aspirational goals of zero waste, carbon neutrality, and 100 percent sourcing of more responsibly produced products.

Big companies had made big sustainability promises before. Back in 2001, British Petroleum announced a "beyond petroleum" campaign. Ford had proclaimed in 1999 that it would "bring about the demise of the internal combustion engine," and had pledged in 2004 to spend half of its R&D budget on making its vehicles and its factories run cleaner. But these announcements were more about public relations than about the pursuit of business earnings and power. British Petroleum continued to rely on fossil fuels. And Ford stayed at the bottom of fuel-efficiency rankings for automakers.

The approach of General Electric and Walmart in 2005 was different. They were aiming to use corporate sustainability as a strategic tool to change practices to enhance financial strength and earnings potential—and thus to generate business value. This was more than just public relations or marketing. And it went beyond a risk-management program to protect a brand's reputation. Even more significant, this approach was not just looking to advance the bottom-line earnings through "eco-efficiency"—an idea that was increasingly popular among companies after the 1992 Earth Summit in Rio de Janeiro—but was also striving to achieve top-line "green growth" by producing more goods from less resources and with less waste.

General Electric and Walmart were aiming to pursue environmental objectives through the entire corporate structure to gain competitive advantages and increase sales and profits. "Green is green," General Electric's chief executive officer, Jeffrey Immelt, explained when announcing Ecomagination. "We are launching Ecomagination not because it's trendy or moral but because it will accelerate our growth." Before long, it wasn't just niche green brand leaders such as Body Shop, Patagonia, Ben & Jerry's, Whole Foods, and Interface Carpets that were embracing corporate sustainability. Big-box retailers and brand manufacturers in all consumer-goods sectors—from apparel and electronics to food and beverage to household and personal care products—were aiming to integrate eco-business into their guiding strategy. Today just about every big brand has a sustainability program. ([The following table] provides a sample.) And corporate executives are jockeying to position themselves as "thought-and-action" sustainability leaders who are setting a "future-friendly" direction for producers and consumers.

CLAIMS AND COMMITMENTS

Almost every day, it seems, a big brand makes another sustainability claim or "commitment." Coca-Cola is promising water neutrality. McDonald's is promising sustainable sourcing of beef, coffee, fish, chicken, and cooking oil. Unilever is promising 100 percent sustainable agricultural sourcing and has set a deadline of 2020. H&M is promising to eliminate all hazardous chemicals from its apparel manufacturing, and Nestlé is promising zero deforestation from its activities. Adidas, Puma, and Nike are promising to eliminate all toxic discharges from their factories, and Walmart, Tesco, Disney, Google, and Carrefour are promising to become carbon neutral.

And this is just a few of the claims and commitments. Dell now advertises that it offers free recycling of its products, and claims that it no longer allows "e-waste" to be exported to developing countries. IBM is claiming that it will reduce energy use worldwide through its "smart-grid" programs. And Procter & Gamble is setting—and claiming to meet—targets so that one day it will power all of its operations with 100 percent renewable energy, make all of its products with recyclable materials, and avoid sending any manufacturing and product waste to landfills.

WHY NOW?

What explains this recent rise of eco-business programs and promises? Companies are responding in part to state regulations and international laws. Some are also using sustainability language and programming to respond to environmental advocacy groups, consumers, investors, and employees as environmentalism broadens in diverse forms across diverse groups. But . . . the full explanation for the accelerating turn to eco-business must look at how the above factors are converging with changes in the world economy. These changes include the rise of global retailing, as well as growing populations and resource scarcities, high and volatile commodity prices, the 2007–2009 global economic downturn, and escalating ecological stressors such as climate change. Especially important for encouraging and enabling the increasing use of eco-business as a tool of corporate growth has been the well-documented globalization of production and the shift toward consumer goods moving along lengthening, dynamic supply chains through the surging economies of China, Brazil, and India.

Growth of eco-business programs

Company	Sustainability program	Year launched	Promises or goals
Sainsbury	20 by 20 Sustainability Plan	2011	Reach 20 sustainability targets for products, communities, and employees by 2020.
McDonald's	Sustainable Land Management Commitment	2011	Ensure that food served in McDonald's restaurants is sourced from certified sustainable sources.
Best Buy	Greener Together	2010	Encourage consumers to reduce, reuse, and trade in "end of life" electronics.
Procter & Gamble	Sustainability Vision	2010	Design products that maximize the conservation of resources.
Unilever	Sustainable Living Plan	2010	Decouple business growth from environmental impact.
PepsiCo	Performance with Purpose	2009	Deliver sustainable growth.
FedEx	Earth Smart	2009	Extend the depth and breadth of how sustainability is integrated in to the company.
Nike	Considered Design	2008	Performance without compromising sustainability.
IBM	Smarter Planet	2008	Apply smart technology systems to sustainability solutions.
Starbucks	Shared Planet	2008	Aspire to environmental stewardship, ethical sourcing, and community involvement.
Marks & Spencer	Plan A	2007	Become the world's most sustainable retailer by 2015.
Coca-Cola	Live Positively	2007	Make a positive difference in the world.
Johnson & Johnson	Healthy Planet	2006	Safeguard the health of people and the planet.
Walmart	Sustainability Commitment	2005	Commit to zero waste, 100% renewable energy, and sustainable sourcing.
General Electric	Ecomagination	2005	Grow through clean energy, clean water, and clean technology.

Sources: Company reports (with goals partly quoted or paraphrased).

The shift toward manufacturing and purchasing in China is particularly notable. To remain competitive all multinational corporations have been moving away from using home suppliers and owning foreign factories and toward working with thousands of small and medium-size suppliers worldwide. Walmart reports that it has about 20,000 suppliers in China alone. China is now central to the world retail economy, with Chinese manufacturers still expanding at home as well as outsourcing more and more to developing countries in search of cheaper labor, natural resources, and infrastructure. Moving into China is also part of an effort by big brands to reach the country's rapidly growing middle class. By mid 2010, Walmart had 189 stores in 101 cities across China: a steady increase after opening its first Supercenter and Sam's Club in Shenzhen in 1996. Carrefour has announced that it will add 20–25 stores a year indefinitely. H&M is opening new outlets every week. IKEA is working to more than double its number of stores to 17. Starbucks is planning to expand from 459 stores (in 2010) to 1,500 stores by 2015. And this is just a sampling of big brands' expansion plans.

China's rise is creating some new dependencies and vulnerabilities for big brands. For example, by 2011, although having only 30 percent of global reserves, China was mining and refining at least 95 percent of the world's rare earth metals (seventeen elements that are needed to make a wide variety of products, ranging from Apple's iPhone to Toyota's Prius). The Chinese government has not been afraid to exercise this power—in 2010 it enforced a two-month ban on rare earth shipments to Japan during a territorial dispute.

These changes in the world economy are pushing big brands to search for greater efficiencies and resource security. They are looking to find better ways to maintain quality and reliable supplies within lower-cost but higher-risk global supply chains. And they are launching new growth strategies to capture markets in high-growth emerging economies. Eco-business, more and more big brands are finding, is an effective way to control supply chains, pursue efficiencies and competitive advantages, and generate business value (e.g., reputation, sales, profits, and growth).

THE BUSINESS OF ECO-BUSINESS

Eco-business efforts do vary across product segments, sectors, countries, and companies, from determined and sustained to weak and ad hoc. Many factors contribute to differences across and between manufacturers and retailers. These include the origins and size of firms, the legal context of the primary operations, the technological complexity of the main products, and the intricacy of supply chains. Inconsistencies of commitments and actions continue within big-brand companies, too, leading to confusing proclamations that certain companies (e.g., Walmart and Coca-Cola) represent the best and the worst in the world.

However, what is consistent across all the big brands is how eco-business is helping to improve product-design and production processes and to turn waste streams into profit streams. Measured on the basis of per unit of output, energy, water, material use, and waste output intensity do seem to be lessening, if sometimes only fractionally. Big brands are winning awards (with valuable reputational spinoffs) for these efforts. In 2011, Unilever received the International Green Award for "true innovation, thought leadership, and commitment to sustainable values that are integrated throughout the value chain." The multi-stakeholder panel of judges praised the company for being "an organization at the cutting edge of change and a beacon that others aspire to follow." *Newsweek* rated IBM as America's greenest company in 2011. (Dell had ranked first in 2010.) The magazine *Corporate Knights* ranked Johnson & Johnson as the world's second "most sustainable company" in 2011—a position General Electric had held in 2010. Companies are also shining a spotlight on themselves with industry awards. The business-led World Environment Center, for example, has awarded its International Corporate Achievement in Sustainable Development prize to several of its member companies, including Marks & Spencer (2008), Coca-Cola (2009), Walmart (2010), Nestlé (2011), and IBM (2012).

Much of what big brands are doing still involves enhancing the eco-efficiency of production to improve bottom-line earnings. Hurdles such as managing up-front costs, payback periods, access to capital, and uncertainty about how to measure the savings continue to challenge efficiency efforts. Yet finding ways to make a product with less resources, energy, and waste remains central to efforts to turn eco-business into savings and lower costs—and thus profit and competitive advantage. This became even more important during the global economic downturn of 2007–2009, and since then it has remained crucial for business success as brand companies look for efficiencies to help them ride out ongoing slowdowns in consumption. Striving for more eco-efficiency to improve the bottom line, however, is only part of what is encouraging ecobusiness. It is very much about enhancing the growth-oriented top line, too. Nike, the world's largest apparel firm, sees great potential here: "[T]he opportunity is greater than ever for sustainability principles and practices to deliver business returns and become a driver of growth."

The competition for revenues and markets is especially fierce in emerging economies, such as China and India, where companies are infusing traditional brands and products with "sustainability purpose" (e.g., hydration, mobility, connectivity, nourishment, and well-being) to capture new consumers. But eco-business is increasingly important in more mature markets, such as the United States, too. In 2008 alone, American consumers doubled their spending on "sustainable products and services" to about US$500 billion, according to the market-research firm Penn Schoen Berland. Big brands are extracting even greater bottom-line and top-line value, however, from the eco-business of supply chains. . . .

The growth of eco-business is further concentrating the power and extending the governance scale and reach of private environmental authority. Transnational retail governance has the potential to produce global change faster than previous forms of environmental governance. Noting such capacity is not meant to suggest that this is good for societies or for ecosystems: without a doubt the politics of eco-business can harm local suppliers, developing economies, and the global environment. Identifying and better understanding this governing authority could, however, open up opportunities to channel it toward more social and ecological purposes.

The power of big brands across economies and cultures is unparalleled in history—and it is growing quickly. Procter & Gamble, PepsiCo, Nestlé, and other companies buy worldwide and sell into virtually every market. Nestlé sells about 10,000 different products, and in 2010 it netted $36 billion in profits on $115 billion in revenues. That works out to about a billion Nestlé products sold per day. Big brands are striving in particular to reach consumers in developing economies where growth forecasts look highly promising. In India, Hindustan Unilever (52 percent of which is owned by Unilever) already controls many of India's top consumer brands. In 2009, it added 500,000 new stores to the more than 6.1 million outlets it already had, achieving a growth in sales volume that year of 14 percent (a year in which retailers faced slower growth across most of the developed world). In China, Procter & Gamble holds the top spot in every category of consumer products in which its brands compete. In 2010, P&G announced plans to invest an additional $1 billion or so in China over the next five years.

The reach and the influence of mass retailers such as Walmart, Tesco, and Best Buy are also increasing. Around 50 retailers are on the Fortune Global 500 list of the world's biggest companies by revenue turnover. Walmart is at the top. Walmart is now one of China's largest trading partners; only entire economies, including the United States, Japan, South Korea, Taiwan, and Germany, are ahead of it. And it is still growing quickly, with more than $440 billion in sales in fiscal year 2012 (ending January 31) across more than 10,000 outlets (under 69 different banners) in 27 countries. The fastest expansion is in the emerging economies. In the period 2005–2010, Walmart invested $3.8 billion in Brazil alone, and in 2011 it announced plans to add another 80 stores to the 450 it already had in Brazil. Carrefour (the world's second-biggest retailer, headquartered in France) has an even bigger presence in Brazil.

The governing reach of big brands is now deeply global. States can ignore, and often fall far short of meeting, international obligations. And companies everywhere tend to evade and soften government rules. Depending on the political context, they may use lawyers, bribes, or violence to do so. Yet a company that disobeys or ignores a big-brand chain leader runs the risk of being switched for a more compliant supplier. . . .

PARTNERING WITH POWER

Gerald Butts, president and CEO of World Wildlife Fund Canada, has called the Coca-Cola Company "literally more important, when it comes to sustainability, than the United Nations." The reason for him is simple: raw purchasing power: "Coke is the No. 1 purchaser of aluminum on the face of the earth. . . . The No. 1 purchaser of sugar cane. The No. 3 purchaser of citrus. The second-largest purchaser of glass, and the fifth-largest purchaser of coffee."

Given this, he sees great value in joining forces with Coca-Cola. "We could spend 50 years," he goes on, "lobbying 75 national governments to change the regulatory framework for the way these commodities are grown and produced. Or these folks at Coke could make a decision that they're not going to purchase anything that isn't grown or produced in a certain way—and the whole global supply chain changes overnight. And that in a nutshell is why we're in a partnership."

Even the traditionally anti-corporate organization Greenpeace has been working with Coca-Cola since 2009 on reducing greenhouse gas emissions. "Corporations," Greenpeace USA acknowledges, "can be extraordinarily dynamic, powerful, and swift allies." Some activists see such cooperation as the beginning of a perilous slide toward cooptation. Still, with governments fiscally and jurisdictionally constrained and lagging badly in regulating global environmental problems, many now see partnering with big brands as one of the few ways to improve business accountability, transparency, and management. The Environmental Defense Fund's director of corporate partnerships, Gwen Ruta, justifies the EDF's partnership with McDonald's: "[T]he political system is not moving as quickly as those of us who have environmental aspirations would like—so we need to turn to the levers that we have, and one of the biggest levers is the marketplace, and in particular the clout and power that companies like McDonald's have within their own supply chain."

The first partnership between a Fortune 500 company and environmental non-governmental organization (NGO), set up in 1990, was between the US-based Environmental Defense Fund and McDonald's to phase out styrofoam "clamshell" packaging. Some saw the move as a naive step backward. "It's like saying I'm going to join a task force with the Mafia to discuss how to cope with the drug situation," occupational health specialist Samuel Epstein reacted. Such criticism did little to slow the EDF's new and seemingly effective strategy, and since then it has established many other partnerships, including one with Walmart. The EDF has even opened an office next to Walmart's headquarters in Bentonville, Arkansas. David Yarnold, the EDF's executive vice-president, explains why: "[W]hen Walmart makes important decisions, the company moves very quickly. If you are not at the table, you don't get a chance to influence those decisions. By having an office in Bentonville, we'll help to assure that the environment is represented."

Today, partnerships between Fortune 500 companies and NGOs are common. Both big brands and NGOs have been seeking them out. Many activists recognize the irony, and even the hypocrisy, of such deals. But the desire for faster, more immediate, and more wide-ranging change is, more and more, overriding fears that these partnerships are turning environmentalism into a marketing tool. They are also providing financial support to NGOs. The WWF, for example, maintains a worldwide partnership with Coca-Cola; in 2010 worth about $20 million to the WWF. But even in these cases the reason for partnering is more to gain access to power than to receive money. . . .

THE LIMITS OF ECO-BUSINESS

. . . Companies are achieving some eco-business targets and falling short on others. Walmart reached only half of its carbon-reduction target for 2010. Starbucks has so far failed to meet its energy-reduction and recycling targets. IKEA fell short of its 2006 commitment to reach 30 percent sustainable sourcing by 2010. Its proportion of certified chipboard and fiberboard was even further off the mark, at just 10 percent. All are promising to do better. IKEA's reason for the failure to reach its target, however, is revealing of the limits of eco-business: according to IKEA's global forestry manager, it was impossible to source sustainable wood in a way to keep prices low enough to sustain the company's rapid growth.

The *total* environmental impacts of consumption, moreover, continue to increase even as the per-unit energy, material, water, and waste impacts of producing, consuming, and disposing of some consumer goods are declining. The same big brands trumpeting sustainability programs are aggressively marketing "new" products to billions of "new" consumers: diapers, soft drinks, plastic razors, flip-flops, bottled water—the list could go on and on. According to Stacy Mitchell, the author of *Big-Box Swindle*, "Walmart is accelerating the cycle of consumption, speeding up how fast products move from factory to shelf to house to landfill. Even if Walmart does reduce the resources used to make a T-shirt or a television set, those gains will be more than outstripped by growth in the number of T-shirts and TVs we're consuming. It's one step forward and three steps back. . . ."

Eco-business may even accelerate a decline in global environmental conditions as the same processes that are enhancing the efficiency and control of business push up consumption. The ultimate goal of eco-business is more consumption of brands and discount goods, and big brands are investing savings to expand and grow—especially in developing markets. "Sustainability is a business strategy, not a charitable giving strategy," explains Beth Keck, Walmart's senior director of sustainability. "We're thinking about sustainability from the customer's point of view. We don't want customers to have to choose between products that are sustainable or products that are affordable." Absolute environmental gains are an incidental outcome rather than the goal of eco-business. It doesn't aim to curtail consumption to stop ecological loss; it helps to ensure that any loss doesn't impede more goods and more growth.

Eco-business is not about transforming the world economy that underpins today's global environmental crisis. It is about advancing the growth of ever-larger businesses. It assumes—indeed it needs—increasing production and consumption for its dynamism and rationale. Scaling back consumerism or eliminating brands or products with high social costs are not part of what eco-business is aiming to change. Consumers are the ultimate source of brand power: more consumers, buying more brands, creates more power. . . .

Turning sustainability into eco-business, moreover, is altering the nature of environmentalism, increasing its power to accelerate some forms of change, but limiting what is on the table to question, challenge, and alter. Sustainability as an idea can be radical: not just calling for changes in the rules of the game (i.e., market dynamics), but also to the game itself (i.e., the global economy). It can, for instance, challenge individuals to reduce consumption. It can challenge businesses to stop certain practices, eliminate certain products, and produce more durable goods. And it can challenge public and private organizations to operate systems within ecological and social principles, and not just within economic ones. The big brands' takeover of sustainability, however, is shifting the purpose and goal of sustainability governance toward the need to create business value as an outcome of pursuing sustainability. And the levers of change within resulting governance mechanisms are increasingly under the control of large private organizations. States and NGOs can advance some causes by stepping strategically on these levers. But eco-business on its own cannot—and never will—alter the underlying logic of accelerating consumerism and unequal globalization behind the increasing power of big brands. . . .

17

Environmental Economics 101

Overcoming Market Failures

Paul Krugman

If you listen to climate scientists—and despite the relentless campaign to discredit their work, you should—it is long past time to do something about emissions of carbon dioxide and other greenhouse gases. If we continue with business as usual, they say, we are facing a rise in global temperatures that will be little short of apocalyptic. And to avoid that apocalypse, we have to wean our economy from the use of fossil fuels, coal above all.

But is it possible to make drastic cuts in greenhouse-gas emissions without destroying our economy?

Like the debate over climate change itself, the debate over climate economics looks very different from the inside than it often does in popular media. The casual reader might have the impression that there are real doubts about whether emissions can be reduced without inflicting severe damage on the economy. In fact, once you filter out the noise generated by special-interest groups, you discover that there is widespread agreement among environmental economists that a market-based program to deal with the threat of climate change—one that limits carbon emissions by putting a price on them—can achieve large results at modest, though not trivial, cost. There is, however, much less agreement on how fast we should move, whether major conservation efforts should start almost immediately or be gradually increased over the course of many decades. . . .

ENVIRONMENTAL ECON 101

If there's a single central insight in economics, it's this: There are mutual gains from transactions between consenting adults. If the going price of widgets is $10 and I buy a widget, it must be because that widget is worth more than $10 to me. If you sell a widget at that price, it must be because it costs you less than $10 to make it. So buying and selling in the widget market works to the benefit of both buyers and sellers. More than that, some careful analysis shows that if there is effective competition in the widget market, so that the price ends up matching the number of widgets people want to buy to the number of widgets other people want to sell, the outcome is to maximize the total gains to producers and consumers. Free markets are "efficient"—which, in economics-speak as opposed to plain English, means that nobody can be made better off without making someone else worse off.

Now, efficiency isn't everything. In particular, there is no reason to assume that free markets will deliver an outcome that we consider fair or just. So the case for market efficiency says nothing about whether we should have, say, some form of guaranteed health insurance, aid to the poor and so forth. But the logic of basic economics says that we should try to achieve social goals through "aftermarket" interventions. That is, we should let markets do their job, making efficient use of the nation's resources, then utilize taxes and transfers to help those whom the market passes by.

But what if a deal between consenting adults imposes costs on people who are not part of the exchange? What if you manufacture a widget and I buy it, to our mutual benefit, but the process of producing that widget involves dumping toxic sludge into other people's drinking water? When there are "negative externalities"—costs that economic actors impose on others without paying a price for their actions—any presumption that the market economy, left to its own devices, will do the right thing goes out the window. So what should we do? Environmental economics is all about answering that question.

One way to deal with negative externalities is to make rules that prohibit or at least limit behavior that imposes especially high costs on others. That's what we did in the first major wave of environmental legislation in the early 1970s: cars were required to meet emission standards for the chemicals that cause smog, factories were required to limit the volume of effluent they dumped into waterways and so on. And this approach yielded results; America's air and water became a lot cleaner in the decades that followed.

But while the direct regulation of activities that cause pollution makes sense in some cases, it is seriously defective in others, because it does not offer any scope for flexibility and creativity. Consider the biggest environmental issue of the 1980s—acid rain. Emissions of sulfur dioxide from power plants, it turned out, tend to combine with water downwind and produce flora- and wildlife-destroying sulfuric acid. In 1977, the government made its first stab at confronting the issue, recommending that all new coal-fired plants have scrubbers to remove sulfur dioxide from their emissions. Imposing a tough standard on all plants was problematic, because retrofitting some older plants would have been extremely expensive. By regulating only new plants, however, the government passed up the opportunity to achieve fairly cheap pollution control at plants that were, in fact, easy to retrofit. Short of a de facto federal takeover of the power industry, with federal officials issuing specific instructions to each plant, how was this conundrum to be resolved?

Enter Arthur Cecil Pigou, an early-20th-century British don, whose 1920 book, "The Economics of Welfare," is generally regarded as the ur-text of environmental economics. . . .

What Pigou enunciated was a principle: economic activities that impose unrequited costs on other people should not always be banned, but they should be discouraged. And the right way to curb an activity, in most cases, is to put a price on it. So Pigou proposed that people who generate negative externalities should have to pay a fee reflecting the costs they impose on others—what has come to be known as a Pigovian tax. The simplest version of a Pigovian tax is an effluent fee: anyone who dumps pollutants into a river, or emits them into the air, must pay a sum proportional to the amount dumped.

Pigou's analysis lay mostly fallow for almost half a century, as economists spent their time grappling with issues that seemed more pressing, like the Great Depression. But with the rise of environmental regulation, economists dusted off Pigou and began pressing for a "market-based" approach that gives the private sector an incentive, via prices, to limit pollution, as opposed to a "command and control" fix that issues specific instructions in the form of regulations.

The initial reaction by many environmental activists to this idea was hostile, largely on moral grounds. Pollution, they felt, should be treated like a crime rather than something you have the right to do as long as you pay enough money. Moral concerns aside, there was also considerable skepticism about whether market incentives would actually be successful in reducing pollution. . . .

What has caught on instead is a variant that most economists consider more or less equivalent: a system of tradable emissions permits, aka cap and trade. In this model, a limited number of licenses to emit a specified pollutant, like sulfur dioxide, are issued. A business that wants to create more pollution than it is licensed for can go out and buy additional licenses from other parties; a firm that has more licenses than it intends to use can sell its surplus. This gives everyone an incentive to reduce pollution, because buyers would not have to acquire as many licenses if they can cut back on their emissions, and sellers can unload more licenses if they do the same. In fact, economically, a cap-and-trade system produces the same incentives to reduce pollution as a Pigovian tax, with the price of licenses effectively serving as a tax on pollution. . . .

[E]xperience suggests that market-based emission controls work. Our recent history with acid rain shows as much. The Clean Air Act of 1990 introduced a cap-and-trade system in which power plants could buy and sell the right to emit sulfur dioxide, leaving it up to individual companies to manage their own business within the new limits. Sure enough, over time sulfur-dioxide emissions from power plants were cut almost in half, at a much lower cost than even optimists expected; electricity prices fell instead of rising. Acid rain did not disappear as a problem, but it was significantly mitigated. The results, it would seem, demonstrated that we can deal with environmental problems when we have to.

So there we have it, right? The emission of carbon dioxide and other greenhouse gases is a classic negative externality—the "biggest market failure the world has ever seen," in the words of Nicholas Stern, the author of a report on the subject for the British government. Textbook economics and real-world experience tell us that we should have policies to discourage activities that generate negative externalities and that it is generally best to rely on a market-based approach. . . .

Is a cap-and-trade program along the lines of the model used to reduce sulfur dioxide the right way to go?

Serious opposition to cap and trade generally comes in two forms: an argument that more direct action—in particular, a ban on coal-fired power plants—would be more effective and an argument that an emissions tax would be better than emissions trading. . . . There's something to each of these positions, just not as much as their proponents think.

When it comes to direct action, you can make the case that economists love markets not wisely but too well, that they are too ready to assume that changing people's financial incentives fixes every problem. In particular, you can't put a price on something unless you can measure it accurately, and that can be both difficult and expensive. So sometimes it's better simply to lay down some basic rules about what people can and cannot do.

Consider auto emissions, for example. Could we or should we charge each car owner a fee proportional to the emissions from his or her tailpipe? Surely not. You would have to install expensive monitoring equipment on every car, and you would also have to worry about fraud. It's almost certainly better to do what we actually do, which is impose emissions standards on all cars.

Is there a comparable argument to be made for greenhouse-gas emissions? My initial reaction, which I suspect most economists would share, is that the very scale and complexity of the situation requires a market-based solution, whether cap and trade or an emissions tax. After all, greenhouse gases are a direct or indirect byproduct of almost everything produced in a modern economy, from the houses we live in to the cars we drive. Reducing emissions of those gases will require getting people to change their behavior in many different ways, some of them impossible to identify until we have a much better grasp of green technology. So can we really make meaningful progress by telling people specifically what will or will not be permitted? Econ 101 tells us—probably correctly—that the only way to get people to change their behavior appropriately is to put a price on emissions so this cost in turn gets incorporated into everything else in a way that reflects ultimate environmental impacts.

When shoppers go to the grocery store, for example, they will find that fruits and vegetables from farther away have higher prices than local produce, reflecting in part the cost of emission licenses or taxes paid to ship that produce. When businesses decide how much to spend on insulation, they will take into account the costs of heating and air-conditioning that include the price of emissions licenses or taxes for electricity generation. When electric utilities have to choose among energy sources, they will have to take into account the higher license fees or taxes associated with fossil-fuel consumption. And so on down the line. A market-based system would create decentralized incentives to do the right thing, and that's the only way it can be done.

That said, some specific rules may be required. James Hansen, the renowned climate scientist who deserves much of the credit for making global warming an issue in the first place, has argued forcefully that most of the climate-change problem comes down to just one thing, burning coal, and that whatever else we do, we have to shut down coal burning over the next couple decades. My economist's reaction is that a stiff license fee would strongly discourage coal use anyway. But a market-based system might turn out to have loopholes—and their consequences could be dire. So I would advocate supplementing market-based disincentives with direct controls on coal burning.

What about the case for an emissions tax rather than cap and trade? There's no question that a straightforward tax would have many advantages over legislation like Waxman-Markey, which is full of exceptions and special situations. But that's not really a useful comparison: of course an idealized emissions tax looks better than a cap-and-trade system that has already passed the House with all its attendant compromises. The question is whether the emissions tax that could actually be put in place is better than cap and trade. There is no reason to believe that it would be—indeed, there is no reason to believe that a broad-based emissions tax would make it through Congress. . . .

The bottom line, then, is that while climate change may be a vastly bigger problem than acid rain, the logic of how to respond to it is much the same. What we need are market incentives for reducing greenhouse-gas emissions—along with some direct controls over coal use—and cap and trade is a reasonable way to create those incentives. . . .

THE COSTS OF INACTION

. . . At this point, the projections of climate change, assuming we continue business as usual, cluster around an estimate that average temperatures will be about 9 degrees Fahrenheit higher in 2100 than they were in 2000. That's a lot—equivalent to the difference in average temperatures between New York and central Mississippi. Such a huge change would have to be highly disruptive. And the troubles would not stop there: temperatures would continue to rise.

Furthermore, changes in average temperature will by no means be the whole story. Precipitation patterns will change, with some regions getting much wetter and others much drier. Many modelers also predict more intense storms. Sea levels would rise, with the impact intensified by those storms: coastal flooding, already a major source of natural disasters, would become much more frequent and severe. And there might be drastic changes in the climate of some regions as ocean currents shift. It's always worth bearing in mind that London is at the same latitude as Labrador; without the Gulf Stream, Western Europe would be barely habitable.

While there may be some benefits from a warmer climate, it seems almost certain that upheaval on this scale would make the United States, and the world as a whole, poorer than it would be otherwise. How much poorer? If ours were a preindustrial, primarily agricultural society, extreme climate change would be obviously catastrophic. But we have an advanced economy, the kind that has historically shown great ability to adapt to changed circumstances. If this sounds similar to my argument that the costs of emissions limits would be tolerable, it ought to: the same flexibility that should enable us to deal with a much higher carbon prices should also help us cope with a somewhat higher average temperature.

But there are at least two reasons to take sanguine assessments of the consequences of climate change with a grain of salt. One is that, as I have just pointed out, it's not just a matter of having warmer weather—many of the costs of climate change are likely to result from droughts, flooding and severe storms. The other is that while modern economies may be highly adaptable, the same may not be true of ecosystems. The last time the earth experienced warming at anything like the pace we now expect was during the Paleocene-Eocene Thermal Maximum, about 55 million years ago, when temperatures rose by about 11 degrees Fahrenheit over the course of around 20,000 years (which is a much slower rate than the current pace of warming). That increase was associated with mass extinctions, which, to put it mildly, probably would not be good for living standards.

So how can we put a price tag on the effects of global warming? The most widely quoted estimates, like those in the Dynamic Integrated Model of Climate and the Economy, known as DICE, used by Yale's William Nordhaus and colleagues, depend upon educated guesswork to place a value on the negative effects of global warming in a number of crucial areas, especially agriculture and coastal protection, then try to make some allowance for other possible repercussions. Nordhaus has argued that a global temperature rise of 4.5 degrees Fahrenheit—which used to be the consensus projection for 2100—would reduce gross world product by a bit less than 2 percent. But what would happen if, as a growing number of models suggest, the actual temperature rise is twice as great? Nobody really knows how to make that extrapolation. For what it's worth, Nordhaus's model puts losses from a rise of 9 degrees at about 5 percent of gross world product. Many critics have argued, however, that the cost might be much higher.

Despite the uncertainty, it's tempting to make a direct comparison between the estimated losses and the estimates of what the mitigation policies will cost: climate change will lower gross world product by 5 percent, stopping it will cost 2 percent, so let's go ahead. Unfortunately the reckoning is not that simple for at least four reasons.

First, substantial global warming is already "baked in," as a result of past emissions and because even with a strong climate-change policy the amount of carbon dioxide in the atmosphere is most likely to continue rising for many years. So even if the nations of the world do manage to take on climate change, we will still have to pay for earlier inaction. As a result, Nordhaus's loss estimates may overstate the gains from action.

Second, the economic costs from emissions limits would start as soon as the policy went into effect and under most proposals would become substantial within around 20 years. If we don't act, meanwhile, the big costs would probably come late this century (although some things, like the transformation of the American Southwest into a dust bowl, might come much sooner). So how you compare those costs depends on how much you value costs in the distant future relative to costs that materialize much sooner.

Third, and cutting in the opposite direction, if we don't take action, global warming won't stop in 2100: temperatures, and losses, will continue to rise. So if you place a significant weight on the really, really distant future, the case for action is stronger than even the 2100 estimates suggest.

Finally and most important is the matter of uncertainty. We're uncertain about the magnitude of climate change, which is inevitable, because we're talking about reaching levels of carbon dioxide in the atmosphere not seen in millions of years. . . .

You might think that this uncertainty weakens the case for action, but it actually strengthens it. As Harvard's Martin Weitzman has argued in several influential papers, if there is a significant chance of utter catastrophe, that chance—rather than what is most likely to happen—should dominate cost-benefit calculations. And utter catastrophe does look like a realistic possibility, even if it is not the most likely outcome.

Weitzman argues—and I agree—that this risk of catastrophe, rather than the details of cost-benefit calculations, makes the most powerful case for strong climate policy. . . .

Still that leaves a big debate about the pace of action.

THE RAMP VERSUS THE BIG BANG

Economists who analyze climate policies agree on some key issues. There is a broad consensus that we need to put a price on carbon emissions, that this price must eventually be very high but that the negative economic effects from this policy will be of manageable size. In other words, we can and should act to limit climate change. But there is a ferocious debate among knowledgeable analysts about timing, about how fast carbon prices should rise to significant levels.

On one side are economists who have been working for many years on so-called integrated-assessment models, which combine models of climate change with models of both the damage from global warming and the costs of cutting emissions. For the most part, the message from these economists is a sort of climate version of St. Augustine's famous prayer, "Give me chastity and continence, but not just now." Thus Nordhaus's DICE model says that the price of carbon emissions should eventually rise to more than $200 a ton, effectively more than quadrupling the cost of coal, but that most of that increase should come late this century, with a much more modest initial fee of around $30 a ton. Nordhaus calls this recommendation for a policy that builds gradually over a long period the "climate-policy ramp."

On the other side are some more recent entrants to the field, who work with similar models but come to different conclusions. Most famously, Nicholas Stern, an economist at the London School of Economics, argued in 2006 for quick, aggressive action to limit emissions, which would most likely imply much higher carbon prices. This alternative position doesn't appear to have a standard name, so let me call it the "climate-policy big bang."

I find it easiest to make sense of the arguments by thinking of policies to reduce carbon emissions as a sort of public investment project: you pay a price now and derive benefits in the form of a less-damaged planet later. And by later, I mean much later; today's emissions will affect the amount of carbon in the atmosphere decades, and possibly centuries, into the future. So if you want to assess whether a given investment in emissions reduction is worth making, you have to estimate the damage that an additional ton of carbon in the atmosphere will do, not just this year but for a century or more to come; and you also have to decide how much weight to place on harm that will take a very long time to materialize.

The policy-ramp advocates argue that the damage done by an additional ton of carbon in the atmosphere is fairly low at current concentrations; the cost will not get really large until there is a lot more carbon dioxide in the air, and that won't happen until late this century. And they argue that costs that far in the future should not have a large influence on policy today. They point to market rates of return, which indicate that investors place only a small weight on the gains or losses they expect in the distant future, and argue that public policies, including climate policies, should do the same.

The big-bang advocates argue that government should take a much longer view than private investors. Stern, in particular, argues that policy makers should give the same weight to future generations' welfare as we give to those now living. Moreover, the proponents of fast action hold that the damage from emissions may be much larger than the policy-ramp analyses suggest, either because global temperatures are more sensitive to greenhouse-gas emissions than previously thought or because the economic damage from a large rise in temperatures is much greater than the guesstimates in the climate-ramp models. . . .

Personally, I lean toward the big-bang view. Stern's moral argument for loving unborn generations as we love ourselves may be too strong, but there's a compelling case to be made that public policy should take a much longer view than private markets. Even more important, the policy-ramp prescriptions seem far too much like conducting a very risky experiment with the whole planet. Nordhaus's preferred policy, for example, would stabilize the concentration of carbon dioxide in the atmosphere at a level about twice its preindustrial average. In his model, this would have only modest effects on global welfare; but how confident can we be of that? How sure are we that this kind of change in the environment would not lead to catastrophe? Not sure enough, I'd say, particularly because, as noted above, climate modelers have sharply raised their estimates of future warming in just the last couple of years.

So what I end up with is basically Martin Weitzman's argument: it's the nonnegligible probability of utter disaster that should dominate our policy analysis. And that argues for aggressive moves to curb emissions, soon.

THE POLITICAL ATMOSPHERE

. . . [T]he issue isn't going away. There's a pretty good chance that the record temperatures the world outside Washington has seen so far this year will continue, depriving climate skeptics of one of their main talking points. And in a more general sense, given the twists and turns of American politics in recent years . . . there has to be a real chance that political support for action on climate change will revive.

If it does, the economic analysis will be ready. We know how to limit greenhouse-gas emissions. We have a good sense of the costs—and they're manageable. All we need now is the political will.

18

Capitalism vs. Climate

Naomi Klein*

There is a question from a gentleman in the fourth row.

He introduces himself as Richard Rothschild. He tells the crowd that he ran for county commissioner in Maryland's Carroll County because he had come to the conclusion that policies to combat global warming were actually "an attack on middle-class American capitalism." His question for the panelists, gathered in a Washington, DC, Marriott Hotel in late June, is this: "To what extent is this entire movement simply a green Trojan horse, whose belly is full with red Marxist socioeconomic doctrine?"

Here at the Heartland Institute's Sixth International Conference on Climate Change, the premier gathering for those dedicated to denying the overwhelming scientific consensus that human activity is warming the planet, this qualifies as a rhetorical question. Like asking a meeting of German central bankers if Greeks are untrustworthy. Still, the panelists aren't going to pass up an opportunity to tell the questioner just how right he is.

Chris Horner, a senior fellow at the Competitive Enterprise Institute who specializes in harassing climate scientists with nuisance lawsuits and Freedom of Information fishing expeditions, angles the table mic over to his mouth. "You can believe this is about the climate," he says darkly, "and many people do, but it's not a reasonable belief." Horner, whose prematurely silver hair makes him look like a right-wing Anderson Cooper, likes to invoke Saul Alinsky: "The issue isn't the issue." The issue, apparently, is that "no free society would do to itself what this agenda requires. . . . The first step to that is to remove these nagging freedoms that keep getting in the way."

Claiming that climate change is a plot to steal American freedom is rather tame by Heartland standards. Over the course of this two-day conference, I will learn that Obama's campaign promise to support locally owned biofuels refineries was really about "green communitarianism," akin to the "Maoist" scheme to put "a pig iron furnace in everybody's backyard" (the Cato Institute's Patrick Michaels). That climate change is "a stalking horse for National Socialism" (former Republican senator and retired astronaut Harrison Schmitt). And that environmentalists are like Aztec priests, sacrificing countless people to appease the gods and change the weather (Marc Morano, editor of the denialists' go-to website, ClimateDepot.com).

Most of all, however, I will hear versions of the opinion expressed by the county commissioner in the fourth row: that climate change is a Trojan horse designed to abolish capitalism and replace it with some kind of eco-socialism. As conference speaker Larry Bell succinctly puts it in his new book *Climate of Corruption,* climate change "has little to do with the state of the environment and much to do with shackling capitalism and transforming the American way of life in the interests of global wealth redistribution."

Yes, sure, there is a pretense that the delegates' rejection of climate science is rooted in serious disagreement about the data. And the organizers go to some lengths to mimic credible scientific conferences. . . . But the scientific theories presented here are old and long discredited. And no attempt is made to explain why each speaker seems to contradict the next. (Is there no warming, or is there warming but it's not a problem? And if there is no warming, then what's all this talk about sunspots causing temperatures to rise?)

In truth, several members of the mostly elderly audience seem to doze off while the temperature graphs are projected. They come to life only when the rock stars of the movement take the stage—not the C-team scientists but the A-team ideological warriors like Morano and Horner. This is the true purpose of the gathering: providing a forum for die-hard denialists to collect the rhetorical baseball bats with which they will club environmentalists and climate scientists in the weeks and months to come. The talking points first tested here will jam the comment sections beneath every article and You-Tube video that contains the phrase "climate change" or "global warming." They will also exit the mouths of hundreds of right-wing commentators and politicians—from Republican presidential candidates like Rick Perry and Michele Bachmann all the way down to county commissioners like Richard Rothschild. In an interview outside the sessions, Joseph Bast, president of the Heartland Institute, proudly takes credit for "thousands of articles and op-eds and speeches . . . that were informed by or motivated by somebody attending one of these conferences."

The Heartland Institute, a Chicago-based think tank devoted to "promoting free-market solutions," has been holding these confabs since 2008, sometimes twice a year. And the strategy appears to be working. At the end of day one, Morano—whose claim to fame is having broken the Swift Boat Veterans for Truth story that sank John Kerry's 2004 presidential campaign—leads the gathering through a series of victory laps. Cap and trade: dead! Obama at the Copenhagen summit: failure! The climate movement: suicidal! He even projects a couple of quotes from climate activists beating up on themselves (as progressives do so well) and exhorts the audience to "celebrate!"

There were no balloons or confetti descending from the rafters, but there may as well have been.

When public opinion on the big social and political issues changes, the trends tend to be relatively gradual. Abrupt shifts, when they come, are usually precipitated by dramatic events. Which is why pollsters are so surprised by what has happened to perceptions about climate change over a span of just four years. A 2007 Harris poll found that 71 percent of Americans believed that the continued burning of fossil fuels would cause the climate to change. By 2009 the figure had dropped to 51 percent. In June 2011 the number of Americans who agreed was down to 44 percent—well under half the population. According to Scott Keeter, director of survey research at the Pew Research Center for People and the Press, this is "among the largest shifts over a short period of time seen in recent public opinion history."

Even more striking, this shift has occurred almost entirely at one end of the political spectrum. As recently as 2008 . . . the issue still had a veneer of bipartisan support in the United States. Those days are decidedly over. Today, 70–75 percent of self-identified Democrats and liberals believe humans are changing the climate—a level that has remained stable or risen slightly over the past decade. In sharp contrast, Republicans, particularly Tea Party members, have overwhelmingly chosen to reject the scientific consensus. In some regions, only about 20 percent of self-identified Republicans accept the science.

Equally significant has been a shift in emotional intensity. Climate change used to be something most everyone said they cared about—just not all that much. When Americans were asked to rank their political concerns in order of priority, climate change would reliably come in last.

But now there is a significant cohort of Republicans who care passionately, even obsessively, about climate change—though what they care about is exposing it as a "hoax" being perpetrated by liberals to force them to change their light bulbs, live in Soviet-style tenements and surrender their SUVs. For these right-wingers, opposition to climate change has become as central to their worldview as low taxes, gun ownership and opposition to abortion. Many climate scientists report receiving death threats, as do authors of articles on subjects as seemingly innocuous as energy conservation. (As one letter writer put it to Stan Cox, author of a book critical of air-conditioning, "You can pry my thermostat out of my cold dead hands.")

This culture-war intensity is the worst news of all, because when you challenge a person's position on an issue core to his or her identity, facts and arguments are seen as little more than further attacks, easily deflected. . . .

[T]he effects of the right-wing climate conspiracies reach far beyond the Republican Party. The Democrats have mostly gone mute on the subject, not wanting to alienate independents. And the media and culture industries have followed suit. . . .

This uneasy silence has persisted through the end of the hottest decade in recorded history and yet another summer of freak natural disasters and record-breaking heat worldwide. Meanwhile, the fossil fuel industry is rushing to make multibillion-dollar investments in new infrastructure to extract oil, natural gas and coal from some of the dirtiest and highest-risk sources on the continent (the $7 billion Keystone XL pipeline being only the highest-profile example). In the Alberta tar sands, in the Beaufort Sea, in the gas fields of Pennsylvania and the coalfields of Wyoming and Montana, the industry is betting big that the climate movement is as good as dead. . . .

All of this means that the climate movement needs to have one hell of a comeback. For this to happen, the left is going to have to learn from the right. Denialists gained traction by making climate about economics: action will destroy capitalism, they have claimed, killing jobs and sending prices soaring. But at a time when a growing number of people agree with the protesters at Occupy Wall Street, many of whom argue that capitalism-as-usual is itself the cause of lost jobs and debt slavery, there is a unique opportunity to seize the economic terrain from the right. This would require making a persuasive case that the real solutions to the climate crisis are also our best hope of building a much more enlightened economic system—one that closes deep inequalities, strengthens and transforms the public sphere, generates plentiful, dignified work and radically reins in corporate power. It would also require a shift away from the notion that climate action is just one issue on a laundry list of worthy causes vying for progressive attention. Just as climate denialism has become a core identity issue on the right, utterly entwined with defending current systems of power and wealth, the scientific reality of climate change must, for progressives, occupy a central place in a coherent narrative about the perils of unrestrained greed and the need for real alternatives.

Building such a transformative movement may not be as hard as it first appears. Indeed, if you ask the Heartlanders, climate change makes some kind of left-wing revolution virtually inevitable, which is precisely why they are so determined to deny its reality. Perhaps we should listen to their theories more closely—they might just understand something the left still doesn't get.

The deniers did not decide that climate change is a left-wing conspiracy by un-covering some covert socialist plot. They arrived at this analysis by taking a hard look at what it would take to lower global emissions as drastically and as rapidly as climate science demands. They have concluded that this can be done only by radically reordering our economic and political systems in ways antithetical to their "free market" belief system. As British blogger and Heartland regular James Delingpole has pointed out, "Modern environmentalism successfully advances many of the causes dear to the left: redistribution of wealth, higher taxes, greater government intervention, regulation." Heartland's Bast puts it even more bluntly: For the left, "Climate change is the perfect thing. . . . It's the reason why we should do everything [the left] wanted to do anyway."

Here's my inconvenient truth: they aren't wrong. Before I go any further, let me be absolutely clear: as 97 percent of the world's climate scientists attest, the Heartlanders are completely wrong about the science. The heat-trapping gases released into the atmosphere through the burning of fossil fuels are already causing temperatures to increase. If we are not on a radically different energy path by the end of this decade, we are in for a world of pain.

But when it comes to the real-world consequences of those scientific findings, specifically the kind of deep changes required not just to our energy consumption but to the underlying logic of our economic system, the crowd gathered at the Marriott Hotel may be in considerably less denial than a lot of professional environmentalists, the ones who paint a picture of global warming Armageddon, then assure us that we can avert catastrophe by buying "green" products and creating clever markets in pollution.

The fact that the earth's atmosphere cannot safely absorb the amount of carbon we are pumping into it is a symptom of a much larger crisis, one born of the central fiction on which our economic model is based: that nature is limitless, that we will always be able to find more of what we need, and that if something runs out it can be seamlessly replaced by another resource that we can endlessly extract. But it is not just the atmosphere that we have exploited beyond its capacity to recover—we are doing the same to the oceans, to fresh-water, to topsoil and to biodiversity. The expansionist, extractive mindset, which has so long governed our relationship to nature, is what the climate crisis calls into question so fundamentally. The abundance of scientific research showing we have pushed nature beyond its limits does not just demand green products and market-based solutions; it demands a new civilizational para-digm, one grounded not in dominance over nature but in respect for natural cycles of renewal—and acutely sensitive to natural limits, including the limits of human intelligence.

So in a way, Chris Horner was right when he told his fellow Heartlanders that climate change isn't "the issue." In fact, it isn't an issue at all. Climate change is a message, one that is telling us that many of our culture's most cherished ideas are no longer viable. These are profoundly challenging revelations for all of us raised on Enlightenment ideals of progress, unaccustomed to having our ambitions confined by natural boundaries. And this is true for the statist left as well as the neoliberal right.

While Heartlanders like to invoke the specter of communism to terrify Americans about climate action . . . , the reality is that Soviet-era state socialism was a disaster for the climate. It devoured resources with as much enthusiasm as capitalism, and spewed waste just as recklessly: before the fall of the Berlin Wall, Czechs and Russians had even higher carbon footprints per capita than their counterparts in Britain, Canada and Australia. And while some point to the dizzying expansion of China's renewable energy programs to argue that only centrally controlled regimes can get the green job done, China's command-and-control economy continues to be harnessed to wage an all-out war with nature, through massively disruptive mega-dams, superhighways and extraction-based energy projects, particularly coal.

It is true that responding to the climate threat requires strong government action at all levels. But real climate solutions are ones that steer these interventions to systematically disperse and devolve power and control to the community level, whether through community-controlled renewable energy, local organic agriculture or transit systems genuinely accountable to their users.

Here is where the Heartlanders have good reason to be afraid: arriving at these new systems is going to require shredding the free-market ideology that has dominated the global economy for more than three decades. What follows is a quick-and-dirty look at what a serious climate agenda would mean in the following six arenas: public infrastructure, economic planning, corporate regulation, international trade, consumption and taxation. For hard-right ideologues like those gathered at the Heartland conference, the results are nothing short of intellectually cataclysmic.

1. REVIVING AND REINVENTING THE PUBLIC SPHERE

After years of recycling, carbon offsetting and light bulb changing, it is obvious that individual action will never be an adequate response to the climate crisis. Climate change is a collective problem, and it demands collective action. One of the key areas in which this collective action must take place is big-ticket investments designed to reduce our emissions on a mass scale. That means subways, streetcars and light-rail systems that are not only everywhere but affordable to everyone; energy-efficient affordable housing along those transit lines; smart electrical grids carrying renewable energy; and a massive research effort to ensure that we are using the best methods possible.

The private sector is ill suited to providing most of these services because they require large up-front investments and, if they are to be genuinely accessible to all, some very well may not be profitable. They are, however, decidedly in the public interest, which is why they should come from the public sector. . . .

2. REMEMBERING HOW TO PLAN

In addition to reversing the thirty-year privatization trend, a serious response to the climate threat involves recovering an art that has been relentlessly vilified during these decades of market fundamentalism: planning. Lots and lots of planning. And not just at the national and international levels. Every community in the world needs a plan for how it is going to transition away from fossil fuels, what the Transition Town movement calls an "energy descent action plan." In the cities and towns that have taken this responsibility seriously, the process has opened rare spaces for participatory democracy, with neighbors packing consultation meetings at city halls to share ideas about how to reorganize their communities to lower emissions and build in resilience for tough times ahead.

Climate change demands other forms of planning as well—particularly for workers whose jobs will become obsolete as we wean ourselves off fossil fuels. A few "green jobs" trainings aren't enough. These workers need to know that real jobs will be waiting for them on the other side. That means bringing back the idea of planning our economies based on collective priorities rather than corporate profitability—giving laid-off employees of car plants and coal mines the tools and resources to create jobs, for example, with Cleveland's worker-run green co-ops serving as a model. . . .

3. REINING IN CORPORATIONS

A key piece of the planning we must undertake involves the rapid re-regulation of the corporate sector. Much can be done with incentives: subsidies for renewable energy and responsible land stewardship, for instance. But we are also going to have to get back into the habit of barring outright dangerous and destructive behavior. That means getting in the way of corporations on multiple fronts, from imposing strict caps on the amount of carbon corporations can emit, to banning new coal-fired power plants, to cracking down on industrial feedlots, to shutting down dirty-energy extraction projects like the Alberta tar sands (starting with pipelines like Keystone XL that lock in expansion plans).

Only a very small sector of the population sees any restriction on corporate or consumer choice as leading down Hayek's road to serfdom—and, not coincidentally, it is precisely this sector of the population that is at the forefront of climate change denial.

4. RELOCALIZING PRODUCTION

If strictly regulating corporations to respond to climate change sounds somewhat radical it's because, since the beginning of the 1980s, it has been an article of faith that the role of government is to get out of the way of the corporate sector—and nowhere more so than in the realm of international trade. The devastating impacts of free trade on manufacturing, local business and farming are well known. But perhaps the atmosphere has taken the hardest hit of all. The cargo ships, jumbo jets and heavy trucks that haul raw resources and finished products across the globe devour fossil fuels and spew greenhouse gases. And the cheap goods being produced—made to be replaced, almost never fixed—are consuming a huge range of other nonrenewable resources while producing far more waste than can be safely absorbed. . . .

Climate change does not demand an end to trade. But it does demand an end to the reckless form of "free trade" that governs every bilateral trade agreement as well as the World Trade Organization. This is more good news— for unemployed workers, for farmers unable to compete with cheap imports, for communities that have seen their manufacturers move offshore and their local businesses replaced with big boxes. But the challenge this poses to the capitalist project should not be underestimated: it represents the reversal of the thirty-year trend of removing every possible limit on corporate power.

5. ENDING THE CULT OF SHOPPING

The past three decades of free trade, deregulation and privatization were not only the result of greedy people wanting greater corporate profits. They were also a response to the "stagflation" of the 1970s, which created intense pressure to find new avenues for rapid economic growth. The threat was real: within our current economic model, a drop in production is by definition a crisis—a recession or, if deep enough, a depression, with all the desperation and hardship that these words imply.

This growth imperative is why conventional economists reliably approach the climate crisis by asking the question, How can we reduce emissions while maintaining robust GDP [gross domestic product] growth? The usual answer is "decoupling"—the idea that renewable energy and greater efficiencies will allow us to sever economic growth from its environmental impact. And "green growth" advocates like Thomas Friedman tell us that the process of developing new green technologies and installing green infrastructure can provide a huge economic boost, sending GDP soaring and generating the wealth needed to "make America healthier, richer, more innovative, more productive, and more secure."

But here is where things get complicated. There is a growing body of economic research on the conflict between economic growth and sound climate policy. . . .

The bottom line is that an ecological crisis that has its roots in the overconsumption of natural resources must be addressed not just by improving the efficiency of our economies but by reducing the amount of material stuff we produce and consume. . . .

The way out is to embrace a managed transition to another economic paradigm, using all the tools of planning discussed above. Growth would be reserved for parts of the world still pulling themselves out of poverty. Meanwhile, in the industrialized world, those sectors that are not governed by the drive for increased yearly profit (the public sector, co-ops, local businesses, nonprofits) would expand their share of overall economic activity, as would those sectors with minimal ecological impacts (such as the caregiving professions). A great many jobs could be created this way. But the role of the corporate sector, with its structural demand for increased sales and profits, would have to contract.

So when the Heartlanders react to evidence of human-induced climate change as if capitalism itself were coming under threat, it's not because they are paranoid. It's because they are paying attention.

6. TAXING THE RICH AND FILTHY

About now a sensible reader would be asking, How on earth are we going to pay for all this? The old answer would have been easy: we'll grow our way out of it. Indeed, one of the major benefits of a growth-based economy for elites is that it allows them to constantly defer demands for social justice, claiming that if we keep growing the pie, eventually there will be enough for everyone. That was always a lie, as the current inequality crisis reveals, but in a world hitting multiple ecological limits, it is a nonstarter. So the only way to finance a meaningful response to the ecological crisis is to go where the money is.

That means taxing carbon, as well as financial speculation. It means increasing taxes on corporations and the wealthy, cutting bloated military budgets and eliminating absurd subsidies to the fossil fuel industry. And governments will have to coordinate their responses so that corporations will have nowhere to hide (this kind of robust international regulatory architecture is what Heartlanders mean when they warn that climate change will usher in a sinister "world government").

Most of all, however, we need to go after the profits of the corporations most responsible for getting us into this mess. . . .

Just as tobacco companies have been obliged to pay the costs of helping people to quit smoking, and BP has had to pay for the cleanup in the Gulf of Mexico, it is high time for the "polluter pays" principle to be applied to climate change. Beyond higher taxes on polluters, governments will have to negotiate much higher royalty rates so that less fossil fuel extraction would raise more public revenue to pay for the shift to our postcarbon future (as well as the steep costs of climate change already upon us). Since corporations can be counted on to resist any new rules that cut into their profits, nationalization—the greatest free-market taboo of all—cannot be off the table. . . .

So let's summarize. Responding to climate change requires that we break every rule in the free-market playbook and that we do so with great urgency. We will need to rebuild the public sphere, reverse privatizations, relocalize large parts of economies, scale back overconsumption, bring back long-term planning, heavily regulate and tax corporations, maybe even nationalize some of them, cut military spending and recognize our debts to the global South. Of course, none of this has a hope in hell of happening unless it is accompanied by a massive, broad-based effort to radically reduce the influence that corporations have over the political process. That means, at a minimum, publicly funded elections and stripping corporations of their status as "people" under the law. In short, climate change supercharges the pre-existing case for virtually every progressive demand on the books, binding them into a coherent agenda based on a clear scientific imperative.

More than that, climate change implies the biggest political "I told you so" since Keynes predicted German backlash from the Treaty of Versailles. Marx wrote about capitalism's "irreparable rift" with "the natural laws of life itself," and many on the left have argued that an economic system built on unleashing the voracious appetites of capital would overwhelm the natural systems on which life depends. And of course indigenous peoples were issuing warnings about the dangers of disrespecting "Mother Earth" long before that. The fact that the airborne waste of industrial capitalism is causing the planet to warm, with potentially cataclysmic results, means that, well, the naysayers were right. And the people who said, "Hey, let's get rid of all the rules and watch the magic happen" were disastrously, catastrophically wrong.

There is no joy in being right about something so terrifying. But for progressives, there is responsibility in it, because it means that our ideas—informed by indigenous teachings as well as by the failures of industrial state socialism—are more important than ever. It means that a green-left worldview, which rejects mere reformism and challenges the centrality of profit in our economy, offers humanity's best hope of overcoming these overlapping crises.

But imagine, for a moment, how all of this looks to a guy like Heartland president Bast, who studied economics at the University of Chicago and described his personal calling to me as "freeing people from the tyranny of other people." It looks like the end of the world. It's not, of course. But it is, for all intents and purposes, the end of *his* world. Climate change detonates the ideological scaffolding on which contemporary conservatism rests. There is simply no way to square a belief system that vilifies collective action and venerates total market freedom with a problem that demands collective action on an unprecedented scale and a dramatic reining in of the market forces that created and are deepening the crisis. . . .

NOTE

*This is an excerpt of the article "Capitalism vs. the Climate," originally published in *The Nation* magazine, November 28, 2011 (copyright Naomi Klein).

Section 5 Exercise

What's for Dinner?

Money makes the world go around. This is a truism for many who counsel using economic forces to shape environmental conditions. They recognize that purchasing power can shape production practices and thus influence resource extraction, waste generation, and environmental well-being in general. Such voices also recognize that some buying decisions are better in an environmental sense than others. Buy green and save the planet! There is something to this. Buying and riding a bike is better than buying and driving a car, for instance, in terms of greenhouse-gas emissions, energy use, air and water pollution, and mineral extraction.

Yet there are limits to such individualized decisions. What if the way your city is laid out makes it unsafe to ride a bike? Or what if economic circumstances force you to live far from your job and thus a car is essential for employment? One's ability to make environmentally responsible purchasing decisions then becomes more limited. Furthermore, such choices are challenging in that it is not always clear that one decision is better, in an environmental sense, than another. Paper or plastic bags? Conventional apples from Upstate New York or organic apples from New Zealand? What about moving beyond environmental considerations to take account of the broader economic, political, or social consequences of your purchases?

For this exercise we will explore how economic conditions shape purchasing choices, and the potentials and limitations inherent in voting with your dollars.

Step 1: Plan an environmentally friendly dinner for some of your friends or classmates (and, ideally, host that dinner). Keep a journal where you address the following questions: What did (or will) you buy? Why? How much did cost influence your decisions? How different is your environmentally friendly menu from what you would typically purchase and serve? Also, see if you can flesh out some of the broader environmental implications of your meal. Consider how you got to the store. How was your food prepared, cooked, and served? What people in what places were responsible for growing, processing, transporting, and selling the food that you purchased?

Step 2: In your journal or in a class discussion, consider how much difference taking this action made. How far in a green direction did your purchase move the world?

Step 3: While your purchasing power may have had some impact, it should be clear that any effect was limited. Why? What, then, would it take to engage with economic actors in order to have a wider impact? Could your purchases alone change an individual store? Could they change the food system? What kinds of actions would be needed to change the larger structure in which the store and you are located—global capitalism?

Section 6

Civil Society

In the last two sections we explored environmental governance in the state system and world economy. Civil society is the third realm of governance, and in the following pages we investigate how it shapes environmental affairs. Civil society is the arena wherein we engage in activities that are distinct from our obedience to governmental decrees or economic incentives but that still have public import. The concept of civil society goes back to Aristotle, who used the term *koinōnía politikḗ* to refer to a community that is defined by a set of shared norms and values through which individuals pursue the same goal: common well-being. Civil society, as it is understood today, is the place where we associate with like-minded people and express our concerns; it is where we form groups to practice religion or share in recreational activities; it is where we socialize and engage in cultural life.

Civil society is made up of schools, the media, scientific associations, artist communities, and politically engaged nongovernmental organizations (NGOs) such as Greenpeace, Amnesty International, and Doctors Without Borders. NGOs, in particular, are immensely important to the practice of global environmental politics, and the political roles of NGOs are given a prominent place in the excerpts that make up this section. That said, it is crucial to recognize that the political dimension of civil society is not monopolized by the NGOs, but is evident in the way that all civil-society actors exert power. In this sense, civil society is not simply a realm in which people voluntarily come together; it also serves as an influence on what people think and how they act. The introduction to the preceding section pointed out that individuals respond to a range of economic incentives. Consider now how much we also respond to customs, mores, codes of good conduct, and fashion trends. Think about how our choices of entertainment and friendships, and even our sense of self, are swayed by fads or other cultural movements. The power of culture—both within and across countries—is particularly influential and relevant for understanding global environmental politics.

Civil-society activities depend on bonds between people. Therefore, there has tended to be a geographic dimension to them. People throughout history have interacted most closely with families and immediate neighbors, and lines of connection and webs of affection have tended to be strongest closest to home. The same goes, it should be said, for state and economic action, in that most power in each of these realms has traditionally been directed within the borders of particular countries. However, given globalization, these realms now extend far beyond territorial borders and have become transnational if not global in scope. Thus, today, in addition to there being an *international* state system and *world* economy, there is also a *global* civil society—a realm where people engage in voluntary associations across borders. Because norms, fads, and mores not only whip around the world but also shape the way people think and act, they represent a hugely important form of global environmental governance. How does it shape environmental conditions? How do we find those levers of power strewn throughout the transnational cultural realm that can be employed in the service of global environmental protection?

There are, of course, no straightforward answers. The selections in this section variously applaud, unpack, and problematize the roles of civil-society actors in this increasingly complex global network. The first selection is from entrepreneur and author **Paul Hawken,** an outspoken booster of grassroots environmental action. In this excerpt, from a commencement address, he urges the graduating class to join a growing effort to bring about social and environmental justice that is "unparalleled in history." For Hawken, global civil society is already responding productively to global environmental challenges. It simply needs more active members.

Paul Wapner also finds much promise in the activities of global civil society, but believes that NGOs and other civil-society actors can be more influential if they focus on a particular dimension of civic politics. Many NGOs seek change by lobbying governments or corporations to adopt certain measures. Wapner recognizes the importance of such efforts but argues that NGOs would be even more influential if they deliberately and aggressively aimed at altering the structures of cultural life. Ultimately, he suggests, the manner by which NGOs shape cultural understandings of environmental dilemmas may have more political relevance than state- or corporate-directed forms of NGO engagement. Put differently, Wapner sees the promise of global civil society but believes it can be best realized through more deliberate cultural political efforts.

While Hawken and Wapner recognize the potential of global civil society to shape the environmental condition in positive ways, not all is unproblematic in the world of civic environmental action. Journalist **Johann Hari** offers a biting critique of some of the most important environmental NGOs, claiming that a number of them are far too cozy with the very polluters they are meant to be fighting. Major NGOs, he suggests, have an economic and political stake in maintaining the status quo, such that they work now, at best, as incremental reformers. Hari insists that NGOs should instead be taking a more radical stand to better what he sees as a "broken system."

19

The Power of Environmental Activism

Paul Hawken

When I was invited to give this speech, I was asked if I could give a simple short talk that was "direct, naked, taut, honest, passionate, lean, shivering, startling, and graceful." No pressure there.

Let's begin with the startling part. . . . [Y]ou are going to have to figure out what it means to be a human being on earth at a time when every living system is declining, and the rate of decline is accelerating. Kind of a mind-boggling situation . . . but not one peer-reviewed paper published in the last thirty years can refute that statement. Basically, civilization needs a new operating system, you are the programmers, and we need it within a few decades.

This planet came with a set of instructions, but we seem to have misplaced them. Important rules like don't poison the water, soil, or air, don't let the earth get overcrowded, and don't touch the thermostat have been broken. Buckminster Fuller said that spaceship earth was so ingeniously designed that no one has a clue that we are on one, flying through the universe at a million miles per hour, with no need for seatbelts, lots of room in coach, and really good food—but all that is changing.

There is invisible writing on the back of the diploma you will receive, and in case you didn't bring lemon juice to decode it, I can tell you what it says: You are Brilliant, and the Earth is Hiring. The earth couldn't afford to send recruiters or limos to your school. It sent you rain, sunsets, ripe cherries, night blooming jasmine, and that unbelievably cute person you are dating. Take the hint. And here's the deal: Forget that this task of planet-saving is not possible in the time required. Don't be put off by people who know what is

188

not possible. Do what needs to be done, and check to see if it was impossible only after you are done.

When asked if I am pessimistic or optimistic about the future, my answer is always the same: If you look at the science about what is happening on earth and aren't pessimistic, you don't understand the data. But if you meet the people who are working to restore this earth and the lives of the poor, and you aren't optimistic, you haven't got a pulse. What I see everywhere in the world are ordinary people willing to confront despair, power, and incalculable odds in order to restore some semblance of grace, justice, and beauty to this world. The poet Adrienne Rich wrote, "So much has been destroyed I have cast my lot with those who, age after age, perversely, with no extraordinary power, reconstitute the world." There could be no better description. Humanity is coalescing. It is reconstituting the world, and the action is taking place in schoolrooms, farms, jungles, villages, campuses, companies, refugee camps, deserts, fisheries, and slums.

You join a multitude of caring people. No one knows how many groups and organizations are working on the most salient issues of our day: climate change, poverty, deforestation, peace, water, hunger, conservation, human rights, and more. This is the largest movement the world has ever seen. Rather than control, it seeks connection. Rather than dominance, it strives to disperse concentrations of power. Like Mercy Corps, it works behind the scenes and gets the job done. Large as it is, no one knows the true size of this movement. It provides hope, support, and meaning to billions of people in the world. Its clout resides in idea, not in force. It is made up of teachers, children, peasants, businesspeople, rappers, organic farmers, nuns, artists, government workers, fisherfolk, engineers, students, incorrigible writers, weeping Muslims, concerned mothers, poets, doctors without borders, grieving Christians, street musicians, the President of the United States of America, and as the writer David James Duncan would say, the Creator, the One who loves us all in such a huge way.

There is a rabbinical teaching that says if the world is ending and the Messiah arrives, first plant a tree, and then see if the story is true. Inspiration is not garnered from the litanies of what may befall us; it resides in humanity's willingness to restore, redress, reform, rebuild, recover, reimagine, and reconsider. "One day you finally knew what you had to do, and began, though the voices around you kept shouting their bad advice," is Mary Oliver's description of moving away from the profane toward a deep sense of connectedness to the living world.

Millions of people are working on behalf of strangers, even if the evening news is usually about the death of strangers. This kindness of strangers has religious, even mythic origins, and very specific eighteenth-century roots. Abolitionists were the first people to create a national and global movement to defend the rights of those they did not know. Until that time, no group had filed a grievance except on behalf of itself. The founders of this movement were largely unknown—Granville Clark, Thomas Clarkson, Josiah Wedgwood—and their goal was ridiculous on the face of it: at that time three out of four people in the world were enslaved. Enslaving each other was what human beings had done for ages. And the abolitionist movement was greeted with incredulity. Conservative spokesmen ridiculed the abolitionists as liberals, progressives, do-gooders, meddlers, and activists. They were told they would ruin the economy and drive England into poverty. But for the first time in history a group of people organized themselves to help people they would never know, from whom they would never receive direct or indirect benefit. And today tens of millions of people do this every day. It is called the world of non-profits, civil society, schools, social entrepreneurship, non-governmental organizations, and companies who place social and environmental justice at the top of their strategic goals. The scope and scale of this effort is unparalleled in history.

The living world is not "out there" somewhere, but in your heart. What do we know about life? In the words of biologist Janine Benyus, life creates the conditions that are conducive to life. I can think of no better motto for a future economy. We have tens of thousands of abandoned homes without people and tens of thousands of abandoned people without homes. We have failed bankers advising failed regulators on how to save failed assets. We are the only species on the planet without full employment. Brilliant. We have an economy that tells us that it is cheaper to destroy earth in real time rather than renew, restore, and sustain it. You can print money to bail out a bank but you can't print life to bail out a planet. At present we are stealing the future, selling it in the present, and calling it gross domestic product. We can just as easily have an economy that is based on healing the future instead of stealing it. We can either create assets for the future or take the assets of the future. One is called restoration and the other exploitation. And whenever we exploit the earth we exploit people and cause untold suffering. Working for the earth is not a way to get rich, it is a way to be rich.

The first living cell came into being nearly 40 million centuries ago, and its direct descendants are in all of our bloodstreams. Literally you are breathing molecules this very second that were inhaled by Moses, Mother Teresa, and Bono. We are vastly interconnected. Our fates are inseparable. We are here because the dream of every cell is to become two cells. And dreams come true. In each of you are one quadrillion cells, 90 percent of which are not human cells. Your body is a community, and without those other microorganisms you would perish in hours. Each human cell has 400 billion molecules conducting millions of processes between trillions of atoms. The total cellular activity in one human body is staggering: one septillion actions at any one moment, a one with twenty-four zeros after it. In a millisecond, our body has undergone ten times more processes than there are stars in the universe, which is exactly what Charles Darwin foretold when he said science would discover that each living creature was a "little universe, formed of a host of self-propagating organisms, inconceivably minute and as numerous as the stars of heaven."

So I have two questions for you all: First, can you feel your body? Stop for a moment. Feel your body. One septillion activities going on simultaneously, and your body does this so well you are free to ignore it, and wonder instead when this speech will end. You can feel it. It is called life. This is who you are. Second question: who is in charge of your body? Who is managing those molecules? Hopefully not a political party. Life is creating the conditions that are conducive to life inside you, just as in all of nature. Our innate nature is to create the conditions that are conducive to life. What I want you to imagine is that collectively humanity is evincing a deep innate wisdom in coming together to heal the wounds and insults of the past.

Ralph Waldo Emerson once asked what we would do if the stars only came out once every thousand years. No one would sleep that night, of course. The world would create new religions overnight. We would be ecstatic, delirious, made rapturous by the glory of God. Instead, the stars come out every night and we watch television.

This extraordinary time when we are globally aware of each other and the multiple dangers that threaten civilization has never happened, not in a thousand years, not in ten thousand years. Each of us is as complex and beautiful as all the stars in the universe. We have done great things and we have gone way off course in terms of honoring creation. You are graduating to the most amazing, stupefying challenge ever bequested to any generation. The generations before you failed. They didn't stay up all night. They got distracted and lost sight of the fact that life is a miracle every moment of your existence. Nature beckons you to be on her side. You couldn't ask for a better boss. The most unrealistic person in the world is the cynic, not the dreamer. Hope only makes sense when it doesn't make sense to be hopeful. This is your century. Take it and run as if your life depends on it.

20

Forcing Cultural Change

Paul Wapner

Most scholars ignore the cultural dimension of NGO work either because it seemingly lacks political significance or because alterations in cultural life are difficult to gauge. This article addresses both these concerns in an effort to develop analysis that can more fully appreciate NGO cultural efforts. With regard to the first issue, the article demonstrates that, from the perspective of long-term change, NGO cultural challenges may have more political signifi-cance than direct and obvious forms of political activism and engagement. With regard to the second, notwithstanding formidable methodological challenges, there are ways to measure shifts in broad ideational frameworks—even across borders—and scholars can adopt these in productive ways. The article advances both of these points in an effort to appreciate both the political dimensions of culture and the cultural dimensions of NGO politics. . . .

ENVIRONMENTAL NGOS AND CULTURAL CHANGE

States and firms greatly influence behavior throughout the world and this is the reason why NGOs pressure them to adopt environmentally-friendly poli-cies or procedures. But NGOs direct their efforts at other actors as well. It is in this latter sense that one begins to appreciate the cultural dimension of their work. In addition to states and firms, NGOs try to persuade ordinary citizens throughout the world to care about, and take action to protect, envi-ronmental well-being. Such action involves not only educating people about given problems but also engaging widespread value systems and cultivating new understandings of personal identity. NGOs attempt, in other words, to disseminate an "ecological sensibility" among all people in the hope that this will inspire many to act more responsibly toward the environment. This type of action forms the bulk of their cultural politics.

There is a long, theoretical tradition that sees human beings as fundamentally social animals who need each other and find themselves constituted by social interaction. People adopt ethical and practical orientations toward the world through social experience and are conditioned by the socio-historical context within which they find themselves. Social institutions go by many names. Some refer to them as "discourses," emphasizing the role language plays in constructing social life; others speak of them as "cultural systems," highlighting the patterned and persistent quality of norms, values and symbols that constitute cultural life; still others refer to them as internalized "social fields," drawing attention to the networked relations and distribution of power that shape cultural understandings. Behind all such appellations is the idea that people (and social organizations) are not autonomous entities who can construct lives as they individually see fit. Rather, they are social beings constructed by exterior social forces that condition their view of the world and inform their actions.

The lynchpin behind NGO cultural politics is that social institutions are dynamic and change over time. Moreover, they change not simply as a matter of course, but through the concerted efforts of people seeking new understandings and different social conditions. Finally, they change not only by altering material conditions—as if social institutions were mere superstructural reflections—but also by directly engaging the cultural attributes that constitute them. This entails reformatting, as it were, the ideational codes of conduct, systems of understanding, or ruling discourses of people throughout the world with regard to environmental issues. To be sure, there is nothing straightforward or easy about such a politics. It involves an ability to identify the ideational structures that inform widespread practices and to find ways to manipulate them. Environmental NGOs have found creative ways of doing this.

In parts of Asia, there is a tradition of ingesting wild plants and animals to boost one's health. Because of increasing demand, this tradition threatens particular species and biological diversity more generally. For example, many East Asians believe that the bile from bear gallbladders acts as a health restorative, working as an antidote to liver cancer, hemorrhoids and conjunctivitis. According to the Hong Kong office of the World Wide Fund for Nature, people collect the bile by holding bears in captivity and slowly draining their bile intravenously in a way that keeps the bears alive while still producing enough bile to sell. The widely-held belief that ingesting bear bile provides health benefits threatens bears throughout the world. . . . Similar belief systems threaten tigers, rhinoceros and other living things thought to have health benefits.

Environmental NGOs work to reduce demand for bears, tigers and rhinos by engaging in a host of activities. Many of these involve lobbying states and intervening in international regimes. One of the more impressive efforts along these lines . . . involves NGOs working to strengthen compliance with CITES. Through a special arrangement with the Convention on International Trade in Endangered Species (CITES) Secretariat, NGOs help track the movement of endangered species across borders and provide personnel to investigate possible violations of the treaty. NGOs play an indispensable role through such efforts. Nonetheless, NGOs recognize that this work has its limitations. No matter how stringent international regimes are, if cultural understandings still support the exploitation of endangered species, bears, tigers and other living entities will always be at risk. As a result, NGOs try directly to change cultural practices.

The World Wide Fund for Nature (WWF), for instance, has been engaged in an ongoing dialogue with consumers and medical practitioners throughout East Asia to alter the way they understand endangered species and the necessity of using such species for medicinal purposes. This has involved a dual strategy of, on the one hand, trying to re-acculturate people to different understandings of health and the use of plants and animals, and, on the other, convincing medical practitioners and consumers of the benefits of synthetic substitutes. The first involves changing the ideational context within which some traditional Eastern medicine operates. It aims to persuade people to disbelieve existing medical promises. In this capacity, WWF publicizes medical evidence that contradicts longstanding local ideas. (It also, by the way, publicizes ecological information explaining the biophysical role certain animals play within their environments and their endangered status.) The second entails accommodating that tradition through technological intervention. It tries to assure medical practitioners that synthetic substitutes are functionally equivalent to the original source. The purpose of both strategies is to change the way people understand their own health and the ruling discourses that inform local medicinal practices. As such, both represent attempts to engage the cultural dimension of collective life.

One need not go to the East to discover the impact of cultural forces on environmental affairs. Particular understandings of nature animate all societies and, in an increasingly interdependent world, do so across borders. NGOs try to change or modify such understandings in support of environmental well-being. One of the more obvious efforts along these lines is the ongoing campaign to endear people to certain animals and inspire them to value the preservation of species rather than their consumption. Environmentalists have worked for years to instill such compassion in people for whales, wolves, harp seals, elephants, tigers and so on.

Modern environmentalism cut its teeth on campaigning on behalf of whales. . . . For . . . decades, organizations such as the Sea Shepherds Conservation Society, Friends of the Earth, Greenpeace, WWF and others have tried to change the way people think about and act toward whales. This has involved educating the public about the anthropomorphic qualities of whales and using this link as a way to generate respect and win protection for whales. Activists have done this by, for example, using photographs, films and audio recordings to advertise whales' evident intelligence, gentleness and unique vocalizations now known as whale "songs." Additionally, NGOs have undertaken direct actions to stop the killing of whales in the oceans and have projected images of such actions through the media to the world's publics at large. . . . Due in large measure to NGO efforts, many people throughout the world no longer view whales merely as resources. Indeed, many now see whales in an almost mystical light, deserving a privileged status among large animals. . . .

Environmental NGOs undertake direct action and work to shift cultural understandings in all environmental issue areas. Groups like RAN, Greenpeace, EarthFirst! and Friends of the Earth have been known to parachute from the top of smokestacks, block trains carrying CFCs, float hot-air balloons into nuclear test sites, and scale and unfurl banners on skyscrapers in an effort to bring greater awareness and instill greater concern about environmental issues. Organizations such as Centre for Science and Environment, National Wildlife Federation and the Green Belt Movement publish magazines, support films and host educational enterprises to heighten environmental awareness. Through all these efforts, NGOs work the cultural dimension of global collective life. They manipulate cultural frames of reference to sway public thought and action.

ENVIRONMENTAL NGOS, STATES, ECONOMIC ACTORS AND SOCIAL MORES: CULTURAL POLITICS REVISITED

NGOs identify and manipulate cultural frames of reference in an effort to persuade ordinary citizens throughout the world to adopt environmentalist values. . . . This type of politics takes on additional meaning, however, insofar as states and economic actors are themselves embedded in broad cultural institutions and are thus vulnerable to widespread cultural change. States and economic actors, like individuals, are not static entities with given interests. Rather, they develop identities and concerns over time and in different socio-historical contexts. Put differently, they are constructed and motivated by cultural frames of reference. As a result, their nature, purposes, behavior and self-understanding get redefined as cultural frames themselves change. When NGOs try to shift the terms of cultural reference, then, they are not merely targeting ordinary citizens but are influencing the ideational structure within which states and corporations also operate. NGOs target widely-shared orientations in an attempt to disseminate an ecological sensibility in the broadest and most politically expansive sense of this phrase. They hope that, in so doing, they will manipulate states, economic actors and ordinary people to adopt more ecologically sound practices.

The flip-side of this type of politics is the recognition that states and corporations are not just passive consumers of ideational norms but are themselves active cultural agents. States rule primarily through law backed by force. Most states possess a monopoly of legitimate use of violence within a given territory and this allows them to direct widespread behavior. Such power, however, is not merely material, although it relies on the threat and, at times, use of coercion, but has a cultural dimension to it as well. . . . States, in other words, play a key role in generating cultural institutions.

The same can be said of economic actors. Economic life involves the process of production, distribution, exchange and consumption, and each of these has to do with the way humans materially sustain themselves. However, the activities of production, distribution, and so forth are about more than material survival and the satisfaction of physical needs; they extend into cultural life as well. The way a society produces or exchanges goods, for instance, largely animates the way it understands itself and operates. It gives rise to, or sets the parameters of, certain identities that, in turn, create interests that translate into actual behavior. Economic actors, like states (and individuals and NGOs themselves), are cultural agents. . . .

One can gain a fuller understanding of the cultural dimension of NGO politics by taking seriously the multifaceted character of states, economic actors and individual citizen practices. That each of these engender cultural institutions speaks to the overlaps that exist between different spheres of collective life. Governmental or state activity, for example, at both the domestic and international levels, is neither separate nor immune from economic and cultural dynamics. Rather, in many ways it mirrors the qualities and patterns of economic and cultural activity. One can say the same thing about economic processes and cultural institutions: they are infused with qualities and patterns that animate states and the international state-system. Another way to say this is that the cultural, governmental and economic dimensions of collective life, while analytically distinguishable, cannot be empirically separated. . . .

This interconnectedness helps explain why one can say that NGO cultural politics may be more politically significant than NGO policy efforts. Students of politics have long had what could be called a "cash register" notion of political significance. They notice much political activity though they measure its ultimate meaning in terms of changing state behavior. States are, by most counts, the most important governors of widespread thought and behavior, and the state-system remains the most obvious and effective form of political organization at the international level. As a result, political action becomes effective ultimately when it moves such organizations. The state and the state-system sit at the end of the line like a cash register does in a store, gauging the political value of all that goes before them. Without the register, political action loses importance; without the register, action may be sociologically interesting but politically insignificant. This view greatly skews political analysis.

Scholars nonetheless justify this view by identifying state action with "hard," in contrast to "soft," law and privileging it as a form of effective governance. State directives, policies and programs enjoy the designation of hard law because they possess legal status and can thus be backed up with coercion. Customs, norms, values, principles and the like, that make up cultural life, embody no such status and thus have, theoretically, less of a pull on people's minds and actions. With this distinction in mind, many scholars claim that state laws are not only more powerful than norms but more primary in the sense of generating norms themselves. That is, laws serve as the "base" while values, codes of conduct and shared principles constitute the "superstructure." This orientation clearly privileges state action, regarding it as the *sine qua non* of politics.

An appreciation for cultural politics turns this view on its head, arguing that social mores are more fundamental to social change. Governmental decrees, from this perspective, are not the source of change but are merely reflections of it. Laws and policies arise out of, or give authoritative expression to, norms that already enjoy widespread acceptance. Social mores are primary political agents. This view, in contrast to the one above, sees norms constituting the base of political life with laws being the superstructure.

Obviously, neither of these positions is completely accurate. It thus makes sense to consider at least both factors in political analysis. Indeed, some argue that they are in dialectical relation to each other. As legal scholar Christopher Stone puts it, "in general, laws and cultural norms are mutually reinforcing. Formal laws arise from cultures, and command obedience in proportion to their coherence with fundamental beliefs of the culture. Cultures, however, are not static. Law, and especially the activities of law making and legal reform, are among the forces that contribute to cultural evolution." For my purposes, rather than weigh-in on one side or the other, I want simply to underline the agency that accompanies cultural change and to make the argument that, in the long run, cultural change may be more significant than changes in specific laws or regulations. I qualify my argument by using the word "may" because its persuasiveness turns on one's understanding of how power operates.

Government laws can come and go with different administrations; and cultural codes may shift with the winds of moral fashion. Nonetheless, as numerous social theorists tell us, the governing mechanisms of the latter have a deeper pull on people insofar as they operate in a constitutive rather than a regulative manner. Political scientists are keen on following Weber in saying that power is the ability to get someone to do something against their will. Power, in this sense, rests on the assumption that actors are given entities with stable identities and interests, and denotes an ability to control and dominate such actors. The notion of power behind cultural norms differs from this understanding insofar as it starts with different assumptions and denotes other governing abilities. Cultural norms work with, rather than against, someone's will. Another way of saying this is that norms, values, principles and other cultural expressions work through persuasion and socialization rather than coercion; they enlist subjects in their own subjectification rather than bringing force to bear upon them. The assumption behind this idea of power is that actors are not stable entities with given identities and interests but rather are constantly being constructed in the midst of social interaction. . . .

ASSESSING TRANSNATIONAL CULTURAL CHANGE

Scholars have difficulty appreciating the political effectiveness of NGO cultural efforts because cultural changes are difficult to assess. This is especially
the case with broad, historically significant types of change. How, in fact, can
one notice and measure cultural change? . . .

Students of domestic contentious politics have long distinguished
between social movements and social movement organizations (SMOs). A
movement is a distinct type of social interaction rather than an organization
as such. It refers to a cluster of political practices in which sustained challenge
is mounted against existing power-holders and ruling ideas. A SMO, in contrast, is a discrete organization that mobilizes as an expression of, and to give
expression to, a social movement. SMOs are made-up of volunteers or paid
staff who design, coordinate and carry out explicit public displays of challenge.
In Gamson's phrase, SMOs are "movement carriers."

One can make the same distinction at the global level between transnational social movements and transnational social movement organizations
(TSMOs). TSMOs, like their domestic counterparts, give organizational form
to transnational social movements insofar as they direct public expression
of political challenges. The transnational groups that I have been discussing
throughout this article, such as Greenpeace, WWF, Chipko Movement, Rainforest Action Network and Friends of the Earth are examples of TSMOs. And
their domestic counterparts, such as the Greenbelt Movement, Sierra Club,
Australian Conservation Foundation and Co-op America, represent SMOs
that are tightly networked with TSMOs. All of these are part and parcel with
the environmental movement more generally. That is, each gives expression
to, and is an expression of, the broad challenge environmentalism poses to
power-holders and ruling ideas.

With this in mind, it is possible to chart, if only in broad terms, the cultural effects of environmental NGOs. To do so, one can use what sociologists
call a "fluid" or "public discourse" approach to social change. This orientation
takes the notion of movement seriously and gauges the significance of NGOs'
cultural efforts through the increased codification of the larger movements of
which particular NGOs are a part. It measures and assesses NGO work by
attending to broad cultural expressions that exhibit cognitive, affective, and
evaluative shifts in societies. It concentrates on and tries to measure the impact
of changes in meaning of hitherto uncontested, widespread understandings.
A fluid approach, in other words, interprets NGO efforts by noticing and
analyzing, "cultural drifts," "societal moods," or "public orientations" felt and
expressed by people in diverse ways. These include changes in lifestyle, art,
consumer habits, fashion and so forth.

There are many measures of such change. One of the easiest to appreciate
is, what Gamson, Giugni, Hanagan and others call "incorporation." This refers
to the assimilation or institutionalization of movement actors or ideas into

existing social arrangements. Social movements begin as criticisms of the exist-ing order. They take issue with or see an injustice in particular contemporary circumstances. As such, they arise at the margins of society and hold grievances against what is considered mainstream. Initially, many movements are seen as illegitimate in the sense that they complain against what others take to be right, proper, just or appropriate. They gain legitimacy as society sympathizes with their critique and the positions they advance become part of mainstream culture. This is not always obvious insofar as observers often have a hard time noticing new ideas before they become part and parcel of everyday life.

One sees incorporation of environmentalism to the degree that certain environmentalist phrases and ideals have become part of mainstream public life throughout the world. When the modern environmental movement emerged in the 1960s and 1970s, people worried about industrial pollution, dwindling resources and other challenges to the First World. Environmental concern was considered a luxury issue that only the wealthier nations could address. Given that one needs to eat before one can worry about, for example, stratospheric ozone depletion, environmentalism was very much a First World concern. Indeed, at the 1972 United Nations Conference on the Human Environment (UNCHE), the first large-scale international meeting to address environmen-tal issues, only two developing countries sent heads of state and discussions focused primarily on the environmental threats faced by industrialized states.

Shortly after UNCHE, a whole new breed of environmentalism emerged. It became increasingly clear that environmental protection was not a luxury to be pursued only by the wealthy. Many recognized, for example, that poverty is its own form of environmental degradation, as the poor rightfully exploit the environment to meet basic needs. Others acknowledged that population control and pollution-reducing technologies emerge in affluent societies and thus to protect the environment throughout the world entails promoting some type of economic growth to the poorest nations of the world. Still others saw that the wealthy do, in fact, generate the bulk of the world's environmental harm and thus feared that, as Third World states developed, they would place greater burdens on the earth's ecosystems. These types of concerns led many to explore the linkages between economic development and environmental protection.

In the mid-1970s, the idea of "sustainable development" emerged as an answer to this quest. First used in the Cocoyo declaration on environment and development, and then later given greater exposure by the International Union for the Conservation of Nature and Natural Resources (IUCN) in its 1980 World Conservation Strategy, the term came clearly into its own when the World Commission on Environment and Development made the idea famous with its publication of *Our Common Future*. The Commission defined the term as meeting the needs of the present generation without compromising the ability of future generations to meet their needs and advertised it as the central approach to environmental protection. The idea of sustainable devel-opment provided the fundamental framework for the 1992 United Nations

Conference on Environment and Development (UNCED) and continues to inform almost all environmental and development thought and action. Indeed, one cannot conceptualize environmental issues anymore without direct and constant reference to the idea of sustainable development.

The widespread acceptance of the term sustainable development provides one indication of the environmental movement's incorporation into mainstream society. NGOs such as IUCN worked hard to promote the idea, which includes a critique of contemporary business as usual and an ideal of how to proceed. The term, as such, is really an invention of environmentalists and, although it has been used to support policies and projects that many environmentalists find abhorrent, its widespread usage indicates some form of successful cultural change. It indicates a change in meaning in both the ideas of development and environmental protection and thus represents a cultural shift or alteration in public discourse.

A second and related indication of incorporation has to do with a shift in the "balance of legitimacy." Like other movements, the modern environmental one emerged as a marginal voice in public life. Until the 1960s, much of the industrialized world was pleased with the gifts of science and engineering, and held great faith in technological progress. "Better living through chemistry" was a mantra of the 1950s and early 1960s, with the synthetic revolution revamping everyday life by increasing comfort, security and convenience. The environmental movement arose partly as a critique of the synthetic revolution. Early modern environmentalists questioned the engines and ultimate character of industrialized society as modern life bulldozed forests, polluted rivers and streams, created air pollution and threatened supplies of natural resources. While this voice had its predecessors in earlier thinkers, it emerged in the mid-1960s as a new movement that, along with the anti-war movement in the US and student protest movement in Europe, questioned social authority. As such, it was primarily a youth-based movement expressing the criticisms and dreams of a marginal group in society.

Throughout the 1980s and 1990s, this changed dramatically. Many more people now express concern about environmental quality; in fact, people from various age groups claim that they are willing to make personal economic sacrifices to enjoy better environmental conditions and express deep commitments to environmental protection. Even more striking is that this trend exists throughout the world. Pollsters have found that people in both the North and South know and express concern about environmental issues, and share a willingness to make personal financial sacrifices to improve environmental quality.

Indications of environmental movement incorporation go well beyond opinion polls. Environmentalism has become mainstream. It informs fashion, music, art and literature. Moreover, being "green," as it were, is now almost a prerequisite of high-minded citizenship and has become an informal litmus test for politicians. One can no longer, for example, claim openly to be anti-environmental and hope to gain much support. The mainstreaming of environmentalism is so pervasive that many worry about the critical challenge of the movement itself. A number of scholars now argue that environmental-ism has been so integrated into societies throughout the world that its critical messages have been co-opted and thus are no longer effective. Surely such worry indicates successful incorporation even if it raises concern about the continued potential of the movement inducing change.

A related indicator of incorporation goes beyond the appropriation of values and orientations of the environmental movement to encompass the ac-ceptance of environmental NGOs themselves into the formal political process. The proliferation of Green parties and their formal incorporation into polities throughout the world underscores how far environmentalism has come over the past few decades. Moreover, many green parties emerged out of specific envi-ronmental NGOs. And, that these groups now find organizational expression in the formal political process demonstrates that the framework for political acceptability has changed in terms of both supporters of these parties and their official recognition. This represents a significant cultural shift.

In addition to gaining legitimacy as political parties, environmental NGOs have also acquired much respect as "interest mediators." Many envi-ronmental NGOs are seen as reliable intermediaries to channel widespread concern and to cooperate with states, IGOs and multilateral organizations in the area of environmental quality. Put differently, environmental NGOs have become significant partners in environmental governance. States look to them for their scientific expertise and their abilities to network with multiple actors throughout societies and thus to be effective mechanisms for promoting certain actions on behalf of environmental well-being. (It should be noted that some critics acknowledge this and find it troubling.) Political incorporation provides an imperfect but nonetheless significant benchmark for witnessing the effects of NGO efforts. Focusing upon it, then, provides partial evidence of the success of environmental NGO cultural politics. . . .

This article explores the cultural dimension of environmental NGO politics. It describes those NGO activities that target the constitutive quality of norms, values and predispositions in an effort to use cultural attributes as levers for political change. NGOs assume that, while cultural life is tightly woven into all aspects of collective life, it can also be manipulated in the sense of political change. . . .

Protecting the global environment is an immense challenge that calls for discovering and enlisting multiple mechanisms of governance. NGOs work for global environmental protection by lobbying states, pressuring corporations and engaging social mores. Scholars have long dismissed this last element because it is too difficult to address analytically and to work with methodologically. This article attempts to alleviate some of those problems. Normatively, the hope is that by clarifying this type of politics, scholars will devote more effort to understanding it and practitioners will more self-consciously undertake it.

21

The Wrong Kind of Green

Johann Hari

Why did America's leading environmental groups jet to Copenhagen and lobby for policies that will lead to the faster death of the rainforests—and runaway global warming? Why are their lobbyists on Capitol Hill dismissing the only real solutions to climate change as "unworkable" and "unrealistic," as though they were just another sooty tentacle of Big Coal?

At first glance, these questions will seem bizarre. Groups like Conservation International are among the most trusted "brands" in America, pledged to protect and defend nature. Yet as we confront the biggest ecological crisis in human history, many of the green organizations meant to be leading the fight are busy shoveling up hard cash from the world's worst polluters—and burying science-based environmentalism in return. . . .

I have spent the past few years reporting on how global warming is remaking the map of the world. I have stood in half-dead villages on the coast of Bangladesh. . . . I have stood on the edges of the Arctic and watched glaciers that have existed for millenniums crash into the sea. I have stood on the borders of dried-out Darfur and heard refugees explain, "The water dried up, and so we started to kill each other for what was left."

While I witnessed these early stages of ecocide, I imagined that American green groups were on these people's side in the corridors of Capitol Hill, trying to stop the Weather of Mass Destruction. But it is now clear that many were on a different path—one that began in the 1980s, with a financial donation.

Environmental groups used to be funded largely by their members and wealthy individual supporters. They had only one goal: to prevent environmental destruction. Their funds were small, but they played a crucial role in saving vast tracts of wilderness and in pushing into law strict rules forbidding air and water pollution. But Jay Hair—president of the National Wildlife Federation from 1981 to 1995—was dissatisfied. He identified a huge new source of revenue: the worst polluters.

Hair found that the big oil and gas companies were happy to give money to conservation groups. Yes, they were destroying many of the world's pristine places. Yes, by the late 1980s it had become clear that they were dramatically destabilizing the climate—the very basis of life itself. But for Hair, that didn't make them the enemy; he said they sincerely wanted to right their wrongs and pay to preserve the environment. He began to suck millions from them, and in return his organization and others, like The Nature Conservancy (TNC), gave them awards for "environmental stewardship."

Companies like Shell and British Petroleum (BP) were delighted. They saw it as valuable "reputation insurance": every time they were criticized for their massive emissions of warming gases, or for being involved in the killing of dissidents who wanted oil funds to go to the local population, or an oil spill that had caused irreparable damage, they wheeled out their shiny green awards, purchased with "charitable" donations, to ward off the prospect of government regulation. At first, this behavior scandalized the environmental community. Hair was vehemently condemned as a sellout and a charlatan. But slowly, the other groups saw themselves shrink while the corporate-fattened groups swelled—so they, too, started to take the checks.

Christine MacDonald, an idealistic young environmentalist, discovered how deeply this cash had transformed these institutions when she started to work for Conservation International in 2006. She told me, "About a week or two after I started, I went to the big planning meeting of all the organization's media teams, and they started talking about this supposedly great new project they were running with BP. But I had read in the newspaper the day before that the EPA [Environmental Protection Agency] had condemned BP for running the most polluting plant in the whole country. . . . But nobody in that meeting, or anywhere else in the organization, wanted to talk about it. It was a taboo. You weren't supposed to ask if BP was really green. They were 'helping' us, and that was it."

She soon began to see . . . how this behavior has pervaded almost all the mainstream green organizations. They take money, and in turn they offer praise, even when the money comes from the companies causing environmental devastation. To take just one example, when it was revealed that many of IKEA's dining room sets were made from trees ripped from endangered forests, the World Wildlife Fund leapt to the company's defense, saying—wrongly—that IKEA "can never guarantee" this won't happen. Is it a coincidence that WWF is a "marketing partner" with IKEA, and takes cash from the company?

Likewise, the Sierra Club was approached in 2008 by the makers of Clorox bleach, who said that if the Club endorsed their new range of "green" household cleaners, they would give it a percentage of the sales. The Club's Corporate Accountability Committee said the deal created a blatant conflict of interest—but took it anyway. Executive director Carl Pope defended the move in an e-mail to members, in which he claimed that the organization had carried out a serious analysis of the cleaners to see if they were "truly superior." But it hadn't. The Club's Toxics Committee co-chair, Jessica Frohman, said, "We never approved the product line." Beyond asking a few questions, the committee had done nothing to confirm that the product line was greener than its competitors' or good for the environment in any way.

The green groups defend their behavior by saying they are improving the behavior of the corporations. But as these stories show, the pressure often flows the other way: the addiction to corporate cash has changed the green groups at their core. As MacDonald says, "Not only do the largest conservation groups take money from companies deeply implicated in environmental crimes; they have become something like satellite PR offices for the corporations that support them." . . .

This pattern was bad enough when it affected only a lousy household cleaning spray, or a single rare forest. But today, the stakes are unimaginably higher. We are living through a brief window of time in which we can still prevent runaway global warming. We have emitted so many warming gases into the atmosphere that the world's climate scientists say we are close to the climate's "point of no return." Up to 2 degrees Celsius of warming, all sorts of terrible things happen—we lose the islands of the South Pacific, we set in train the loss of much of Florida and Bangladesh, terrible drought ravages central Africa—but if we stop the emissions of warming gases, we at least have a fifty-fifty chance of stabilizing the climate at this higher level. This is already an extraordinary gamble with human safety, and many climate scientists say we need to aim considerably lower: 1.5 degrees or less.

Beyond 2 degrees, the chances of any stabilization at the hotter level begin to vanish, because the earth's natural processes begin to break down. The huge amounts of methane stored in the Arctic permafrost are belched into the atmosphere, causing more warming. The moist rainforests begin to dry out and burn down, releasing all the carbon they store into the air, and causing more warming. These are "tipping points": after them, we can't go back to the climate in which civilization evolved.

So in an age of global warming, the old idea of conservation—that you preserve one rolling patch of land, alone and inviolate—makes no sense. If the biosphere is collapsing all around you, you can't ring-fence one lush stretch of greenery and protect it: it too will die.

You would expect the American conservation organizations to be joining the great activist upsurge demanding we stick to a safe level of carbon dioxide in the atmosphere: 350 parts per million (ppm), according to professor and NASA climatologist James Hansen. And—in public, to their members—they often are supportive. On its website the Sierra Club says, "If the level stays higher than 350 ppm for a prolonged period of time . . . it will spell disaster for humanity as we know it."

But behind closed doors, it sings from a different song-sheet. Kieran Suckling, executive director of the Center for Biological Diversity, in Arizona, which refuses funding from polluters, has seen this from the inside. He told me, "There is a gigantic political schizophrenia here. The Sierra Club will send out e-mails to its membership saying we have to get to 350 parts per million and the science requires it. But in reality they fight against any sort of emission cuts that would get us anywhere near that goal."

For example, in 2009 the EPA moved to regulate greenhouse gases under the Clean Air Act, which requires the agency to ensure that the levels of pollutants in the air are "compatible with human safety"—a change the Sierra Club supported. But the Center for Biological Diversity petitioned the EPA to take this commitment seriously and do what the climate science says really is "compatible with human safety": restore us to 350 ppm. Suckling explains, "I was amazed to discover the Sierra Club opposed us bitterly. They said it should not be done. In fact, they said that if we filed a lawsuit to make EPA do it, they would probably intervene on EPA's side. They threw climate science out the window."

Indeed, the Sierra Club's chief climate counsel, David Bookbinder, ridiculed the center's attempts to make 350 ppm a legally binding requirement. He said it was "truly a pointless exercise" and headed to "well-deserved bureaucratic oblivion"—and would only add feebly that "350 may be where the planet should end up," but not by this mechanism. He was quoted in the media alongside Bush administration officials who shared his contempt for the center's proposal.

Why would the Sierra Club oppose a measure designed to prevent environmental collapse? The Club didn't respond to my requests for an explanation. Climate scientists are bemused. When asked about this, Hansen said, "I find the behavior of most environmental NGOs to be shocking. . . . I [do] not want to listen to their lame excuses for their abominable behavior." It is easy to see why groups like Conservation International, which take money from Big Oil and Big Coal, take backward positions. Their benefactors will lose their vast profits if we make the transition away from fossil fuels—so they fall discreetly silent when it matters. But while the Sierra Club accepts money from some corporations, it doesn't take cash from the very worst polluters. So why is it, on this, the biggest issue of all, just as bad?

It seems its leaders have come to see the world through the funnel of the US Senate and what legislation it can be immediately coaxed to pass. They say there is no point advocating a strategy that senators will reject flat-out. They have to be "politically realistic" and try to advocate something that will appeal to Blue Dog Democrats.

This focus on inch-by-inch reform would normally be understandable: every movement for change needs a reformist wing. But the existence of tipping points—which have been overwhelmingly proven by the climate science—makes a mockery of this baby-steps approach to global warming. If we exceed the safe amount of warming gases in the atmosphere, then the earth will release its massive carbon stores and we will have runaway warming. After that, any cuts we introduce will be useless. You can't jump halfway across a chasm: you still fall to your death. It is all or disaster.

By definition, if a bill can pass through today's corrupt Senate, then it will not be enough to prevent catastrophic global warming. Why? Because the bulk of the Senate—including many Democrats—is owned by Big Oil and Big Coal. They call the shots with their campaign donations. Senators will not defy their benefactors. So if you call only for measures the Senate could pass tomorrow, you are in effect giving a veto over the position of the green groups to the fossil fuel industry.

Yet the "conservation" groups in particular believe they are being hard-headed in adhering to the "political reality" that says only cuts far short of the climate science are possible. They don't seem to realize that in a conflict between political reality and physical reality, physical reality will prevail. The laws of physics are more real and permanent than any passing political system. You can't stand at the edge of a rising sea and say, "Sorry, the swing states don't want you to happen today. Come back in fifty years."

A classic case study of this inside-the-Beltway mentality can be found in a blog written by David Donniger, policy director of the climate center at the Natural Resources Defense Council (NRDC), after the collapse of the Copenhagen climate summit. The summit ended with no binding agreement for any country to limit its emissions of greenhouse gases, and a disregard of the scientific targets. Given how little time we have, this was shocking. Donniger was indeed furious—with the people who were complaining. He decried the "howls of disaster in European media, and rather tepid reviews in many U.S. stories." He said people were "holding the accord to standards and expectations that no outcome achievable at Copenhagen could reasonably have met—or even should have met."

This last sentence is very revealing. Donniger believes it is "reasonable" to act within the constraints of the US and global political systems, and un-reasonable to act within the constraints of the climate science. The greens, he suggests, are wrong to say their standards should have been met at this meet-ing; the deal is "not weak." After fifteen climate summits, after twenty years of increasingly desperate scientific warnings about warming, with the tipping points drawing ever closer, he says the world's leaders shouldn't be on a faster track and that the European and American media should stop whining. Re-member, this isn't an oil company exec talking; this is a senior figure at one of the leading environmental groups.

There is a different way for green groups to behave. If the existing political system is so corrupt that it can't maintain basic human safety, they should be encouraging their members to take direct action to break the Big Oil deadlock. This is precisely what has happened in Britain—and it has worked. Direct-action protesters have physically blocked coal trains and new airport runways . . . and as a result, airport runway projects that looked certain are falling by the wayside, and politicians have become very nervous about authorizing any new coal power plants. The more mainstream British climate groups are not reluctant to condemn the Labour government's environmental failings in the strongest possible language. Compare the success of this direct confrontation with the utter failure of the US groups' work-within-the-system approach. As James Hansen has pointed out, the British model offers real hope rather than false hope. . . .

By pretending the broken system can work—and will work, in just a moment, after just one more Democratic win, or another, or another—the big green groups are preventing the appropriate response from concerned citizens, which is fury at the system itself. They are offering placebos to calm us down when they should be conducting and amplifying our anger at this betrayal of our safety by our politicians. The US climate bills are long-term plans: they lock us into a woefully inadequate schedule of carbon cuts all the way to 2050. So when green groups cheer them on, they are giving their approval to a path to destruction—and calling it progress. . . .

How do we retrieve a real environmental movement, in the very short time we have left? Charles Komanoff, who worked as a consultant for the Natural Resources Defense Council for thirty years, says, "We're close to a civil war in the environmental movement. For too long, all the oxygen in the room has been sucked out by this beast of these insider groups, who achieve almost nothing. . . . We need to create new organizations that represent the fundamentals of environmentalism and have real goals."

Some of the failing green groups can be reformed from within. The Sierra Club is a democratic organization, with the leadership appointed by its members. There are signs that members are beginning to put the organization right after the missteps of the past few years. Carl Pope is being replaced by Mike Brune, formerly of the Rainforest Action Network—a group much more aligned with the radical demands of the climate science. But other organizations—like Conservation International and TNC—seem incapable of internal reform and simply need to be shunned. They are not part of the environmental movement: they are polluter-funded leeches sucking on the flesh of environmentalism, leaving it weaker and depleted.

Already, shining alternatives are starting to rise up across America. . . . [T]he brilliant 350.org has formed a huge network of enthusiastic activists who are demanding our politicians heed the real scientific advice—not the parody of it offered by the impostors. They have to displace the corrupt conservationists as the voice of American environmentalism, fast.

This will be a difficult and ugly fight, when we need all our energy to take on the forces of ecocide. But these conservation groups increasingly resemble the forces of ecocide draped in a green cloak. If we don't build a real, unwavering environmental movement soon, we had better get used to a new sound—of trees crashing down and an ocean rising, followed by the muffled, private applause of America's "conservationists."

Section 6 Exercise

Unpacking the NGO World and Taking Action

OPTION 1

Environmental NGOs focus on a wide range of different issues and adopt various strategies for advancing global environmental protection. Furthermore, some utilize conventional means of political persuasion while others employ more radical methods. This exercise invites you to become familiar with the array of environmental NGOs and analyze the strategic quality of their efforts.

Visit the websites of three environmental NGOs. These can be large, established ones that work globally (like Greenpeace, Friends of the Earth, or World Wildlife Fund) or smaller ones that focus on more local issues (like Anacostia Watershed Society, Appalachian Voices, or National Black Environmental Justice Network). Write a short description of each, explaining the issues they focus on and the strategies each employs. How does each group work for political change? Do they, for instance, lobby government officials, pressure corporations, seek to change cultural understandings, undertake specific projects, or model appropriate lifestyle change?

Next, choose one organization that particularly appeals to you and write a cover letter seeking a job or internship. (Consult the website to address the letter to a particular person at the organization—the head of either the human resources department or the particular section of the organization for which you would like to work.)

In your letter, answer the following questions. What is it about the NGO's focus and orientation that fits with your own outlook? What special skills do you offer that would be valuable to the organization? In what specific ways do you imagine contributing to the NGO's work?

OPTION 2 (FOR THE AMBITIOUS)

Pull together a group of four or five people. Collectively, identify one issue that you think is particularly important to the sustainability of your campus or community. Next, consider possible actions that can better the situation. Come up with a plan of action on that issue over the course of a semester or quarter. Then go to work implementing your plan.

You'll need to ask some focused questions of one another and others on your campus as you construct your action steps. For instance, you'll need to ask what's already being done to advance sustainability on the campus. Who are the chief players, and who among those players is most influential? What student groups are advancing sustainability and what administrative initiatives are in the works? What forms of action are likely to be most meaningful and impactful on your particular campus? How can your efforts link up with the efforts of others on your campus or in the wider world? What kinds of resources and support will you need to bring about the kinds of change you wish to see?

Once your sustainability initiative is completed (whether successful or not), write up the story of your effort and seek to have it published in your school newspaper, in a relevant newsletter, or on a relevant blog.

Section 7

Race, Class, and Geopolitical Difference

The preceding three sections examined the state, economy, and civil society as separate but overlapping domains that contribute to global environmental governance. Throughout our treatment, we have assumed that people and organizations come together in each of these realms as equals. That is, when speaking about states, we failed to differentiate between powerful and weak ones. In discussing the economy, we spoke as if all consumers have equal access to the market and as if corporations are equal in their environmental impact. Likewise, in discussing global civil society, we have assumed that the realm is open to all bidders, no matter one's social position.

The world, however, is not a place of equals; inequality reigns. Inequality expresses itself as people experience unfair treatment because of their economic status, racial identity, gender, or sexual orientation. Furthermore, this takes on global proportions as states, corporations, and nongovernmental actors with the most power have an outsized influence on global environmental relations. In this section we examine difference directly and seek to understand how it structures environmental harm and governance.

While it is true that nation-states are sovereign in the eyes of international law, unequal distribution of power makes clear that some states are "more sovereign" than others and have a greater ability to shape international affairs. Nowhere is this more obvious than in the North-South divide. The North, which consists of the developed world, has a disproportional amount of economic and military might, and this enables it to advance its interests and visions. The South, which consists of the developing world, is relatively poor in sheer economic and military power, and thus often must accommodate itself to the designs and preferences of the North.

This divide is not simply about the ability to get one's way. It also depicts fundamentally different views of the problem toward which global environmental governance must direct itself. For many in the North, global environmental issues are about the degradation of the planet's ecosystems—the quality of air, water, soil, and so forth—something for which everybody is responsible. In contrast, for many in the South, global environmental issues are about people's unequal access to resources and the material privation of the world's poor—something that stems primarily from the selfish actions of the world's rich countries. India's former prime minister Indira Gandhi famously said that "poverty is the worst form of pollution." She was pointing out how the unwillingness of the international community to join together to meet basic human needs is the most shameful type of assault, and how poverty stands at the center of much environmental degradation.

Moreover, the poor, because they lack political power, are often on the receiving end of the world's environmental harms. Poor communities serve as waste dumps for toxic substances from the world's wealthy regions; the problems associated with climate change fall in an outsized way on the poor; and so forth. This is why, for Gandhi and others, development represents the key to environmental well-being. Environmentalism, in other words, must aim to lift up the impoverished. For some, this means that economic growth must proceed at any cost. These "market optimists" believe that more aggregate wealth brings about more opportunities for tackling the world's environmental problems. For others, finding a way to protect the environment while also enabling the global poor to live decent lives entails curtailing the excessive consumption of the global rich. Anything else, suggests this line of reasoning, is morally and pragmatically suspect.

Since the mid-1980s the international community has tried to marry the South's call for development with the North's concern for ecology via the idea of "sustainable development." Sustainable development, as the World Commission on Environment and Development made clear in a famous report published in 1987, titled *Our Common Future,* involves "meet[ing] the needs of the present without compromising the ability of future generations to meet their own needs." It stands on three legs: economic development, environmental protection, and social justice—or economy, ecology, and equity. Country representatives met in Rio de Janeiro in 1992 for the United Nations Conference on Environment and Development, again in Johannesburg in 2002 for the World Summit on Sustainable Development, and yet again in Rio for the 2012 United Nations Conference on Sustainable Development. In each of these meetings and through myriad additional efforts, states, corporations, activist organizations, and other groups have worked to figure out and give expression to sustainable development. To be sure, there remains no consensus on how to marry ecology, economy, and equity, but sustainable development remains a central informing aspiration of global environmental governance.

The following selections provide insight into the challenges of sustainable development and the entire issue of inequality in global environmental affairs. We begin with economist **Herman E. Daly**, who introduces the idea that economic growth without concern for ecological limits is the epitome of unsustainability. For too long, the world has equated development with growth and has assumed that, as long as economies are growing, societies are developing. Daly challenges this view. He explains that development is not about getting economically bigger, but rather socially better. This is good news since, according to Daly, the world cannot afford (ecologically) to keep materially growing—in the sense of using more and more resources—but certainly can and must embrace forms of economic activity that improve the quality of life. Daly explains how the global North and South can pursue meaningful sustainable development.

Jonathan Rowe continues this discussion by asking a fundamental question: What is an economy for? He shows that current ways of measuring development and growth tend to encourage investment in the wrong kinds of goods and services, and ultimately support forms of exchange that continually exploit the underprivileged and the nonhuman world.

The inequalities that mark the struggle for sustainable development express themselves in the way the international community addresses global environmental problems. Philosopher **Peter Singer** sheds light on this by explaining what a fair agreement for addressing climate change would look like. He suggests that all people have a right to the atmosphere and thus any fair agreement must call upon the richest and most developed nations—those who have contributed most to the buildup of greenhouse gases—to take the lead in reducing emissions and help less developed countries adapt to climate change.

Indian researchers and activists **Anil Agarwal** and **Sunita Narain** make Singer's case in a classic article that argues for global climate equity. The crux of their argument is that countries have vastly different populations in terms of both numbers of people and percentage of the world's poor. For instance, the United States currently has around 4.5% of the world's people yet produces close to 18% of the world's emissions of carbon dioxide. Meanwhile, India, with 17% of the global population, is responsible for just 5.5% of the world's carbon dioxide emissions. Furthermore, there are many more poor people in India than in the United States. Thus, it is unfair to measure global carbon emissions along the lines of individual countries—an almost universal practice (typified by measurements presented by the World Resources Institute in Agarwal and Narain's article). Rather, fairness requires apportioning climate rights and responsibilities on a per capita basis and distinguishing between "luxury" emissions (coming from cars and factories) and "survival" emissions (associated with growing rice and other agricultural activities). To not do so is to deepen global inequalities and move the world further along an unsustainable path.

This section's final selection, by sociologist **Robert Bullard**, shows that inequality and injustice take place not only between countries and the world's rich and poor, but also within states and along racial lines. Focusing on the United States, Bullard demonstrates that minorities suffer the brunt of environmental harm. They disproportionately live in neighborhoods with higher levels of water and air pollution, toxic industries, and dangerous facilities such as garbage incinerators. This doesn't happen as a matter of course, but rather is fully in line with a history of internal colonialism and racism, and suggests that environmental well-being will never fully be realized until we learn to share the burdens of industrial society and stop racist practices of dumping on the most vulnerable.

22

The Delusion of Sustainable Growth

Herman E. Daly

Impossibility statements are the very foundation of science. It is impossible to: travel faster than the speed of light; create or destroy matter-energy; build a perpetual motion machine, etc. By respecting impossibility theorems we avoid wasting resources on projects that are bound to fail. Therefore economists should be very interested in impossibility theorems, especially the one to be demonstrated here, namely that it is impossible for the world economy to grow its way out of poverty and environmental degradation. In other words, sustainable growth is impossible.

In its physical dimensions the economy is an open subsystem of the earth ecosystem, which is finite, nongrowing, and materially closed. As the economic subsystem grows it incorporates an ever greater proportion of the total ecosystem into itself and must reach a limit at 100 percent, if not before. Therefore its growth is not sustainable. The term "sustainable growth" when applied to the economy is a bad oxymoron—self-contradictory as prose, and unevocative as poetry.

CHALLENGING THE ECONOMIC OXYMORON

Economists will complain that growth in GNP [gross national product] is a mixture of quantitative and qualitative increase and therefore not strictly subject to physical laws. They have a point. Precisely because quantitative and qualitative change are very different it is best to keep them separate and call them by the

215

different names already provided in the dictionary. To grow means "to increase naturally in size by the addition of material through assimilation or accretion." To develop means "to expand or realize the potentialities of; to bring gradually to a fuller, greater, or better state." When something grows it gets bigger. When something develops it gets different. The earth ecosystem develops (evolves), but does not grow. Its subsystem, the economy, must eventually stop growing, but can continue to develop. The term "sustainable development" therefore makes sense for the economy, but only if it is understood as "development without growth"—i.e., qualitative improvement of a physical economic base that is maintained in a steady state by a throughput of matter-energy that is within the regenerative and assimilative capacities of the ecosystem. Currently the term "sustainable development" is used as a synonym for the oxymoronic "sustainable growth." It must be saved from this perdition.

Politically it is very difficult to admit that growth, with its almost religious connotations of ultimate goodness, must be limited. But it is precisely the nonsustainability of growth that gives urgency to the concept of sustainable development. The earth will not tolerate the doubling of even one grain of wheat 64 times, yet in the past two centuries we have developed a culture dependent on exponential growth for its economic stability (Hubbert, 1976). Sustainable development is a cultural adaptation made by society as it becomes aware of the emerging necessity of nongrowth. Even "green growth" is not sustainable. There is a limit to the population of trees the earth can support, just as there is a limit to the populations of humans and of automobiles. To delude ourselves into believing that growth is still possible and desirable if only we label it "sustainable" or color it "green" will just delay the inevitable transition and make it more painful.

LIMITS TO GROWTH?

If the economy cannot grow forever then by how much can it grow? Can it grow by enough to give everyone in the world today a standard of per capita resource use equal to that of the average American? That would turn out to be a factor of seven, a figure that is neatly bracketed by the Brundtland Commission's call (Brundtland et al., 1987) for the expansion of the world economy by a factor of five to ten. The problem is that even expansion by a factor of four is impossible if Vitousek et al. (1986, pp. 368–373) are correct in their calculation that the human economy currently preempts one-fourth of the global net primary product of photosynthesis (NPP). We cannot go beyond 100 percent, and it is unlikely that we will increase NPP since the historical tendency up to now is for economic growth to reduce global photosynthesis. Since land-based ecosystems are the more relevant, and we preempt 40 percent of land-based NPP, even the factor of four is an overestimate. Also, reaching 100 percent is unrealistic since we are incapable of bringing under direct human management all the species that make up the ecosystems upon which we depend. Furthermore it is ridiculous to urge the preservation of biodiversity without being willing to halt the economic growth that requires human take-over of places in the sun occupied by other species.

If growth up to the factor of five to ten recommended by the Brundt-land Commission is impossible, then what about just sustaining the present scale—i.e., zero net growth? Every day we read about stress-induced feedbacks from the ecosystem to the economy, such as greenhouse [gas] buildup, ozone layer depletion, acid rain, etc., which constitute evidence that even the present scale is unsustainable. How then can people keep on talking about "sustain-able growth" when: (a) the present scale of the economy shows clear signs of unsustainability, (b) multiplying that scale by a factor of five to ten as recom-mended by the Brundtland Commission would move us from unsustainability to imminent collapse, and (c) the concept itself is logically self-contradictory in a finite, nongrowing ecosystem? Yet sustainable growth is the buzz word of our time. Occasionally it becomes truly ludicrous, as when writers gravely speak of "sustainable growth in the rate of increase of economic activity." Not only must we grow forever, we must accelerate forever! This is hollow political verbiage, totally disconnected from logical and physical first principles.

ALLEVIATING POVERTY, NOT ANGELIZING GNP

The important question is the one that the Brundtland Commission leads up to, but does not really face: How far can we alleviate poverty by development without growth? I suspect that the answer will be a significant amount, but less than half. One reason for this belief is that if the five- to tenfold expansion is really going to be for the sake of the poor, then it will have to consist of things needed by the poor—food, clothing, shelter—not information services. Basic goods have an irreducible physical dimension and their expansion will require growth rather than development, although development via improved efficiency will help. In other words, the reduction in resource content per dollar of GNP observed in some rich countries in recent years cannot be heralded as severing the link between economic expansion and the environment, as some have claimed. Angelized GNP will not feed the poor. Sustainable development must be development without growth—but with population control and wealth redistribution—if it is to be a serious attack on poverty.

In the minds of many people, growth has become synonymous with increase in wealth. They say that we must have growth to be rich enough to afford the cost of cleaning up and curing poverty. That all problems are easier to solve if we are richer is not in dispute. What is at issue is whether growth at the present margin really makes us richer. There is evidence that in the US it now makes us poorer by increasing costs faster than it increases benefits (Daly and Cobb, 1989, appendix). In other words we appear to have grown beyond the optimal scale.

DEFINING THE OPTIMAL SCALE

The concept of an optimal scale of the aggregate economy relative to the ecosystem is totally absent from current macroeconomic theory. The aggregate economy is assumed to grow forever. Microeconomics, which is almost entirely devoted to establishing the optimal scale of each microlevel activity by equating costs and benefits at the margin, has neglected to inquire if there is not also an optimal scale for the aggregate of all micro activities. A given scale (the product of population times per capita resource use) constitutes a given throughput of resources and thus a given load on the environment, and can consist of many people each consuming little, or fewer people each consuming correspondingly more.

An economy in sustainable development adapts and improves in knowledge, organization, technical efficiency, and wisdom; and it does this without assimilating or accreting, beyond some point, an ever greater percentage of the matter-energy of the ecosystem into itself, but rather stops at a scale at which the remaining ecosystem (the environment) can continue to function and renew itself year after year. The nongrowing economy is not static—it is being continually maintained and renewed as a steady-state subsystem of the environment.

What policies are implied by the goal of sustainable development, as here defined? Both optimists and pessimists should be able to agree on the following policy for the US (sustainable development should begin with the industrialized countries). Strive to hold throughput constant at present levels (or reduced truly sustainable levels) by taxing resource extraction, especially energy, very heavily. Seek to raise most public revenue from such resource severance taxes, and compensate (achieve revenue neutrality) by reducing the income tax, especially on the lower end of the income distribution, perhaps even financing a negative income tax at the very low end. Optimists who believe that resource efficiency can increase by a factor of ten should welcome this policy, which raises resource prices considerably and would give powerful incentive to just those technological advances in which they have so much faith. Pessimists who lack that technological faith will nevertheless be happy to see restrictions placed on the size of the already unsustainable throughput. The pessimists are protected against their worst fears; the optimists are encouraged to pursue their fondest dreams. If the pessimists are proven wrong and the enormous increase in efficiency actually happens, then they cannot complain. They got what they most wanted, plus an unexpected bonus. The optimists, for their part, can hardly object to a policy that not only allows but gives a strong incentive to the very technical progress on which their optimism is based. If they are proved wrong at least they should be glad that the throughput-induced rate of environmental destruction has been slowed. Also severance taxes are harder to avoid than income taxes and do not reduce incentives to work.

At the project level there are some additional policy guidelines for sustainable development. Renewable resources should be exploited in a manner such that:

1. harvesting rates do not exceed regeneration rates; and
2. waste emissions do not exceed the renewable assimilative capacity of the local environment.

BALANCING NONRENEWABLE AND RENEWABLE RESOURCES

Nonrenewable resources should be depleted at a rate equal to the rate of creation of renewable substitutes. Projects based on exploitation of nonrenewable resources should be paired with projects that develop renewable substitutes. The net rents from the nonrenewable extraction should be separated into an income component and a capital liquidation component. The capital component would be invested each year in building up a renewable substitute. The separation is made such that by the time the nonrenewable is exhausted, the substitute renewable asset will have been built up by investment and natural growth to the point where its sustainable yield is equal to the income component. The income component will have thereby become perpetual, thus justifying the name "income," which is by definition the maximum available for consumption while maintaining capital intact. It has been shown (El Serafy, 1989, pp. 10–18) how this division of rents into capital and income depends upon: (1) the discount rate (rate of growth of the renewable substitute); and (2) the life expectancy of the nonrenewable resource (reserves divided by annual depletion). The faster the biological growth of the renewable substitute and the longer the life expectancy of the nonrenewable, the greater will be the income component and the less the capital set-aside. "Substitute" here should be interpreted broadly to include any systemic adaptation that allows the economy to adjust the depletion of the nonrenewable resource in a way that maintains future income at a given level (e.g., recycling in the case of minerals). Rates of return for the paired projects should be calculated on the basis of their income component only.

However, before these operational steps toward sustainable development can get a fair hearing, we must first take the conceptual and political step of abandoning the thought-stopping slogan of "sustainable growth."

23

Who Is an Economy For?

Rethinking GDP

Jonathan Rowe

Mr. Chairman and Members of the Committee:

Let's suppose that the head of a federal agency came before this committee and reported with pride that agency employees had burned 10 percent more calories in the workplace than they did the year before. Not only that—they had spent 10% more money too.

I have a feeling you would want to know more. What were these employees doing when they burnt those calories? What did they spend that money on? Most important, what were the *results*? Expenditure is a means not an end; and to assess the health of an agency, or system, or whatever, you need to know what it has accomplished, not just how much motion it has generated and money it has spent.

The point seems obvious. Yet Congress does this very thing every day, and usually many times a day, when it talks about this thing called "the economy." The administration and the media do it too. Every time you say that the "economy" is up, or that you want to "stimulate" it, or get it going again, or whatever words you use, this is what you actually are saying. You are urging more expenditure and motion without regard to what that expenditure is and what it might accomplish—and without regard to what it might crowd out or displace in the process.

That term "the economy": what it means, in practice, is the Gross Domestic Product or GDP. It's just a big statistical pot that includes all the money spent in a given period of time. (I'm simplifying but that's the gist.) If the pot is bigger than it was the previous quarter, or year, then you cheer. If it isn't bigger, or bigger enough, then you get [Federal Reserve chair Ben] Bernanke up here and ask him what the heck is going on.

The *what* of the economy makes no difference in these councils. It never seems to come up. The money in the big pot could be going to cancer treatments or casinos, violent video games or usurious credit card rates. It could go toward the $9 billion or so that Americans spend on gas they burn while they sit in traffic and go nowhere; or the billion plus that goes to drugs such as Ritalin and Prozac that schools are stuffing into kids to keep them quiet in class.

The money could be the $20 billion or so that Americans spend on divorce lawyers each year; or the $5 billion on identity theft; or the billions more spent to repair property damage caused by environmental pollution. The money in the pot could betoken social and environmental breakdown—misery and distress of all kinds. It makes no difference. You don't ask. All you want to know is the total amount, which is the GDP. So long as it is growing then everything is fine.

We aren't here today to talk about an obscure technical measure. This isn't stuff for the folks in the back room. We are talking about what you mean when you use that term "the economy." Few words induce such a reverential hush in these halls. Few words are so laden with authority and portent. When you say "the economy" is up then no news is brighter. When you argue that a proposal will help the economy or hurt it, then you have played the ultimate trump card in your polemical decks, bin Laden possibly excepted. . . .

This is not an argument against growth by the way. To be reflexively against growth is as numb-minded as to be reflexively for it. Those are theological positions. I am arguing for an empirical one. Let's find out what is growing, and the effects. Tell us what this growth is, in concrete terms. Then we can begin to say whether it has been good or not.

The failure to do this is insane, literally. It is an insanity that is embedded in the political debate, and in media reportage; and it leads to fallacy in many directions. We hear for example that efforts to address climate change will hurt "the economy." Do they mean that if we clean up the air we will spend less money treating asthma in young kids? That Americans will spend fewer billions of dollars on gasoline to sit in traffic jams? That they will spend less on coastal insurance if the sea level stops rising?

There is a basic fallacy here. The atmosphere is part of the economy too—the real economy that is, though not the artificial construct portrayed in the GDP. It does real work, as we would discover quickly if it were to collapse. Yet the GDP does not include this work. If we burn more gas, the expenditure gets added to the GDP. But there is no corresponding subtraction for the toll this burning takes on the thermostatic and buffering functions that the atmosphere provides. (Nor is there a subtraction for the oil we take out of the ground.)

Yet if we burn less gas, and thus maintain the crucial functions of the atmosphere, we say "the economy" has suffered, even though the real economy has been enhanced. With families it's the same thing. By the standard of the GDP, the worst families in America are those that actually function as families—that cook their own meals, take walks after dinner and talk together instead of just farming the kids out to the commercial culture.

Cooking at home, talking with kids, walking instead of driving, involve less expenditure of money than do their commercial counterparts. Solid marriages involve less expenditure for counseling and divorce. Thus they are threats to the economy as portrayed in the GDP. By that standard, the best kids are the ones that eat the most junk food and exercise the least, because they will run up the biggest medical bills for obesity and diabetes.

This kind of thinking has been guiding the economic policy minds of this country for the last sixty years at least. Is it surprising that the family structure is shaky, real community is in decline, and kids have become Petri dishes of market-related dysfunction and disease? The nation has been driving by an instrument panel that portrays such things as growth and therefore good. It is not accidental that the two major protest movements of recent decades—environmental and pro-family—both deal with parts of the real economy that the GDP leaves out and that the commercial culture that embodies it tends to erode or destroy.

How did we get to this strange pass, in which up is down and down is up? How did it happen that the nation's economic hero is a terminal cancer patient going through a costly divorce? How is it that Congress talks about stimulating "the economy" when much that actually will be stimulated is the destruction of things it says it cares about on other days? How did the notion of economy become so totally uneconomic?

It's a long story, but for the present purpose it probably starts in Ireland in the 1640s. British troops just had repressed another uprising there, and the Cromwell government had devised a final solution to put its Irish problem to rest. The government would remove a significant portion of the populace—Catholics in particular—to a remote part of the island. Then it would redistribute their lands to British troops, thus providing compensation to them, and also an occupational presence for the benefit of the government in London.

The task of creating an inventory of the lands went to an army surgeon by the name of William Petty. Petty was a quick study, and also a man with an eye for the main chance. He classified much land as marginal that actually was quite good. Then he got himself appointed to the panel that made the distributions, and bestowed much of that land upon himself.

Petty's survey was the first known attempt in Western history to create a total inventory of a nation's wealth. It was not done for the well-being of the Irish people, but rather to take their lands away from them. It was an instrument of government policy; and this has been true from that time to the present. Governments have sought to catalogue the national wealth for purposes of taxation, confiscation, planning and mobilization in times of war.

They have not designed these catalogues to be measures of national well-being or of quality of life.

Yet that is how the national wealth inventories have come to be used, and especially the GDP. Somehow, a means of policy has become the end of policy. The tool has become the task. This part of the story begins with the Great Depression.

In the early 1930s, as the U.S. sank deeper into an economic slough, Congress faced an absence of data to help guide the way out. It didn't really know exactly what was happening, and where. There were no systematic figures on unemployment or production. Then–President Hoover had dispatched six employees from the Commerce Department to travel around the country and file reports. These were anecdotal and tended toward the Hoover view that recovery was just around the corner.

Members of Congress wanted more. Senator Robert LaFollette, a Republican, introduced a resolution to require the Commerce Department to develop a spreadsheet—as we would call it today—of economy with its component parts. LaFollette was a Progressive in the original sense. He believed in "scientific management and planning"; and the resolution was to produce a tool to that end. It passed on June 8, 1932, and the work fell to one Simon Kuznets, a professor at the University of Pennsylvania who was working at the National Bureau for Economic Research in New York.

Kuznets was clear that he was producing a policy tool, and not a measure of living standards or well-being. As he put it later in his clinical prose, the goal was to help understand the "relations and relative importance of various parts of the productive system and their responsiveness to various types of stimulae as shown by their changes in the past."

The project was a marvel by today's standards. Kuznets had virtually no budget, and a tiny staff. Data sources were fragmentary. But about a year and a half later, Kuznets submitted his report to Congress. . . . With a brevity and candor that are rare today, Kuznets laid out for Congress the limitations of the accounts he had constructed. He took particular pains to tell you why you should not use these accounts the way you—and the media—have come to use them.

For one thing, the national accounts leave out a crucial dimension of the economy—namely, the part that exists outside the realm of monetary exchange. This includes both the ecosystem and the social system—the life-supporting functions of the oceans and atmosphere for example, and work within families and communities that isn't done for money. The GDP takes no account of these. The result is that when the monetized economy displaces them—as when both parents have to work, or when forest clearing eliminates the cleansing function of trees—the losses are not subtracted against the market gain.

Kuznets was under no such illusion. "The volume of services rendered by housewives and other members of the household toward the satisfaction of wants must be imposing indeed," he writes. There's also the question of what he called "odd jobs," or what we would call the "underground economy." He knew that these played a large role in the economy. He also grasped, more broadly, that the quality and importance of a function does not depend upon the amount of money paid for it—or whether any money was paid at all. The care of a mother or father is not inferior to that of a day care worker just because they do not charge a price for their services.

This recognition undercuts a basic assumption behind the GDP—namely, that the contribution of an activity can be gauged solely from its market price. But there's a practical problem, Kuznets observed. Accounts require data; and there is by definition little data on the underground economy and on non-market exchange. As a result, the national accounts include only the slice of economic reality that falls within the bandwidth that economists are able to grasp—that is, recorded expenditures of money.

Then there's the thorny question of constructive versus destructive activities within the realm of monetized exchange. Once you have decided to count only that which is transacted through money, do you make the further assumption that everything transacted for money counts on the plus side of the ledger? Is something beneficial just because money changes hands when it passes from a seller to a buyer?

The mentality that lies behind the GDP assumes that it does. We all are "rational," and so any choice we make in the market is by definition one that makes our lives better. Kuznets focused on one obvious exception: activities that are illegal, such as gambling (when it is) and drugs. To assume that such expenditures add to the national well-being would undercut the rationale for making them illegal in the first place. The GDP is an instrument of the state, after all, and so Kuznets drew the line there.

He was aware of how arbitrary this is from an economic standpoint. Why exactly does legal gambling add to well-being if the illegal kind does not? Or what about alcohol? Given the assumption that legality confers benediction, the economy had a huge boost at the end of Prohibition, simply because the drinking that formally was illegal now was deemed OK. But booze still was booze. If the government can increase the growth rate by jiggering the metrics in this way, that does not increase confidence in the validity of measure.

But legality is the easy part. Just beneath it lies a deeper issue—namely, the assumption that every purchase is beneficial simply because someone has paid the purchase price. The exclusion of illegal activities, Kuznets said, "does not imply . . . that all lawful pursuits are necessarily serviceable from the social viewpoint." He left the question there, a chasm that an honest inquiry has to address.

There are so many examples of expenditure that goes into the GDP that has a questionable claim to the stature of growth and good, even from the standpoint of those who make it. For example, much consumption is compulsory, in that buyers have little choice. There is fraud, such as the way seniors are cheated in reverse mortgage scams. There's also products that are designed to lock buyers into an endless stream of high-priced replacements, such as inkjet printer cartridges that are designed to resist refilling.

Or what about car bumpers that are designed not to bump, so that a mild fender bender turns into a $5,000 repair bill? Or the usurious charges and fees that are built into credit cards. Not all Americans confronted with these regard them as "consumption choices" that propel them further up the mountain of more. . . .

Yet another reason is what economists call "distribution." The GDP makes no distinction between a $500.00 dinner in Manhattan and the hundreds of more humble meals that could be provided for that same amount. An Upper East Side socialite who buys a pair of $800.00 pumps from Manolo Blahnik appears to contribute forty times more to the national well-being than does the mother who buys a pair of $20.00 sneakers at Payless for her son. "Economic welfare cannot be adequately measured unless the personal distribution of income is known," [wrote Kuznets].

As included in the national accounts, an accretion of luxury buying at the top covers up a lack of necessary buying at the bottom. As the income scale becomes more skewed, as it has in the U.S., the cover-up becomes even greater. In this respect the GDP serves as a statistical laundry operation that hides the suffering at the bottom. . . .

Another problem has to do with work, and the toll it takes on those who do it. Kuznets called this the "reverse side of income, that is, the intensity and unpleasantness of effort going into the earning of income." That earning comes at a cost of wear and tear upon the body and psyche. If the GDP subtracts depreciation on buildings and equipment, should there not be a corresponding subtraction for the wearing out of people?

What about the loss in the value of their skills as one technology displaces another? In the current accounting, this toll often gets added to the GDP rather than subtracted, in the form of medications, expenditures for retraining, and day care for children as parents work longer hours. Most workers would regard such outlays as costs not gains.

Had Kuznets been writing today, moreover, he probably would have added another kind of depletion—that of natural resources. It sounds incredible, but when this nation drills its oil and mines its coal, the national accounts treat this as an addition to the national wealth rather than a subtraction from it. The result is like a car with a gas gauge that goes up as the fuel tank gets lower. The national accounts portray a nation getting richer, when in fact it is draining itself dry.

Kuznets concluded his report with words that ought to be inscribed on the walls in every office on Capitol Hill, and over every computer screen within a twenty mile radius. "The welfare of a nation can, therefore, scarcely be inferred from a measurement of national income as defined above."

I'm going to repeat that in case anyone missed it:

The welfare of a nation can, therefore, scarcely be inferred from a measurement of national income as defined above.

That's what the man who invented the GDP—its predecessor, more precisely—told Congress regarding the use of his invention. Yet Congress has done exactly what Kuznets urged it not to do. Congress and everybody else.

How exactly that came about is another long story. It began with the gradual seep of the new accounts into the political arena. In his 1936 re-election campaign, Franklin Roosevelt noted that the economy—as defined by the national accounts—had increased under his watch. It was a number: who could resist? The likely source was FDR's close advisor Harry Hopkins, whose office was a hub for the young economists who came to Washington to join the New Deal. But in the passage across 15th Street from the Commerce Department to the White House, Kuznets' numbers were turning in to precisely what he said they shouldn't be.

Then came World War II, when the national accounts played a central role in the mobilization effort. A bitter debate erupted in Washington over the nation's production goals. Corporate leaders insisted that the mobilization must come out of the existing level of production. They didn't want to be stuck with excess capacity when the war was over. Kuznets and others argued to the contrary that the U.S. had vast troves of untapped capacity; and they used the national accounts to prove it. . . .

This was heady stuff, and it was just a start. As the war was winding down, the accounts served again to guide the shift back to a peacetime basis without relapse into the dreaded Depression. Consumption was the key; the Cold War, with its Pentagon spending, was not yet in prospect. As war production diminished, shoppers would have to pick up the slack. The national accounts showed exactly how it could be done. As John Kenneth Galbraith put it in a series of articles for *Fortune* Magazine, "One good reason for expecting prosperity after the war is the fact that we can lay down its specifications."

The new Keynesian economists such as Galbraith were now the Merlins of prosperity, and the national accounts were their magic wand. Consumption itself was taking on a heroic stature; the returning troops were handing off the mantle of national purpose to the shoppers who would replace them in keeping the industrial machinery in motion. (The heroic imagery persists in media accounts today, as when we read that consumers will provide the "engine" for recovery, or that they will "pull" the nation out of its recession.)

In this atmosphere, it was perhaps inevitable that the map of the nation's capacity would become a totem to its economic success. But Simon Kuznets watched it happen with increasing dismay. (Galbraith came to have second thoughts as well.) Kuznets was a quiet academic who was loath to mount a soapbox. But he asserted over and over that those who had seized upon his handiwork had missed the point.

In 1962 he wrote an article in the *New Republic* magazine on the question of growth. In evaluating growth, he said, "distinctions must be kept in mind between quantity and quality of growth, between its costs and return, and between the short and the long run."

Kuznets continued, "goals for 'more' growth should specify more growth of what and for what. It is scarcely helpful to urge that the over-all growth rate be raised to *x* percent a year, without specifying the components of the product that should grow at increased rates to yield this acceleration." If you are going to "stimulate" the economy, in other words, could we at least have a little debate over what exactly you are going to stimulate?

That is the challenge that you face today. You might think of it as a broken feedback loop. If you had a gas gauge that went up as you drove, eventually you would run out of gas. If you have an index of economic well-being that goes up as families and communities cease to function, then you will keep doing the things that cause this dysfunction to increase. If your measures portray resource depletion as wealth increases, then you will continue to borrow from the future and to drain America first. . . .

This is the most important thing. The purpose of an economy is to meet human needs in such a way that life becomes in some respect richer and better in the process. It is not simply to produce a lot of stuff. Stuff is a means, not an end. Yet current modes of economic measurement focus almost entirely on means.

For example, an automobile is productive if it produces transportation. Yet today we look only at the cars produced per hour worked. More cars can mean more traffic and therefore a transportation system that is less productive. The medical system is the same way. The aim should be healthy people, not the sale of more medical services and drugs. Yet today, we assess the economic contribution of the medical system on the basis of treatment rather than results.

Economists see nothing wrong with this. They see no problem that the medical system is expected to produce 30–40 percent of new jobs over the next 30 years. "We have to spend our money on something," shrugged a Stanford economist to the *New York Times*. This is more insanity. Next we will be hearing about "disease-led recovery." To stimulate the economy we will have to encourage people to be sick so that the economy can be well. . . .

24

One Atmosphere, Two Worlds

Peter Singer

WHAT IS AN EQUITABLE DISTRIBUTION?

In the second of the three televised debates held during the 2000 U.S. presidential election, the candidates were asked what they would do about global warming. George W Bush said:

> I'll tell you one thing I'm not going to do is I'm not going to let the United States carry the burden for cleaning up the world's air, like the Kyoto treaty would have done. China and India were exempted from that treaty. I think we need to be more even-handed.

There are various principles of fairness that people often use to judge what is fair or "even-handed." In political philosophy, it is common to follow Robert Nozick in distinguishing between "historical" principles and "time-slice" principles. An historical principle is one that says: we can't decide, merely by looking at the present situation, whether a given distribution of goods is just or unjust. We must also ask how the situation came about; we must know its history. Are the parties entitled, by an originally justifiable acquisition and a chain of legitimate transfers, to the holdings they now have? If so, the present distribution is just. If not, rectification or compensation will be needed to produce a just distribution. In contrast, a time-slice principle looks at the existing distribution at a particular moment and asks if that distribution satisfies some principles of fairness, irrespective of any preceding sequence of events. I shall look at both of these approaches in turn.

A Historical Principle: "The Polluter Pays"
or "You Broke It, Now You Fix It"

Imagine that we live in a village in which everyone puts their wastes down a giant sink. No one quite knows what happens to the wastes after they go down the sink, but since they disappear and have no adverse impact on anyone, no one worries about it. Some people consume a lot, and so have a lot of waste, while others, with more limited means, have barely any, but the capacity of the sink to dispose of our wastes seems so limitless that no one worries about the difference. As long as that situation continues, it is reasonable to believe that, in putting waste down the sink, we are leaving "enough and as good" for others, because no matter how much we put down it, others can also put as much as they want, without the sink overflowing. . . .

Now imagine that conditions change, so that the sink's capacity to carry away our wastes is used up to the full, and there is already some unpleasant seepage that seems to be the result of the sink's being used too much. This seepage causes occasional problems. When the weather is warm, it smells. A nearby water hole where our children swim now has algae blooms that make it unusable. Several respected figures in the village warn that unless usage of the sink is cut down, all the village water supplies will be polluted. At this point, when we continue to throw our usual wastes down the sink we are no longer leaving "enough and as good" for others, and hence our right to unchecked waste disposal becomes questionable. For the sink belongs to us all in common, and by using it without restriction now, we are depriving others of their right to use the sink in the same way without bringing about results none of us wants. We have an example of the well-known "tragedy of the commons." The use of the sink is a limited resource that needs to be shared in some equitable way. But how? A problem of distributive justice has arisen.

Think of the atmosphere as a giant global sink into which we can pour our waste gases. Then once we have used up the capacity of the atmosphere to absorb our gases without harmful consequences, it becomes impossible to justify our usage of this asset by the claim that we are leaving "enough and as good" for others. The atmosphere's capacity to absorb our gases has become a finite resource on which various parties have competing claims. The problem is to allocate those claims justly. . . .

The average American, by driving a car, eating a diet rich in the products of industrialized farming, keeping cool in summer and warm in winter, and consuming products at a hitherto unknown rate, uses more than fifteen times as much of the global atmospheric sink as the average Indian. Thus Americans, along with Australians, Canadians, and to a lesser degree Europeans, effectively deprive those living in poor countries of the opportunity to develop along the lines that the rich ones themselves have taken. If the poor were to behave as the rich now do, global warming would accelerate and almost certainly bring widespread catastrophe. . . .

[S]ince the wealth of the developed nations is inextricably tied to their prodigious use of carbon fuels (a use that began more than 200 years ago and continues unchecked today), it is a small step from here to the conclusion that the present global distribution of wealth is the result of the wrongful expropriation by a small fraction of the world's population of a resource that belongs to all human beings in common.

For those whose principles of justice focus on historical processes, a wrongful expropriation is grounds for rectification or compensation. What sort of rectification or compensation should take place in this situation?

One advantage of being married to someone whose hair is a different color or length from your own is that, when a clump of hair blocks the bath outlet, it's easy to tell whose hair it is. "Get your own hair out of the tub" is a fair and reasonable household rule. Can we, in the case of the atmosphere, trace back what share of responsibility for the blockage is due to which nations? It isn't as easy as looking at hair color, but a few years ago researchers measured world carbon emissions from 1950 to 1986 and found that the United States, with about 5 percent of the world's population at that time, was responsible for 30 percent of the cumulative emissions, whereas India, with 17 percent of the world's population, was responsible for less than 2 percent of the emissions. It is as if, in a village of 20 people all using the same bathtub, one person had shed 30 percent of the hair blocking the drain hole and three people had shed virtually no hair at all. . . . In these circumstances, one basis of deciding who pays the bill for the plumber to clear out the drain would be to divide it up proportionately to the amount of hair from each person that has built up over the period that people have been using the tub, and has caused the present blockage. . . .

At present rates of emissions—even including emissions that come from changes in land use like clearing forests—contributions of the developing nations to the atmospheric stock of greenhouse gases will not equal the built-up contributions of the developed nations until about 2038. If we adjust this calculation for population—in other words, if we ask when the contributions of the developing nations per person will equal the per person contributions of the developed nations to the atmospheric stock of greenhouse gases—the answer is: not for at least another century.

If the developed nations had had, during the past century, per capita emissions at the level of the developing nations, we would not today be facing a problem of climate change caused by human activity, and we would have an ample window of opportunity to do something about emissions before they reached a level sufficient to cause a problem. So, to put it in terms a child could understand, as far as the atmosphere is concerned, the developed nations broke it. If we believe that people should contribute to fixing something in proportion to their responsibility for breaking it, then the developed nations owe it to the rest of the world to fix the problem with the atmosphere.

Time-Slice Principles

The historical view of fairness just outlined puts a heavy burden on the developed nations. In their defense, it might be argued that at the time when the developed nations put most of their cumulative contributions of greenhouse gases into the atmosphere, they could not know of the limits to the capacity of the atmosphere to absorb those gases. It would therefore be fairer, it may be claimed, to make a fresh start now and set standards that look to the future, rather than to the past.

There can be circumstances in which we are right to wipe the slate clean and start again. A case can be made for doing so with respect to cumulative emissions that occurred before governments could reasonably be expected to know that these emissions might harm people in other countries. . . . At least since 1990, however, when the Intergovernmental Panel on Climate Change published its first report, solid evidence about the hazards associated with emissions has existed. To wipe the slate clean on what happened since 1990 seems unduly favorable to the industrialized nations that have, despite that evidence, continued to emit a disproportionate share of greenhouse gases. Nevertheless, in order to see whether there are widely held principles of justice that do not impose such stringent requirements on the developed nations as the "polluter pays" principle, let us assume that the poor nations generously overlook the past. We would then need to look for a time-slice principle to decide how much each nation should be allowed to emit.

An Equal Share for Everyone

If we begin by asking, "Why should anyone have a greater claim to part of the global atmospheric sink than any other?" then the first, and simplest response is: "No reason at all." In other words, everyone has the same claim to part of the atmospheric sink as everyone else. This kind of equality seems self-evidently fair, at least as a starting point for discussion, and perhaps, if no good reasons can be found for moving from it, as an end point as well.

If we take this view, then we need to ask how much carbon each country would be allowed to emit and compare that with what they are now emitting. The first question is what total level of carbon emission is acceptable. The Kyoto Protocol aimed to achieve a level for developed nations that was 5 percent below 1990 levels. Suppose that we focus on emissions for the entire planet and aim just to stabilize carbon emissions at their present levels. Then the allocation per person conveniently works out at about 1 metric ton per year. This therefore becomes the basic equitable entitlement for every human being on this planet.

Now compare actual per capita emissions for some key nations. The United States currently produces more than 5 tons of carbon per person per year. Japan and Western European nations have per capita emissions that range from 1.6 tons to 4.2 tons, with most below 3 tons. In the developing world, emissions average 0.6 tons per capita, with China at 0.76 and India at 0.29. This means that to reach an "even-handed" per capita annual emission limit of 1 ton of carbon per person, India would be able to increase its carbon emissions to more than three times what they now are. China would be able to increase its emissions by a more modest 33 percent. The United States, on the other hand, would have to reduce its emissions to no more than one-fifth of present levels. . . .

25

Environmental Colonialism

The Perverse Politics of Climate Change

**Anil Agarwal
and Sunita Narain**

The idea that developing countries like India and China must share the blame for heating up the Earth and destabilizing its climate—as espoused in a recent study published in the United States by the World Resources Institute in collaboration with the United Nations Environment Program—is an excellent example of environmental colonialism. India and China may account for more than one-third of the world's population, but are these two nations really responsible for flushing one-third of the muck and dirt into the world's air and oceans?

The report of the World Resources Institute (WRI), a Washington-based private research group, is based less on science than politically motivated mathematics. Its main intention seems to be to blame developing countries for global warming and to perpetuate the current global inequity in the use of the Earth's environment and its resources.

The big fear is that global warming could destabilize the world's climate, increase floods and droughts, melt the polar ice caps, raise sea levels and inundate large parts of countries like India, Bangladesh and the Maldives.

The exercise of blaming developing countries has already begun. Until recently, it was widely accepted that developed countries of the West consume most of the world's fossil fuels and produce most of the carbon dioxide—the main agents of global warming. In recent years, however, Western nations have been carrying out a sustained propaganda campaign alleging that deforestation in developing countries, and the generation of methane through irrigated rice farming and the raising of cattle, is also contributing to global warming. This has shifted the onus onto developing countries. . . .

[T]he World Resources Institute and the United Nations Environment Program jointly released the annual report, World Resources 1990–91, that stated for the first time that India, China and Brazil are among the top five countries responsible for the accumulation of these gases in the Earth's atmosphere.

COOKING THE FIGURES

The figures used by WRI to calculate the quantity of carbon dioxide and methane produced by each country are extremely questionable. Heavy emphasis has been placed on comparisons of carbon dioxide produced by deforestation and methane generated by rice fields and livestock to carbon dioxide produced by burning fossil fuels like oil and coal—an emphasis that tends to underplay the impact of the developed countries.

The methane issue raises further questions of justice and morality. Can we really equate the carbon dioxide contributions of gas guzzling automobiles in Europe and North America (or, for that matter, anywhere in the Third World) with the methane emissions of water buffalo and rice fields of subsistence farmers in West Bengal or Thailand? Do these people not have a right to live? No effort has been made in WRI's report to separate the "survival emissions" of the poor from the "luxury emissions" of the rich.

OLD NUMBERS; NEW RECIPE

A study conducted by India's Centre for Science and Environment (CSE), which uses WRI's data for each country's gaseous emissions, concludes that developing countries are responsible for only 16 percent of the carbon dioxide accumulating in the Earth's atmosphere. The WRI report claims a Third World share of 48 percent. Similarly, developing countries were not found to be responsible for any excess methane accumulation, although WRI claims a Third World share of 56 percent.

This difference is explained by a simple fact: no country can be blamed for the gases accumulating in the Earth's atmosphere until each country's share in the Earth's cleansing ability has been apportioned on an equitable and fair basis. Since most of the cleansing is done by the oceans and the troposphere, the Earth has to be treated as a common heritage of humankind. Good environmental management demands that nations should learn to live within the Earth's ability to absorb these gaseous wastes.

Since there is no reason to believe that any human being in any part of the world is more or less important than another, CSE has apportioned the world's restoration ability to each country in proportion to its share of the world's population. Thus India, with 16 percent of the world's population, gets 16 percent of the Earth's natural air and ocean "sinks" for carbon dioxide and methane absorption. Describing these emissions as "permissible," CSE finds that India is producing carbon dioxide just equal to six percent of the world's natural sinks and methane equal to 14 percent of the natural sinks. How, then, can India be blamed for any of the excess carbon dioxide or methane that is accumulating in the Earth's atmosphere?

The same scenario is true for China, Pakistan, Sri Lanka, Egypt, Kenya, Nigeria, Tanzania, Zimbabwe and Chile. Meanwhile, almost all Western countries are emitting well beyond their "permissible shares" of the Earth's carbon dioxide and methane sinks. In Europe, only Portugal and Albania are emitting carbon dioxide within their limits. Clearly, it is Western wastes and willful over-consumption of the world's natural resources that are polluting the Earth and threatening the global environment.

What WRI has done instead is to calculate the percentage of India's total emissions of carbon dioxide and methane before they are absorbed and then hold India responsible for the same quantitative share of the gases actually accumulating in the Earth's atmosphere. This manner of calculating each nation's responsibility is extremely unfair and amounts to a scientific sleight of hand.

According to the WRI-UNEP [United Nations Environment Programme] calculations, the US, which produces 14.4 percent of the world's annual output of carbon dioxide, becomes responsible for only 14.4 percent of the carbon dioxide that is actually accumulating every year. The CSE's analysis, however, indicates the United States, with only 4.73 percent of the world's population, emits as much as 26 percent of the carbon dioxide and 20 percent of the methane that is absorbed every year.

It is the production of carbon dioxide and methane by countries like the US and Japan—totally out of proportion to their populations and that of the world's absorptive capacity—that is responsible for accumulation of excess, unabsorbed carbon dioxide and methane in the atmosphere. In addition, these countries emit large quantities of chlorofluorocarbon (CFC) gases that do not get absorbed at all. Japan accounts for 7.4 percent and the US for 25.8 percent of the world's CFC use. Meanwhile India, with 3.4 times the population of the US, gets less than one fourth of the US' share of the planet's natural sink.

India and China account for less than 0.5 percent of net emissions to the atmosphere, while WRI claims they together contribute about ten percent. The CSE analysis shows India to be the world's lowest per capita net emitter of greenhouse gases.

A mere 15 nations—nine industrialized and six developing countries —account for more than 83 percent of the net emissions of all greenhouse gases which are accumulating in the atmosphere. Industrialized countries have together exceeded their permissible quotas of carbon dioxide by 2839 million tons of carbon equivalent—50 percent of excess global CO_2 emissions. The WRI-UNEP method of calculating pollution is extremely unfair because it favors the biggest polluters—i.e., the bigger the polluter, the larger the share of the sink it gets.

Because of these inequities, CSE has proposed a two-tiered system of usage charges and fines to bring rationality to the global use of the atmosphere.

EMISSIONS & OMISSIONS

CSE's method offers a better way of calculating each country's responsibility for global warming. Not only do developing countries get a fair share of the Earth's natural cleansing ability, but several industrialized countries also benefit. Using CSE's analysis, France's contribution to all greenhouse gases goes down by 43 percent, Japan's and Italy's by 36 percent, the United Kingdom's by 12 percent, and West Germany's by four percent.

On the other hand, Saudi Arabia's share goes up by 131 percent, Canada's by 110 percent, Australia's by 78 percent, and the US share jumps 53 percent. Since the US is the largest emitter of greenhouse gases, this increase overshadows that of all other countries.

The WRI-UNEP figures for methane and carbon dioxide emissions are based on just a handful of Western measurements of cattle and rice field emissions that have then been projected over the entire world. The existing data on deforestation rates are also extremely shaky. Brazil, a frequent target of WRI criticism for deforestation, has accused the organization of inflating its deforestation rates by 300 to 400 percent.

The entire WRI-UNEP study appears designed to bolster both foreign and domestic policy interests of Western nations whose governments would like to convince their environmentalists that their nations are not to blame and cannot do much locally unless they rope in the hapless Third World.

RENTING SINK SPACE?

An interesting implication of CSE's study is that it opens the way for developing countries to bill the Western nations for the latter's excess emissions. Since India is using only a small share of its global pollution sink, Western nations might be required to pay for polluting India's unused portion of the Earth's "cleansing commons." Using a figure of $15 per ton of carbon emitted, India could expect to receive $8.3 billion a year from the West under this arrangement.

Similarly, China, Pakistan, Nigeria, Bangladesh, Egypt, Kenya, Tanzania and Sri Lanka would also receive billions of dollars. The top 15 polluting nations would have to pay individual developing countries a total of $20 billion per year.

Such a system of "tradable emissions" would be an ideal market economy solution to control global warming. It would work both ways by giving countries like India the monetary incentive to keep their emissions as low as possible. At the same time, it would provide countries like the US with a financial stimulus to reduce their emissions as fast as possible.

Countries that exceed their permissible emissions (even after they have purchased the unused shares of developing countries) should be forced to pay damages to a Climate Protection Fund. Such a fund—which has already been proposed by numerous experts and environmentalists—would amass up to $90 billion per year on the basis of contributions received from just 15 of the worst-polluting Western nations. These funds should be used to compensate countries adversely affected by global warming (like India, Bangladesh or the Maldives) and to develop alternate, non-polluting energy technologies as a common resource for humankind.

None of this means that India should not regenerate its environment nor that it should not become more efficient in its use of energy. This will be our best defense against global warming. If the diverse ecosystems of India are functioning at the optimum levels of productivity, the effects of the expected changes in the global climate will become somewhat manageable. But if, as today, our land and water resource base remains highly stressed and degraded, climatic perturbations will throw society into a state of total chaos.

However, it is vital for a country like India to take bold steps to advance the interests of the Third World. It is vital that developing nations fight for a fair share of the Earth's environment and the benefits of the global commons. Only then will "our common future" be secured.

It is time for the Third World to ask the West: "Whose future generations are we seeking to protect—the Western World's or the Third World's?"

26

Environmental Racism and the Environmental Justice Movement

Robert Bullard

Communities are not all created equal. In the United States, for example, some communities are routinely poisoned while the government looks the other way. Environmental regulations have not uniformly benefited all segments of society. People of color (African Americans, Latinos, Asians, Pacific Islanders, and Native Americans) are disproportionately harmed by industrial toxins on their jobs and in their neighborhoods. These groups must contend with dirty air and drinking water—the byproducts of municipal landfills, incinerators, polluting industries, and hazardous waste treatment, storage, and disposal facilities.

Why do some communities get "dumped on" while others escape? Why are environmental regulations vigorously enforced in some communities and not others? Why are some workers protected from environmental threats to their health while others (such as migrant farmworkers) are still being poisoned? How can environmental justice be incorporated into the campaign for environmental protection? What institutional changes would enable the United States to become a just and sustainable society? . . .

INTERNAL COLONIALISM AND WHITE RACISM

The history of the United States has long been grounded in white racism. The nation was founded on the principles of "free land" (stolen from Native Americans and Mexicans), "free labor" (cruelly extracted from African slaves), and "free men" (white men with property). From the outset, institutional racism shaped the economic, political, and ecological landscape, and buttressed the exploitation of both land and people. Indeed, it has allowed communities of color to exist as internal colonies characterized by dependent (and unequal) relationships with the dominant white society or "Mother Country." In their 1967 book, *Black Power,* Carmichael and Hamilton were among the first to explore the "internal" colonial model as a way to explain the racial inequality, political exploitation, and social isolation of African Americans. As Carmichael and Hamilton write:

> The economic relationship of America's black communities [to white society] . . . reflects their colonial status. The political power exercised over those communities goes hand in glove with the economic deprivation experienced by the black citizen.
>
>   Historically, colonies have existed for the sole purpose of enriching, in one form or another, the "colonizer"; the consequence is to maintain the economic dependency of the "colonized" (pp. 16–17).

Generally, people of color in the United States—like their counterparts in formerly colorized lands of Africa, Asia, and Latin America—have not had the same opportunities as whites. The social forces that have organized oppressed colonies internationally still operate in the "heart of the colonizer's mother country" (Blauner 1972, p. 26). For Blauner, people of color are subjected to five principal colonizing processes: they enter the "host" society and economy involuntarily; their native culture is destroyed; white-dominated bureaucracies impose restrictions from which whites are exempt; the dominant group uses institutionalized racism to justify its actions; and a dual or "split labor market" emerges based on ethnicity and race. Such domination is also buttressed by state institutions. Social scientists Omi and Winant (1986, pp. 76–78) go so far as to insist that "every state institution is a racial institution." Clearly, whites receive benefits from racism, while people of color bear most of the cost.

ENVIRONMENTAL RACISM

Racism plays a key factor in environmental planning and decisionmaking. Indeed, environmental racism is reinforced by government, legal, economic, political, and military institutions. It is a fact of life in the United States that the mainstream environmental movement is only beginning to wake up to. Yet, without a doubt, racism influences the likelihood of exposure to environmental and health risks and the accessibility of health care. Racism provides whites of all class levels with an "edge" in gaining access to a healthy physical environment. This has been documented again and again.

    Whether by conscious design or institutional neglect, communities of color in urban ghettos, in rural "poverty pockets," or on economically impoverished Native-American reservations face some of the worst environmental devastation in the nation. Clearly, racial discrimination was not legislated out of existence in the 1960s. While some significant progress was made during this decade, people of color continue to struggle for equal treatment in many areas, including environmental justice. Agencies at all levels of government, including the federal EPA, have done a poor job protecting people of color from the ravages of pollution and industrial encroachment. It has thus been an up-hill battle convincing white judges, juries, government officials, and policymakers that racism exists in environmental protection, enforcement, and policy formulation.

The most polluted urban communities are those with crumbling infrastructure, ongoing economic disinvestment, deteriorating housing, inadequate schools, chronic unemployment, a high poverty rate, and an overloaded health-care system. Riot-torn South Central Los Angeles typifies this urban neglect. It is not surprising that the "dirtiest" zip code in California belongs to the mostly African-American and Latino neighborhood in that part of the city (Kay 1991a). In the Los Angeles basin, over 71 percent of the African Americans and 50 percent of the Latinos live in areas with the most polluted air, while only 34 percent of the white population does (Ong and Blumenberg 1990; Mann 1991). This pattern exists nationally as well. As researchers Wernette and Nieves note:

> In 1990, 437 of the 3,109 counties and independent cities failed to meet at least one of the EPA ambient air quality standards . . . 57 percent of whites, 65 percent of African Americans, and 80 percent of Hispanics live in 437 counties with substandard air quality. Out of the whole population, a total of 33 percent of whites, 50 percent of African Americans, and 60 percent of Hispanics live in the 136 counties in which two or more air pollutants exceed standards. The percentage living in the 29 counties designated as nonattainment areas for three or more pollutants are 12 percent of whites, 20 percent of African Americans, and 31 percent of Hispanics (pp. 16–17).

Income alone does not account for these above-average percentages. Housing segregation and development patterns play a key role in determining where people live. Moreover, urban development and the "spatial configuration" of communities flow from the forces and relationships of industrial production which, in turn, are influenced and subsidized by government policy (Feagin 1988; Gottdiener 1988). There is widespread agreement that vestiges of race-based decisionmaking still influence housing, education, employment, and criminal justice. The same is true for municipal services such as garbage pickup and disposal, neighborhood sanitation, fire and police protection, and library services. Institutional racism influences decisions on local land use, enforcement of environmental regulations, industrial facility siting, management of economic vulnerability, and the paths of freeways and highways.

People skeptical of the assertion that poor people and people of color are targeted for waste-disposal sites should consider the report the Cerrell Associates provided the California Waste Management Board. In . . . *Political Difficulties Facing Waste-to-Energy Conversion Plant Siting,* they offered a detailed profile of those neighborhoods more likely to organize effective resistance against incinerators. The policy conclusion based on this analysis is clear. As the report states:

> All socioeconomic groupings tend to resent the nearby siting of major facilities, but middle and upper socioeconomic strata possess better resources to effectuate their opposition. Middle and higher socioeconomic strata neighborhoods should not fall within the one-mile and five-mile radius of the proposed site (p. 43).

Where then will incinerators or other polluting facilities be sited? For Cerrell Associates, the answer is low-income, disempowered neighborhoods with a high concentration of nonvoters. The ideal site, according to their report, has nothing to do with environmental soundness but everything to do with lack of social power. Communities of color in California are far more likely to fit this profile than are their white counterparts.

Those still skeptical of the existence of environmental racism should also consider the fact that zoning boards and planning commissions are typically stacked with white developers. Generally, the decisions of these bodies reflect the special interests of the individuals who sit on these boards. People of color have been systematically excluded from these decisionmaking boards, commissions, and governmental agencies (or allowed only token representation). Grassroots leaders are now demanding a shared role in all the decisions that shape their communities. They are challenging the intended or unintended racist assumptions underlying environmental and industrial policies.

TOXIC COLONIALISM ABROAD

To understand the global ecological crisis, it is important to understand that the poisoning of African Americans in South Central Los Angeles and of Mexicans in border *maquiladoras* have their roots in the same system of economic exploitation, racial oppression, and devaluation of human life. The quest for solutions to environmental problems and for ways to achieve sustainable development in the United States has considerable implications for the global environmental movement.

Today, more than 1,900 *maquiladoras,* assembly plants operated by American, Japanese, and other foreign countries, are located along the 2,000-mile U.S.-Mexico border (Center for Investigative Reporting 1990; Sanchez 1990; Zuniga 1992, p. 22A). These plants use cheap Mexican labor to assemble products from imported components and raw materials, and then ship them back to the United States (Witt 1991). Nearly half a million Mexicans work in the *maquiladoras.* They earn an average of $3.75 a day. While these plants bring jobs, albeit low-paying ones, they exacerbate local pollution by over-crowding the border towns, straining sewage and water systems, and reducing air quality. All this compromises the health of workers and nearby community residents. The Mexican environmental regulatory agency is understaffed and ill-equipped to adequately enforce the country's laws (Working Group on Canada-Mexico Free Trade 1991).

The practice of targeting poor communities of color in the Third World for waste disposal and the introduction of risky technologies from industrialized countries are forms of "toxic colonialism," what some activists have dubbed the "subjugation of people to an ecologically-destructive economic order by entities over which the people have no control" (Greenpeace 1992, p. 3). The industrialized world's controversial Third World dumping policy was made public by the release of an internal December 12, 1991, memorandum authored by Lawrence Summers, chief economist of the World Bank. It shocked the world and touched off a global scandal. Here are the highlights:

> *"Dirty" Industries:* Just between you and me, shouldn't the World Bank be en-couraging MORE migration of the dirty industries to the LDCs [Less Developed Countries]? I can think of three reasons:
>
>   1) The measurement of the costs of health impairing pollution depends on the foregone earnings from increased morbidity and mortality. From this point of view a given amount of health impairing pollution should be done in the country with the lowest cost, which will be the country with the lowest wages. I think the economic logic behind dumping a load of toxic waste in the lowest wage country is impeccable and we should face up to that.
>
>   2) The costs of pollution are likely to be non-linear as the initial increments of pollution probably have very low cost. I've always thought that under-polluted areas in Africa are vastly UNDER-polluted; their air quality is probably vastly inefficiently low compared to Los Angeles or Mexico City. Only the lamentable facts that so much pollution is generated by non-tradable industries (transport, electrical generation) and that the unit transport costs of solid waste are so high prevent world welfare-enhancing trade in air pollution and waste.
>
>   3) The demand for a clean environment for aesthetic and health reasons is likely to have very high income elasticity. The concern over an agent that causes a one in a million change in the odds of prostate cancer is obviously going to be much higher in a country where people survive to get prostate cancer than in a country where under 5 [year-old] mortality is 200 per thousand. Also, much of the concern over industrial atmosphere discharge is about visibility impairing particulates. These discharges may have very little direct health im-pact. Clearly trade in goods that embody aesthetic pollution concerns could be welfare enhancing. While production is mobile the consumption of pretty air is a non-tradable.

The problem with the arguments against all of these proposals for more pol-lution in LDCs (intrinsic rights to certain goods, moral reasons, social concerns, lack of adequate markets, etc.) could be turned around and used more or less effectively against every Bank proposal. . . .

BEYOND THE RACE VS. CLASS TRAP

Whether at home or abroad, the question of who *pays* and who *benefits* from current industrial and development policies is central to any analysis of en-vironmental racism. In the United States, race interacts with class to create special environmental and health vulnerabilities. People of color, however, face elevated toxic exposure levels even when social class variables (income, education, and occupational status) are held constant (Bryant and Mohai 1992). Race has been found to be an independent factor, not reducible to class, in predicting the distribution of 1) air pollution in our society (Freeman 1972; Gianessi, Peskin, and Wolff 1979; Gelobter 1988; Wernette and Nieves 1992); 2) contaminated fish consumption (West, Fly, and Marans 1990); 3) the location of municipal landfills and incinerators (Bullard 1983, 1987, 1990, 1991a); 4) the location of abandoned toxic waste dumps (United Church of Christ Commission for Racial Justice 1987); and 5) lead poisoning in children (Agency for Toxic Substances and Disease Registry 1988).

Lead poisoning is a classic case in which race, not just class, determines exposure. It affects between three and four million children in the United States—most of whom are African Americans and Latinos living in urban areas. Among children five years old and younger, the percentage of African Americans who have excessive levels of lead in their blood far exceeds the percentage of whites at all income levels (Agency for Toxic Substances and Disease Registry 1988, p. I–12).

The federal Agency for Toxic Substances and Disease Registry found that for families earning less than $6,000 annually an estimated 68 percent of African-American children had lead poisoning, compared with 36 percent for white children. For families with incomes exceeding $15,000, more than 38 percent of African-American children have been poisoned, compared with 12 percent of white children. African-American children are two to three times more likely than their white counterparts to suffer from lead poisoning independent of class factors.

One reason for this is that African Americans and whites do not have the same opportunities to "vote with their feet" by leaving unhealthy physical environments. The ability of an individual to escape a health-threatening en-vironment is usually correlated with income. However, racial barriers make it even harder for millions of African Americans, Latinos, Asians, Pacific Islanders, and Native Americans to relocate. Housing discrimination, redlining, and other market forces make it difficult for millions of households to buy their way out of polluted environments. For example, an affluent African-American family (with an income of $50,000 or more) is as segregated as an African-American family with an annual income of $5,000 (Denton and Massey 1988; Jaynes and Williams 1989). Thus, lead poisoning of African-American children is not just a "poverty thing."

White racism helped create our current separate and unequal communities. It defines the boundaries of the urban ghetto, *barrio,* and reservation, and influences the provision of environmental protection and other public services. Apartheid-type housing and development policies reduce neighborhood options, limit mobility, diminish job opportunities, and decrease environmental choices for millions of Americans. It is unlikely that this nation will ever achieve lasting solutions to its environmental problems unless it also addresses the system of racial injustice that helps sustain the existence of powerless communities forced to bear disproportionate environmental costs.

THE LIMITS OF MAINSTREAM ENVIRONMENTALISM

Historically, the mainstream environmental movement in the United States has developed agendas that focus on such goals as wilderness and wildlife preservation, wise resource management, pollution abatement, and population control. It has been primarily supported by middle- and upper-middle-class whites. Although concern for the environment cuts across class and racial lines, ecology activists have traditionally been individuals with above-average education, greater access to economic resources, and a greater sense of personal power (Buttel and Flinn 1978; Morrison 1980, 1986; Dunlap 1987; Bullard, 1990; Bullard and Wright 1987; Bachrach and Zautra 1985; Mohai, 1985, 1990).

Not surprisingly, mainstream groups were slow in broadening their base to include poor and working-class whites, let alone African Americans and other people of color. Moreover, they were ill-equipped to deal with the environmental, economic, and social concerns of these communities. During the 1960s and 1970s, while the "Big Ten" environmental groups focused on wilderness preservation and conservation through litigation, political lobbying, and technical evaluation, activists of color were engaged in mass direct action mobilizations for basic civil rights in the areas of employment, housing, education, and health care. Thus, two parallel and sometimes conflicting movements emerged, and it has taken nearly two decades for any significant convergence to occur between these two efforts. In fact, conflicts still remain over how the two groups should balance economic development, social justice, and environmental protection.

In their desperate attempt to improve the economic conditions of their constituents, many African-American civil rights and political leaders have directed their energies toward bringing jobs to their communities. In many instances, this has been achieved at great risk to the health of workers and the surrounding communities. The promise of jobs (even low-paying and hazardous ones) and of a broadened tax base has enticed several economically impoverished, politically powerless communities of color both in the United States and around the world (Center for Investigative Reporting and Bill Moyers 1990; Bullard 1990; Bryant and Mohai 1992). Environmental job blackmail is a fact of life. You can get a job, but only if you are willing to do work that will harm you, your families, and your neighbors.

Workers of color are especially vulnerable to job blackmail because of the greater threat of unemployment they face compared to whites and because of their concentration in low-paying, unskilled, nonunionized occupations. For example, they make up a large share of the nonunion contract workers in the oil, chemical, and nuclear industries. Similarly, over 95 percent of migrant farm-workers in the United States are Latino, African-American, Afro-Caribbean, or Asian, and African Americans are overrepresented in high-risk, blue-collar, and service occupations for which a large pool of replacement labor exists. Thus, they are twice as likely to be unemployed as their white counterparts. Fear of unemployment acts as a potent incentive for many African-American workers to accept and keep jobs they know are health threatening. Workers will tell you that "unemployment and poverty are also hazardous to one's health." An inherent conflict exists between the interests of capital and that of labor. Employers have the power to move jobs (and industrial hazards) from the Northeast and Midwest to the South and Sunbelt, or they may move the jobs offshore to Third World countries where labor is even cheaper and where there are even fewer health and safety regulations. Yet, unless an environmental movement emerges that is capable of addressing these economic concerns, people of color and poor white workers are likely to end up siding with corporate managers in key conflicts concerning the environment.

Indeed, many labor unions already moderate their demands for improved work-safety and pollution control whenever the economy is depressed. They are afraid of layoffs, plant closings, and the relocation of industries. These fears and anxieties of labor are usually built on the false but understandable assumption that environmental regulations inevitably lead to job loss (Brown 1980, 1987).

The crux of the problem is that the mainstream environmental movement has not sufficiently addressed the fact that social inequality and imbalances of social power are at the heart of environmental degradation, resource depletion, pollution, and even overpopulation. The environmental crisis can simply not be solved effectively without social justice. As one academic human ecologist notes, "Whenever [an] in-group directly and exclusively benefits from its own overuse of a shared resource but the costs of that overuse are 'shared' by out-groups, then in-group motivation toward a policy of resource conservation (or sustained yields of harvesting) is undermined" (Catton 1982).

Section 7 Exercise

A Toxic Thank-You

Architect William McDonough is fond of gesturing to an image of the globe and requesting that his audience point to *away* in the picture. The point, of course, is that there is no "away" when it comes to our wastes. When we throw things "away" they end up in specific places and affect particular people.

This exercise awakens us to the inequalities that mark our environmental lives.

To prepare for the exercise, please view the short online film "The Story of Stuff" (Annie Leonard, 2007) available at http://storyof stuff.org/movies/story-of-stuff/.

(Note that this exercise is designed for a campus setting but can easily be reconfigured as an individual experiment.)

Step 1: Collect and carry around with you every piece of trash you produce over a five-day period. Separate different materials—recyclable, organic, etc.—into different plastic bags and carry these with you as you go through your days. Then bring your bags to class.

Step 2: Analyze your trash with other members of your class. What do you have the most of?

Pass the bags around so each person receives a bag that someone else generated. Look at the trash you received. How does it feel to have to deal with someone else's refuse?

Then, take responsibility for discarding the trash in an appropriate fashion on campus.

Step 3: Work in groups to figure out what happens to the trash once you throw it away. Does your campus recycle? If so, where is the recycling plant? Does it incinerate? If so, where is the incinerator located? Does trash get buried? If so, where is the landfill?

Pick one form of disposal and research who lives in the vicinity of the recycling, incineration, or landfill site.

Step 4: Write these people a letter as a way to relate to those who live "downstream." What will you tell them? Do you want to thank them for dealing with your campus's waste? Would you like to apologize for sending toxic substances? What would a "hello" say?

Part III

**From Person to Planet:
Into a Livable Future**

Section 8

Thinking Strategically

This book is subtitled "From Person to Planet" for a reason. Among its major motivating questions is, How can individuals respond meaningfully to the environmental situation? Where does a person sit in relation to concerns of planetary scope and scale? We, the book's editors, believe that knowledge is power and that it generates responsibility. Once we know about environmental issues, we cannot in good conscience turn away in ignorance. That would deprive us of living authentic lives. Much of the book up to this point has been about the various drivers of environmental harm and the large-scale routes to more effective environmental governance. In this section we explore in a more direct way the challenge of assuming environmental responsibility. We examine how an individual or group can best conceptualize and engage with global environmental-protection efforts.

There is a long and heated debate about this. It is between those who think that changing our individual lives is the best and most responsible route to environmental protection and those who argue for changing structures of power. Those advocating the first position call for reducing one's ecological footprint—consuming less, using earth-friendly technologies, eating sustainably grown food, and so forth. They see environmental harm originating with individuals and global environmental degradation as the accumulated effect of more than seven billion people living ecologically unsustainable lives (or at least a large portion of the world's people doing so). For them, lifestyle change is, at a minimum, a necessary although perhaps insufficient avenue to meaningful environmental change. Without people taking personal responsibility for individual ecological behavior, sustainability is a hollow aspiration.

On the other side are those who look at lifestyle change as spitting in the wind. To them, there will never be enough people willing to undertake significant personal change to make a difference.

251

The issues we're dealing with are too huge: climate change, ozone depletion, freshwater scarcity, and loss of biological diversity. A person could reduce their ecological footprint to zero, but this would not impact global issues a whit. Rather, the most important thing to do is to change the structures of power—the economic, political, technological, and social systems that drive unsustainability. This involves altering government policies, shifting economic incentives, redirecting technological innovation, and redefining international development. These changes would really matter. They would enlist the mechanisms of governance discussed in previous sections and employ them in the service of large-scale environmental protection.

Who is right? To us, this seems like the wrong question. A more useful way to think about "what is to be done" revolves around how to live strategically—how to make plans and take actions that enhance one's personal life *and* our collective lives. These days, strategy gets a bad rap. It is associated with instrumentality and getting what one wants, often independent of the effect on others. But strategy is about not only finding a means to an end, but also discerning what that end should be. In this section, we explore the question of how to make a difference through the lens of discernment. The aim is to provide a menu of political thinking and invite reflection on how each of us can find our unique way of addressing environmental dilemmas.

Systems theorist **Donella H. Meadows**, in the first reading, offers some classic advice about how to engineer social change. Meadows identifies a range of leverage points—"points of power"—that are present in social systems, and ranks them from least to most important. Her intent is to show that if we aim to bring about some form of social shift, our attentions are best directed toward those places in a social system where our efforts will be magnified. A leverage point is like the diminutive rudder on a great ship. Sometimes a relatively small force applied to just the right location in the right manner can have an outsized impact.

Environmental-studies professor **Michael F. Maniates** takes aim at what he calls the "individualization of responsibility" around environmental concerns. He suggests that the mainstream message seems to be that the environmental situation is caused by individual failings and that our best response is individual action: "Plant a tree, ride a bike, save the world!" Maniates argues that this individualizing tendency is dangerous, limiting the ability of the environmental movement to confront adequately the deeply rooted drivers of environmental harm. He urges us, ultimately, to think and act collectively as citizens rather than individually as consumers.

Global environmental politics professor **Paul Wapner** and economist **John Willoughby** similarly point to limits inherent in certain kinds of individual action. They start with the IPAT equation, discussed in the introduction to Section 3 of this book. If, based on IPAT, the global environmental challenges are seen as being driven largely by higher levels of population and consumption, then it would seem reasonable to ask people to have fewer children and spend less money. Yet, as Wapner and Willoughby show, adopting such individual choices can have counterproductive—even perverse—impacts. Having fewer kids, for instance, means that adults end up with more disposable income to invest or spend in ways that can lead to harmful environmental outcomes. Like Maniates, these authors recognize that all responses to the environmental situation are at some level individual actions. However, when we think of ourselves *solely* as individuals and eschew taking collective action, we are missing opportunities for greater impact.

Author **Michael Pollan** takes a significantly different tack by addressing a straightforward, hardheaded question: Why bother? The environmental challenge can seem so vast, and our individual capacities to take action so comparatively limited, that it can be tempting to throw up one's hands. Pollan challenges such an understanding. He argues that climate change and, by extension, other global environmental challenges are at root a "crisis of lifestyle." The deteriorating environmental situation is the product of countless individual choices and actions. We are all complicit. Given that, he suggests that to imagine some piece of legislation or a new technology or a corporation will come along and save us is to shirk our personal responsibilities, and in fact is an extension of the thinking that got us into this mess in the first place. Pollan argues that we must imagine we can live differently, then take the steps, as individuals, necessary to make that different way of living a reality.

There is much agreement among the different authors excerpted in this section. Each raises questions about the value of an environmental politics built solely on asking individuals to do small, simple things. The authors challenge us instead to consider how our individual and collective actions can be directed toward the conditions that produce environmental harm and that hold an unsustainable world so firmly in place. In this sense the authors give us one way to understand what it means to think strategically: How can I make the *most* difference?

There is another aspect to strategic thinking, though, that should not be ignored. It boils down to this: How can I ensure that my life has meaning? Implicit in each of this chapter's excerpts, and in many of the other selections in this book, is the idea that taking on the world's environmental challenges is more than a job—more than something that can be relegated to the 9-to-5 world. For the authors excerpted in this section and for many others, environmental action is a *vocation.* To paraphrase writer Frederick Buechner, a vocation is where our most passionate gladness meets the world's deepest need. It is where the things we do in our lives line up in meaningful and fulfilling ways with issues of deep importance. The readings that follow, then, offer some guidance not just about how to be an effective agent of change, but also about how to find worth in the effort.

27

Leverage Points

Toward a Sustainable World

Donella H. Meadows*

Folks who do systems analysis have a great belief in "leverage points." These are places within a complex system (a corporation, an economy, a living body, a city, an ecosystem) where a small shift in one thing can produce big changes in everything.

This idea is not unique to systems analysis—it's embedded in legend. The silver bullet, the trimtab, the miracle cure, the secret passage, the magic password, the single hero or villain who turns the tide of history. The nearly effortless way to cut through or leap over huge obstacles. We not only want to believe that there are leverage points, we want to know where they are and how to get our hands on them. Leverage points are points of power. . . .

The systems analysts I know have come up with no quick or easy formulas for finding leverage points. When we study a system, we usually learn where leverage points are. But a new system we've never encountered? Well, our counterintuitions aren't that well developed. Give us a few months or years to do some computer modeling and we'll figure it out. And we know from bitter experience that, because of counterintuitiveness, when we do discover the system's leverage points, hardly anybody will believe us.

Very frustrating, especially for those of us who yearn not just to understand complex systems, but to make the world work better. . . .

[W]hat you are about to read is a work in progress. It's not a simple, sure-fire recipe for finding leverage points. Rather, it's an invitation to think more broadly about the many ways there might be to get systems to change. . . .

Places to Intervene in a System
(in increasing order of effectiveness)

12. Constants, parameters, numbers (such as subsidies, taxes, standards)
11. The sizes of buffers and other stabilizing stocks, relative to their flows.
10. The structure of material stocks and flows (such as transport networks, population age structures)
9. The lengths of delays, relative to the rate of system change
8. The strength of negative feedback loops, relative to the impacts they are trying to correct against
7. The gain around driving positive feedback loops
6. The structure of information flows (who does and does not have access to what kinds of information)
5. The rules of the system (such as incentives, punishments, constraints)
4. The power to add, change, evolve, or self-organize system structure
3. The goals of the system
2. The mindset or paradigm out of which the system—its goals, structure, rules, delays, parameters—arises
1. The power to transcend paradigms

To explain parameters, stocks, delays, flows, feedback, and so forth, I need to start with a basic diagram.

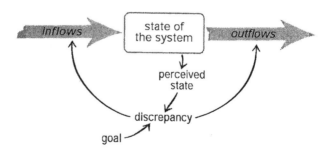

The "state of the system" is whatever standing stock is of importance: amount of water behind the dam, amount of harvestable wood in the forest, number of people in the population, amount of money in the bank, whatever. System states are usually physical stocks, but they could be nonmaterial ones as well: self-confidence, degree of trust in public officials, perceived safety of a neighborhood.

There are usually **inflows** that increase the stock and **outflows** that decrease it. Deposits increase the money in the bank; withdrawals decrease it. River inflow and rain raise the water behind the dam; evaporation and discharge through the spillway lower it. Births and immigrations increase the population, deaths and emigrations reduce it. Political corruption decreases trust in public officials; experience of a well-functioning government increases it. . . .

The rest of the diagram shows the information that causes the flows to change, which then cause the stock to change. If you're about to take a bath, you have a desired water level in mind (your goal). You plug the drain, turn on the faucet, and watch until the water rises to your chosen level (until the discrepancy between the goal and the perceived state of the system is zero). Then you turn the water off.

If you start to get into the bath and discover that you've underestimated your volume and are about to produce an overflow, you can open the drain for awhile, until the water goes down to your desired level.

Those are two **negative feedback loops**, or correcting loops, one controlling the inflow, one controlling the outflow, either or both of which you can use to bring the water level to your goal. Notice that the goal and the feedback connections are not visible in the system. If you were an extraterrestrial trying to figure out why the tub fills and empties, it would take awhile to figure out that there's an invisible goal and a discrepancy-measuring process going on in the head of the creature manipulating the faucets. But if you watched long enough, you could figure that out.

Very simple so far. Now let's take into account that you have two taps, a hot and a cold, and that you're also adjusting for another system state: temperature. Suppose the hot inflow is connected to a boiler way down in the basement, four floors below, so it doesn't respond quickly. And you're making faces at yourself in the mirror and not paying close attention to the water level. The system begins to get complex, and realistic, and interesting.

Mentally change the bathtub into your checking account. Write checks, make deposits, add a faucet that keeps dribbling in a little interest and a special drain that sucks your balance even drier if it ever goes dry. Attach your account to a thousand others and let the bank create loans as a function of your combined and fluctuating deposits. Link a thousand of those banks into a federal reserve system. You begin to see how simple stocks and flows, plumbed together, make up systems way too complex to figure out.

That's why leverage points are not intuitive. And that's enough systems theory to proceed to the list.

12. CONSTANTS, PARAMETERS, NUMBERS

"Parameters" in systems jargon are the numbers that determine how much of a discrepancy turns which faucet how fast. Maybe the faucet turns hard, so it takes awhile to get the water flowing or to turn it off. Maybe the drain is blocked and can allow only a small flow, no matter how open it is. Maybe the faucet can deliver with the force of a fire hose. These considerations are a matter of numbers, some of which are physically locked in and unchangeable, but most of which are popular intervention points.

Consider the national debt. It's a negative bathtub, a money hole. The annual rate at which it sinks is called the deficit. Tax income makes it rise, government expenditures make it fall. Congress and the President spend most of their time arguing about the many, many parameters that open and close tax faucets and spending drains. Since those faucets and drains are connected to us, the voters, these are politically charged parameters. But, despite all the fireworks, and no matter which party is in charge, the money hole keeps getting deeper, just at different rates (and even when, as in 1999, the parties are arguing about how to spend a nonexistent "surplus"). . . .

Parameters are the points of least leverage on my list of interventions. Diddling with the details, arranging the deck chairs on the Titanic. Probably 90—no 95—no 99 percent of our attention goes to parameters, but there's not a lot of leverage in them.

Not that parameters aren't important. They can be, especially in the short term and to the individual who's standing directly in the flow. People care deeply about parameters and fight fierce battles over them. But they *rarely change behavior.* If the system is chronically stagnant, parameter changes rarely kick-start it. If it's wildly variable, they don't usually stabilize it. If it's growing out of control, they don't brake it.

Whatever cap we put on campaign contributions, it doesn't clean up politics. The Feds fiddling with the interest rate haven't made business cycles go away. (We always forget that reality during upturns, and are shocked, shocked by the downturns.) After decades of the strictest air pollution standards in the world, Los Angeles air is less dirty, but it isn't clean. Spending more on police doesn't make crime go away.

Since I'm about to get into some examples where parameters are leverage points, let me insert a big caveat here. Parameters become leverage points when they go into ranges that kick off one of the items later on this list. Interest rates, for example, or birth rates, control the gains around positive feedback loops. System goals are parameters that can make big differences. Sometimes a system gets onto a chaotic edge, where the tiniest change in a number can drive it from order to what appears to be wild disorder.

These critical numbers are not nearly as common as people seem to think they are. Most systems have evolved or are designed to stay far out of critical parameter ranges. Mostly, the numbers are not worth the sweat put into them. . . .

11. THE SIZES OF BUFFERS AND OTHER STABILIZING STOCKS, RELATIVE TO THEIR FLOWS

Consider a huge bathtub with slow in- and outflows. Now think about a small one with very fast flows. That's the difference between a lake and a river. You hear about catastrophic river floods much more often than catastrophic lake floods, because stocks that are big, relative to their flows, are more stable than small ones. In chemistry and other fields, a big, stabilizing stock is known as a buffer.

The stabilizing power of buffers is why you keep money in the bank rather than living from the flow of change through your pocket. It's why stores hold inventory instead of calling for new stock just as customers carry the old stock out the door. It's why we need to maintain more than the minimum breeding population of an endangered species. Soils in the eastern U.S. are more sensitive to acid rain than soils in the west, because they haven't got big buffers of calcium to neutralize acid.

Often you can stabilize a system by increasing the capacity of a buffer. But if a buffer is too big, the system becomes inflexible. It reacts too slowly. And big buffers of some sorts, such as water reservoirs or inventories, cost a lot to build or maintain. . . .

There's leverage, sometimes magical, in changing the size of buffers. But buffers are usually physical entities, not easy to change. The acid absorption capacity of eastern soils is not a leverage point for alleviating acid rain damage. The storage capacity of a dam is literally cast in concrete. So I have put buffers at the less influential end of the list of leverage points.

10. THE STRUCTURE OF MATERIAL STOCKS AND FLOWS AND NODES OF INTERSECTION

The plumbing structure, the stocks and flows and their physical arrangement, can have an enormous effect on how the system operates. When the Hungarian road system was laid out so all traffic from one side of the nation to the other has to pass through central Budapest, that determined a lot about air pollution and commuting delays that are not easily fixed by pollution control devices, traffic lights, or speed limits. The only way to fix a system that is laid out wrong is to rebuild it, if you can. . . .

Physical structure is crucial in a system, but rarely a leverage point, because changing it is rarely simple. The leverage point is in proper design in the first place. After the structure is built, the leverage is in understanding its limitations and bottlenecks and refraining from fluctuations or expansions that strain its capacity.

9. THE LENGTHS OF DELAYS, RELATIVE TO THE RATE OF SYSTEM CHANGES

Remember that bathtub on the fourth floor I mentioned, with the water heater in the basement? I actually experienced one of those once, in an old hotel in London. It wasn't even a bathtub, it was a shower—no buffering capacity. The water temperature took at least a minute to respond to my faucet twists. Guess what my shower was like.

Right, oscillations from hot to cold and back to hot, punctuated with expletives.

Delays in feedback loops are common causes of oscillations. If you're trying to adjust a system state to your goal, but you only receive delayed information about what the system state is, you will overshoot and undershoot. Same if your information is timely, but your response isn't. For example, it takes several years to build an electric power plant, and then that plant lasts, say, thirty years. Those delays make it impossible to build exactly the right number of plants to supply a rapidly changing demand. Even with immense effort at forecasting, almost every centralized electricity industry in the world experiences long oscillations between overcapacity and undercapacity. A system just can't respond to short-term changes when it has long-term delays. That's why a massive central-planning system, such as the Soviet Union or General Motors, necessarily functions poorly. . . .

I would list delay length as a high leverage point, except for the fact that delays are not often easily changeable. Things take as long as they take. You can't do a lot about the construction time of a major piece of capital, or the maturation time of a child, or the growth rate of a forest. It's usually easier to slow down the change rate, so that inevitable feedback delays won't cause so much trouble. That's why growth rates are higher up on the leverage-point list than delay times. . . .

[I]f there is a delay in your system that can be changed, changing it can have big effects. Watch out! Be sure you change it in the right direction! (For example, the great push to reduce information and money transfer delays in financial markets is just asking for wild gyrations.)

8. THE STRENGTH OF NEGATIVE FEEDBACK LOOPS, RELATIVE TO THE IMPACTS THEY ARE TRYING TO CORRECT AGAINST

Now we're beginning to move from the physical part of the system to the information and control parts, where more leverage can be found.

Negative feedback loops are ubiquitous in systems. Nature evolves them and humans invent them as controls to keep important system states within safe bounds. A thermostat loop is the classic example. Its purpose is to keep the system state called "room temperature" fairly constant at a desired level. Any negative feedback loop needs a goal (the thermostat setting), a monitoring and signaling device to detect excursions from the goal (the thermostat), and a response mechanism (the furnace and/or air conditioner, fans, heat pipes, fuel, etc.).

A complex system usually has numerous negative feedback loops that it can bring into play, so it can self-correct under different conditions and impacts. Some of those loops may be inactive much of the time, like the emergency cooling system in a nuclear power plant, or your ability to sweat or shiver to maintain your body temperature. They may not be very visible. But their presence is critical to the long-term welfare of the system.

One of the big mistakes we make is to strip away these "emergency" response mechanisms because they aren't used often and they appear to be costly. In the short term, we see no effect from doing this. In the long term, we drastically narrow the range of conditions over which the system can survive. One of the most heartbreaking ways we do this is in encroaching on the habitats of endangered species. Another is in encroaching on our own time for rest, recreation, socialization, and meditation.

The "strength" of a negative loop—its ability to keep its appointed stock at or near its goal—depends on the combination of all its parameters and links—the accuracy and rapidity of monitoring, the quickness and power of response, the directness and size of corrective flows. Sometimes there are leverage points here.

Take markets, for example, the negative feedback systems that are all but worshipped by economists—and they can indeed be marvels of self-correction, as prices vary to moderate supply and demand and keep them in balance. The more the price—the central piece of information signaling both producers and consumers—is kept clear, unambiguous, timely, and truthful, the more smoothly markets will operate. Prices that reflect full costs will tell consumers how much they can actually afford and will reward efficient producers.

Companies and governments are fatally attracted to the price leverage point, of course, all of them determinedly pushing it in the wrong direction with subsidies, fixes, externalities, taxes, and other forms of confusion.

These folks are trying to weaken the feedback power of market signals by twisting information in their favor. The real leverage here is to keep them from doing it. Hence the necessity of anti-trust laws, truth-in-advertising laws, attempts to internalize costs (such as pollution taxes), the removal of perverse subsidies, and other ways to level market playing fields. . . .

The strength of a negative feedback loop is important *relative to the impact it is designed to correct*. If the impact increases in strength, the feedbacks have to be strengthened too. A thermostat system may work fine on a cold winter day, but open all the windows and its corrective power will fail. Democracy worked better before the advent of the brainwashing power of centralized mass communications. Traditional controls on fishing were sufficient until radar spotting and drift nets and other technologies made it possible for a few actors to wipe out the fish. The power of big industry calls for the power of big government to hold it in check; a global economy makes necessary a global government.

Here are some examples of strengthening feedback controls to improve a system's self-correcting abilities:

- preventive medicine, exercise, and good nutrition to bolster the body's ability to fight disease;
- integrated pest management to encourage natural predators of crop pests;
- the Freedom of Information Act to reduce government secrecy;
- monitoring systems to report on environmental damage;

- protection of whistleblowers;
- impact fees, pollution taxes, and performance bonds to recapture the externalized public costs of private benefits.

7. THE GAIN AROUND DRIVING POSITIVE FEEDBACK LOOPS

A negative feedback loop is self-correcting; a *positive feedback loop* is self-reinforcing. The more it works, the more it gains power to work some more. The more people catch the flu, the more they infect other people. The more babies are born, the more people grow up to have babies. The more money you have in the bank, the more interest you earn, the more money you have in the bank. The more the soil erodes, the less vegetation it can support, the fewer roots and leaves to soften rain and run-off, the more soil erodes. The more high-energy neutrons in the critical mass, the more they knock into nuclei and generate more.

Positive feedback loops are sources of growth, explosion, erosion, and collapse in systems. A system with an unchecked positive loop ultimately will destroy itself. That's why there are so few of them. Usually a negative loop will kick in sooner or later. The epidemic will run out of infectable people—or people will take increasingly strong steps to avoid being infected. The death rate will rise to equal the birth rate—or people will see the consequences of unchecked population growth and have fewer babies. The soil will erode away to bedrock—or people will stop overgrazing, put up check dams, plant trees, and stop the erosion.

In all these examples, the first outcome is what will happen if the positive loop runs its course, the second is what will happen if there is an intervention to reduce its self-multiplying power. Reducing the gain around a positive loop—slowing the growth—is usually a more powerful leverage point in systems than strengthening negative loops, and much preferable to letting the positive loop run.

Population and economic growth rates are leverage points, because slowing them gives the many negative loops—technology and markets and other forms of adaptation, all of which have limits and delays—time to function. It's the same as slowing the car when you're driving too fast, rather than calling for more responsive brakes or technical advances in steering. . . .

6. THE STRUCTURE OF INFORMATION FLOWS

There was this subdivision of identical houses, the story goes, except that for some reason the electric meter in some of the houses was installed in the basement and in others it was installed in the front hall, where the residents could see it constantly, going round faster or slower as they used more or less electricity. With no other change, with identical prices, electricity consumption was 30 percent lower in the houses where the meter was in the front hall.

We systems-heads love that story because it's an example of a high leverage point in the information structure of the system. It's not a parameter adjustment, not a strengthening or weakening of an existing loop. It's a *new loop,* delivering information to a place where it wasn't going before and therefore causing people to behave differently.

A more recent example is the Toxic Release Inventory, the U.S. government's requirement, instituted in 1986, that every factory releasing hazardous air pollutants report those emissions publicly every year. Suddenly every community could find out precisely what was coming out of the smokestacks in town. There was no law against those emissions, no fines, no determination of "safe" levels, just information. But by 1990, emissions dropped 40 percent. They have continued to go down since, not so much because of citizen outrage as because of corporate shame. One chemical company that found itself on the Top Ten Polluters list reduced its emissions by 90 percent, just to "get off that list."

Missing feedback is one of the most common causes of system malfunction. Adding or restoring information can be a powerful intervention, usually much easier and cheaper than rebuilding physical infrastructure. . . .

We humans have a systematic tendency to avoid accountability for our own decisions. That's why so many feedback loops are missing—and why this kind of leverage point is so often popular with the masses, unpopular with the powers that be, and effective, if you can get the powers that be to permit it to happen (or go around them and make it happen anyway).

5. THE RULES OF THE SYSTEM

The rules of the system define its scope, its boundaries, its degrees of freedom. Thou shalt not kill. Everyone has the right of free speech. Contracts are to be honored. The President serves four-year terms and cannot serve more than two of them. Nine people on a team, you have to touch every base, three strikes and you're out. If you get caught robbing a bank, you go to jail. . . .

To demonstrate the power of rules, I like to ask my students to imagine different ones for a college. Suppose the students graded the teachers, or each other. Suppose there were no degrees: you come to college when you want to learn something, and you leave when you have learned it. Suppose tenure were awarded to professors according to their ability to solve real-world problems, rather than publishing academic papers. Suppose a class was graded as a group, instead of as individuals.

As we try to imagine restructured rules like these and what our behavior would be under them, we come to understand the power of rules. They are high leverage points. Power over the rules is real power. That's why lobbyists congregate when Congress writes laws, and why the Supreme Court, which interprets and delineates the Constitution—the rules for writing the rules—has even more power than Congress. If you want to understand the deepest malfunctions of systems, pay attention to the rules, and to who has power over them. . . .

4. THE POWER TO ADD, CHANGE, EVOLVE, OR SELF-ORGANIZE SYSTEM STRUCTURE

The most stunning thing living systems and social systems can do is to change themselves utterly by creating whole new structures and behaviors. In biological systems that power is called evolution. In human society it's called technical advance or social revolution. In systems lingo, it's called **self-organization**.

Self-organization means changing any aspect of a system lower on this list: adding completely new physical structures, such as brains or wings or computers; adding new negative or positive loops: making new rules. The ability to self-organize is the strongest form of system resilience. A system that can evolve can survive almost any change, by changing itself. The human immune system has the power to develop new responses to (some kinds of) insults it has never before encountered. The human brain can take in new information and pop out completely new thoughts. . . .

Further investigation of self-organizing systems reveals that the divine creator, if there is one, did not have to produce evolutionary miracles. He, she, or it just had to write marvelously clever rules for self-organization. These rules basically govern how, where, and what the system can add onto or subtract from itself under what conditions. . . .

Self-organization is basically the combination of an evolutionary raw material—a highly variable stock of information from which to select possible patterns—and a means for experimentation, for selecting and testing new patterns. For biological evolution the raw material is DNA, one source of variety is spontaneous mutation, and the testing mechanism is something like punctuated Darwinian selection. For technology, the raw material is the body of understanding people have accumulated and stored in libraries and in brains. The source of variety is human creativity (whatever that is) and the selection mechanism can be whatever the market will reward or whatever governments and foundations will fund or whatever meets human needs or solves an immediate problem.

When you understand the power of system self-organization, you begin to understand why biologists worship biodiversity even more than economists worship technology. The wildly varied stock of DNA, evolved and accumulated over billions of years, is the source of evolutionary potential, just as science libraries and labs and universities where scientists are trained are the source of technological potential. Allowing species to go extinct is a systems crime, just as randomly eliminating all copies of particular science journals, or particular kinds of scientists, would be.

The same could be said of human cultures, of course, which are the store of behavioral repertoires, accumulated over not billions, but hundreds of thousands of years. They are a stock out of which social evolution can arise. Unfortunately, people appreciate the precious evolutionary potential of cultures even less than they understand the preciousness of every genetic variation in the world's ground squirrels. I guess that's because one aspect of almost every culture is the belief in the utter superiority of that culture.

Insistence on a single culture shuts down learning. Cuts back resilience. Any system, biological, economic, or social, that becomes so encrusted that it cannot self-evolve, a system that systematically scorns experimentation and wipes out the raw material of innovation, is doomed over the long term on this highly variable planet.

3. THE GOALS OF THE SYSTEM

The goal of a system is a leverage point superior to the self-organizing ability of a system. For example, if the goal is to bring more and more of the world under the control of one particular central planning system (the empire of Genghis Khan, the world of Islam, the People's Republic of China, Walmart, Disney, whatever), then everything further down the list, physical stocks and flows, feedback loops, information flows, even self-organizing behavior, will be twisted to conform to that goal.

That's why I can't get into arguments about whether genetic engineering is a "good" or a "bad" thing. Like all technologies, it depends upon who is wielding it, with what goal. The only thing one can say is that if corporations wield it for the purpose of generating marketable products, that is a very different goal, a different selection mechanism, a different direction for evolution than anything the planet has seen so far. . . .

Whole system goals are not what we think of as goals in the human-motivational sense. They are not so much deducible from what anyone says as from what the system *does*. Survival, resilience, differentiation, evolution are system-level goals.

Even people within systems don't often recognize what whole-system goal they are serving. To make profits, most corporations would say, but that's just a rule, a necessary condition to stay in the game. What is the *point* of the game?

To increase stockholder wealth, most everyone would say, and that is a powerful, behavior-shaping goal. But there is an even larger one, formally espoused by no one, but obvious when one looks at the actual behavior of the system. To grow, to increase market share, to bring the world (customers, suppliers, regulators) more and more under the control of the corporation, so that its operations become ever more shielded from uncertainty. John Kenneth Galbraith recognized that corporate goal—to engulf everything—long ago.

It's the goal of a cancer cell too. Actually it's the goal of every living population, and only a bad one when it isn't balanced by higher-level negative feedback loops that never let an upstart power-driven entity control the world. The goal of keeping the market competitive has to trump the goal of each corporation to eliminate its competitors (and brainwash its customers and swallow its suppliers), just as in ecosystems, the goal of keeping populations in balance and evolving has to trump the goal of each population to reproduce without limit and control all the resource base.

I said earlier that changing the players in the system is a low-level intervention, as long as the players fit into the same old system. The exception to that rule is at the top, where a single player can have the power to change the system's goal. I have watched in wonder as—only very occasionally—a new leader in an organization, from Dartmouth College to Nazi Germany, comes in, enunciates a new goal, and swings hundreds or thousands or millions of perfectly intelligent, rational people off in a new direction. . . .

2. THE MINDSET OR PARADIGM OUT OF WHICH THE SYSTEM ARISES

[One] of Jay Forrester's famous systems sayings goes: It doesn't matter how the tax law of a country is written. There is a shared idea in the minds of the society about what a "fair" distribution of the tax load is. Whatever the rules say, by fair means or foul, by complications, cheating, exemptions or deductions, by constant sniping at the rules, actual tax payments will push right up against the accepted idea of "fairness."

The shared idea in the minds of society, the great big unstated assumptions—unstated because unnecessary to state; everyone already knows them—constitute that society's paradigm, or deepest set of beliefs about how the world works.

There is a difference between nouns and verbs. Money measures something real and has real meaning (therefore people who are paid less are literally worth less). Growth is good. Nature is a stock of resources to be converted to human purposes. Evolution stopped with the emergence of *Homo sapiens.* One can "own" land. Those are just a few of the paradigmatic assumptions of our current culture, all of which have utterly dumfounded other cultures, who thought them not the least bit obvious.

Paradigms are the sources of systems. From them, from shared social agreements about the nature of reality, come system goals and information flows, feedbacks, stocks, flows and everything else about systems. . . .

The ancient Egyptians built pyramids because they believed in an afterlife. We build skyscrapers because we believe that space in downtown cities is enormously valuable. (Except for blighted spaces, often near the skyscrapers, which we believe are worthless.) Whether it was Copernicus and Kepler showing that the earth is not the center of the universe, or Einstein hypothesizing that matter and energy are interchangeable, or Adam Smith postulating that the selfish actions of individual players in markets wonderfully accumulate to the common good, people who have managed to intervene in systems at the level of paradigm have hit a leverage point that totally transforms systems.

You could say paradigms are harder to change than anything else about a system, and therefore this item should be lowest on the list, not second-to-highest. But there's nothing necessarily physical or expensive or even slow in the process of paradigm change. In a single individual it can happen in a millisecond. All it takes is a click in the mind, a falling of scales from eyes, a new way of seeing. Whole societies are another matter. They resist challenges to their paradigm harder than they resist anything else. Societal responses to paradigm challenge have included crucifixions, burnings at the stake, concentration camps, and nuclear arsenals.

So how do you change paradigms? Thomas Kuhn, who wrote the seminal book about the great paradigm shifts of science, has a lot to say about that. In a nutshell, you keep pointing at the anomalies and failures in the old paradigm, you keep speaking louder and with assurance from the new one, you insert people with the new paradigm in places of public visibility and power. You don't waste time with reactionaries; rather you work with active change agents and with the vast middle ground of people who are open-minded. . . .

1. THE POWER TO TRANSCEND PARADIGMS

There is yet one leverage point that is even higher than changing a paradigm. That is to keep oneself unattached in the arena of paradigms, to stay flexible, to realize that *no* paradigm is "true," that every one, including the one that sweetly shapes your own worldview, is a tremendously limited understanding of an immense and amazing universe that is far beyond human comprehension. It is to "get" at a gut level the paradigm that there are paradigms, and to see that that itself is a paradigm, and to regard that whole realization as devastatingly funny. . . .

It is in this space of mastery over paradigms that people throw off addictions, live in constant joy, bring down empires, found religions, get locked up or "disappeared" or shot, and have impacts that last for millennia.

A FINAL CAUTION

. . . Magical leverage points are not easily accessible, even if we know where they are and which direction to push on them. There are no cheap tickets to mastery. You have to work at it, whether that means rigorously analyzing a system or rigorously casting off your own paradigms and throwing yourself into the humility of Not Knowing. In the end, it seems that power has less to do with pushing leverage points than it does with strategically, profoundly, madly letting go.

NOTE

*This is an abridged version of the text. The full version is available at http://www
.donellameadows.org/wp-content/userfiles/Leverage_Points.pdf.

28

Plant a Tree, Buy a Bike, Save the World?

Michael F. Maniates

One of the must successful modern-day children's stories is *The Lorax,* Seuss's tale of a shortsighted and voracious industrialist who clear-cuts vast tracks of Truffula trees to produce "Thneeds" for unquenchable consumer markets. The Lorax, who "speaks for the trees" and the many animals who make the Truffula forest their home, politely but persistently challenges the industrialist, a Mr. Once-ler, by pointing out again and again the terrible toll his business practices are taking on the natural landscape. The Once-ler remains largely deaf to the Lorax's protestations. "I'm just meeting consumer demand," says the Once-ler; "if I didn't, someone else would." When, finally, the last Truffula tree is cut and the landscape is reduced to rubble, the Once-ler—now out of business and apparently penniless—realizes the error of his ways. Years later, holed up in the ruins of his factory amidst a desolate landscape, he recounts his foolishness to a passing boy and charges him with replanting the forest.

The Lorax is fabulously popular. Most of the college students with whom I work—and not just the ones who think of themselves as environmentalists—know it well and speak of it fondly. My children read it in school. There is a 30-minute animated version of the book, which often finds its way onto television. . . .

All this for a tale that is, well, both dismal and depressing. The Once-ler is a stereotypical rapacious businessman. He succeeds in enriching himself by laying ruin to the landscape. The Lorax fails miserably in his efforts to challenge the interlocking processes of industrial capitalism and consumerism that turn his Eden into a wasteland. The animals of the story are forced to flee to uncertain futures. At the end of the day the Lorax's only satisfaction is the privilege of being able to say "I told you so," but this—and the Once-ler's slide into poverty—has got to be small consolation. The conclusion sees a small boy with no evident training in forestry or community organizing unpromisingly entrusted with the last seed of a critical species. He's told to "Plant a new Truffula. Treat it with care. Give it clean water. And feed it fresh air. Grow a forest. Protect it from axes that hack. Then the Lorax and all of his friends may come back." His chances of success are by no means high.

So why the amazing popularity of *The Lorax*? Why do so many find it to be "the environmental book for children"—and, seemingly, for grown-ups too—"by which all others must be judged?" One reason is its overarching message of environmental stewardship and faith in the restorative powers of the young. The book recounts a foolish tragedy that can be reversed only by a new and, one hopes, more enlightened generation. Surely another reason is the comfortable way in which the book—which adults can easily trivialize as children's literature—permits us to look squarely at a set of profoundly uncomfortable dynamics we know to be operating but find difficult to confront: consumerism, the concentration of economic power, the mindless degradation of the environment, the seeming inability of science (represented by the fact-spouting Lorax himself) and objective fact to slow the damage. The systematic undermining of environmental systems fundamental to human well-being is scary stuff, though no more so than one's own sense of personal impotence in the face of such destruction. Seuss's clever rhyming schemes and engaging illustrations, wrapped around the 20th century tale of economic expansion and environmental degradation, provide safe passage through a topic we know is out there but would rather avoid.

There's another reason, though, why the book is so loved. By ending with the charge to plant a tree, *The Lorax* both echoes and amplifies an increasingly dominant, largely American response to the contemporary environmental crisis. This response half-consciously understands environmental degradation as the product of *individual* shortcomings (the Once-ler's greed, for example), best countered by action that is staunchly *individual* and typically *consumer-based* (buy a tree and plant it!) It embraces the notion that knotty issues of consumption, consumerism, power and responsibility can be resolved neatly and cleanly through enlightened, uncoordinated consumer choice. Education is a critical ingredient in this view—smart consumers will make choices, it's thought, with the larger public good in mind. Accordingly, this dominant response emphasizes (like the Lorax himself) the need to speak politely, and individually, armed only with facts.

For the lack of a better term, call this response the *individualization of responsibility*. When responsibility for environmental problems is individualized, there is little room to ponder institutions, the nature and exercise of political power, or ways of collectively changing the distribution of power and influence in society—to, in other words, "think institutionally." Instead, the serious work of confronting the threatening socio-environmental processes that *The Lorax* so ably illuminates falls to individuals, acting alone, usually as consumers. We are individualizing responsibility when we agonize over the "paper or plastic" choice at the checkout counter, knowing somehow that neither is right given larger institutions and social structures. We think aloud with the neighbor over the back fence about whether we should buy the new Honda or Toyota hybrid engine automobile now or wait a few years until they work the kinks out, when really what we wish for is clean, efficient, and effective public transportation of the sort we read about in science fiction novels when we were young—but which we can't vote for with our consumer dollars since, for reasons rooted in power and politics, it's not for sale. So we ponder the "energy stickers" on the ultra-efficient appliances at Sears, we diligently compost our kitchen waste, we try to ignore the high initial cost and buy a few compact-fluorescent lightbulbs. . . .

The Lorax is not why the individualization of responsibility dominates the contours of contemporary American environmentalism. Several forces, described later in this article, are to blame. They include the historical baggage of mainstream environmentalism, the core tenets of liberalism, the dynamic ability of capitalism to commodify dissent, and the relatively recent rise of global environmental threats to human prosperity. Seuss's book simply bas been swept up by these forces and adopted by them. Seuss himself would probably be surprised by the near deification of his little book; and his central character, a Lorax who politely sought to hold a corporate CEO accountable, surely would be appalled that his story is being used to justify individual acts of planting trees as the primary response to the threat of global climate change. . . .

Skeptics may reasonably question if the individualization of responsibility is so omnipresent to warrant . . . concern. As I argue in the next section of this article, it is: the depoliticization of environmental degradation is in full swing across a variety of fronts and shows little sign of abating. I continue with a review of the forces driving this individualization; it in particular implicates the rise of global environmental problems and the construction of an individualized politics around them. How might these forces be countered? How can the politics of individualization be transcended? How might our environmental imagination be expanded? I wrestle with these questions in the final section of this article by focusing on the IPAT formula—a dominant conceptual lens within the field of environmental policy and politics, which argues that "environmental impact" = "population" × "affluence" × "technology."

A DANGEROUS NARROWING?

A few years back Peter Montague, editor of the internet-distributed *Rachel's Environmental and Health Weekly*, took the Environmental Defense Fund (EDF) to task for its annual calendar, which this powerful and effective organization widely distributes to its more than 300,000 members and many non-members too. What drew Montague's ire was the final page of EDF's . . . calendar, which details a 10-point program to "save the Earth." (EDF's phrase): 1. Visit and help support our national parks; 2. Recycle newspapers, glass, plastic and aluminum; 3. Conserve energy and use energy-efficient lighting; 4. Keep tires properly inflated to improve gas mileage and extend tire life; 5. Plant trees; 6. Organize a Christmas tree recycling program in your community; 7. Find an alternative to chemical pesticides for your lawn; 8. Purchase only those brands of tuna marked "dolphin-safe;" 9. Organize a community group to clean. up a local stream, highway, park, or beach; and 10. Become a member of EDF. Montague's reaction was terse and pointed:

> What I notice here is the complete absence of any ideas commensurate the size and nature of the problems faced by the world's environment. I'm not against recycling Christmas trees—if you MUST have one—but who can believe that recycling Christmas trees—or supporting EDF as it works overtime to amend and re-amend the Clean Air Act—is part of any serious effort to "save the Earth?" I am forced to conclude once again that the mainstream environmental movement in the U.S. has run out of ideas and has no worthy vision.

Shortly after reading Montague's disturbing and, for me, surprising rejection of 10 very sensible measures to protect the environment, I walked into an introductory course on environmental problems that I often team-teach with colleagues in the environmental science department. The course challenges students to consider not only the physical cause-and-effect relationships that manifest themselves as environmental degradation, but also to think critically about the struggles for power and influence that underlie most environmental problems. That day, near the end of a very productive semester, my colleague divided the class of about 45 students into smaller "issue groups" (energy, water, agriculture, etc.) and asked each group to develop a rank-order list of "responses" or "solutions" to environmental threats specific to that issue. He then brought the class back together, had each group report, and tabulated their varied "solutions." From this group of 45, the fourth must recommended solution to mounting environmental degradation was to ride a bike rather than drive a car. Number three on the list was to recycle. The second most preferred action was "plant a tree" and the top response was, again, "plant a tree" (the mechanics of tabulating student preference across the issue groups permitted a singularly strong preference to occupy two slots).

When we asked our students—who were among the brightest and best prepared of the many with whom we'd worked over the years—why, after thirteen weeks of intensive study of environmental problems, they were so reluctant to consider as "solutions" broader changes in policy and institutions, they shrugged. Sure, we remember studying these kinds of approaches in class, they said, but such measures were, well, fuzzy, mysterious, messy, and "idealistic." . . .

As I reflect now on these past events, I wonder if they're getting the wrong message, ubiquitous as it has become. Consider the following:

- ... A colleague recently received a small box in the mail with an attached sticker that read "Environmental Solutions—Not Just Problems." Inside was a peat pot filled with soil in which was growing a pine-tree seedling, together with a piece of paper about 2" square that said "Rather than sensationalize the problems in our world, *Environmental Science* provides your students with the tools to develop their own opinions and focus on solutions. Keeping with this theme, you and your students can decide where to best plant the enclosed seedling and watch it grow throughout the year." The seedling and associated materials was a promotion for one of the most widely used environmental-science textbooks at the undergraduate level.
- These days, my students argue that the best way to reverse environmental degradation is to educate the young children now in school. When pressed, they explain that only a sea-change in the choices individual consumers are making will staunch the ecological bleeding we're now facing—and it's too late to make much of a dent in the consumer preferences of young adults like themselves.
- The biggest environmental issue to hit our community in the last decade has been the threatened demise, for lack of funding, of "drop off" centers for recycled products. Primary-school students have distributed their art work around the theme of "Save the Planet—Recycle" and letters to the editor speak gravely of myriad assaults on the planet and the importance of "buying green" and recycling if we're to stop the destruction. And this is not a phenomenon limited to small-town America; a friend visiting Harvard University recently sent me a copy of a flyer, posted over one of the student copy machines, with a line drawing of planet earth and the slogan "Recycle and Do Your Part to Save the Planet." Recycling is a prime example of the individualization of responsibility. ...

In our struggle to bridge the gap between our morals and our practices, we stay busy—but busy doing that with which we're most familiar and comfortable: consuming our way (we hope) to a better America and a better world. When confronted by environmental ills—ills many confess to caring deeply about—Americans seem capable of understanding themselves only as consumers who must buy "environmentally sound" products (and then recycle them), rather than as citizens who might come together and develop political muscle sufficient to alter institutional arrangements that drive a pervasive consumerism. The relentless ability of contemporary capitalism to commodify dissent and sell it back to dissenters is surely one explanation for the elevation of consumer over citizen. But another factor, no doubt, is the growing suspicion of and unfamiliarity with processes of citizen-based political action among masses of North Americans. The interplay of State and Market after World War II has whittled the obligations of citizenship down to the singular and highly individualized act of voting in important elections. The increasing fragmentation and mobility of everyday life undermines our sense of neighborhood and community, separating us from the small arenas in which we might practice and refine our abilities as citizens. We build shopping malls but let community play-grounds deteriorate and migrate to sales but ignore school-board meetings. Modern-day advances in entertainment and communication increasingly find us sitting alone in front of a screen, making it all seem fine. We do our political bit in the election booth, then get back to "normal."

Given our deepening alienation from traditional understandings of active citizenship, together with the growing allure of consumption-as-social-action, it's little wonder that at a time when our capacity to imagine an array of ways to build a just and ecologically resilient future must expand, it is in fact narrowing. At a moment when we should be vigorously exploring multiple paths to sustainability, we are obsessing over the cobblestones of but one path. This collective obsessing over an array of "green consumption" choices and opportunities to recycle is noisy and vigorous, and thus comes to resemble the foundations of meaningful social action. But it isn't, not in any real and lasting way that might alter institutional arrangements and make possible radically new ways of living that seem required.

ENVIRONMENTALISM AND THE FLIGHT FROM POLITICS

The individualization of responsibility for environmental ills and the piecemeal, counterproductive actions it produces have not gone unnoticed by analysts of contemporary environmental politics. Over a decade ago, for example, social ecologist Murray Bookchin vigorously argued that:

> It is inaccurate and unfair to coerce people into believing that they are *personally* responsible for present-day ecological disasters because they consume too much or proliferate too readily. This privatization of the environmental crisis, like the New Age cults that focus on personal problems rather than on social dislocations, has reduced many environmental movements to utter ineffectiveness and threatens to diminish their credibility with the public. If "simple living" and militant recycling are the main solutions to the environmental crisis, the crisis will certainly continue and intensify.

More recently, Paul Hawken, the co-founder of the environmentally conscious Smith and Hawken garden-supply company and widely published analyst of "eco-commerce," confessed that:

... it [is] clear to me ... that there [is] no way to "there" from here, that all companies are essentially proscribed from becoming ecologically sound, and that awards to institutions that had ventured to the environmental margins only underlined the fact that commerce and sustainability were antithetical by design, not by intention. Management is being told that if it wakes up and genuflects, pronouncing its amendes honorable, substituting paper for polystyrene, we will be on the path to an environmentally sound world. *Nothing could be farther from the truth. The problem isn't with half measures, but the illusion they foster that subtle course corrections can guide us to the good life that will include a "conserved nature" and cozy shopping malls.*

Bookchin and Hawken are reacting, in large measure, to the notable transformation in how Americans understand and attack environmental problems that occurred in the 1980s. The '80s was a decade in which re-energized, politically conservative forces in the US promoted the rhetoric of returning power and responsibility to the individual, while simultaneously curtailing the role of government in an economy that was increasingly characterized as innately self-regulating and efficient. Within this context, responsibility for creating and fixing environmental problems was radically reassigned, from government, corporations, and the environmentally shortsighted policies they were thought to have together fostered, to individual consumers and their decisions in the marketplace. . . .

Others pin the blame for the individualization of responsibility on the bureaucratic calcification of mainstream, "inside the beltway" environmental groups. Buffeted by backlash in the 1980s, laboring hard to fend off challenges to existing environmental regulations in the 1990s, and unsure about how to react to widespread voter apathy in the 2000s, mainstream environmental groups in the US have consolidated and "hunkered down." To survive as non-profit organizations without government financing (as is common in other countries), these US NGOs have had to avoid any costly confrontation with real power while simultaneously appearing to the public as if they are vigorously attacking environmental ills. The result: 10 easy steps to save the planet of the sort proffered each year by the Environmental Defense Fund.

Other scholars draw attention to the classical liberal underpinnings of environmentalism that bias environmentalism towards timid calls for personal responsibility and green consumerism. As Paul Wapner, a professor at American University notes,

Liberal environmentalism is *so* compatible with contemporary material and cultural currents that it implicitly supports the very things that it should be criticizing. Its technocratic, scientistic, and even economistic character gives credence to a society that measures the quality of life fundamentally in terms of economic growth, control over nature, and the maximization of sheer efficiency in everything we do. By working to show that environmental protection need not compromise these maxims, liberal environmentalism fails to raise deeper issues that more fundamentally engage the dynamics of environmental degradation.

And yet mainstream environmentalism has not always advanced an individualized consumeristic strategy for redressing environmental ills. . . . Throughout the 20th century, in fact, mainstream environmentalism has demonstrated an ability to foster multiple and simultaneous interpretations on where we are and where we are heading.

But that ability has, today, clearly become impaired. Although public support for things environmental has never been greater, it is so because the public increasingly understands environmentalism as an individual, rational, cleanly apolitical process that can deliver a future that works without raising voices or mobilizing constituencies. As individual consumers and recyclers we are supplied with ample and easy means of "doing our bit." The result, though, is often dissonant and sometimes bizarre: consumers wearing "save the earth" T-shirts, for example, speak passionately against recent rises in gasoline prices when approached by television news crews; shoppers drive all over town in their gasoline-guzzling SUVs in search of organic lettuce or shade-grown coffee; and diligent recyclers expend far more fossil-fuel energy on the hot water spent to meticulously clean a tin can than is saved by its recycling. . . .

Ironically, those laboring to highlight global environmental ills, in the hope that an aroused public would organize and embark upon collective, political action, aided and abetted this process of individualization. They paved the way for the likes of Rainforest Crunch ice cream ("buy it and a portion of the proceeds will go to save the rainforests") because they were insufficiently attentive to a fundamental social arithmetic: heightened concern about any social ill, erupting at a time of erosion of public confidence in political institutions and citizen capacities to effect change, will prompt masses of people to act, but in that one arena of their lives where they command the most power and feel the most competent—the sphere of consumption. . . .

It's more than coincidental that as our collective perception of environmental problems has become more global, our prevailing way of framing environmental problem-solving has become more individualized. In the end, individualizing responsibility does not work—you can't plant a tree to save the world—and as citizens and consumers slowly come to discover this fact their cynicism about social change will only grow: "you mean after fifteen years of washing out these crummy jars and recycling them, environmental problems are still getting worse—geesh, what's the use?" Individualization, by implying that any action beyond the private and the consumptive is irrelevant, insulates people from the empowering experiences and political lessons of collective struggle for social change and reinforces corrosive myths about the difficulties of public life. By legitimating notions of consumer sovereignty and a self-balancing and autonomous market, it also diverts attention from political arenas that matter. In this way, individualization is both a symptom and a source of waning citizen capacities to participate meaningfully in processes of social change. If consumption, in all its complexity, is to be confronted, the forces that systematically individualize responsibility for environmental degradation must be challenged.

IPAT, AND BEYOND

But how? One approach would focus on undermining the dominant frameworks of thinking and talking that make the individualization of responsibility appear so natural and "common sense." Among other things, this means taking on "IPAT."

At first glance it would seem that advocates of a consumption angle on environmental degradation should naturally embrace IPAT (impact = population × affluence × technology). The "formula" argues, after all, that one cannot make sense of, much less tackle, environmental problems unless one takes into account all three of the proximate causes of environmental degradation. Population growth, resource-intensive and highly polluting technologies, and affluence (that is, levels of consumption) together conspire to undermine critical ecological processes upon which human well-being depends. Focusing on one or two of these three factors, IPAT tells us, will ultimately disappoint.

IPAT is a powerful conceptual framework, and those who would argue the importance of including consumption in the environmental-degradation equation have not been reluctant to invoke it. They note, correctly so, that the "A" in IPAT has for too long been neglected in environmental debates and policy action. However, although IPAT provides intellectual justification for positioning consumption center-stage, it also comes with an underlying set of assumptions—assumptions that reinforce an ineffectual Loraxian flight from politics.

A closer look at IPAT shows that the formula distributes widely all culpability for the environmental crisis (akin to the earlier mentioned "New Age Environmentalism"). Population size, consumption levels, and technology choice are all to blame. Responsibility for environmental degradation nicely splits, moreover, between the so-called developed and developing world: if only the developing world could get its population under control and the developed world could tame its overconsumption and each could adopt green technologies, then all would be well. Such a formulation is, on its face, eminently reasonable, which explains why IPAT stands as such a tempting platform from which advocates of a consumption perspective might press their case.

In practice, however, IPAT amplifies and privileges an "everything is connected to everything else" biophysical, ecosystem-management understanding of environmental problems, one that obscures the exercise of power while systematically disempowering citizen actors. When everything is connected to everything else, knowing how or when or even why to intervene becomes difficult; such "system complexity" seems to overwhelm any possibility of planned, coordinated, effective intervention. Additionally, there is not much room in IPAT's calculus for questions of agency, institutions, political power, or collective action. . . .

Proponents of a consumption angle on environmental degradation must cultivate alternatives to IPAT and conventional development models that focus on, rather than divert attention from, politically charged elements of commercial relations. Formulas like IPAT are handy in that they focus attention on key elements of a problem. In that spirit, then, I propose a variation: "IWAC," which is environmental Impact = quality of Work $\times$ meaningful consumption Alternatives $\times$ political Creativity. If ideas have power, and if acronyms package ideas, then alternative formulations like IWAC could prove useful in shaking the environmentally-inclined out of their slumber of individualization. And this could only be good for those who worry about consumption.

Take "work" for example. IPAT systematically ignores work while IWAC embraces it. As *The Atlantic Monthly* senior editor Jack Beatty notes, "radical talk" about work—questions about job security, worker satisfaction, downsizing, overtime, and corporate responsibility—is coming back strong into public discourse. People who might otherwise imagine themselves as apolitical care about the state of work, and they do talk about it. IWAC taps into this concern, linking it to larger concerns about environmental degradation by suggesting that consumeristic impulses are linked to the routinization of work and, more generally, to the degree of worker powerlessness within the workplace. . . .

Likewise, the "A" in IWAC, "alternatives," expands IPAT's "T" in new directions by suggesting that the public's failure to embrace sustainable technologies has more to do with institutional structures that restrict the aggressive development and wide dissemination of sustainable technologies than with errant consumer choice. The marketplace, for instance, presents us with red cars and blue ones, and calls this consumer choice, when what sustainability truly demands is a choice between automobiles and mass transit systems that enjoy a level of government support and subsidy that is presently showered upon the automotive industry. With "alternatives," spirited conversation can coalesce around questions like: Do consumers confront real, or merely cosmetic choice? Is absence of choice the consequence of an autonomous and distant set of market mechanisms? Or is the self-interested exercise of political and economic power at work? And how would one begin to find out? . . .

And then there is the issue of public imagination and collective creativity, represented by the "C" in IWAC. "Imagination" is not a word one often sees in reflections on environmental politics; it lies among such terms as love, caring, kindness, and meaning that raise eyebrows when introduced into political discourse and policy analysis. . . .

[However,] ideas and the images that convey them have power; and though subtle, such power can and is exercised to channel ideas into separate tracks labeled "realistic" and "idealistic." Once labeled, what is taken to be impossible or impractical—"idealistic," in other words—can no longer serve as a staging ground for struggle. . . .

A proverbial fork in the road looms large for those who would seek to cement consumption into the environmental agenda. One path of easy walking leads to a future where "consumption" in its environmentally undesirable forms—"overconsumption," "commodification," and "consumerism"—has found a place in environmental debates. Environmental groups will work hard to "educate" the citizenry about the need to buy green and consume less and, by accident or design, the pronounced asymmetry of responsibility for and power over environmental problems will remain obscure. Consumption, ironically, could continue to expand as the privatization of the environmental crisis encourages upwardly spiraling consumption, so long as this consumption is "green." This is the path of business-as-usual.

The other road, a rocky one, winds towards a future where environmentally concerned citizens come to understand, by virtue of spirited debate and animated conversation, the "consumption problem." They would see that their individual consumption choices are environmentally important, but that their control over these choices is constrained, shaped, and framed by institutions and political forces that can be remade only through collective citizen action, as opposed to individual consumer behavior. This future world will not be easy to reach. Getting there means challenging the dominant view—the production, technological, efficiency-oriented perspective that infuses contemporary definitions of progress—and requires linking explorations of consumption to politically charged issues that challenge the political imagination. Walking this path means becoming attentive to the underlying forces that narrow our understanding of the possible.

To many, alas, an environmentalism of "plant a tree, save the world" appears to be apolitical and non-confrontational, and thus ripe for success. Such an approach is anything but, insofar as it works to constrain our imagination about what is possible and what is worth working towards. It is time for those who hope for renewed and rich discussion about "the consumption problem" to come to grips with this narrowing of the collective imagination and the growing individualization of responsibility that drives it, and to grapple intently with ways of reversing the tide.

29

The Poverty of Lifestyle Change

Paul Wapner
and John Willoughby

Many environmentalists point to overpopulation and overconsumption as the fundamental causes of environmental harm. They argue that there are simply too many human beings, in terms of sheer numbers, and too many of us who overuse the earth's resources (and thus generate significant amounts of waste) to live ecologically sustainable lives. The fundamental tasks of environmentalism, then, are to lower population rates and curtail consumption. These twin objectives have defined much of the environmental movement for decades, and both trajectories course through contemporary environmentalism, urging us all to cut back: to curtail our numbers and our appetites.

Lowering population and curbing consumption are not simply governmental or corporate tasks, but also involve individual lifestyle choices. The decisions we each make in terms of whether to have children and, if so, how many, and what level of material comfort to experience translate into widespread fertility and consumption patterns. As the environmental movement has been explaining since its inception over a century ago, environmental protection entails, as the saying goes, "walking lightly on the earth." And, as the surge of such best-selling books as *Voluntary Simplicity* and *50 Simple Things You Can Do to Save the Earth* explain, this is something we can *all* learn to do.

While acting at the microlevel to reduce family size and consume less is almost dogma among environmentalists, there are reasons to question their admonitions, or at least to specify the conditions under which such activities would genuinely make a difference in terms of environmental well-being. In this article we argue that prescriptions that call for individually reducing consumption and having fewer children are valid only under highly restricted conditions, conditions that are generally unacknowledged by environmental researchers and activists. In fact, we show that the conditions are so narrow that, for most people most of the time, lifestyle changes are ecologically irrelevant.

Many environmentalists call for reducing family size and consuming less because they see these as ways to decrease the total amount of spending within an economy. Reduced spending limits the demand for resources and the production of waste, and thus contributes to environmental well-being. As we will demonstrate, however, while less spending within an economy may, in fact, minimize environmental harm, it is not the case that cutting back on individual consumption or having a smaller family will reduce overall spending. In most cases, such actions will simply shift the locus of spending. If a family, for example, continues to receive the same amount of income but decides to buy fewer products or have fewer children (and thus forgo the consumption associated with additional family members), they have more savings at their disposal. In fact, much of the literature advocating less consumption and greater consumer simplicity emphasizes the bonus of extra savings. It is crucial to recognize, however, that savings do not simply sit in banks or other financial portfolios; rather, they are deployed by financial institutions to fund investment projects. Consequently, because purchasing power is fungible, it makes little difference ecologically if one saves or invests money rather than spends it. For, aside from placing money under one's mattress, it will most likely be used by investors to create more economic wealth, and this will be done primarily by funding practices that use resources and create waste.

In this essay, we demonstrate that unless one invests savings in particular, very circumscribed ways (to be explained), one is not necessarily supporting environmental protection. Money withheld from one sector simply gets channeled into another. To the degree that this is the case, the irony of environmentalism is that the very practices that seemingly hold promise for environmental protection at the individual level become a matter of merely shifting the locale of environmental harm. Lifestyle changes that emphasize greater efficiency, less consumption, and genuine personal sacrifice may feel good and make for good press, but they rarely help the earth. . . .

REDUCING ENVIRONMENTAL DESTRUCTION

What happens when individuals choose not to have children or to have fewer of them for environmentalist reasons? And what happens when people curtail their consumption habits in the name of environmental protection? Do these efforts actually improve environmental well being? The real answer, not surprisingly, is, "It depends." It depends upon what people do with the economic benefits they reap from having fewer children or buying fewer things. Redirecting such benefits, in the form of additional money, into traditional savings and investment mechanisms could, in fact, undermine the most ecologically friendly intentions.

Let's say that my partner and I choose not to have children because we wish to reduce the sheer number of people putting demands on the earth. What then happens? In the most immediate way, this removes one person from consumptive practices and will prevent an entire line of individuals in the future from consuming. However, it also enables a different set of pressures to be exerted on the earth. In the language of economics, the opportunity cost of having children is the foregone purchasing power that one could use to buy an alternative set of commodities, to increase savings, or to finance personally directed investment projects. By not having children, I will presumably have more disposable income. If I spend this money on material goods for myself and my partner—say, a bigger house, an additional car, a better music system, and so forth—then there is a real question whether I have, in fact, reduced pressure on the environment. But what if my environmentally conscious partner and I did reduce consumption and thus increase savings? Would this individual action reduce pressure on the environment?

The most basic way to save money is to place it in an interest-bearing checking, savings, money market, or certificate of deposit account in a bank. Does such saving, however, remove money from circulation or otherwise prevent its translation into materiality and greater environmental stress? Banks make profits by practicing "fractional reserve banking." This means that banks lend more funds than they hold as deposits. In normal times, this practice is not irresponsible because only a small fraction of deposits is withdrawn in any given day. Thus, in the United States banks can lend approximately ten times their holdings. The stability of this system of finance is further buttressed by governmental regulations, which guarantee the security of deposits, enable investigation of bank lending practices, and set the fraction of deposits that banks must keep in reserve.

With fractional reserve banking, every dollar one chooses not to spend on personal consumption gives banks that many more financial resources for private and commercial loans. These loans are often used to start or expand businesses or to support large consumer expenditures, all of which generally have material consequences. To be sure, many loans are used to purchase "services" such as education, health care, and entertainment. But to the degree that these services rest on some resource use and waste generation, or that expenditures on such services provide more income for service providers (who then go ahead and spend money on material goods), it is unclear that saving actually reduces environmental damage. Even bank loans for purposes that do not directly lead to expanded production can have negative environmental consequences. For example, if banks make advances to a government to pay off previously held debt, this financial infusion might permit the government to expand expenditure that, in turn, may boost economic production, which then places more stress on the environment.

The same dynamic is at work with other forms of investment and saving. Stocks and bonds, for example, although they are often only traded, provide more financial resources for further private and commercial productive activity. The stock market, for instance, consists of buying and selling shares of certain publicly traded companies. When a company initially goes public, it sells shares and is able to use that income for company expenditures, which leads directly to expanded economic activity. Once the initial amount of shares exists, the buying and selling of stocks do not generate revenue for the company. From an ecological perspective, this is seemingly good news insofar as it breaks the connection between stock prices and revenue, on the one hand, and manufacturing or other types of material productivity, on the other. However, this ignores the trickle-down effect of wealth generated by the stock market. For instance, if the price of shares that I hold increases and I choose then to sell my stocks, I have generated purchasing power that I can now use for expenditures or other types of saving. In addition, even if I do not sell my shares, the increase in my wealth permits me to increase my borrowing from banks. In both cases, my expenditures probably increase and stimulate production. In short, saving does not in general reduce environmental stress, but simply rechannels expenditures and production patterns.

Taking these points together, decisions to have fewer or no children do not automatically lead to greater environmental wellbeing. Considering what would happen if a group of environmentalists decided to cut back on their use of a key resource can also make this point. Let's say, for example, that I reduce my water consumption in an effort to save fresh water. There is no question that this immediately reduces demand on water and thus helps to conserve a limited resource. But, in the act of doing so, I also pay less to the water utility provider, and thus have more discretionary income. If I spend the money I save by not consuming water on other resource-involved goods or activities, especially ones that indirectly use water (such as many manufactured goods), the net environmental impact of my decision may be hard to discern. If I invest my savings in conventional financial mechanisms, I will probably still end up inducing environmental harm. In short, resource restraint by some may not translate directly into a collective reduction in resource use. This underlines the difficulty of protecting the environment through campaigns to change individual consumption patterns.

OBJECTIONS AND QUALIFICATIONS

Criticisms can be leveled at our argument. Let us anticipate a number of the most important. One criticism is that consumption choices *do*, in fact, make a difference to the degree that they generate investments in, and the production of, environmentally sound technologies that *can* reduce environmental degradation overall. The idea here is that the market operates like a ballot box in which one votes with one's dollars. When I choose to buy one item rather than another, or choose not to buy any items at all, I send a message to the economy that registers in the dynamics of supply and demand. This is the great hope of many ecological modernization theorists. They seek to use market mechanisms to shift toward cleaner and more environmentally benign technologies.

There is much to this argument. Its persuasiveness rests, however, more on public policy choices than on individual lifestyles. If we could develop public policy that encourages the development of environmentally friendly technologies and products, then it might be possible to link increased savings that result from our choices to consume less to an overall improvement to our environment. A number of European countries have shown that investments in green technologies *can,* for example, increase energy efficiency and reduce the generation of greenhouse gases, and these changes have shown up in national measurements of environmental quality. In nearly all cases, however, such positive changes have depended on a change in state policy—not on the aggregation of individual decisions through the marketplace. A political process is necessary to form an environmentalist collective will. . . .

A [second] criticism is that a number of socially responsible investment mechanisms allow investors to place their money in mutual funds that have portfolios screened for companies that engage in seemingly harmful types of commercial activity. These types of funds have been growing over the past few years and now represent a sizeable amount of investment capital. These funds refuse to buy shares of companies associated with, for example, military technologies, nuclear power, tobacco, and so forth. On the face of it, socially responsible investing *does* represent an option for people to channel their money in ways that address their normative commitments, including environmental ones. The trouble is that socially responsible investment firms are not necessarily environmental. They often support social justice concerns that may be of interest to those worried about the environment but, in themselves, are not necessarily environmental in focus. Investing in companies that make books in contrast to those that make bombs is an admirable and important practice. Book-producing companies and the like, however, are not necessarily environmental stewards. In fact, like most commercial enterprises, even socially responsible ones use resources and generate waste.

WHERE DO WE TURN?

Are there any individual choices we can make when we curtail consumption or family size that *would* have a positive environmental impact? Are there places we can put our extra discretionary income that would protect the environment? One can identify a few. First, one can invest in or simply donate money to the poor. According to Ken Conca, Alan Durning, and others, those who most damage the environment are the rich and the poor of the world, with those in the middle living relatively environmentally benign lives. If this is indeed the case, then an argument can be made for shifting finances to the poor, with the hope that this will enable them to be lifted out of poverty and thus live lives that are less stressful on the environment. This can be done with either a more progressive taxation system or a reorganization of government expenditures that place significantly more emphasis on income transfers to the poor. . . .

A second route involves fundamentally questioning unmitigated capitalist development. Global capitalism is partly constituted by the search for not-yet-spent purchasing power for profitable outlets. Money whips around the globe today in search of profitable investment much like a hyper circulation system. The rate, character, and reach of contemporary capitalism refuse many options that would clearly benefit the environment, insofar as they generate multiple shells under which money can be placed and made available to material production. Indeed, any honest analysis of the problem of curtailment must eventually go beyond seeing environmental challenges as mere externalities and identify unbridled capitalism as foundational to the redeployment of finances toward environmentally harmful practices.

Rethinking development and confronting key engines of capitalism are far from easy, even if they seem inescapable. Moreover, it is unclear how rethinking itself will make much of a difference. Yet at the heart of both is the requirement to build political movements that question the logic of unregu- lated capitalist development. In both rich and poor societies of the world, such politics must stress the importance of guaranteeing the satisfaction of human needs to all citizens. Such needs should be defined broadly to include the right to an adequately comfortable material life as well as a politically and spiritually fulfilling one. In rich societies, such a politics would stress the importance of redistribution and the expansion of "nonproductive," "leisure" activities. In poorer societies, the pressure to pursue material growth as rapidly as possible can be reduced if states provide widespread education and health services. Such efforts will not in themselves end, to be sure, ecologically unsound material growth or capitalism per se. They will, however, place pressure upon contempo- rary economic practices and create openings for reorganizing capitalist society.

It is in this context that advocates for a simpler life that places less stress on the environment can link personal lifestyle choice to effective ecological change. Efforts to use fewer resources through the reduction of wasteful con- sumption practices can serve as demonstration projects, as indicators to other people of the efficacy and joy inherent in living "simply." Such demonstrations would evidently play a key role in mobilizing political movements dedicated to resisting unregulated capitalist development.

Short of such transformation, our analysis shows that, at a minimum, it does little good to blame individual choices for environmental degradation, and thus to look to individual choice alone as the best route to environmental well-being. If we had effective public policies that redistributed income, forced polluters to pay for the harm they cause, mandated more environmentally friendly technologies, and reduced the workday in the richer parts of the world, we could change the way we live our material lives. The rich would restrict their consumption without inevitably redirecting residual savings to material production. The poor could afford to make environmentally responsible choices. Polluting forms of production and consumption would decline. Investments in future production methods would take account of the needs to preserve and improve the environment. New types of environmentally friendly leisure activities would emerge. In short, the political economy of capitalism would change. . . .

Our concern is that people make at least two choices when they take personal action to limit their impact on the earth, yet many are conscious of only one. Many people throughout the world are choosing to have smaller families and to use fewer resources (and thereby produce less waste) for environmental reasons. These actions should be applauded. Unfortunately, our responsibilities do not end after this choice. We must also choose what to do with the additional money we often possess as a result of our initial choices. As mentioned, one result of not having children or of reducing consumption is the opportunity to spend and save. To see our actions fully through, we must take environmental responsibility for this opportunity. To the degree that our expenditures and savings go into productive processes that use resources and generate waste beyond essential needs, our efforts will not achieve our intended aims. As we have noted, however, taking environmental responsibility to realize such aims is something that cannot be done easily as individuals or rest on personal abilities to track and manage the consequences of our individual choices. Rather, we can be most effectively responsible only within political economic conditions that deliberately reduce throughput. Ushering in such a system must be part of genuine environmentalism.

Having said this, it would be irresponsible of us to end without saying something about the initial choices themselves. Although these choices may fall short of achieving demonstrable environmental protection, they nonetheless stand as important moral and political actions. This should not be lost in the above analysis.

Environmentalism is not simply about the earth's ecological conditions; it is also about the kinds of people we wish to be. One thing often ignored by analysts is the ethical aspirations of environmentalists. As Leslie Paul Thiele has explained, environmentalism is essentially about extending one's moral concern across time, space, and species; that is, environmentalists wish to leave a healthy planet to future generations, to protect fellow humans who live "downstream" from experiencing the ill effects of environmental degradation, and to protect the nonhuman world. Behind all of this is a moral sensitivity for others. It represents a sense of concern and solidarity with other people and other living beings. That environmentalists of all stripes work to express this concern politically is one of the most admirable dimensions of environmentalism.

When individuals seek to live the change they wish to bring about, or, put differently, when they prefigure the future they want to create, we should all take note. This is especially the case with environmentalists who sacrifice many personal desires for the wellbeing of others. Such action, which includes limiting family size and curtailing consumption, represents important moral behavior, and although it may not translate directly into actual biophysical changes in the world, there is no reason to belittle it. If we are ever to create an ecologically sound world in which social structures and individuals operate in ways that enhance environmental wellbeing, it will be based on, and inspired by, the model of action individual environmentalists undertake in their personal lives. In the context of this article, this means that lifestyle choices can inspire and mobilize people to seek alternative forms of economic activity—specifically ones that do not lead to endless consumption. So, although choosing to have fewer children or fewer things may not directly protect the earth because of the economic trade-offs involved, one should still undertake and support such actions because they can influence economic, social, and political institutions and, at a more basic level, hold the key toward achieving meaningful environmental living.

Meaningful action is a combination of deep commitment and instrumental consequence. In this article we have questioned the instrumental results of personal lifestyle changes aimed at environmental protection. We found a number of significant shortcomings that should give many of us pause in our confidence that our actions are actually making a difference. This does not mean, however, that no change is taking place. Exercising one's political capacity is one of the most admirable and generous forms of living. Deep commitment provides the passion that carries political movements and opens the way for collective change. It can be the bedrock upon which political movements are built. Put differently, our analysis pertains to the economic dimensions of lifestyle change rather than broader sociopolitical ones. People are more than consumers or economic actors, and their actions, while having economic consequences, do not end with economic activity. People are also voters, members of civic organizations, friends, colleagues, advocates of governmental policies and funding, conservationists and developers, and they thus have many ways to educate and inspire one another, and to work politically for environmental protection. Individual lifestyle change can have dramatic effects as it disseminates through the many dimensions and relations of individual life.

It hurts us to call on environmentalists to watch more closely the consequences of their lifestyle changes and to take on the burden of altering the dynamics and structures of capitalist society. They already have enough to do. Our hope, however, is that we have not added burden but rather provided some insight toward more refined instrumental action. Additionally, we hope that those not already taking action will do so in the interest of expressing deep commitment. For both groups, we hope that our analysis points to ways of aligning one's individual actions with efforts aimed more toward structural change. At the end of the day, it is largely the structures of society that pervert or make possible ecologically sound living. Social structures may be encrusted but they are not eternal. Sound environmental action requires that we hasten their transformation.

30

Why Bother?

Michael Pollan

Why bother? That really is the big question facing us as individuals hoping to do something about climate change, and it's not an easy one to answer. I don't know about you, but for me the most upsetting moment in *An Inconvenient Truth* came long after Al Gore scared the hell out of me, constructing an utterly convincing case that the very survival of life on earth as we know it is threatened by climate change. No, the really dark moment came during the closing credits, when we are asked to . . . change our light bulbs. That's when it got really depressing. The immense disproportion between the magnitude of the problem Gore had described and the puniness of what he was asking us to do about it was enough to sink your heart.

But the drop-in-the-bucket issue is not the only problem lurking behind the "why bother" question. Let's say I do bother, big time. I turn my life upside-down, start biking to work, plant a big garden, turn down the thermostat so low I need the Jimmy Carter signature cardigan, forsake the clothes dryer for a laundry line across the yard, trade in the station wagon for a hybrid, get off the beef, go completely local. I could theoretically do all that, but what would be the point when I know full well that halfway around the world there lives my evil twin, some carbon-footprint doppelgänger in Shanghai or Chongqing who has just bought his first car (Chinese car ownership is where ours was back in 1918), is eager to swallow every bite of meat I forswear and who's positively itching to replace every last pound of CO_2 I'm struggling no longer to emit. So what exactly would I have to show for all my trouble?

289

A sense of personal virtue, you might suggest, somewhat sheepishly. But what good is that when virtue itself is quickly becoming a term of derision? And not just on the editorial pages of *The Wall Street Journal* or on the lips of the [former] vice president [Dick Cheney], who famously dismissed energy conservation as a "sign of personal virtue." No, even in the pages of *The New York Times* and *The New Yorker,* it seems the epithet "virtuous," when applied to an act of personal environmental responsibility, may be used only ironically. Tell me: How did it come to pass that virtue—a quality that for most of history has generally been deemed, well, a virtue—became a mark of liberal softheadedness? How peculiar, that doing the right thing by the environment—buying the hybrid, eating like a locavore—should now set you up for the Ed Begley Jr. treatment.

And even if in the face of this derision I decide I am going to bother, there arises the whole vexed question of getting it right. Is eating local or walking to work really going to reduce my carbon footprint? According to one analysis, if walking to work increases your appetite and you consume more meat or milk as a result, walking might actually emit more carbon than driving. A handful of studies have recently suggested that in certain cases under certain conditions, produce from places as far away as New Zealand might account for less carbon than comparable domestic products. True, at least one of these studies was co-written by a representative of agribusiness interests in (surprise!) New Zealand, but even so, they make you wonder. If determining the carbon footprint of food is really this complicated, and I've got to consider not only "food miles" but also whether the food came by ship or truck and how lushly the grass grows in New Zealand, then maybe on second thought I'll just buy the imported chops at Costco, at least until the experts get their footprints sorted out.

There are so many stories we can tell ourselves to justify doing nothing, but perhaps the most insidious is that, whatever we do manage to do, it will be too little too late. Climate change is upon us, and it has arrived well ahead of schedule. Scientists' projections that seemed dire a decade ago turn out to have been unduly optimistic: the warming and the melting is occurring much faster than the models predicted. Now truly terrifying feedback loops threaten to boost the rate of change exponentially, as the shift from white ice to blue water in the Arctic absorbs more sunlight and warming soils everywhere become more biologically active, causing them to release their vast stores of carbon into the air. Have you looked into the eyes of a climate scientist recently? They look really scared.

So do you still want to talk about planting gardens?

I do.

Whatever we can do as individuals to change the way we live at this suddenly very late date does seem utterly inadequate to the challenge. It's hard to argue with Michael Specter, in a recent *New Yorker* piece on carbon footprints, when he says: "Personal choices, no matter how virtuous [N.B.!], cannot do enough. It will also take laws and money." So it will. Yet it is no less accurate or hardheaded to say that laws and money cannot do enough, either; that it will also take profound changes in the way we live. Why? Because the climate-change crisis is at its very bottom a crisis of lifestyle—of character, even. The Big Problem is nothing more or less than the sum total of countless little everyday choices, most of them made by us (consumer spending represents 70 percent of our economy), and most of the rest of them made in the name of our needs and desires and preferences.

For us to wait for legislation or technology to solve the problem of how we're living our lives suggests we're not really serious about changing—something our politicians cannot fail to notice. They will not move until we do. Indeed, to look to leaders and experts, to laws and money and grand schemes, to save us from our predicament represents precisely the sort of thinking—passive, delegated, dependent for solutions on specialists—that helped get us into this mess in the first place. It's hard to believe that the same sort of thinking could now get us out of it.

Thirty years ago, Wendell Berry, the Kentucky farmer and writer, put forward a blunt analysis of precisely this mentality. He argued that the environmental crisis of the 1970s—an era innocent of climate change; what we would give to have back *that* environmental crisis!—was at its heart a crisis of character and would have to be addressed first at that level: at home, as it were. He was impatient with people who wrote checks to environmental organizations while thoughtlessly squandering fossil fuel in their everyday lives—the 1970s equivalent of people buying carbon offsets to atone for their Tahoes and Durangos. Nothing was likely to change until we healed the "split between what we think and what we do." For Berry, the "why bother" question came down to a moral imperative: "Once our personal connection to what is wrong becomes clear, then we have to choose: we can go on as before, recognizing our dishonesty and living with it the best we can, or we can begin the effort to change the way we think and live."

For Berry, the deep problem standing behind all the other problems of industrial civilization is "specialization," which he regards as the "disease of the modern character." Our society assigns us a tiny number of roles: we're producers (of one thing) at work, consumers of a great many other things the rest of the time, and then once a year or so we vote as citizens. Virtually all of our needs and desires we delegate to specialists of one kind or another—our meals to agribusiness, health to the doctor, education to the teacher, entertainment to the media, care for the environment to the environmentalist, political action to the politician.

As Adam Smith and many others have pointed out, this division of labor has given us many of the blessings of civilization. Specialization is what allows me to sit at a computer thinking about climate change. Yet this same division of labor obscures the lines of connection—and responsibility—linking our everyday acts to their real-world consequences, making it easy for me to overlook the coal-fired power plant that is lighting my screen, or the mountaintop in Kentucky that had to be destroyed to provide the coal to that plant, or the streams running crimson with heavy metals as a result.

Of course, what made this sort of specialization possible in the first place was cheap energy. Cheap fossil fuel allows us to pay distant others to process our food for us, to entertain us and to (try to) solve our problems, with the result that there is very little we know how to accomplish for ourselves. Think for a moment of all the things you suddenly need to do for yourself when the power goes out—up to and including entertaining yourself. Think, too, about how a power failure causes your neighbors—your community—to suddenly loom so much larger in your life. Cheap energy allowed us to leapfrog community by making it possible to sell our specialty over great distances as well as summon into our lives the specialties of countless distant others.

Here's the point: Cheap energy, which gives us climate change, fosters precisely the mentality that makes dealing with climate change in our own lives seem impossibly difficult. Specialists ourselves, we can no longer imagine anyone but an expert, or anything but a new technology or law, solving our problems. Al Gore asks us to change the light bulbs because he probably can't imagine us doing anything much more challenging, like, say, growing some portion of our own food. We can't imagine it, either, which is probably why we prefer to cross our fingers and talk about the promise of ethanol and nuclear power—new liquids and electrons to power the same old cars and houses and lives.

The "cheap-energy mind," as Wendell Berry called it, is the mind that asks, "Why bother?" because it is helpless to imagine—much less attempt— a different sort of life, one less divided, less reliant. Since the cheap-energy mind translates everything into money, its proxy, it prefers to put its faith in market-based solutions—carbon taxes and pollution-trading schemes. If we could just get the incentives right, it believes, the economy will properly value everything that matters and nudge our self-interest down the proper channels. The best we can hope for is a greener version of the old invisible hand. Visible hands it has no use for.

But while some such grand scheme may well be necessary, it's doubtful that it will be sufficient or that it will be politically sustainable before we've demonstrated to ourselves that change is possible. Merely to give, to spend, even to vote, is not to do, and there is so much that needs to be done—without further delay. In the judgment of James Hansen, the NASA climate scientist who began sounding the alarm on global warming 20 years ago, we have only 10 years left to start cutting—not just slowing—the amount of carbon we're emitting or face a "different planet." Hansen said this more than two years ago, however; two years have gone by, and nothing of consequence has been done. So: eight years left to go and a great deal left to do.

Which brings us back to the "why bother" question and how we might better answer it. The reasons not to bother are many and compelling, at least to the cheap-energy mind. But let me offer a few admittedly tentative reasons that we might put on the other side of the scale:

If you do bother, you will set an example for other people. If enough other people bother, each one influencing yet another in a chain reaction of behavioral change, markets for all manner of green products and alternative technologies will prosper and expand. (Just look at the market for hybrid cars.) Consciousness will be raised, perhaps even changed: new moral imperatives and new taboos might take root in the culture. Driving an S.U.V. or eating a 24-ounce steak or illuminating your McMansion like an airport runway at night might come to be regarded as outrages to human conscience. Not having things might become cooler than having them. And those who did change the way they live would acquire the moral standing to demand changes in behavior from others—from other people, other corporations, even other countries.

All of this could, theoretically, happen. What I'm describing (imagining would probably be more accurate) is a process of viral social change, and change of this kind, which is nonlinear, is never something anyone can plan or predict or count on. Who knows, maybe the virus will reach all the way to Chongqing and infect my Chinese evil twin. Or not. Maybe going green will prove a passing fad and will lose steam after a few years, just as it did in the 1980s, when Ronald Reagan took down Jimmy Carter's solar panels from the roof of the White House.

Going personally green is a bet, nothing more or less, though it's one we probably all should make, even if the odds of it paying off aren't great. Sometimes you have to act as if acting will make a difference, even when you can't prove that it will. That, after all, was precisely what happened in Communist Czechoslovakia and Poland, when a handful of individuals like Vaclav Havel and Adam Michnik resolved that they would simply conduct their lives "as if" they lived in a free society. That improbable bet created a tiny space of liberty that, in time, expanded to take in, and then help take down, the whole of the Eastern bloc.

So what would be a comparable bet that the individual might make in the case of the environmental crisis? Havel himself has suggested that people begin to "conduct themselves as if they were to live on this earth forever and be answerable for its condition one day." Fair enough, but let me propose a slightly less abstract and daunting wager. The idea is to find one thing to do in your life that doesn't involve spending or voting, that may or may not virally rock the world but is real and particular (as well as symbolic) and that, come what may, will offer its own rewards. Maybe you decide to give up meat, an act that would reduce your carbon footprint by as much as a quarter. Or you could try this: determine to observe the Sabbath. For one day a week, abstain completely from economic activity: no shopping, no driving, no electronics.

But the act I want to talk about is growing some—even just a little—of your own food. Rip out your lawn, if you have one, and if you don't—if you live in a high-rise, or have a yard shrouded in shade—look into getting a plot in a community garden. Measured against the Problem We Face, planting a garden sounds pretty benign, I know, but in fact it's one of the most powerful things an individual can do—to reduce your carbon footprint, sure, but more important, to reduce your sense of dependence and dividedness: to change the cheap-energy mind.

A great many things happen when you plant a vegetable garden, some of them directly related to climate change, others indirect but related nevertheless. Growing food, we forget, comprises the original solar technology: calories produced by means of photosynthesis. Years ago the cheap-energy mind discovered that more food could be produced with less effort by replacing sunlight with fossil-fuel fertilizers and pesticides, with a result that the typical calorie of food energy in your diet now requires about 10 calories of fossil-fuel energy to produce. It's estimated that the way we feed ourselves (or rather, allow ourselves to be fed) accounts for about a fifth of the greenhouse gas for which each of us is responsible.

Yet the sun still shines down on your yard, and photosynthesis still works so abundantly that in a thoughtfully organized vegetable garden (one planted from seed, nourished by compost from the kitchen and involving not too many drives to the garden center), you can grow the proverbial free lunch—CO_2-free and dollar-free. This is the most-local food you can possibly eat (not to mention the freshest, tastiest and most nutritious), with a carbon footprint so faint that even the New Zealand lamb council dares not challenge it. And while we're counting carbon, consider too your compost pile, which shrinks the heap of garbage your household needs trucked away even as it feeds your vegetables and sequesters carbon in your soil. What else? Well, you will probably notice that you're getting a pretty good workout there in your garden, burning calories without having to get into the car to drive to the gym. (It is one of the absurdities of the modern division of labor that, having replaced physical labor with fossil fuel, we now have to burn even more fossil fuel to keep our unemployed bodies in shape.) Also, by engaging both body and mind, time spent in the garden is time (and energy) subtracted from electronic forms of entertainment.

You begin to see that growing even a little of your own food is, as Wendell Berry pointed out 30 years ago, one of those solutions that, instead of begetting a new set of problems—the way "solutions" like ethanol or nuclear power inevitably do—actually beget other solutions, and not only of the kind that save carbon. Still more valuable are the habits of mind that growing a little of your own food can yield. You quickly learn that you need not be dependent on specialists to provide for yourself—that your body is still good for something and may actually be enlisted in its own support. If the experts are right, if both oil and time are running out, these are skills and habits of mind we're all very soon going to need. We may also need the food. Could gardens provide it? Well, during World War II, victory gardens supplied as much as 40 percent of the produce Americans ate.

But there are sweeter reasons to plant that garden, to bother. At least in this one corner of your yard and life, you will have begun to heal the split between what you think and what you do, to commingle your identities as consumer and producer and citizen. Chances are, your garden will re-engage you with your neighbors, for you will have produce to give away and the need to borrow their tools. You will have reduced the power of the cheap-energy mind by personally overcoming its most debilitating weakness: its helplessness and the fact that it can't do much of anything that doesn't involve division or subtraction. The garden's season-long transit from seed to ripe fruit—*will you get a load of that zucchini?!*—suggests that the operations of addition and multiplication still obtain, that the abundance of nature is not exhausted. The single greatest lesson the garden teaches is that our relationship to the planet need not be zero-sum, and that as long as the sun still shines and people still can plan and plant, think and do, we can, if we bother to try, find ways to provide for ourselves without diminishing the world.

Section 8 Exercise

Two Minutes to Sustainability: Moving Governments, the Economy, and the Public

Come to class or gather with friends, ready to discuss a single insight about how to create a more sustainable world. Break into groups of three to five. Each person should prepare and then present a two-minute talk titled "My Big Sustainability Idea." The idea is to set out a particular sustainability-related challenge and offer your proposal for a new way forward.

What's your big sustainability idea? Is it to reform the United Nations? To ask people to eat less shrimp? To raise the cost of airline tickets so that people fly less? To provide incentives for more local food production?

The task requires that you think strategically. What do you care about? What's the true nature of the challenge you are outlining? What kinds of action would have the biggest impact in response?

In your group, someone should take responsibility for holding each presenter strictly to the two-minute timeframe. Each group should then vote to determine the best presentation, then share that presentation with the whole class.

Section 9

Political Imagination

This last section of the volume explores the political imagination. It serves not simply as a conclusion, but also as a review of the entire book. Imagination is not a flight of fancy or form of mental escape. Rather, it is a disciplined ability to make sense of the world, the challenges we face, and the options for building a better future. Thus, imagination has been with us throughout the book as we have worked to understand the nature of global environmental politics.

Think about previous chapters. Whether we were trying to understand humanity's influence on Earth, catalogue global challenges, explain the causes of environmental harm, or study how the international system can respond to environmental degradation, we have had to go beyond our empirical senses to draw mental connections, picture trajectories, conjure causes, or envision institutional or structural arrangements. In each case, we had to leave the physical circumstances of everyday life and create mental images of broader, more meaningful realities.

The imagination is not simply about abstraction, however, and this is where this last section departs from previous ones. Up until now, we have employed the imagination to make sense of environmental affairs. We have used it to visualize concepts aimed at explaining contemporary conditions. At this stage we turn to the imagination not to *account for* but rather to *change* the world. The idea is to envision different arrangements so as to cast a critical gaze at present realities in the interest of creating new ones.

Imagining the contours of a better future is no easy exercise, especially since it involves an element of forecasting. As physicist Niels Bohr has put it, "Prediction is very difficult, particularly if it's about the future." Still, the preceding sections of the book provide some guidance. While a few authors have suggested that answers to environmental dilemmas will emerge from an extension of established ways of doing things—bigger and better-functioning markets, more economic growth, more state-to-state negotiations, and the like—others have argued that answers can come only from a dramatic change in direction.

Wherever we ultimately come down on such questions, it is imperative that we have something toward which to direct our efforts. Does this consist of a world that looks fairly similar to the present but with small tweaks to existing social institutions and behaviors, or a radically different one in which we reformat the template of collective life? The authors in this final section offer clues as to how to engage the political imagination in the service of crafting a vision of a sustainable world. What *should* the world of tomorrow look like? What is possible in ecological and political terms, and what is desirable as we think about the future arrangements of our societies, economies, and politics?

Acts of imagination of this type can be difficult. Throughout this book you have read about power as it relates to environmental affairs. Power is often defined in a coercive fashion, as the ability to get someone to do something against their will. It is a capacity to shape how one acts. But we also know that power does not simply alter our actions; it also shapes and circumscribes our thinking. These days, in the face of immense global environmental dangers, we confront not simply a political, technological or economic crisis, but also a crisis of creativity. We almost cannot picture other ways of doing things. It is as if the magnitude and strength of the "system" is so entrenched historically and functionally that another world is impossible. We live within a mental prison in which our options appear within a narrow window and our politics is about debating whether a few minor adjustments in one direction rather than another make sense. In such a situation, especially given the stakes involved, exercising the political imagination in the service of a livable future is imperative. This involves going beyond abstraction and expanding our mental horizons to awaken ourselves to both what is widely deemed politically possible and what is *necessary* if we are to meaningfully grapple with the environmental dilemma.

Imagination used in the service of environmental well-being requires widening our temporal and spatial coordinates. This means we must project ourselves backward and forward in time, and picture new roles, scopes, and functions for actors and institutions. This is critical since one of the reasons we're in the current environmental mess is that we have been doing the same old things in the same old ways for too long, unable to *imagine* other possibilities. Enlarging our timeframes and spatial sensitivities is a crucial way to liberate ourselves from the momentum of status quo thinking.

Environmental-studies professor **Roderick Frazier Nash** invites a pronounced enlargement of our timeframes by asking us to imagine the world 1,000 years from now. After rehearsing a number of possible scenarios, he offers his preferred future—a world in which human civilization is concentrated in technological islands surrounded by vast expanses of natural landscapes. In such a world, Nash envisions fewer people, abundant resources, and deep happiness. The essay stands as an invitation and a provocation. By letting his imagination fly, he calls on each of us to think carefully about the future toward which our efforts can be directed. What kind of world, collectively, are we trying to bring into being?

Writer **Joanne Harris** casts her imagination into the nearer future, and sees a dystopia of a world beset by the ravages of a changing climate and species extinctions. Describing a barren world where humans live mostly indoors, she explores how curiosity and lamentation might operate on an ecologically changed planet. Harris shows the importance of speculative fiction in opening our eyes to the contours of possible worlds to come, and of the ecological, social, and political implications of collective action (and inaction) in the present day.

Wendell Berry, by contrast, asks us to look back, to recapture and reinvigorate ways of living and knowing that are fast disappearing. Berry draws lessons learned from a life of tending a Kentucky farm that has been in his family for generations. To him, wisdom comes from becoming intimate with a specific place and using low-tech and community-based forms of activity to address not simply our environmental woes, but also economic and educational challenges. Berry teaches that imagination is not just about casting our minds far away and into the distant future. A working political and ecological imagination also requires that we learn the lessons being taught by the places we call home.

Michael Shellenberger and **Ted Nordhaus**, founders of the Breakthrough Institute, call for a different understanding of the way forward. Their argument is this: don't downsize or live more humbly to fit into a particular place, but rather go big by investing in and building high-tech systems to address pressing global environmental challenges. The problems we face, they imply, are too large for small-scale intimacy. We need a technological revolution that will spur economic growth and redirect environmentalism away from a doom-and-gloom mentality about the future and toward an optimistic one that promises realizing humanity's full potential. In contrast to Berry and others who represent a Malthusian perspective, arguing for forms of human existence that fit wholly within ecological limits,

Shellenberger and Nordhaus advance a Promethean one that evinces strong techno-optimism.

Global environmental politics professor **Simon Nicholson** focuses on a specific element of the environmental imagination, geoengineering. Geoengineering represents a host of technological efforts aimed at reformatting the earth's ecosphere to protect against climate change. At this stage, most geoengineering efforts exist in the mind or, at best, on the drawing board. But as Nicholson shows, the way people are imagining them threatens to bring about a dark future. Some actors use the work of geoengineers to paint a picture in which people can continue living energy-intensive lives with no need to sacrifice in the face of global warming. Nicholson shows us that such a portrait hides the severe sacrifices that technological prowess often requires—especially for those on the low end of the power totem pole. In other words, Nicholson unmasks the imaginative visions of climate technocrats and underlines how their schemes will actually exacerbate contemporary injustices, environmental degradation, and social division.

Paul Wapner, another professor of global environmental politics, joins Nicholson's call for caution in the face of technological promise. He sees the many technological fixes that environmentalists like Nordhaus, Shellenberger, and others suggest for addressing climate change as part of a larger intention to master the natural world. Wapner shows the folly of mastery and suggests that humility can provide a moral compass for navigating our climate future. He demonstrates the way the imagination can help us find our collective bearings in a climate-change age.

Finally, we have a commencement address given by novelist and essayist **Barbara Kingsolver**. She tells us of a future filled with promise, a future in which we have overcome the most debilitating and destructive features of established ways of being. The making of such a world, she tells us, is our most worthy calling. It is work that will require vision and sweat. It is also work that calls for an inexhaustible fount of hope—a commodity that, Kingsolver says, you should "rise in the morning and put . . . on again with your shoes."

The future, these authors tell us, is ours to fashion. This book has provided essential tools for making this possible. When we embrace the challenge of building a livable future, we move most meaningfully from person to planet.

31

Island Civilization

1,000 Years into the Future

Roderick Frazier Nash

The new, Third Millennium we are just entering affords an excellent opportunity to think big about the history and future of wilderness and civilization on planet Earth. Of course a millennium is an entirely synthetic (as opposed to astronomical) concept. Measuring time in thousand-year units only began in 1582 when Christian officials arbitrarily fixed a date for the birth of Christ. So there was nothing special about December 31, 999; it wasn't even recognized as the end of the First Millennium. But we made a big deal about the end of the second one a thousand years later on December 31, 1999. Here was an opportunity to transcend our species' characteristic myopia. Rarely do humans make plans more than a couple of years in advance. And we don't do history very well either. Similarly, we don't often think in the wider angles that encompass our species as a whole, but now is an excellent time to begin. One way to look at the opportunity and the responsibility we have with regard to the environment is in terms of legacy. As an historian I am concerned about how the future will regard what happened to the planet on our watch. What will my great grandchildren (and theirs) think when they learn the truth about passenger pigeons, salmon, whales and coral reefs?

My mission in this essay is to review the history of human-nature relations and to extend the discussion into a quite distant future. I want to stretch our minds a bit. What could the human tenure on Earth be like a thousand years from now—at the start of the Fourth Millennium? My proposal involves some

301

really major changes. I expect it to be controversial. At first glance you may think Island Civilization is crazy and impossible, but don't stop with criticism. The whole purpose of this essay is to advance for discussion a strategy for occupation of this planet that will work in the very long run and for the whole ecosystem. This is simply the greatest challenge facing our species, and, in a sense, facing evolution on Earth. If you disagree with some or all of my vision of an Island Civilization, create your own. Particularly, if you think staying the present course is the way to go, put forward your evidence and reasoning. The essential thing is that we occasionally lift our eyes from everyday details and five-year plans to the far horizons of planetary possibility. Having such a goal is a vital first step to solving problems. Without it we lack direction and the means to evaluate options as they come into focus.

As a starting point let's consider wilderness. It's a state of mind, a perception, rather than a geographical reality, and prior to the advent of herding and agriculture about 10,000 years before the present, it didn't exist. But after we began to draw mental lines between ourselves and nature, and to place walls and fences on the land, the idea of controlled versus uncontrolled environments acquired meaning. The root of the word "wilderness" in Old English was something that had its own will. The adjective that came to be used was "wild." For example, wildfire, wild (undammed) rivers, and wildcats that you can't herd. The other important part of the word, "ness," indicates a condition or place. So "wilderness" literally means *self-willed land,* a place where wild (undomesticated) animals roam and where natural processes proceed unencumbered by human interference.

After humans created farms, and literally bet our survival on them instead of on hunting and gathering, uncontrolled nature became the enemy of the new civilization. Pastoral societies, like those that produced the Old and New Testaments, became obsessed with making the crooked straight and the rough places plain. For thousands of years the success of civilization seemed to mandate the destruction of wild places, wild animals and wild peoples. The game plan was to break their "wills." In the Bible "wilderness" was the land God cursed. Its antipode was called "paradise." Adam and Eve lost it when they angered God and found themselves banished into the wild. The first European colonists of the New World carried in their intellectual baggage a full load of bias against wilderness. The last thing settlers of the eastern seaboard had in mind was protecting wild nature or establishing national parks! Indians were savages who needed to be "civilized" or eliminated. After a rocky start, these pioneers became very good at breaking the "will" of uncontrolled land and peoples. Axes, rifles and barbed wire—and more recently railroads, dams and freeways—were the celebrated tools of an environmental transformation that left the wilderness in scattered remnants.

Lost in the celebration of westward expansion, however, was the possible irony in the process. When does success in too great a dose produce failure? We always thought of growth as synonymous with progress, but maybe bigger is not better if it creates a civilization that is unsustainable. Maybe what really needs to be conquered is not wilderness but rather our capitalist-driven culture in its cancer-like tendency to self-destruct.

Americans began to explore these revolutionary ideas as the Second Millennium drew to a close in the nineteenth and twentieth centuries. As early as 1851 Henry David Thoreau thought that wildness held the key to the preservation of the world. George Perkins Marsh, a well-traveled diplomat who spoke twenty-one languages, understood in 1864 in his remarkable book *Man and Nature* that with their improved technology, untempered by ethics, humans had become a new and destructive force of nature. He suspected that what humans assumed to be victory against the forest primeval could result in floods, droughts and desertification that defeat their dreams of progress and prosperity. Beginning in the 1870s, John Muir reversed thousands of years of Judeo-Christian attitude by publicizing mountain forests as temples and cathedrals. What shocked Americans of this generation the most was the United States Census' pronouncement in 1890 that there was no more frontier. With the Indians crushed, the buffalo almost gone and big, industrial cities losing their luster, it was possible to think that the cherished civilizing process could go too far. The appearance in the early twentieth century of best-selling books with a primitivistic slant like Jack London's *The Call of the Wild* (1903) and Edgar Rice Burroughs' *Tarzan* (1913) indicated that the relative valuations of wilderness and civilization were changing.

As the twentieth century began a scarcity theory of value began to reshape the relative importance of wilderness and civilization in the United States. It explains the national angst over the ending of the frontier. Attitude toward wilderness was passing over a tipping point from liability to asset. Of course the pioneers did not go camping for fun! Wilderness appreciation, and later preservation, began in the cities where wild country was perceived as a relative novelty and substantially less threatening.

The rationale of the early movement for wilderness was almost entirely anthropocentric. Scenery, recreation and the economics of a new nature-based tourism underlay the growing popularity of wild places. More sophisticated, but no less utilitarian, were ideas of wilderness as a church, a museum of national history, a stimulant to a unique art and literature and a psychological aid. These were good arguments for their time and they underlay the establishment of the first national parks and wilderness. The Wilderness Act of 1964 was revolutionary but, make no mistake, its point was the benefit of people.

A new, biocentric rationale for wilderness emerged in the last fifty years of the Second Millennium. At its core was the idea that wilderness had intrinsic value, that its protection was not about *us* at all! Rather, it was a place where our species took a badly needed "time out" from our ten thousand year old obsession with the control and modification of the planet. In honoring wilderness we manifested a capacity for restraint. Preserved wilderness was a gesture of planetary modesty, a way to share the spaceship on which all life travels together. . . .

The appearance of biocentrism and environmental ethics was encouraging, but an avalanche of evidence suggested that civilization continued to wreak havoc with natural rhythms and balances as the Third Millennium began. Awareness of the problems has penetrated deeply into contemporary thought and discussion. Accelerated human-caused decline in biodiversity amounts in the opinion of many biologists to a Sixth Great Extinction. More humans than existed since the start of the species occupied the planet in 1950 and population surged upward at a billion every fifteen years. Sprawling into open space at the rate in the United States alone of 6,000 acres each day, people dominated most of the preferred locales in the temperate latitudes. Climate change now seems to be at least partially human-induced. Fresh water, soil, forest and food issues make headlines daily. Lurking just over the horizon are concerns over massive epidemics and the dark, cold specter of a nuclear war that would take down most life on the planet. Civilization, in a word, appears vulnerable. Making the point explicit, Jared Diamond's book *Collapse* (2005) underscores the lack of sustainability in many human cultures over the last 10,000 years, and suggests strongly that we are not exempt. There will be a resolution of environmental problems, he argues, if not by intelligent choice then by ecological disaster and social disintegration. My proposal for Island Civilization, below, responds to the concerns Diamond raises.

As for wilderness, where most of the thirty-odd million species sharing Earth reside, it's now an endangered geographical species. Only about two percent of the contiguous forty-eight states are legally wild, and the same amount is paved! Much of the American landscape has been modified to some degree. And the United States is a leader in national parks and wilderness preservation and is only a little more than a century beyond its frontier era. In other, older regions—France and Japan come to mind—environmental control is near total. At least in the temperate latitudes we are dealing with remnants of a once-wild world, and we face irreversible decisions about their future on a planet that suddenly seems small and vulnerable. In a century wilderness could disappear or become so fragmented as to be ecologically meaningless. Some now view this not just as a violation of the rights of humans to enjoy wild nature but of the rights of other species and self-willed environments themselves.

Looking toward the Fourth Millennium, a thousand years ahead, there seem to be several ways that the natural world we evolved in could end. The *wasteland scenario* anticipates a trashed, poisoned and used-up planet that can support only a pathetic remnant of its once-miraculous biodiversity and civilization. Humans have proved to be terrible neighbors to most of the rest of life on the planet. We did not share well. Growth was confused with progress. Centuries of deficit environmental financing of too large and sprawling a civilization have brought the ecosystem, ourselves included of course, to its knees. Maybe, in the height of ingratitude and irresponsibility, we have abandoned and discarded this planet. A vanguard of humans, no wiser for their history, treks through the stars seeking new frontiers to plunder. Perhaps wilderness conditions eventually return to what Alan Weisman calls a world without humans, but the setback to evolution would be profound and slow in healing.

The second possible future is the *garden scenario.* Imagine by the Fourth Millennium human control of nature is total, but this time it's beneficent. Our species has occupied and modified every square mile and every planetary process from the oceans to weather to the creation and evolution of life. It is finally, as some feared, all about us. We're no longer part of nature; we've stepped off, or more exactly, over the biotic team. Scores or even hundreds of billions of people occupy this planetary garden. Dammed rivers flow clean and cold (but without much diversity of life) and waving fields of grain stretch to the horizon. The only big animals around are those we eat! Maybe such a world could be made sustainable for a few species, but the wilderness, and the diversity of life that depends on it, is long gone. So maybe environmental health long thought linked to the normal and natural functioning of ecosystems. The gardeners of Eden may not be quite as *sapient* apes as they imagined and become victims of homogenization, biotic impoverishment and their own excessive appetites.

There is a third scenario that has captured the imagination of some thoughtful environmental philosophers. It might be called the *future primitive.* It involves writing off technological civilization as a 10,000 year bad experiment. Either by choice or necessity small numbers of humans resume the kind of hunter and gatherer existence that indeed worked quite well for our species for millions of years. But the downside is that the extraordinary achievements and breathtaking potential of civilization are lost. A better goal, I feel, is that of Henry David Thoreau who wished "to secure all the advantages" of civilization "without suffering any of the disadvantages." Don't humans have as much right to fulfill their evolutionary potential as other species? The vital proviso is that in so doing we don't compromise or eliminate the opportunity of other members of the biotic community to fulfill theirs. This means not discarding technology but using it responsibly.

The fourth scenario for the Fourth Millennium I call *Island Civilization.* It's a vision, a dream if you prefer Martin Luther King's rhetoric, and it means clustering on a planetary scale. Boundaries are drawn around the human presence not around wilderness. Advanced technology permits humans to reduce their environmental impact. For the first time in human history, better tools mean peace rather than war with nature. Of course Island Civilization means the end of the idea of integrating our civilization into nature. The divorce that began with herding and agriculture is final! Since we proved clever enough to create our environment, rather than adapt to what nature provided, we've taken that option to the logical extreme. We impact only a tiny part of the planet. The rest is self-willed. The matrix is wild not civilized.

Of course a change like this one involves compromises with human freedom. On a finite planet, shared with millions of other species, only limited numbers of humans can enjoy unlimited opportunities. The first step toward Island Civilization is to check population growth and turn it back to a total of about 1.5 billion. . . . Of course this can be done! Here's one problem for which we know the cause and the solution. It's the motivation that is thus far lacking. A new, expanded earth ethic and plain fear about the crash of a bloated species might change things around. The essential first step is to put nature above people: "Earth First!" was the name Dave Foreman, Mike Roselle and their colleagues gave to their program in 1980. As it is, humans increase and multiply at the rate of 10,000 per hour, a rate that wipes out any gains friends of wildlife and wilderness try to make today.

The other need for restraint is in the realm of living space. We've historically demanded too much of a planet we supposedly share with other species. We've pushed the wild things into the least desirable corners of the environment. It's time our species took some of the "marginal" lands that we can modify with our intelligence. The fact is that we've been horrible roommates in the earth household. What species would support an endangered species act for us? One version of Island Civilization might mandate that the 1.5 billion people live in five hundred concentrated habitats scattered widely over Earth. Food production, energy generation, waste treatment and cultural activities take place in 100-mile closed-circle units supporting three million humans. "Cities" cannot begin to describe the new living arrangements that the architects and engineers of the Fourth Millennium could create. They might be on the poles, around mountains, in the air, underground and undersea. Rivers might run through some of them. Others might float in water or in the air. There would be cultural exchange, of course, but no need for global trade in food, energy or materials among the islands. Economies would be relocalized; the concept of "hundred mile meals" would be a reality. We would get back to an arrangement that worked well on a small scale for Greek city-states, medieval monasteries and pueblos of the Southwest. Sure, wild nature will be heavily impacted on the islands we occupy, but isn't that fairer and better than a planet-wide sacrifice to a single species? The concept of an island means that human impact is completely contained. The kind of sprawl from which the planet suffers today would be gone. And, I am hoping, no more war. At least border tensions and territorial expansion would not be factors!

Exciting as the possibilities are for this new way for humans to live, it is what's outside the islands (or more clearly what is *not* outside them!) that is especially compelling. The human presence has imploded. Fences are down. Dams are gone. Roads, railroads, pipelines, telephone lines, ocean-going ships indeed all terrestrial forms of transportation could be unnecessary in a millennium. I'm counting on amazing new technology to make all this possible. Nuclear fusion may be just the tip of the new technological iceberg. Utopian science fiction? Well, consider what was said about television and computers a century ago. And the pace of technological change is accelerating dramatically. Of course I can't prove marvels such as transportation by teleportation will exist in a thousand years, but by the same token you can't deny they won't. Turn our best minds loose on the technological challenges of Island Civilization (rather than repairing the old, dead-end paths) and miracles will happen. It is not necessary to go back to the Pleistocene to live with a low ecological impact. Technology is essentially neutral; it's what we do with it that is the problem. So why not expand our ethics, end mind pollution and take the high tech road to minimal impact? The result could be the conservation biology dream. The frontier reappears, and this time it is permanent. Rivers are full of salmon and the deer and antelope play on the plains. The big predators are back too and, without human interference, perhaps evolving into some of the Pleistocene megafauna we never got to know. As we were before herding and agriculture, say 10,000 BC, humans in the year 3010 are once again good neighbors in the ecological community. *Homo sapiens* is healthy and enjoying its version of liberty and the pursuit of happiness and so are all the other components of the natural world.

But what, the question frequently arises, are your options if you don't want to live on densely populated islands in a matrix of wilderness? The short response is that if you wanted to live a technological lifestyle in the Fourth Millennium you wouldn't have a choice. According to the terms of a new, ecological contract, we'd surrender some freedoms like herding cows on the open range or living in a sprawling ski resort. (If you wanted to ski you'd chose to live on the island built into, say, part of the Alps.) But you could leave the islands to enjoy minimum-impact vacations in high-quality wilderness. You could even live out there for a while or forever. The condition is that you'd have to do it as part of the wilderness. That means a resumption of the old pre-pastoral ways. No herds or settling down, no towns and walls, not even cottages in the woods. Those who opted off the island would take only what they needed from nature; profits and growth would not figure into the equation. We would have finally learned what the 1964 Wilderness Act meant about people being "visitors" who do not remain in someone else's home. Perhaps humans of the distant future could choose on a seasonal basis between ways of life centered on computers or campfires. And young people of that society might be encouraged to take a two-year mission into the wild. Completely out of contact with the civilized islands, they would learn the old hunting/gathering ways and the old land ethics. Here is where some humans might go back to the Pleistocene and live in the "future primitive" way I described a bit earlier. But is it possible people could support themselves out there for that long, living off the land? The answer is of course they could, considering that the healthy land and sea on which our ancestors built a very sustainable culture for hundreds of thousands of years was back again.

Island Civilization is a response to the history of *Homo sapiens* on Earth. For some five million years the planet was self-willed. Humans were just another hunter and gatherer and population remained small and stable. It was a successful lifestyle that weathered just as severe climate changes as the one that scares us now. About 10,000 years before the present our species began to experiment with controlling nature and reshaping our habitat. More precisely, humans stopped adapting to their environment and began to create it. Parts of this experiment resulted in impressive pinnacles of evolutionary achievement. But over time irony kicked in. Human success, especially the idea that bigger was better, carried the seeds of its own destruction as well as that of many other life forms. From the standpoint of the rest of life, the growth of our civilization amounts to a cancer in the ecosystem. We no longer belong to the ecological team; we've checked off the biotic ark! Isn't this exactly what biologist Edward O. Wilson meant in saying "Darwin's dice have rolled badly for Earth"? Island Civilization makes the needed correction. It permits human beings to realize their cultural and technological potential while safeguarding the same right of self-realization for all the other beings. . . .

So we stand at a crossroads not merely of human history but of the entire evolutionary process. Life evolved from stardust, water and fire over billions of years until one clever species developed the capacity to bring down the whole biological miracle. But amidst the fear associated with this reality of a sinking ark, there is one comfort. Earth is not threatened as in the age of the dinosaurs by an errant asteroid, a death star. Now we are the death star, but we are also capable of changing its course. And it may be appropriate at this point in the paper to observe that the environmental movement has been mostly negative. It's against things. With Island Civilization I am trying to look at the half-full part of the glass. I am not just talking about problems. Island Civilization is something to be **for.**

Imagine, in conclusion, this planet, in the desperate frame of mind contemporary conditions warrant, submitting a "personals" advertisement to a hypothetical, intergalactic cyberdating service, a kind of eHarmony.com for the universe.

> TEMPERATE BUT ENDANGERED PLANET
> ENJOYS WEATHER, PHOTOSYNTHESIS, EVOLUTION,
> CONTINENTAL DRIFT
> SEEKS CARING LONG-TERM RELATIONSHIP WITH
> COMPASSIONATE LIFEFORM

Well, maybe it could still be us! Maybe biocentric ethics and respect for self-willed nature (along with a healthy dose of fear for our future!) could turn us from cancerous to caring. Maybe we should answer that personals ad. Earth might just be ready to receive a proposal for Island Civilization.

32

A Is for Acid Rain, B Is for Bee

Joanne Harris

You never went out on rainy days. Health and Safety wouldn't let you. Instead, you played games online, or read books, or talked to your friends on your smartie, or even watched a movie—they still had live movies in those days, before ceegee took over for good (so much safer than real life, of course, but somehow not as exciting). In those days before the Cloud, you actually still *went* to school, instead of doing it all from home, and friends were people you saw every day, and games were what you played outside—that is, if it wasn't raining.

In a minute. Come here first. I hardly ever see you, kid. Yes, that's right. Climb onto my knee. Let me tell you a story. What about? Well, let me see. Do you like animals? No, *not* ceegee animals. I mean actual, real-life animals. Tigers and elephants and whales and such.

No kid, I've never seen a tiger. But listen and I'll tell you about the time I once saw a bee. You know what a bee is, don't you, kid?

No, don't say *bug*. It's an *insect*.

Why? Well, a *bug* is something gone wrong. A glitch in a machine. A cockroach is a bug, I guess. A bee—well that was something else: a living cog in a machine more complex than the Cloud itself—

What's a cog? Another time. Let me tell you about the bee. It was in the summer of—well, never mind. A long time ago, when I was your age. I used to go to school just round the corner, where the Parklands building is now. My school was called Saint Oswald's. Even in those days, it was pretty old. There was even an actual park nearby, with trees and grass and everything. We used

309

to have a lot more of that in those days. Now you don't really get it much, because of the rain. And flowers too. In those days flowers grew mostly *outside.*

That was where the bees came in. Of course, they were pretty rare even then. People said they were dying out. Some kind of disease, or the rain, or the sun, or maybe smarties, which some people said were interfering with the special signals the bees gave out to find their way back to where they lived.

In any case, we hadn't seen a real live bee for years and years. But by then I guess must of us didn't know what a bee looked like anyway. Trust me, those cartoon bees in stripy sweaters that you see in books and games look nothing like the real thing, so you can't really blame folk for getting confused. But that day, we *all* saw the bee, Philip and Johnny and Frankie and me. For all we knew it might have been the very last bee in the whole world. In any case, we never saw another one after that, and by the time I left school, the park was gone to make way for these apartment blocks. Couple of years later, the school went the same way. It was a very old building. It never passed Health and Safety tests. Still, we kind of liked it. Parklands Estate, they call it now. There hasn't been a park there in fifty years.

I know, I know. The bee. Well, in those days, some of us kids still *walked* to school. A lot of people thought that was wrong: Health and Safety did, of course, and the Social Services. But it was only ten minutes through the park, and I guess my parents thought it would be OK, as long as it didn't look like rain, and as long as we didn't loiter.

That day was fine. Not a cloud in sight. No, not *that* Cloud; we used to call that the Internet in those days, before it really took off. Clouds were just what you saw in the sky on days when it wasn't raining. No, that doesn't happen much now. Listen, do you want to hear this story or don't you? Right, then. We were walking to school. It was warm, and you could smell the flowers. Yes, smartass, they used to smell. Like what? No, not *quite* like that. They had all kinds of different smells, and that was why bees used to like them. Why? Because it means pollen, that's why, and pollen means making honey. You know all about honey, right? Yes, of course, you learnt it at school. Let me guess—in history.

Well, kid, in my day you could still buy honey online, from abroad, but it was really expensive, and I only had it once or twice. No, it wasn't yucky at all. I know it kind of sounds that way. Bee-spit. But it wasn't. It wasn't like anything you've ever tasted, or ever will.

What's it like? Like an *old* taste, somehow, like living history on your tongue. And it smelt of flowers, and sunlight, and air, and it was sweet enough to make you feel a little dizzy, a little drunk; and there was all kinds of secret stuff in there they never learnt to synthesize; and all of that comes out of flowers and grass, and only the bees knew the secret.

Well, Philip and Johnny and Frankie and me, we were in no hurry to get to school. We stopped for five minutes in the park—I didn't have a smartie then, and we couldn't play games without one. But we could still play football, the old-fashioned way, with a regular ball, and Johnny used to bring one hidden in his schoolbag. Of course, we wouldn't have got away with that at school. Health and Safety didn't allow it. But in the park, you could still run about, and to be fair, although I fell over quite a *lot,* it never did more damage than a few grass stains on my knees.

It was there that we all saw the bee that day. Philip had managed to kick the ball into one of the flower beds, and we all ran up to retrieve it. It was sitting in a big patch of some kind of tall pink flowers, and Phil reached in to get it back, lost his balance, grabbed one of the stems and—

'Ouch! Damn thing! It *stung* me!'

'Must be a rose,' said Frankie. Roses had thorns in those days, you know; not like the ones you can buy in the shops. They had a scent in those days, too, and I guess the bees must have liked them. Because there it was on the flower, the bee; no bigger than my fingertip, and nothing like the ceegeed bees you see in animations. For a start, it was brown, not yellow; a kind of tabby brown, with delicate stripy markings, and when you looked at it really closely you could see that it was *furry,* somehow, with little feathery feelers. This, and not the rose bush, was what had stung Philip; this single bee, now clinging onto the palm of his hand and arching its back like an acrobat—because bees were able to *sting,* you know—only in self-defense, I guess, but Phil had put his hand on it, and it got him good. He shook off the bee, and I saw the mark, as big as a pound coin, I guess, and his fingers already beginning to swell. He wasn't crying—well, not yet—but I could see it hurt a *lot.*

'They say when a bee stings you, you die!' said Johnny, not helping the situation much.

Philip's eyes got very big.

'No, dummy, it's the *bee* that dies,' said Frankie, who was a smartass, like you.

'What if I've got an allergy?' said Phil. 'You can get them to bee stings.'

'In that case, you're a goner,' said Frankie.

Philip started to cry for real.

'No way,' I said. 'A tiny thing like that?'

'That sting could get infected,' said Frankie. 'We ought to tell Health and Safety. Or—'

'Listen,' I said. 'It's making a noise.'

It was true; the bee was *buzzing.* At first, it sounded like a circular saw heard from a million miles away. Then it rose and became a whine; intermittent; protesting.

'Kill it!' said Johnny.

'No way,' I said. I took it gently between my hands.

'It'll sting you,' said Philip.

'No it won't. A bee can only sting once.'

Well, kid, in the end we had to take Phil to the walk-in center to get an anti-allergy shot. We got into terrible trouble at school. After that, we weren't allowed to walk to school through the park any more.

But I kept the bee in my pencil case, hoping it might somehow survive It didn't, of course. Frankie was right. It's the bee, and not the person, who dies. Pity. I'd always wanted a pet.

I never saw another bee. They all turned out to be hover-flies. Or wasps, which can sting you as often as they feel like it. But I told Mrs. Teague about it at school, and she showed me an old glass collecting case from on top of a pile of stuff to throw out.

'People used to collect insects,' she said. 'These were collected a long time ago, before it became illegal. For some reason, this box has survived. I think someone left it to the school, an old man who used to live nearby. He was a lepidopterist. That means he collected butterflies. But he also collected other insects. Perhaps you'd like to have this.'

And so I took the glass case. I never told anyone about it. For a start, Health and Safety would have said that it was unhygienic; I might have picked up some kind of disease or allergy from those dusty old things. For a long time I kept it under my bed, and looked at it in secret. There were thirty-five specimens in that case, all held in place by long steel pins and labelled in tiny brown writing. *Bumble bee. Carpenter bee. Stingless bee. Leafcutter bee. Orchid bee. Cuckoo bee. Hornfaced bee. Orchard bee.* And here, at the end of a row, *my* bee: *Apis Mellifera,* the European honeybee, banded in brown and honey-gold under a layer of feathery dust. All of them extinct now, as well as a lot of the plants they served. Funny to think that only fifty years ago, those bees were flying all over the place, making honey, building nests, making that funny buzzing sound and flitting from flower to flower.

What's that, kid? No, I don't have the collecting case any more. The rules on that kind of thing are too strict. I'd have to have a license. But I do remember all their names. Would you like to hear them? Yes, I know. I'm repeating myself. But it's so good to see you. We so rarely see children around here nowadays. Why? Oh, Health and Safety, I guess. Unless there's some other reason, kid. Allergies, maybe. Acid rain.

What? Is visiting time over so soon? Well, maybe next time you'll stay longer. Tell your mother I love her, kid. Tell her to call me once in a while. I still have dreams about that case, you know; those carefully labelled specimens. I once read somewhere that there used to be nine hundred thousand insect species in the world, and more being discovered every day. Now so many seem to be gone. Except for the cockroaches, that is. They'll always be around.

What happened to make things change this way? Were we somehow responsible? Of course, there's no actual proof that we did anything at all. No one knows why the bees died out, or whether their disappearance had anything at all to do with allergies, acid rain, the disappearance of our parks or the fact that I can sometime spend days or weeks before seeing even a single kid. And yet, I can't help thinking. Maybe the earth is allergic to *us*—maybe we're the insects, and all this is the final stage in a long, slow process of rejection.

We used to be kings of this world, kid. Or so we thought. But kings get overturned in the end, and sometimes all it takes is a stone to bring down the oldest of empires. We always thought the cockroaches would end up ruling the world. Perhaps they will. Rain doesn't hurt them, they're immune to UV. They don't even have any allergies. Next to them, we're soft and weak. They're bound to do better than we did.

We used to be kings of the world, once.

Not any more, kid. Not any more.

33

The Future Is Local

Wendell Berry

I live in and have known all my life the northern corner of Henry County, Kentucky. The country here is narrowly creased and folded; it is a varied landscape whose main features are these:

(1) A rolling upland of which some of the soil is excellent and some, because of abuse, is less so. This upland is well suited to mixed farming which was, in fact, traditional to it, but which is less diversified now than it was twenty-five years ago. Some row-cropping is possible here, but even the best-lying ridges are vulnerable to erosion and probably not more than 10% should be broken in any year. It is a kind of land that needs grass and grazing animals, and it is excellent for this use.

(2) Wooded bluffs where the upland breaks over into the valleys of the creeks and the Kentucky River. Along with virtually all of this region, most of these bluffs have been cleared and cropped at one time or another. They should never have been cropped, and because of their extreme vulnerability to erosion they should be logged only with the greatest skill and care. Most of these bluffs are now forested, though not many old growth stands remain.

(3) Slopes of gentler declivity below the bluffs. Some of these slopes are grassed, and, with close care, are maintainable as pasture. Until World War II they were periodically cropped, in a version of slash-and-burn agriculture, which resulted in serious damage by erosion. Now much of this land is covered with trees thirty or forty years old.

(4) Finally, there are the creek and river bottoms, some of which are subject to flooding at varying frequencies. Much of this land is suitable for

intensive row-cropping, which, under the regime of industrial agriculture, has sometimes been too intensive.

Within these four general divisions, this country is extremely diverse. To familiarity and experience, the landscape divides into many small facets or aspects differentiated by the kind or quality of soil, and by slope, exposure, drainage, rockiness, etc. In the two centuries during which European races have occupied this part of the country, the best of the land has sometimes been well used, under the influence of good times and good intentions. But virtually none of it has escaped ill use under the influence of bad times or ignorance, need or greed. Some of it—the steeper, more marginal areas—has never been well used. Of virtually all of this land it may be said that the national economy has prescribed ways of use but not ways of care. It is now impossible to imagine any immediate way that most of this land might receive excellent care. The economy, as it now is, prescribes plunder of the land owners and abuse of the land.

The connection of the American economy to this place—in comparison, say, to the connection of the American economy to just about any university—has been unregarding and ungenerous. Indeed, the connection has been almost entirely exploitive. It has never been more exploitive than it is now. Increasingly, from the beginning, most of the money made on the products of this place has been made in other places. Increasingly the ablest young people of this place have gone away to receive a college education, which has given them a "professional status" too often understood as a license to predatorize such places as this one that they came from. The destruction of the human community, the local economy, and the natural health of such a place as this is now looked upon, not as a "trade-off," a possibly regrettable "price of progress," but as a good, virtually a national goal.

Recently I heard, on an early morning radio program, a university economist explaining the benefits of off-farm work for farm women: that farm women are increasingly employed off the farm, she said, has made them "full partners" in the farm's economy. Never mind that this is a symptom of economic desperation and great unhappiness on the farm. And never mind the value, which was more than economic, of these women's previous contribution *on* the farm to the farm family's life and economy—which was, many of them would have said, a full partnership. *Now* they are "earning 45% of total family income," *now* they are playing "a major role." The 45% and the "major role" are allowed to defray all other costs. That the farm family now furnishes labor and (by its increased consumption) income to the economy that is destroying it is seen simply as an improvement. Thus the abstract and extremely tentative value of money is thoughtlessly allowed to replace the particular and fundamental values of the lives of household and community. Obviously, we need to stop thinking about the economic functions of individuals for a while, and try to learn to think of the economic functions of communities and households. We need to try to understand the long-term economies of places—places, that is, that are considered as dwelling places for humans and their fellow creatures, not as exploitable resources.

What happens when farm people take up "off-farm work"? The immediate result is that they must be replaced by chemicals and machines and other purchases from an economy adverse and antipathetic to farming, which means that the remaining farmers are put under yet greater pressure to abuse their land. If under the pressure of an adverse economy, the soil erodes, soil and water and air are poisoned, the woodlands are wastefully logged, and everything not producing an immediate economic return is neglected, that is apparently understood by most of the society as merely the normal cost of production.

One thing that this means is that the land and its human communities are not being thought about in places of study and leadership, and this failure to think is causing damage. But if one lives in a country place, and if one loves it, one must think about it. Under present circumstances, it is not easy to imagine what might be a proper human economy for the country I have just described. And yet, if one loves it, one must make the attempt; if one loves it, in fact, the attempt is irresistible.

Two facts are immediately apparent. One is that the present local economy, based exclusively on the export of raw materials, like the economies of most rural places, is ruinous. Another is that the influence of a complex, aggressive national economy upon a simple, passive local economy will also be ruinous. In a varied and versatile countryside, fragile in its composition and extremely susceptible to abuse, requiring close human care and elaborate human skills, able to produce a great variety of products from its soils, what is needed, obviously, is a highly diversified local economy.

We should be producing the fullest variety of foods to be consumed locally, in the countryside itself and in nearby towns and cities: meats, grains, table vegetables, fruits and nuts, dairy products, poultry and eggs. We should be harvesting a sustainable yield of fish from our ponds and streams. Our woodlands, managed for continuous yields, selectively and carefully logged, should be yielding a variety of timber for a variety of purposes: firewood, fence posts, lumber for building, fine woods for furniture makers.

And we should be adding value locally to these local products. What is needed is not the large factory so dear to the hearts of government "developers" and local "boosters." To set our whole population to making computers or automobiles would be as gross an error as to use the whole countryside for growing corn or Christmas trees or pulpwood; it would discount everything we have to offer as a community and a place; it would despise our talents and capacities as individuals.

We need, instead, a system of decentralized, small-scale industries to transform the products of our fields and woodlands and streams: small creameries, cheese factories, tanneries, grain mills, saw mills, furniture factories, and the like. By "small" I mean simply a size that would not be destructive of the appearance, the health, and the quiet of the countryside. If a factory began to "grow" or to be noisy at night or on Sunday, that would mean that another such factory was needed somewhere else. If waste should occur at any point, that would indicate the need for an enterprise of some other sort. If poison or pollution resulted from any enterprise, that would be understood as an indication that something was absolutely wrong, and a correction would be made. Small scale, of course, makes such changes and corrections more thinkable and more possible than does large scale.

I realize that, by now, my argument has crossed a boundary line of which everyone in our "realistic" society is keenly aware. I will be perceived to have crossed over into "utopianism" or fantasy. Unless I take measures to prevent it, I am going to hear somebody say, "All that would be very vice, if it were possible. Can't you be realistic?"

Well, let me take measures to prevent it. I am not, I admit, optimistic about the success of this kind of thought. Otherwise, my intention, above all, is to be realistic; I wish to be practical. The question here is simply that of convention. Do I want to be realistic according to the conventions of the industrial economy and the military state, or according to what I know of reality? To me, an economy that sees the life of a community or a place as expendable, and reckons its value only as money, is not acceptable because it is *not* realistic. I am thinking as I believe we must think if we wish to discuss the *best* uses of people, places, and things, and if we wish to give affection some standing in our thoughts.

If we wish to make the *best* use of people, places, and things, then we are going to have to deal with a law that reads about like this: as the quality of use increases, the scale of use (that is, the size of operations) will decline, the tools will become simpler, and the methods and the skills will become more complex. That is a difficult law for us to believe, because we have assumed otherwise for a long time, and yet our experience overwhelmingly suggests that it is a law, and that the penalties for disobeying it are severe.

I am making a plea for diversity not only because diversity exists and is pleasant, but because it is necessary and we need more of it. For an example, let me return to the countryside I described at the beginning. From birth, I have been familiar with this place, and have heard it talked about and thought about. For the last twenty-four years I have been increasingly involved in the use and improvement of a little part of it. As a result of some failures and some successes, I have learned some things about it. I am certain, however, that I do not know the best way to use this land. I do not believe that anyone else does. I no longer expect to live to see it come to its best use. But I am beginning to see what is needed, and everywhere the need is for diversity. This is the need of every American rural landscape that I am acquainted with. We need a greater range of species and varieties of plants and animals, of human skills and methods, so that the use may be fitted ever more sensitively and elegantly to the place. Our places, in short, are asking us questions, some of them urgent questions, and we do not have the answers.

The answers, if they are to come, and if they are to work, must be developed in the presence of the user and the land; they must be developed to some degree *by* the user *on* the land. The present practice of handing down from on high policies and technologies developed without consideration of the nature and the needs of the land and the people has not worked, and it cannot work. Good agriculture and forestry cannot be "invented" by self-styled smart people in offices and laboratories and then sold at the highest possible profit to the supposedly dumb country people. That is not the way good land use comes about. And it does not matter how the methodologies so developed and handed down are labeled; whether "industrial" or "conventional" or "organic" or "sustainable," the professional or professorial condescension that is blind to the primacy of the union between the individual people and individual places is ruinous. The challenge to the would-be scientists of an ecologically sane agriculture, as David Ehrenfeld has written, is "to provide unique and particular answers to questions about a farmer's unique and particular land." The proper goal, he adds, is *not* merely to "substitute the cult of the benevolent ecologist for the cult of the benevolent sales representative."

The question of what a beloved country is to be used for quickly becomes inseparable from the questions of who is to use it or who is to prescribe its uses, and what will be the ways of using it. If we speak simply of the use of "a country," then only the first question is asked, and it is asked only by its would-be users. It is not until we speak of "a beloved country"—a particular country, particularly loved—that the question about ways of use will arise. It arises because, loving our country, we see where we are, and we see that present ways of use are not adequate. They are not adequate because such local cultures and economies as we had have been stunted or destroyed. As a nation, we have attempted to substitute the *concepts* of "land use," "agribusiness," "development," and the like, for the *culture* of stewardship and husbandry. And this change is not a result merely of economic pressure and adverse social values; it comes also from the state of affairs in our educational system, especially in our universities. . . .

Without a beloved country as context, the arts and the sciences become oriented to the careers of their practitioners, and the intellectual life to intellectual (and bureaucratic) procedures. And so in the universities we see forming an intellectual elite more and more exclusively accomplished in intellectual procedures: promotion, technological innovation, publication, and grant-getting. The context of a beloved country, moreover, implies an academic standard that is not inflatable or deflatable. The standard—the physical, intellectual, political, ecological, economic, and spiritual health of the country—cannot be too high; it is as high, simply, as we have the love, the vision, and the courage to make it.

I would like my country to be seen and known with an attentiveness that is schooled and skilled. I would like it to be loved with a minutely particular affection and loyalty. I would like the work in it to be practical and loving and respectful and forbearing. In order for these things to happen the sciences and the humanities are going to have to come together again in the presence of the practical problems of individual places, and of local knowledge and local love in individual people—people able to see, know, think, feel, and act coherently and well without the modern instinct of deference to the "outside expert." . . .

Let me give [an] example. My brother, who is a lawyer, recently had as a client an elderly man named Bennie Yeary who had farmed for many years a farm of about three hundred acres of hilly and partly forested land. His farm and the road to his house had been damaged by a power company.

Seeking to determine the value of the land, my brother asked him if he had ever logged his woodlands.

Mr. Yeary answered: "Yes, sir, since 1944 . . . I have never robbed [the land]. I have always just cut a little out where I thought it needed it. I have got as much timber right now, I am satisfied . . . as I had when I started mill runs here in '44."

That we should not rob the land is a principle to be found readily enough in the literary culture. That it came into literature out of the common culture is suggested by the fact that it is commonly phrased in this way by people who have not inherited the literary culture. That we should not rob the land, anyhow, is a principle that can be learned from books. But the ways of living on the land so as not to rob it probably cannot be learned from books, and this is made clear by a further exchange between my brother and Mr. Yeary.

They came to the question of what was involved in the damage to the road, and the old farmer said that the power company had destroyed thirteen or fourteen water breaks. A water break is a low mound of rock and earth built across a hilly road to divert the water out of it. It is a means of preventing erosion both of the roadbed and of the land alongside it, one of the ways of living on the land without robbing it.

"How long . . . had it been since you had those water breaks constructed in there?"

"I had been working on them . . . off and on, for about 12 years, putting them water breaks in. I hauled rocks out of my fields . . . and I would dig out, bury these rocks down, and take the sledgehammer and beat rock in here and make this water break."

The way to make a farm road that will not rob the land cannot be learned from books, then, because the long use of such a road is a part of the proper way of making it, and because the use and improvement of the road are intimately involved with the use and improvement of the place. It is of the utmost importance that the rocks to make the water breaks were hauled from the fields. Mr. Yeary's solution did not, like the typical industrial solution, involve the making of a problem, or a series of problems, elsewhere. It involved the making of a solution elsewhere: the same work that improved the road improved the fields. Such work requires not only correct principles, skill, and industry, but a knowledge of local particulars, and many years; it involves slow, small adjustments in response to questions asked by a particular place.

And this is true in general of the patterns and structures of a proper human use of a beloved country, as examination of the traditional landscapes of the Old World will readily show: they were made by use as much as by skill.

This implication of use in the making of essential artifacts and the maintenance of the landscape—which are to so large an extent the making and the maintenance of culture—brings us to the inescapable final step in an argument for diversity: the realization that without a diversity of people we cannot maintain a diversity of anything else. By a diversity of people I do not mean a diversity of specialists, but a diversity of people elegantly suited to live in their places and to bring them to their best use, whether the use is that of uselessness, as in a place left wild, or that of the highest sustainable productivity. The most abundant diversity of creatures and ways cannot be maintained in preserves, zoos, museums, and the like, but only in the occupations and the pleasures of an appropriately diversified human economy.

The proper ways of using a beloved country are humanities, I think, and are as complex, difficult, interesting, and worthy as any of the rest. But they defy the present intellectual and academic categories. They are *both* science and art, knowing and doing. Indispensable as these ways are to the success of human life, they have no place and no standing in the present structures of our intellectual life. The purpose, indeed, of the present structures of our intellectual life has been to educate them out of existence. I think I know where in any university my brother's client, Mr. Yeary, would be laughed at or ignored or tape-recorded or classified. I don't know where he would be appropriately honored. The scientific disciplines certainly do not honor him, and the "humane" ones almost as certainly do not. We would have to go some distance back in the literary tradition—back to Thomas Hardy, at least, and before Hardy to Wordsworth—to find the due respect paid to such a person. He *has* been educated almost out of existence, and yet an understanding of his importance and worth would renew the life of the mind in this country, in the university and out.

34

Technological Salvation

Michael Shellenberger
and Ted Nordhaus

Sometime around 2014, Italy will complete construction of seventy-eight mobile floodgates aimed at protecting Venice's three inlets from the rising tides of the Adriatic Sea. The massive doors—twenty meters by thirty meters, and five meters thick—will, most of the time, lie flat on the sandy seabed between the lagoon and the sea. But when a high tide is predicted, the doors will empty themselves of water and fill with compressed air, rising up on hinges to keep the Adriatic out of the city. Three locks will allow ships to move in and out of the lagoon while the gates are up.

Nowhere else in the world have humans so constantly had to create and re-create their infrastructure in response to a changing natural environment than in Venice. The idea for the gates dates back to the 1966 flood, which inundated 100 percent of the city. Still, it took from 1970 to 2002 for the hydrologist Robert Frassetto and others to convince their fellow Italians to build them. Not everyone sees the oscillating and buoyant floodgates as Venice's salvation. After the project was approved, the head of World Wildlife Fund Italy said, "Today the city's destiny rests on a pretentious, costly, and environmentally harmful technological gamble."

In truth, the grandeur that is Venice has always rested—quite literally— on a series of pretentious, costly, and environmentally harmful technological gambles. Her buildings rest upon pylons made of ancient larch and oak trees ripped from inland forests a thousand years ago. Over time, the pylons were petrified by the saltwater, infill was added, and cathedrals were constructed.

Little by little, technology helped transform a town of humble fisherfolk into the city we know today.

Saving Venice has meant creating Venice, not once, but many times since its founding. And that is why her rescue from the rising seas serves as an apt metaphor for solving this century's formidable environmental problems. Each new act of salvation will result in new unintended consequences, positive and negative, which will in turn require new acts of salvation. What we call "saving the Earth" will, in practice, require creating and re-creating it again and again for as long as humans inhabit it.

Many environmentally concerned people today view technology as an affront to the sacredness of nature, but our technologies have always been perfectly natural. Our animal skins, our fire, our farms, our windmills, our nuclear plants, and our solar panels—all 100 percent natural, drawn, as they are, from the raw materials of the Earth.

Furthermore, over the course of human history, those technologies have not only been created by us, but have also helped create us. Recent archaeological evidence suggests that the reason for our modern hands, with their opposable thumbs and shorter fingers, is that they were better adapted for tool use. Ape hands are great for climbing trees but not, it turns out, for striking flint or making arrowheads. Those prehumans whose hands could best use tools gained an enormous advantage over those whose hands could not.

As our hands and wrists changed, we increasingly walked upright, hunted, ate meat, and evolved. Our upright posture allowed us to chase down animals we had wounded with our weapons. Our long-distance running was aided by sweat glands replacing fur. The use of fire to cook meat allowed us to consume much larger amounts of protein, which allowed our heads to grow so large that some prehumans began delivering bigger-brained babies prematurely. Those babies, in turn, were able to survive because we were able to fashion still more tools, made from animal bladders and skins, to strap the helpless infants to their mothers' chests. Technology, in short, made us human.

Of course, as our bodies, our brains, and our tools evolved, so too did our ability to radically modify our environment. We hunted mammoths and other species to extinction. We torched whole forests and savannas in order to flush prey and clear land for agriculture. And long before human emissions began to affect the climate, we had already shifted the albedo of the Earth by replacing many of the world's forests with cultivated agriculture. While our capabilities to alter our environment have, over the last century, expanded substantially, the trend is long-standing. The Earth of one hundred or two hundred or three hundred years ago was one that had already been profoundly shaped by human endeavor.

None of this changes the reality and risks of the ecological crises humans have created. Global warming, deforestation, overfishing, and other human activities—if they don't threaten our very existence—certainly offer the possibility of misery for many hundreds of millions, if not billions, of humans and are rapidly transforming nonhuman nature at a pace not seen for many hundreds of millions of years. But the difference between the new ecological crises and the ways in which humans and even prehumans have shaped nonhuman nature for tens of thousands of years is one of scope and scale, not kind.

Humans have long been cocreators of the environment they inhabit. Any proposal to fix environmental problems by turning away from technology risks worsening them, by attempting to deny the ongoing coevolution of humans and nature.

Nevertheless, elites in the West—who rely more heavily on technology than anyone else on the planet—insist that development and technology are the causes of ecological problems but not their solution. They claim that economic sacrifice is the answer, while living amid historic levels of affluence and abundance. They consume resources on a vast scale, overwhelming whatever meager conservations they may partake in through living in dense (and often fashionable) urban enclaves, driving fuel-efficient automobiles, and purchasing locally grown produce. Indeed, the most visible and common expressions of faith in ecological salvation are new forms of consumption. Green products and services—the Toyota Prius, the efficient washer/dryer, the LEED-certified office building—are consciously identified by consumers as things they do to express their higher moral status.

The same is true at the political level, as world leaders, to the cheers of the left-leaning postmaterial constituencies that increasingly hold the balance of political power in many developed economies, offer promise after promise to address climate change, species extinction, deforestation, and global poverty, all while studiously avoiding any action that might impose real cost or sacrifice upon their constituents. While it has been convenient for many sympathetic observers to chalk up the failure of such efforts to corporate greed, corruption, and political cowardice, the reality is that the entire postmaterial project is, confoundingly, built upon a foundation of affluence and material consumption that would be considerably threatened by any serious effort to address the ecological crises through substantially downscaling economic activity.

It's not too difficult to understand how this hypocrisy has come to infiltrate such a seemingly well-meaning swath of our culture. As large populations in the developed North achieved unprecedented economic security, affluence, and freedom, the project that had centrally occupied humanity for thousands of years—emancipating ourselves from nature, tribalism, peonage, and poverty—was subsumed by the need to manage the unintended consequences of modernization itself, from local pollution to nuclear proliferation to global warming.

Increasingly skeptical of capitalist meritocracy and economic criteria as the implicit standards of success at the individual level and the defining measure of progress at the societal level, the post–World War II generations have redefined normative notions of well-being and quality of life in developed societies. Humanitarianism and environmentalism have become the dominant social movements, bringing environmental protection, preservation of quality of life, and other "life-political" issues, in the words of British sociologist Anthony Giddens, to the fore.

The rise of the knowledge economy—encompassing medicine, law, finance, media, real estate, marketing, and the nonprofit sector—has further accelerated the West's growing disenchantment with modern life, especially among the educated elite. Knowledge workers are more alienated from the products of their labor than any other class in history, unable to claim some role in producing food, shelter, or even basic consumer products. And yet they can afford to spend time in beautiful places—in their gardens, in the countryside, on beaches, and near old-growth forests. As they survey these landscapes, they tell themselves that the best things in life are free, even though they have consumed mightily to travel to places where they feel peaceful, calm, and far from the worries of the modern world.

These postmaterial values have given rise to a secular and largely inchoate ecotheology, complete with apocalyptic fears of ecological collapse, disenchanting notions of living in a fallen world, and the growing conviction that some kind of collective sacrifice is needed to avoid the end of the world. Alongside those dark incantations shine nostalgic visions of a transcendent future in which humans might, once again, live in harmony with nature through a return to small-scale agriculture, or even to hunter-gatherer life.

The contradictions between the world as it is—filled with the unintended consequences of our actions—and the world as so many of us would like it to be result in a pseudorejection of modernity, a kind of postmaterialist nihilism. Empty gestures are the defining sacraments of this ecotheology. The belief that we must radically curtail our consumption in order to survive as a civilization is no impediment to elites paying for private university educations, frequent jet travel, and iPads.

Thus, ecotheology, like all dominant religious narratives, serves the dominant forms of social and economic organization in which it is embedded. Catholicism valorized poverty, social hierarchy, and agrarianism for the masses in feudal societies that lived and worked the land. Protestantism valorized industriousness, capital accumulation, and individuation among the rising merchant classes of early capitalist societies and would define the social norms of modernizing industrial societies. Today's secular ecotheology values creativity, imagination, and leisure over the work ethic, productivity, and efficiency in societies that increasingly prosper from their knowledge economies while outsourcing crude, industrial production of goods to developing societies. Living amid unprecedented levels of wealth and security, ecological elites reject economic growth as a measure of well-being, tell cautionary tales about modernity and technology, and warn of overpopulation abroad now that the societies in which they live are wealthy and their populations are no longer growing.

Such hypocrisy has rarely been a hindrance to religion and, indeed, contributes to its power. One of the most enduring characteristics of human civilization is the way ruling elites espouse beliefs radically at odds with their own behaviors. The ancient Greeks recited the cautionary tales of Prometheus and Icarus while using fire, dreaming of flight, and pursuing technological frontiers. Early agriculturalists told the story of the fall from Eden as a cautionary tale against the very agriculture they practiced. European Christians espoused poverty and peacemaking while accumulating wealth and waging war.

In preaching antimodernity while living as moderns, ecological elites affirm their status at the top of the postindustrial knowledge hierarchy. Affluent developed-world elites offer both their less well-to-do countrymen and the global poor a laundry list of don'ts—don't develop like we developed, don't drive tacky SUVs, don't overconsume—that engender resentment, not emulation, from fellow citizens at home and abroad. That the ecological elites hold themselves to a different standard while insisting that all are equal is yet another demonstration of their higher status, for they are thus unaccountable even to reality.

Though it poses as a solution, today's nihilistic ecotheology is actually a significant obstacle to dealing with ecological problems created by modernization—one that must be replaced by a new, creative, and life-affirming worldview. After all, human development, wealth, and technology liberated us from hunger, deprivation, and insecurity; now they must be considered essential to overcoming ecological risks.

There's no question that humans are radically remaking the Earth, but fears of ecological apocalypse—of condemning this world to fiery destruction—are unsupported by the sciences. Global warming may bring worsening disasters and disruptions to rainfall, snowmelts, and agriculture, but there is little evidence to suggest it will deliver the end of modernization. Even the most catastrophic United Nations scenarios predict rising economic growth. While wealthy environmentalists claim to be especially worried about the impact of global warming on the poor, it is rapid, not retarded, development that is most likely to protect the poor against natural disasters and agricultural losses.

What modernization may threaten most is not human civilization, but the survival of those nonhuman species and environments we care about. While global warming dominates ecological discourse, the greatest threats to nonhumans remain our direct changes to the land and the seas. The world's great, diverse, and ancient forests are being converted to tree plantations, farms, and ranches. Humans are causing massive, unprecedented extinctions on Earth due to habitat destruction. We are on the verge of losing primates in the wild. We have so overfished the oceans that most of the big fish are gone.

The apocalyptic vision of ecotheology warns that degrading nonhuman natures will undermine the basis for human civilization, but history has shown the opposite: the degradation of nonhuman environments has made us rich. We have become rather adept at transferring the wealth and diversity of nonhuman environments into human ones. The solution to the unintended consequences of modernity is, and has always been, more modernity—just as the solution to the unintended consequences of our technologies has always been more technology. The Y2K computer bug was fixed by better computer programming, not by going back to typewriters. The ozone-hole crisis was averted not by an end to air conditioning but rather by more advanced, less environmentally harmful technologies.

The question for humanity, then, is not whether humans and our civilizations will survive, but rather what kind of a planet we will inhabit. Would we like a planet with wild primates, old-growth forests, a living ocean, and modest rather than extreme temperature increases? Of course we would—virtually everybody would. Only continued modernization and technological innovation can make such a world possible.

Putting faith in modernization will require a new secular theology consistent with the reality of human creation and life on Earth, not with some imagined dystopia or utopia. It will require a worldview that sees technology as humane and sacred, rather than inhumane and profane. It will require replacing the antiquated notion that human development is antithetical to the preservation of nature with the view that modernization is the key to saving it. Let's call this "modernization theology."

Where ecotheology imagines that our ecological problems are the consequence of human violations of a separate "nature," modernization theology views environmental problems as an inevitable part of life on Earth. Where the last generation of ecologists saw a natural harmony in Creation, the new ecologists see constant change. Where ecotheologians suggest that the unintended consequences of human development might be avoidable, proponents of modernization view them as inevitable, and positive as often as negative. And where the ecological elites see the powers of humankind as the enemy of Creation, the modernists acknowledge them as central to its salvation.

Modernization theology should thus be grounded in a sense of profound gratitude to Creation—human and nonhuman. It should celebrate, not desecrate, the technologies that led our prehuman ancestors to evolve. Our experience of transcendence in the outdoors should translate into the desire for all humans to benefit from the fruits of modernization and be able to experience similar transcendence. Our valorization of creativity should lead us to care for our cocreation of the planet.

The risks now faced by humanity are increasingly ones of our own making—and ones over which we have only partial, tentative, and temporary control. Various kinds of liberation—from hard agricultural labor and high infant mortality rates to tuberculosis and oppressive traditional values—bring all kinds of new problems, from global warming and obesity to alienation and depression. These new problems will largely be better than the old ones, in the way that obesity is a better problem than hunger, and living in a hotter world is a better problem than living in one without electricity. But they are serious problems nonetheless.

The good news is that we already have many nascent, promising technologies to overcome ecological problems. Stabilizing greenhouse gas emissions will require a new generation of nuclear power plants to cheaply replace coal plants as well as, perhaps, to pull carbon dioxide out of the atmosphere and power desalination plants to irrigate and grow forests in today's deserts. Pulling frontier agriculture back from forests will require massively increasing agricultural yields through genetic engineering. Replacing environmentally degrading cattle ranching may require growing meat in laboratories, which will gradually be viewed as less repulsive than today's cruel and deadly methods of meat production. And the solution to the species extinction problem will involve creating new habitats and new organisms, perhaps from the DNA of previously extinct ones.

In attempting to solve these problems, we will inevitably create new ones. One common objection to technology and development is that they will bring unintended consequences, but life on Earth has always been a story of unintended consequences. The Venice floodgates offer a pointed illustration. Concerns raised by the environmental community that the floodgates would impact marine life have been borne out—only not in the way they had feared. Though the gates are still under construction, marine biologists have announced that they have already become host to many coral and fish species, some of which used to be found only in the southern Mediterranean or Red Sea.

Other critics of the gates have questioned what will happen if global warming should raise sea levels higher than the tops of the gates. If this should become inevitable, it is unlikely that Venetians would abandon their city. Instead, they may attempt to raise it. One sweetly ironic proposal would levitate the city by blowing carbon dioxide emissions two thousand feet below the lagoon floor. Some may call such strong faith in the technological fix an instance of hubris, but others will simply call it compassion.

The French anthropologist Bruno Latour has some interesting thoughts on the matter. According to Latour, Mary Shelley's *Frankenstein* is not a cautionary tale against hubris, but rather a cautionary tale against irrational fears of imperfection. Dr. Frankenstein is an antihero not because he created life, but rather because he fled in horror when he mistook his creation for a monster—a self-fulfilling prophecy. The moral of the story, where saving the planet is concerned, is that we should treat our technological creations as we would treat our children, with care and love, lest our abandonment of them turn them into monsters.

"The sin is not to wish to have dominion over nature," Latour writes, "but to believe that this dominion means emancipation and not attachment." In other words, the term "ecological hubris" should not be used to describe the human desire to remake the world, but rather the faith that we can end the cycle of creation and destruction.

35

Geoengineering

Reformatting the Planet for Climate Protection?

Simon Nicholson

Over the last handful of years, a set of radical ideas that have long been confined to the fringes of climate change discussions have begun to edge toward center stage. The ideas are known collectively as geoengineering proposals—sweeping technological schemes designed to counteract the effects of planetary warming.

Many of the best-known geoengineering proposals read like science fiction. One widely circulated idea is to launch giant mirror arrays or sunshades into near-Earth orbit, in an attempt to reflect some amount of solar radiation. Other lines of research suggest that a similar effect could be achieved by depositing fine reflective particles of sulfur dioxide in the stratosphere or by deploying a host of ocean-going ships to spray cloud-whitening saltwater high into the sky. At the same time there are ongoing efforts to develop vast machines designed to suck carbon dioxide (CO_2) out of the air, to produce carbon-capturing cement, to lock carbon into soil, and to perfect the dropping of massive quantities of soluble iron into the oceans to encourage great carbon-inhaling blooms of plankton.

Yet even while many geoengineering proposals sound fantastical, the field is beginning to receive sustained attention from serious people and groups. The Intergovernmental Panel on Climate Change (IPCC) has convened expert meetings to consider the topic. So too have other important scientific bodies around the world. In the United States, government agencies from the Pentagon to the Department of Energy have advocated that federal dollars be devoted to geoengineering research, and research teams in universities and the private sector in many countries are looking to move beyond theorizing about global climate control to technological development and deployment. . . .

Dreams of weather and climate control are hardly new. Ancient traditions had a variety of rituals aimed at calling forth favorable weather. Since the beginning of the science age, numerous attempts have been made to create or dissipate rain, to still hurricanes, and to manage ice flows. This has not always been a venerable undertaking. Weather and climate manipulation has throughout history been a field replete with more than its share of tricksters and dreamers. Today a fresh cadre of would-be climate engineers is emerging. They have newly honed scientific understandings, increasing amounts of money, and strengthening political winds at their backs. So what, then, is to be made of geoengineering? Is it a new form of hucksterism? A dangerous folly? Or does geoengineering have some ultimately positive role to play in the transition to a sustainable future?

Answering such questions is hardly straightforward. One important thing to keep in mind is that not all geoengineering proposals are alike. A catchall category like this hides some very important distinctions. Some geoengineering ideas threaten to unleash extraordinarily high environmental or social costs or promise to concentrate political power in a troubling fashion. Other proposals, if developed in sensible and sensitive ways, hold out some real hope for a world adjusting to a changing climate. Making sense of geoengineering demands a separation of the reality from the hype—and a separation of the ideas that are altogether too risky from those that appear a good deal more benign.

A LOOK AT THE GEOENGINEERING LANDSCAPE

In November 2007, the U.S. National Aeronautics and Space Administration (NASA) hosted a meeting of handpicked scientists at the Ames Research Center in San Francisco, California. The meeting was called to look at the innocuous-sounding enterprise of "managing solar radiation."

The gathering brought together an array of geoengineering luminaries. While their main goal was development of a scientific research agenda for this developing field, a central theme over the two days of conversation was impatience and frustration with the traditional suite of measures put forward to tackle climate change. United Nations–sponsored political negotiations, carbon trading schemes, attempts to promote alternative energies—all were seen by those in attendance as doomed to fail or to be progressing far too slowly to avert disaster. . . .

Such views are the entry point into the world of geoengineering. By just about any available measure, the climate situation is worsening. As Arctic ice melts, sea levels rise, wildfires increase in frequency and severity, and storms worsen, there is a growing sense in influential quarters that political and social strategies aimed at reducing GHG emissions are proving hopelessly ineffective. The stage is set for a shift in focus to dramatic, technology-based climate stabilization measures.

The technological strategies under consideration fall into two basic categories. The first are the kinds of solar radiation management (SRM) techniques that were under explicit consideration at the Ames meeting. SRM techniques are concerned with blocking or reflecting sunlight. Such a feat could, in theory, be achieved by boosting Earth's surface albedo—its reflectivity—using any of a variety of methods or by preventing some portion of solar radiation from ever reaching the earth's surface. The second category is carbon dioxide removal (CDR). Strategies under this heading are concerned with drawing CO_2 out of the atmosphere and locking it into long-term storage. . . .

[R]esearch into these . . . ideas has already begun. There is much hope in the geoengineering community that a real, workable techno-fix can be developed. Still, very few are pretending that the task is an easy engineering puzzle. At the Ames meeting . . . , for instance, hope for a technological breakthrough to tackle climate change was apparently tempered with a well-honed appreciation for the extraordinary nature of the challenge. We can just hope that there was also a strong sense of irony present in the meeting room, given this anecdote related by James Fleming, who was present at the meeting: "Even as [conference participants] joked about a NASA staffer's apology for her inability to control the temperature in the meeting room, others detailed their own schemes for manipulating the earth's climate."

Affixing a thermostat to the planet's climate system should be considered no small task for a species that struggles to control the temperatures in its meeting spaces.

PARSING GEOENGINEERING'S COSTS

So, can human beings willfully use large-scale technologies to cool the planet? The answer is almost certainly yes. A different and altogether trickier question is, Should we? Is the geoengineering path really worth pursuing?

For some, the answer is a resounding "of course." Richard Branson, for instance, chairman of Virgin Atlantic airlines and a host of other companies, is a well-known proponent of geoengineering: "If we could come up with a geoengineering answer to this problem, then [international climate change meetings like] Copenhagen wouldn't be necessary. . . . We could carry on flying our planes and driving our cars." Branson is investing more than words in pursuit of a solution that would leave his core business—flying people around the world—intact. In 2007 he kicked off the $25 million Virgin Earth Challenge, an ongoing search for commercially viable ways to pull carbon out of the atmosphere.

Others, including the vast majority of scientists involved in geoengineering research, are far more circumspect. Hugh Hunt, a professor of engineering at Cambridge University, who is part of a team working on delivery systems to introduce reflective particles into the stratosphere, has summed up the general feeling among scientists working on geoengineering in this way: "I know this [talk of geoengineering] is all unpleasant. Nobody wants it, but nobody wants to put high doses of poisonous chemicals into their bodies, either. That is what chemotherapy is, though, and for people suffering from cancer those poisons are often their only hope. Every day, tens of thousands of people take them willingly—because they are very sick or dying. This is how I prefer to look at the possibility of engineering the climate. It isn't a cure for anything. But it could very well turn out to be the least bad option we are going to have." . . .

Talk of geoengineering is gaining traction at least in part because of Richard Branson's line of argument. That is, geoengineering has the appearance of an easy, sacrifice-free approach to tackling climate change. Finding ways to reduce the world's dependence on fossil fuels is hard and messy. In contrast, developing some kind of geoengineering techno-fix looks easy and clean. Yet it is critically important to recognize that there are sacrifices, some obvious and some harder to spot, associated with the bulk of the geoengineering schemes under serious consideration—sacrifices that can be summarized as material, political, and existential.

Material Sacrifices. Perhaps the most obvious cause for concern is that geoengineering interventions could go catastrophically wrong. The great historian of technology Henry Petroski has argued in a series of books that failure is in the very nature of technological design. He once noted that while the object of engineering design is to reduce the possibility of failure, "the truly fail-proof design is chimerical." In fact, Petroski has shown in a persuasive fashion that technological development has in a very basic sense depended on failure, since the lessons learned from failed design can often teach a great deal more than successful machines and structures.

Given the scope of the geoengineering endeavor, however, that calculus cannot apply. A problem with a new design for a television set or a new line of running shoes may provoke irritation. A problem with a space mirror or stratospheric sulfur deployment, on the other hand, could have truly devastating, irreparable consequences. With many of the geoengineering proposals on the table, there is scant room for error. This is a worrying notion, particularly if influential elites become hell-bent on deploying geoengineering options, since as environmental studies professor Roger Pielke, Jr., has put it, "There is no practice planet Earth on which such technologies can be implemented, evaluated, and improved." . . .

Along with the danger of things going wrong, there are also massive challenges associated with things going exactly as planned. Even if executed without a hitch, certain geoengineering schemes would entail extraordinarily complex trade-offs. Under an SRM scenario, rainfall—even if it were not reduced—would almost certainly be redistributed by any radical intervention in the climate system. . . . These most promising of SRM techniques, in other words, would force those who seek to use them to choose among competing environmental disasters.

With this in mind, geoengineering is, it must be said, too grand a name for the enterprise. "Geo-tinkering" is closer to the mark. The climate system is incompletely understood. Any intervention would be tentative at best, with catastrophic failures likely. And this is taking account just of the problems that are relatively easy to forecast. Complex technologies and technological systems have a habit of "biting back," as historian Edward Tenner once put it, in ways hard to predict and sometimes hard to respond to.

Given the stakes and challenges, 40 years ago British meteorologist H. H. Lamb suggested that before embarking down the geoengineering path, "an essential precaution [is] to wait until a scientific system for forecasting the behavior of the natural climate . . . has been devised and operated successfully for, perhaps, a hundred years."

Political Sacrifices. Waiting 100 years for greater levels of scientific certainty is sage advice, but it is unlikely to be followed. This is because the political pressure to rapidly deploy geoengineering technologies may become overwhelming as the effects of climate change grow more pronounced. Mustering the political will to generate large-scale social change in response to climate change is proving, to state the obvious, difficult. However, should melting ice drive rapid sea level rise, or should climate-related food and water pressures cause great suffering in industrial countries (rather than just in developing ones, as at present), or should some other fast-moving climate calamity force the hand of rich-country elites, then swift technology-based action may suddenly be demanded.

Deploying geoengineering technologies under such circumstances would likely be met with more limited social and political resistance than might be expected, given that geoengineering fits into a broader narrative about using technologies to solve complex problems and that geoengineering approaches require little buy-in or behavior change by the public.

Scientists are eager to start with small-scale geoengineering experiments rather than be forced into large-scale development. If political pressure mounts, though, starting small would be hard. If geoengineering comes to be seen as a last-gasp option, the impetus will be toward rapid, full-scale deployment. There is no guarantee in such a situation that those who end up with their metaphoric hands on the planet's thermostat would act in the global interest rather than following some other calculus. Imagine for a moment that the U.S. government could deploy stratospheric sulfur for the direct short-term benefit of the North American continent. What if that deployment threatened African rainfall patterns? Or imagine a time when the United States is having a rotten summer while Europe is experiencing a heat wave: Who gets to adjust the mirror? What, to play this scenario out, of the legal costs to societies when every bad harvest or vacation spoiled by too much rain is thought to be the fault of distant geoengineers?

Space mirrors, stratospheric sulfur schemes, and the like all require concentration of materials and political authority. By this measure, many geoengineering schemes have a distinctly anti-democratic flavor. Who, then, gets to call the shots in a geoengineered world? Who will receive the benefits? What of small countries with limited economic means and limited political voice? What of villages that happen to be situated on top of the perfect location for underground carbon storage? The questions that can be raised about such activities are endless.

The history of weather modification efforts and of technological development more generally suggests that tussles over mirror alignment might be the smallest of our problems. Militarization could be a far bigger challenge. The militaries of the world's great powers have long looked to weather modification as a potentially potent weapon of war. Given such a history, James Fleming has suggested that "it is virtually impossible to imagine governments resisting the temptation to explore military uses of any climate-altering technology."

Finally, there is a very real danger that a focus on geoengineering saps the political will for other forms of action. It is, tragically, in our collective nature to hope for a miracle. It is in the natures of our politicians and business leaders to promise one. This is the case despite repeated injunctions from scientists to continue work on traditional mitigation efforts even as research on geoengineering technologies advances.

Existential Sacrifices. This leads to a third category of geoengineering sacrifice—a category that we might call "existential." The ability to control the weather was once the prerogative of a divine creator. Now it is a technique within the reach of the world's governments, large corporations, and even wealthy individuals. The transgression of previously sacred and inviolable boundaries that is the product of such a development may seem abstract in the face of climate change, but it is actually profoundly important.

This is because more technology alone does not, despite narratives to the contrary, equal progress. Progress signals movement toward some goal. The large-scale development of geoengineering technologies would render some goals realistic and others unattainable. To imagine that geoengineering is some passive, neutral enterprise, forced on humanity by a changing climate, is to ignore the other options for response that are available and to ignore the role played by the blind worship of technology in creating the current ecological mess.

Now, there is no denying that, as Stewart Brand of the Long Now Foundation has put it, "humanity is stuck with a planet stewardship role." The conversation has to be about what to do with that role. The ultimate ecological question is a deceptively straightforward one: What kind of future will we craft? Because craft it we will. Does that crafting entail a kind of global biospheric management—the geoengineering path—or something else? A different vision of the future would privilege shared sacrifice, directed toward living well and meaningfully within ecological limits. Some geoengineering options close off or render unimaginable such a pathway. Why live differently if space mirrors will come to our rescue? A few geoengineering options, though, may be compatible with a world in which sufficiency rather than domination is the guiding ethic.

Political theorist Langdon Winner once coined a useful phrase that it is worth keeping in mind: *technological somnambulism.* Too often, he suggested, people tend to sleepwalk through the making of technological decisions. With geoengineering, the scope is too vast and the implications too all-encompassing for any kind of passive decision making. The risks and impacts of geoengineering cannot be considered in isolation. They must be compared with the risks of doing nothing in the face of climate change, certainly, but also the risks and benefits that inhere in other forms of response.

THE FUTURE OF PLANETARY ENGINEERING

Is geoengineering something to be avoided at all costs? Or is it, perhaps, "a bad idea whose time has come"? It is relatively easy to poke holes in the geoengineering enterprise. Humanity's track record with large-scale technological deployment hardly gives one faith in the ability of geoengineers to completely and without harm manage the entire climate system. Scientific elites have too often had a misplaced faith in their abilities to cut through complex social problems. The horrors of the early years of the nuclear age and the ongoing blight of global hunger are just two obvious examples.

Still, at the same time as there is cause for real concern about the geoengineering push, doing nothing in the face of climate change is itself not an option. And the track record of recent international climate change meetings and of most efforts to wean individuals and communities from fossil fuel dependence hardly gives cause for optimism. . . .

[Ultimately,] forays into geoengineering could, conceivably, be part of the move to a more just and sustainable social order—but only if the technological development that geoengineering entails is tied to the cultivation of humanity's oldest political virtues, including humility and compassion. A moratorium on geoengineering is doomed to fail. At the same time, pushing ahead with the most outlandish geoengineering schemes is likely to result in catastrophic failure of a wholly different variety. The need is for a middle ground—not geoengineering as techno-fix but rather geoengineering as one small part of an effort to steer the world to a state of rightness and fitness in ecological and social terms.

36

Humility in a Climate Age

Paul Wapner

There is a battle going on for the soul of environmentalism. How it plays out will determine our ability to respond to a whole host of environmental dilemmas, especially climate change. All of us are partners in this struggle, since battle lines are being drawn not simply on the street or in policy debates but also inside each of us. We are torn between two visions of how to relate to the earth. Much depends on how we negotiate our way through the conflict.

One vision sees *Homo sapiens* as merely one of many species, and thus subject to the same biophysical constraints as other creatures: Like the rest of life, we evolved over millennia, and depend fundamentally on the biophysical gifts of the earth. From an environmental perspective, this means that we should try to harmonize ourselves with the natural world—we should use only so many resources and produce only so much waste, and generally strive to fit ourselves into the web of ecological interdependence.

The other vision sees humans as the exceptional species: Yes, we are subject to nature's laws, but these are not inviolate. We can outsmart, work around, or otherwise rise above them by employing our reason and technological abilities. From an environmental perspective, our exceptionalism calls on us not to harmonize ourselves with nature but to rework the natural world in the service of human betterment.

The first view can be called the urge toward *naturalism* whereas the second can be called the urge toward *mastery.*

For decades, environmentalists have primarily expressed the first view in their political orientation and campaigns. They have tended to confront their critics along the naturalism-mastery divide, offering a counter-narrative to the predominant, hubristic attitude of lording over nature and trying to instill a sense of species-humility in the face of growing environmental challenges.

Environmentalism is changing, however, especially in light of the climate crisis. Many are now toning down or outright abandoning a naturalist sensibility for one leaning toward mastery. We see this in the attraction to technological fixes as evident in the resurgence of support for nuclear power, the popularity of carbon sequestration, and the embrace of "green" consumption. Today, some staunch environmentalists are even proposing earth-altering actions to protect ourselves from the dangerous buildup of greenhouse gases, seeking to change the atmosphere itself to accept more carbon dioxide or at least deflect climate change dangers. Proposals include putting up orbiting sunshades to block sunlight, fertilizing the oceans with iron to grow more phytoplankton to absorb carbon dioxide, and pumping sulfur dioxide into the atmosphere to impede solar radiation. Many environmentalists have come reluctantly to recognize that there is simply no way that societies are going to cut back, restrict their imprint on the earth, and otherwise live lightly on the planet enough to mitigate climate change. Too many people need energy and are unwilling to deny themselves the pleasures of material consumption for an orientation of naturalism to take hold widely enough to make a difference. At this stage, they reason, we should ramp up our abilities to outsmart and manipulate nature in the service of protecting ourselves from climate catastrophe. Put differently, many environmentalists are now admitting that global capitalism, incessant technological innovation, endless consumption, and pervasive anthropocentrism are here to stay. Rather than continue to battle against these dynamics in the service of living more harmoniously with the natural world, many argue that it is time to embrace them and align ourselves with their power.

There is much promise to the "new environmentalism." . . . [W]e are all grasping at straws for insight, and the notion that technological fixes could enable us to surmount climate change dangers within the existing world order (and with our lifestyles intact) appears particularly attractive, especially to the privileged among us.

And yet, for all its promise, the new environmentalism raises significant questions. Is it really forward-looking, or will it simply reinforce and accelerate the forces that got us into the climate crisis in the first place? That is, can it usher in a new energy future or will its promise of technical solutions distract us from the difficult work of realigning our lives? Is it so compatible with current economic and social systems that it will merely diversify our energy choices without fashioning a genuinely different orientation to our energy lives? More generally, we need to ask where the new environmentalism will lead us. Will it take us into a technocratic future animated by the type of design and technological optimism associated with Promethean thought that has long animated environmental skeptics, or will it prefigure a more naturalized world, more in line with the precautionary sensibility that has long guided the environmental movement?

There are no easy—and certainly no definitive—answers to such questions. We cannot evaluate the new environmentalism in either/or terms, as if it were *either* helpful *or* not in ushering in a sane climate future. Rather, the effects of the new environmentalism turn on how we translate it into practice. Key to such translation is recognizing that the impulse behind the new environmentalism needs to be in productive tension with conventional environmentalism and the urge to naturalism. As we move deeper into the climate age, we need to revive and embolden the impulse toward naturalism to rein in our hubristic tendencies. Our humanity depends on it.

THE MORAL CHARACTER OF THE TWO ENVIRONMENTALISMS

Environmentalism is many things. At its core, however, it is an ethical movement. As political theorist Leslie Thiele reminds us, it is about extending moral consideration across space, time, and species. It involves caring about the needs and well-being of our fellow human beings, future generations, and the more-than-human world. Addressing climate change is a moral act to the degree that it involves protecting each other and other creatures from climate catastrophe, and ensuring that future human beings will inherit a livable planet. In many ways, the new environmentalism does represent this moral sentiment. Its embrace of technological capability, economic growth, and instrumental rationality represents a commitment to addressing the climate crisis and thus making the world a better place for all living creatures, including future generations.

There is, nonetheless, something unsettling about the moral character of the new environmentalism, especially to the degree that it ignores naturalism. Its promise to deliver a world in which we may continue to indulge all our appetites, desires, and customary practices simply by altering material structures seems morally thin. Such a vision involves technologically engineering the world so individual, environmental decision-making becomes irrelevant. It strives to ensure that we conduct ourselves in an environmentally sound fashion through designed systems of social life. This raises ethical concerns to the degree that it relieves individuals of having to clarify their moral commitments or take deliberate actions to limit themselves in the service of others' well-being.

Ethical action involves deliberation and the conscious choice to restrict acting on one's desires in deference to the welfare of others. The new environmentalism promises gadgets and systems that will absolve us of the need for such reflection and consideration. Most ethical action also entails a sense of humility about oneself and, by extension, the human species. At least since Aristotle, ethicists have considered humility a virtue whose practice deepens the human character and heightens one's moral sensitivity. The new environmentalism dispenses with this to the degree that it calls on us not to respect nature's limits and adjust ourselves to them, but to outsmart and plow through nature's biophysical character with the aim of crafting sustainable lives without requiring, or indeed permitting, the exercise of choice. Humility is thus a casualty of the new environmentalism.

This is not to say, of course, that the new environmentalism is immoral or even amoral. As mentioned, its proponents care deeply about protecting the environment and ensuring that humanity survives and flourishes in the face of grave environmental challenges. Rather, it is to suggest that the new environmentalism is *incompletely* moral. The new environmentalism needs the ethical bearings that sensitivity to naturalism can provide. It needs the sense of humility and the appreciation for the more-than-human world that conventional environmentalism has long valued and championed. This is especially the case at this point in history.

Since the dawn of modernity, the balance between naturalism and mastery has been increasingly weighted toward mastery. Our attempt to decipher nature's ways and manipulate them in the service of human betterment has been accelerating for centuries and shows few signs of abatement. Indeed, we seem continually committed to run roughshod over the nonhuman world. Given this imbalance, this is simply not the time for fully embracing the new environmentalism but rather reviving naturalism, which at its core expresses diffidence concerning human frailty, and the human condition more generally. Naturalism conveys the understanding that we—as individuals and as a species—are not at the center of the universe but simply occupy a distinct place in the order of things.

In many ways, it has been our self-centeredness—our placing ourselves at the core of existence and our willingness to do whatever it takes to advance our interests—that has been the cause of our environmental dilemmas. It is time to regenerate a cautionary attitude toward this sensibility and put it in its proper place. If checked by humility, the new environmentalism can offer wonders without veering off in dangerous and ethically troubling directions. Couched within an effort to balance naturalism and mastery, the new environmentalism can take its rightful place in the evolution of the movement. It can offer promise toward addressing climate change by urging us to explore our technological, scientific, and "economistic" tendencies and capabilities. It will fail us, however, if we don't balance these proclivities and capacities with the moral compass of knowing that, while we may be unique as a species, we are not exempt from nature's laws and imperatives, and we live less than full lives when we forget this. This recognition, paired with the realization that there is more to the cosmos than humans, provides the antidote to the hubris of the mastery narrative—and to our collective ability to address climate change.

The tension between naturalism and mastery is as important to environmentalism as the paradoxes that wrack human life are to human experience. We live best when we refuse to collapse such paradoxes. Likewise, we will live most humanely through the climate age by keeping alive the long environmentalist tradition of harmonizing with the natural world rather than lording over it.

37

How to Be Hopeful

Barbara Kingsolver

The very least you can do in your life is to figure out what you hope for. The most you can do is live inside that hope, running down its hallways, touching the walls on both sides.

Let me begin that way: with an invocation of your own best hopes, thrown like a handful of rice over this celebration. Congratulations, graduates. Congratulations, parents, on the best Mother's Day gift ever. Better than all those burnt-toast breakfasts: these, your children grown tall and competent, educated to within an inch of their lives.

What can I say to people who know almost everything? There was a time when I surely knew, because I'd just graduated from college myself, after writing down the sum of all human knowledge on exams and research papers. But that great pedagogical swilling-out must have depleted my reserves, because decades have passed and now I can't believe how much I don't know. Looking back, I can discern a kind of gaseous exchange in which I exuded cleverness and gradually absorbed better judgment. Wisdom is like frequent-flyer miles and scar tissue; if it does accumulate, that happens by accident while you're trying to do something else. And wisdom is what people will start wanting from you, after your last exam. I know it's true for writers—when people love a book, whatever they say about it, what they really mean is: it was *wise*. It helped explain their pickle. My favorites are the canny old codgers: Neruda, Garcia Marquez, Doris Lessing. Honestly, it is harrowing for me to try to teach 20-year-old students, who earnestly want to improve their writing. The best I can think to tell them is: Quit smoking, and observe posted speed limits. This will improve your odds of getting old enough to be wise.

If I stopped there, you might have heard my best offer. But I am charged with postponing your diploma for about 15 more minutes, so I'll proceed, with a caveat. The wisdom of each generation is necessarily new. This tends to dawn on us in revelatory moments, brought to us by our children. For example: My younger daughter is eleven. Every morning, she and I walk down the lane from our farm to the place where she meets the school bus. It's the best part of my day. We have great conversations. But a few weeks ago as we stood waiting in the dawn's early light, Lily was quietly looking me over, and finally said: "Mom, just so you know, the only reason I'm letting you wear that outfit is because of your age." The *alleged outfit* will not be described here; whatever you're imagining will perfectly suffice. (Especially if you're picturing "Project Runway" meets "Working with Livestock.") Now, I believe parents should uphold respect for adult authority, so I did what I had to do. I hid behind the barn when the bus came.

And then I walked back up the lane in my fly regalia, contemplating this new equation: "Because of your age." It's okay now to deck out and turn up as the village idiot. Hooray! I am old enough. How does this happen? Over a certain age, do you become invisible? There is considerable evidence for this in movies and television. But mainly, I think, you're not expected to know the rules. Everyone knows you're operating on software that hasn't been updated for a good while.

The world shifts under our feet. The rules change. Not the Bill of Rights, or the rules of tenting, but the big unspoken truths of a generation. Exhaled by culture, taken in like oxygen, we hold these truths to be self-evident: You get what you pay for. Success is everything. Work is what you do for money, and that's what counts. How could it be otherwise? And the converse of that last rule, of course, is that if you're not paid to do a thing, it can't be important. If a child writes a poem and proudly reads it, adults may wink and ask, "Think there's a lot of money in that?" You may also hear this when you declare a major in English. Being a good neighbor, raising children: the road to success is not paved with the likes of these. Some workplaces actually quantify your likelihood of being distracted by family or volunteerism. It's called your coefficient of Drag. The ideal number is zero. This is the Rule of Perfect Efficiency.

Now, the rule of "Success" has traditionally meant having boatloads of money. But we are not really supposed to put it in a boat. A house would be the customary thing. Ideally it should be large, with a lot of bathrooms and so forth, but no more than four people. If two friends come over during approved visiting hours, the two children have to leave. The bathroom-to-resident ratio should at all times remain greater than one. I'm not making this up, I'm just observing, it's more or less my profession. As Yogi Berra told us, you can observe a lot just by watching. I see our dream-houses standing alone, the idealized life taking place in a kind of bubble. So you need another bubble, with rubber tires, to convey yourself to places you must visit, such as an office. If you're successful, it will be a large, empty-ish office you don't have to share. If you need anything, you can get it delivered. Play your cards right and you may never have to come face to face with another person. This is the Rule of Escalating Isolation.

And so we find ourselves in the chapter of history I would entitle: Isolation and Efficiency, and How They Came Around to Bite Us in the Backside. Because it's looking that way. We're a world at war, ravaged by disagreements, a bizarrely globalized people in which the extravagant excesses of one culture wash up as famine or flood on the shores of another. Even the architecture of our planet is collapsing under the weight of our efficient productivity. Our climate, our oceans, migratory paths, things we believed were independent of human affairs. Twenty years ago, climate scientists first told Congress that unlimited carbon emissions were building toward a disastrous instability. Congress said, we need to think about that. About ten years later, nations of the world wrote the Kyoto Protocol, a set of legally binding controls on our carbon emissions. The US said, we still need to think about it. Now we can watch as glaciers disappear, the lights of biodiversity go out, the oceans reverse their ancient orders. A few degrees looked so small on the thermometer. We are so good at measuring things and declaring them under control. How could our weather turn murderous, pummel our coasts and push new diseases like dengue fever onto our doorsteps? It's an emergency on a scale we've never known. We've responded by following the rules we know: Efficiency, Isolation. We can't slow down our productivity and consumption, that's unthinkable. Can't we just go home and put a really big lock on the door?

Not this time. Our paradigm has met its match. The world will save itself, don't get me wrong. The term "fossil fuels" is not a metaphor or a simile. In the geological sense, it's over. The internal combustion engine is so 20th Century. Now we can either shift away from a carbon-based economy, or find another place to live. Imagine it: we raised you on a lie. Everything you plug in, turn on or drive, the out-of-season foods you eat, the music in your ears. We gave you this world and promised you could keep it running on: *a fossil substance.* Dinosaur slime, and it's running out. The geologists only disagree on how much is left, and the climate scientists are now saying they're sorry but that's not even the point. We won't get time to use it all. To stabilize the floods and firestorms, we'll have to reduce our carbon emissions by 80 percent, within a decade.

Heaven help us get our minds around that. We're still stuck on a strategy of bait-and-switch: Okay, we'll keep the cars but run them on ethanol made from corn! But—we use petroleum to grow the corn. Even if you like the idea of robbing the food bank to fill up the tank, there is a math problem: it takes nearly a gallon of fossil fuel to render an equivalent gallon of corn gas. By some accounts, it takes more. Think of the Jules Verne novel in which the hero is racing Around the World in 80 Days, and finds himself stranded in the mid-Atlantic on a steamship that's run out of coal. It's day 79. So Phileas Fogg convinces the Captain to pull up the decks and throw them into the boiler. "On the next day the masts, rafts and spars were burned. The crew worked lustily, keeping up the fires. There was a perfect rage for demolition." The Captain remarked, "Fogg, you've got something of the Yankee about you." Oh, novelists. They always manage to have the last word, even when they are dead.

How can we get from here to there, without burning up our ship? That will be central question of your adult life: to escape the wild rumpus of carbon-fuel dependency, in the nick of time. You'll make rules that were previously unthinkable, imposing limits on what we can use and possess. You will radically reconsider the power relationship between humans and our habitat. In the words of my esteemed colleague and friend, Wendell Berry, the new Emancipation Proclamation will not be for a specific race or species, but for life itself. Imagine it. Nations have already joined together to rein in global consumption. Faith communities have found a new point of agreement with student activists, organizing around the conviction that caring for our planet is a moral obligation. Before the last UN Climate Conference in Bali, thousands of U.S. citizens contacted the State Department to press for binding limits on carbon emissions. We're the five percent of humans who have made 50 percent of all the greenhouse gases up there. But our government is reluctant to address it, for one reason: it might hurt our economy.

For a lot of history, many nations said exactly the same thing about abolishing slavery. We can't grant humanity to all people, it would hurt our cotton plantations, our sugar crop, our balance of trade. Until the daughters and sons of a new wisdom declared: We don't care. You have to find another way. Enough of this shame.

Have we lost that kind of courage? Have we let economic growth become our undisputed master again? As we track the unfolding disruption of natural and global stabilities, you will be told to buy into business as usual: You need a job. Trade your future for an entry level position. Do what we did, preserve a profitable climate for manufacture and consumption, at any cost. Even at the cost of the other climate—the one that was hospitable to life as we knew it. Is anyone thinking this through? In the awful moment when someone demands at gunpoint, "Your money or your life," that's not supposed to be a hard question.

A lot of people, in fact, are rethinking the money answer. Looking behind the cash-price of everything, to see what it cost us elsewhere: to mine and manufacture, to transport, to burn, to bury. What did it harm on its way here? Could I get it closer to home? Previous generations rarely asked about the hidden costs. We put them on layaway. You don't get to do that. The bill has come due. Some European countries already are calculating the "climate cost" on consumer goods and adding it to the price. The future is here. We're examining the moralities of possession, inventing renewable technologies, recovering sustainable food systems. We're even warming up to the idea that the wealthy nations will have to help the poorer ones, for the sake of a reconstructed world. We've done it before. That was the Marshall Plan. Generosity is not out of the question. It will grind some gears in the machine of Efficiency. But we can retool.

We can also rethink the big, lonely house as a metaphor for success. You are in a perfect position to do that. You've probably spent very little of your recent life in a free-standing unit with a bathroom-to-resident ratio of greater than one. (Maybe more like 1:200.) You've been living so close to your friends, you didn't have to ask about their problems, you had to step over them to get into the room. As you moved from dormitory to apartment to whatever (and by whatever I think I mean Central Campus) you've had such a full life, surrounded by people, in all kinds of social and physical structures, none of which belonged entirely to you. You're told that's all about to change. That growing up means leaving the herd, starting up the long escalator to isolation.

Not necessarily. As you leave here, remember what you loved most in this place. Not Orgo 2, I'm guessing, or the crazed squirrels or even the bulk cereal in the Freshman Marketplace. I mean the way you lived, in close and continuous contact. This is an ancient human social construct that once was common in this land. We called it a community. We lived among our villagers, depending on them for what we needed. If we had a problem, we did not discuss it over the phone with someone in Bubaneshwar. We went to a neighbor. We acquired food from farmers. We listened to music in groups, in churches or on front porches. We danced. We participated. Even when there was no money in it. Community is our native state. You play hardest for a hometown crowd. You become your best self. You know joy. This is not a guess, there is evidence. The scholars who study social well-being can put it on charts and graphs. In the last 30 years our material wealth has increased in this country, but our self-described happiness has steadily declined. Elsewhere, the people who consider themselves very happy are not in the very poorest nations, as you might guess, nor in the very richest. The winners are Mexico, Ireland, Puerto Rico, the kinds of places we identify with extended family, noisy villages, a lot of dancing. The happiest people are the ones with the most community.

You can take that to the bank. I'm not sure what they'll do with it down there, but you could try. You could walk out of here with an unconventionally communal sense of how your life may be. This could be your key to a new order: you don't need so much stuff to fill your life, when you have people in it. You don't need jet fuel to get food from a farmer's market. You could invent a new kind of Success that includes children's poetry, butterfly migrations, butterfly kisses, the Grand Canyon, eternity. If somebody says "Your money or your life," you could say: Life. And mean it. You'll see things collapse in your time, the big houses, the empires of glass. The new green things that sprout up through the wreck—those will be yours.

The arc of history is longer than human vision. It bends. We abolished slavery, we granted universal suffrage. We have done hard things before. And every time it took a terrible fight between people who could not imagine changing the rules, and those who said, "We already did. We have made the world new." The hardest part will be to convince yourself of the possibilities, and hang on. If you run out of hope at the end of the day, to rise in the morning and put it on again with your shoes. Hope is the only reason you won't give in, burn what's left of the ship and go down with it. The ship of your natural life and your children's only shot. You have to love that so earnestly—you, who were born into the Age of Irony. Imagine getting caught with your Optimism hanging out. It feels so risky. Like showing up at the bus stop as the village idiot. You may be asked to stand behind the barn. You may feel you're not up to the task.

But think of this: what if someone had dared you, three years ago, to show up to some public event wearing a big, flappy dress with sleeves down to your knees. And on your head, oh, let's say, a beanie with a square board on top. And a tassel! Look at you. You are beautiful. The magic is community. The time has come for the square beanie, and you are rocked in the bosom of the people who get what you're going for. You can be as earnest and ridiculous as you need to be, if you don't attempt it in isolation. The ridiculously earnest are known to travel in groups. And they are known to change the world. Look at you. That could be you.

I'll close with a poem:

Hope: An Owner's Manual
Look, you might as well know, this thing
is going to take endless repair: rubber bands,
crazy glue, tapioca, the square of the hypotenuse.
Nineteenth century novels. Heartstrings, sunrise:
all of these are useful. Also, feathers.
To keep it humming, sometimes you have to stand
on an incline, where everything looks possible;
on the line you drew yourself. Or in
the grocery line, making faces at a toddler
secretly, over his mother's shoulder.
You might have to pop the clutch and run
past all the evidence. Past everyone who is
laughing or praying for you. Definitely you don't
want to go directly to jail, but still, here you go,
passing time, passing strange. Don't pass this up.
In the worst of times, you will have to pass it off.
Park it and fly by the seat of your pants. With nothing
in the bank, you'll still want to take the express.
Tiptoe past the dogs of the apocalypse that are sleeping
in the shade of your future. Pay at the window.
Pass your hope like a bad check.
You might still have just enough time. To make a deposit.

Congratulations, graduates.

Section 9 Exercise

Calling All Earthlings: Self and Planetary Stewardship

Close your eyes. Imagine a utopia. What does it look like? How many people are around? How is nature present (or not) in your vision? From where do people get their food, water, and energy? What single element makes your utopian world most desirable?

Then, write for ten minutes without stopping. Dash to your utopia! Discuss.

Credits

The readings included in this volume have been used with permission from the following sources. They appear in condensed form, and all footnotes, endnotes, and references have been omitted.

Section 1

Elizabeth Kolbert. "Enter the Anthropocene—Age of Man." In *National Geographic Magazine* (March 2011). Reprinted with permission of the author.

Charles C. Mann. "State of the Species." In *Orion* (November/December 2012). Reprinted with permission of the author.

Alex Steffen. "Editor's Introduction." In *World Changing: User's Guide for the 21st Century,* edited by Alex Steffen, with Carissa Bluestone, 17–26. New York: Abrams, 2006. Reprinted with permission of the author.

Section 2

Bill McKibben. "Global Warming's Terrifying New Math." In *Rolling Stone* (July 19, 2012). Copyright Rolling Stone LLC 2012. All rights reserved. Reprinted with permission of the publisher.

Stephen M. Meyer. "End of the Wild." In *Boston Review* (April/May 2004): 17–26. Copyright 2006 MIT Press. Reprinted with permission of the publisher.

Maude Barlow. *Blue Covenant: The Global Water Crisis and the Coming Battle for the Right to Water.* New York: The New Press, 2007, 1–33. Reprinted with permission of the publisher.

Lester Brown. "The Great Food Crisis of 2011." In *Foreign Policy* (January 10, 2011). Copyright 2011 *Foreign Policy Magazine.* Reprinted with permission of the publisher.

Section 3

Thomas Friedman. *Hot, Flat, and Crowded (Release 2.0).* New York: Farrar, Straus and Giroux, 2009, 53–71. Copyright 2008 by Thomas L. Friedman. Reprinted with permission of the publisher.

Bill McKibben. *Maybe One: A Case for Smaller Families.* New York: Simon & Schuster, 1998, 66–78; 106–128. Reprinted with permission of the author.

Section 4

Section 5

Section 6

Section 7

Herman E. Daly. "Sustainable Growth: An Impossibility Theorem." In *Development* (1990, nos. 3/4), 45–47. Reprinted with permission of the author.

Jonathan Rowe. Testimony before the United States Senate Committee on Commerce, Science and Transportation, Subcommittee on Interstate Commerce, on "Rethinking the Gross Domestic Product as a Measurement of National Strength." March 12, 2008. Public domain.

Peter Singer. *One World: The Ethics of Globalization.* New Haven: Yale University Press, 2002, 26–37. Reprinted with permission of the publisher.

Anil Agarwal and Sunita Narain. "A Case of Environmental Colonialism." In *Earth Island Journal* 6 no.2 (Spring 1991): 39. Reprinted with permission of the publisher.

Robert Bullard. "Anatomy of Environmental Racism and the Environmental Justice Movement." In *Confronting Environmental Racism: Voices from the Grassroots,* edited by Robert D. Bullard, 15–24. Cambridge: South End Press, 1993. Reprinted with permission of the publisher.

Section 8

Donella H. Meadows. "Leverage Points: Places to Intervene in a System." The Sustainability Institute. 1999. Reprinted with permission of the Donella Meadows Institute.

Michael F. Maniates. "Plant a Tree, Buy a Bike, Save the World?" In *Global Environmental Politics* 1, no. 3 (August 2001), 31–52. Copyright 2001 by the Massachusetts Institute of Technology. Reprinted with permission of the publisher.

Paul Wapner and John Willoughby. "The Irony of Environmentalism: The Ecological Futility but Political Necessity of Lifestyle Change." In *Ethics & International Affairs* 19, no. 3 (December 2005), 77–89. Copyright 2005 Carnegie Council for Ethics in International Affairs. Reprinted by permission of Cambridge University Press.

Michael Pollan. "Why Bother?" In *New York Times Magazine* (April 20, 2008). Reprinted with permission of the publisher. All rights reserved. Copyright by *The New York Times* and protected by the Copyright Laws of the United States. The printing, copying, redistribution, or retransmission of this Content without express written permission is prohibited.

Section 9

Roderick Frazier Nash. "Island Civilization: A Vision for Human Occupancy of Earth in the Fourth Millennium" (revised) (March 2010). Reprinted with permission of the author.

Joanne Harris. "A Is for Acid Rain, B Is for Bee." In *Beacons: Stories from Our Not So Distant Future,* edited by Gregory Norminton, 3–8. London: Oneworld Publications, 2013. Copyright 2013 Johanne Harris. Reprinted with permission of the author.

Wendell Berry. "An Argument for Diversity." In *The Hudson Review* 42, no. 4 (Winter 1990): 537–548. Copyright 1990 by Wendell Berry. Reprinted with permission of the publisher.

Michael Shellenberger and Ted Nordhaus. "Evolve: A Case for Modernization as the Road to Salvation." In *Orion Magazine* (September/October 2011). Copyright 2011 Michael Shellenberger and Ted Nordhaus. Reprinted with permission of the authors.

Simon Nicholson. "The Promises and Perils of Geoengineering." In *State of the World 2013:
      Is Sustainability Still Possible?* 317–331. Washington: Island Press, 2013. Reprinted
      with permission of the Worldwatch Institute.
Paul Wapner. "Humility in a Climate Age." In *Tikkun Magazine* (May/June 2010). Re-
      printed with permission of the publisher.
Barbara Kingsolver. "How to Be Hopeful." Commencement address at Duke University,
      2008. (http://today.duke.edu/2008/05/kingsolver.html.) Copyright 2008 Barbara
      Kingsolver. Reprinted by permission of The Frances Goldin Literary Agency.

About the Editors

Simon Nicholson is assistant professor and director of the Global Environmental Politics program in the School of International Service at American University. His research, teaching, and public engagement center on global food politics and the politics of emerging technologies, with a focus most recently on climate geoengineering technologies. He is coeditor (with Sikina Jinnah) of the forthcoming book *New Earth Politics*.

Paul Wapner is professor of global environmental politics in the School of International Service at American University. He is the author of *Living through the End of Nature: The Future of American Environmentalism* and the award-winning *Environmental Activism and World Civic Politics,* and coeditor of *Principled World Politics: The Challenge of Normative International Relations.* His current research focuses on the effects of climate change on the most vulnerable and the ethics of global climate protection.

About the Authors

Anil Agarwal (1947–2002) was a noted author, activist, and founder of the Centre for Science and Environment, as well as founding editor of *Down to Earth.*

Erik Assadourian is a Senior Fellow at the Worldwatch Institute and director of the Transforming Cultures project.

Maude Barlow is an award-winning author, national chairperson of the Council of Canadians, and cofounder of the Blue Planet Project, an advocacy network for the human right to water.

Wendell Berry is a Kentucky farmer, author, poet, and recipient of the National Humanities Medal.

Lester Brown is founder of the Earth Policy Institute (an organization that seeks to provide a vision for achieving an environmentally sustainable economy) and an inductee into the Earth Hall of Fame, Kyoto.

Robert Bullard is dean of the Barbara Jordan-Mickey Leland School of Public Affairs at Texas Southern University and is often described as the father of environmental justice.

Jennifer Clapp is professor in the Environment and Resource Studies department at the University of Waterloo in Canada.

Herman E. Daly is professor emeritus at the School of Public Policy at University of Maryland, College Park, and was senior economist in the environment department of the World Bank.

Peter Dauvergne is professor of international relations at the University of British Columbia.

Richard Falk is professor emeritus of international law at Princeton University and research professor at the University of California, Santa Barbara.

Thomas Friedman is an author, journalist, and columnist for the *New York Times.* He is a three-time recipient of the Pulitzer Prize.

Johann Hari is a writer and journalist who has written regular columns for the *Independent* and *Huffington Post.*

Joanne Harris is an acclaimed author. Her books are published in more than fifty countries and have won a number of British and international awards.

Paul Harris is professor of global environmental studies at the Hong Kong Institute of Education.

Paul Hawken is an environmentalist, entrepreneur, journalist, and author. He is a founder of the Natural Capital Institute and heads OneSun, Inc., an energy company focused on ultra-low-cost solar.

Barbara Kingsolver is a best-selling author, freelance journalist, and political activist.

Naomi Klein is an award-winning journalist, syndicated columnist, and author.

Elizabeth Kolbert is a multiple-award-winning author, journalist, and staff writer for the *New Yorker.*

Paul Krugman is a *New York Times* columnist and professor of economics and international affairs at the Woodrow Wilson School of Public and International Affairs at Princeton University.

Jane Lister is a research fellow at the Liu Institute for Global Issues at the University of British Columbia, and teaches corporate social responsibility at the Sauder School of Business.

Michael F. Maniates is professor of social science and environmental studies at Yale-NUS College in Singapore.

Charles C. Mann is an award-winning author, journalist, and contributing editor for *Science, Atlantic Monthly,* and *Wired.*

Bill McKibben is an author, activist, journalist, and founder of 350.org.

Donella H. Meadows (1941–2001) was a pioneering environmental scientist, teacher, and writer. She was the founder of the Sustainability Institute, which was renamed the Donella Meadows Institute in 2011.

Stephen M. Meyer (1952–2006) was professor of political science at the Massachusetts Institute of Technology.

Sunita Narain is the director general of the Centre for Science and Environment and publisher of *Down to Earth.*

Roderick Frazier Nash is professor emeritus of history and environmental studies at the University of California, Santa Barbara.

Simon Nicholson is director of the Global Environmental Politics program in the School of International Service at American University.

Ted Nordhaus is an author, an environmental-policy expert, and the chair of The Breakthrough Institute, which he cofounded with Michael Shellenberger in 2003.

Michael Pollan is Knight professor of science and environmental journalism at the University of California, Berkeley. He previously served as executive editor of *Harper's* magazine.

Jonathan Rowe (1946–2011) was an editor at *Washington Monthly* magazine and a staff writer at the *Christian Science Monitor.* He also served on staffs in the US House of Representatives and the US Senate.

Michael Shellenberger is an author, an environmental-policy expert, and the president of The Breakthrough Institute, which he cofounded with Ted Nordhaus.

Peter Singer is Ira W. DeCamp professor of bioethics in the University Center for Human Values at Princeton University. He also holds a part-time position as laureate professor at the University of Melbourne.

Alex Steffen is an award-winning author and "planetary futurist in residence" at the design and innovation company IDEO.

John Tierney is a *New York Times* columnist, noted author, and novelist.

Paul Wapner is professor of global environmental politics in the School of International Service at American University.

John Willoughby is professor of economics in the College of Arts and Sciences at American University.